TORONTO

THE WAY IT WAS

TORONTO

The west side of Jarvis Street, between Cawthra Square and Gloucester, in the early 1940s. The boulevard trees were cut down in the spring of 1947, to allow for road-widening, as part of the plan which eventually connected Jarvis Street with Mount Pleasant Road via Rosedale. The five houses were all built in the late 1880s, almost exactly a century ago, for owners of the ilk of George H. Gooderham, one of the younger sons of the distillery owner. As Jarvis Street changed, the houses' owners left for greener pastures, such as Rosedale and Forest Hill Village; by the 1940s, all of the houses were converted into suites. In 1946, the former Gooderham house, on the far left, at 504 Jarvis (now Angelini's Restaurant) was the Red Triangle Club servicemen's hostel; its next-door neighbour was the Nisei Cooperative residence for Canadians of Japanese ancestry.

THE WAY IT WAS

MICHAEL KLUCKNER

with paintings by the author

WHITECAP BOOKS

Published by Whitecap Books (Toronto) Ltd., Suite 403, 77 Mowat Avenue, Toronto, Ontario M6K 3E3, telephone [416] 534-5320.

Canadian Cataloguing in Publication Data:

Kluckner, Michael
Toronto the way it was

Bibliography: p. 313
Includes index.
ISBN 0-921396-02-3

1. Toronto (Ont.) - History. I. Title.

FC3097.4.K58 1988   971.3'541   C88-094264-9
F1059.5.T6857K58 1988

Printed in Canada by Friesen Printers, Altona, Manitoba

To Christine & Sarah Jane

Contents

Foreword 8
Preface 10
Introduction 13
Old York 17
Downtown 21
   Toronto Transportation Commission 36
   Eaton's 45
   Simpson's 48
   Newspapers 49
   City Hall 54
   Theatres 56
   The Farmers' Bank 60
   The Home Bank 63
   Ryrie Brothers 66
Yonge Street 69
   Eugene O'Keefe 72
   William Lyon Mackenzie 74
   Prohibition 75
   Toronto Hydro 80
   Mary Pickford 84
University Avenue 86
   Queen's Park 88
   University of Toronto 91
   The Free Speech Dispute 96
   Sir Joseph Flavelle 98
   The Great War 100

Industry & the Waterfront 110
   The Electric Diner Murder 114
   Railways 115
   Grant Morden 120
   The Canadian National Exhibition 122
   999 Queen Street West 128
   Massey-Harris 130
Neighbourhoods 133
The Ward & Kensington 134
   W.G. Weston 144
   Goldwin Smith 145
Church Street 148
   The *Ne Temere* Incident 150
   Maple Leaf Gardens 155
Sherbourne Street 156
Jarvis Street 160
Beaches 164
   Woodbine 169
Riverdale & The Danforth 172
Cabbagetown 179
   Gooderham & Worts 188
   Coal 190
   The Consumers' Gas Company 192
   William Davies & Company 194
Parkdale 198
   G.T. Denison III 202
   Sunnyside 205
The Junction 208

Swansea 216
High Park 218
Trinity 219
The Annex 225
   Zebulon Lash 228
   St. George Street 232
Yorkville 234
Rosedale 239
   Chestnut Park 250
   The MacMurchys 255
   Glen Road 256
   Arthur King 258
   "Millionaires' Row" 262
   "Ardwold" 264
   Poplar Plains Road 266
   "Casa Loma" 269
Wychwood Park 274
Deer Park & Moore Park 277
North Toronto 282
Forest Hill Village 287
The Islands 294
Leaside 301
Aviation 304
Metro 307
Appendices
   Painting Sources 310
   The Postcards 312
   Bibliography 313
Index 314

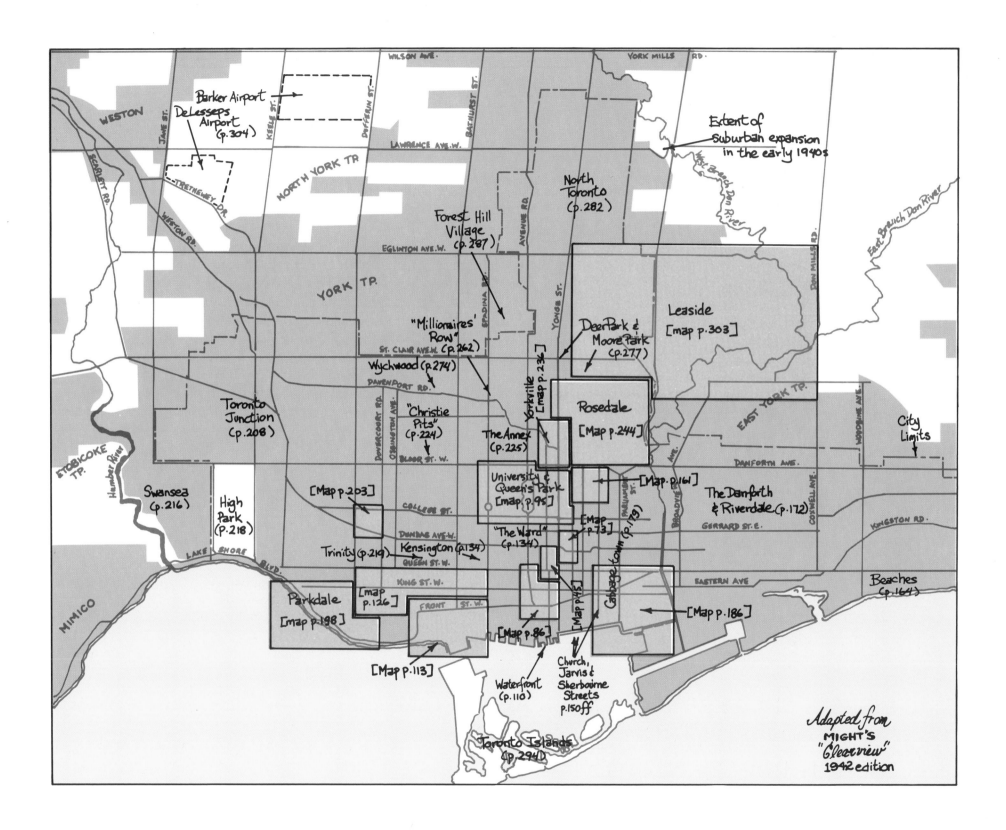

Barker Airport
DeLesseps Airport (p. 304)

WESTON

SCARLETT RD.

JANE ST.

KEELE ST.

TRETHEWEY DR.

WESTON RD.

DUFFERIN ST.

WILSON AVE.

BATHURST ST.

LAWRENCE AVE. W.

NORTH YORK TP.

YORK TP.

Extent of suburban expansion in the early 1940s

West Branch Don River

East Branch Don River

North Toronto (p. 282)

Forest Hill Village (p. 287)

EGLINTON AVE. W.

AVENUE RD.

SPADINA RD.

YONGE ST.

Leaside [map p. 303]

Don Mills Rd.

"Millionaires' Row" (p. 262)

ST. CLAIR AVE. W. (p. 262)

Deer Park & Moore Park (p. 277)

Wychwood (p. 274)

DAVENPORT RD.

DOVERCOURT RD.

OSSINGTON AVE.

Yorkville [Map p. 236]

EAST YORK TP.

City Limits

ETOBICOKE TP.

Humber River

Toronto Junction (p. 208)

"Christie Pits" (p. 224)

BLOOR ST. W.

The Annex (p. 225)

Rosedale [Map p. 244]

Swansea (p. 216)

High Park (p. 218)

[Map p. 203]

COLLEGE ST.

University & Queen's Park [map p. 95]

[Map p. 161]

PARLIAMENT ST.

BROADVIEW AVE.

DANFORTH AVE.

WOODBINE AVE.

The Danforth & Riverdale (p. 172)

KINGSTON RD.

DUNDAS AVE. W.

Trinity (p. 219)

Kensington (p. 134)

QUEEN ST. W.

"The Ward" (p. 134)

[Map p. 73]

GERRARD ST. E.

Cabbage Town (p. 179)

LAKE SHORE BLVD.

KING ST. W.

[map p. 126]

FRONT ST. W.

[Map p. 45]

EASTERN AVE

[Map p. 186]

Beaches (p. 164)

MIMICO

Parkdale [map p. 198]

[Map p. 86]

[Map p. 113]

Waterfront (p. 110)

Church, Jarvis & Sherbourne Streets p. 150 ff

Toronto Islands (p. 294)

Adapted from MIGHT'S "Clearview" 1942 edition

Foreword

I suppose among all man's varied artefacts, nothing is so self-revealing as the city. Come to this planet from the far reaches of the universe, and the city will offer you an instant assessment of humanity's merits and disabilities. That some cities are lovelier than others, some distinctly more interesting, some abruptly created and some matured through long centuries of setback and achievement—that every city is different one from another only makes the form more truly representative of the peculiarly variegated species that invented it.

If I were such a traveller out of a Black Hole somewhere, and I had time only for a single metropolis before the rocket left again, I think I might well choose for my inspection the city of Toronto. There is no pretending that it is the most beautiful of towns, and at the modest age of 154 it has hardly yet acquired the rich patina of antiquity, but in the last decades of the 20th century it has become in many ways a microcosm of its time. Half the world, it often seems, has settled in Toronto, whether by choice or by circumstance; and most of contemporary humanity's aspirations, I think, whether they are expressed in supermarket abundance, political urbanity or a mere yearning for easy-going, mind-your-own-business, evenings-before-the-TV lack of passion, have chosen to settle in this city too.

Michael Kluckner has no extra-territorial status. He needed no rocket to bring him from his home in Vancouver, and as a Canadian himself must share much of the Toronto ethos as his own. Nevertheless, he possesses the one essential qualification for creating a book about any city: he is an outsider.

Ah, what a dismal roster of city books has been written by *insiders*! If there is a more depressing *genre* than that of urban reminiscence, I have yet to find it, and I am not in the least surprised by the prevalence on the shabbier second-hand bookshelves of works with titles like *My Indianapolis*, *Tales of Old Kitchener*, *Main Street Memories*, or *Seventy Years in Manchester*. Hardly more enticing are descriptive books about cities written by local residents, generally far more lavish with the sugar than the salt, and all too often full of affectionate whimsy. I must have twenty or thirty such works in my own library, and give or take a geographical fact or two, their descriptions, like their anecdotes, are more or less interchangeable.

I exaggerate, of course, if only just. Also I have a case to present, for having lived nearly all my life in the bowels of the countryside, I have myself made a career out of describing other people's cities. I cannot claim to have got them always *right*—I remember putting Toronto on the wrong lake once, and Panama City indeed on the wrong ocean. I can claim however all the advantages of detachment. E. M. Forster, describing the Arab quarter of Alexandria, once told his readers that the best way to explore it was "to wander aimlessly about," and this technique, the aimless, rootless, but still determined wander, gives to the stranger a priceless advantage. The resident is not only too embroiled, he is actually too knowledgeable, to lounge about like this; only the visitor, antennae out, emotions ready, can do it properly.

Another text I have honoured in my work comes from the Bible (Psalm 59 Verse 6)—"Grin like a dog and run about the city." I have always interpreted this to imply a certain louche and loping enthusiasm, and again I think it is denied to the resident. The longer you have known a city, and the more profoundly you are concerned with its affairs, the less naturally you can jog chortling through its streets. You may be able to write its economic history, or produce yet another volume of your well-known work about a childhood in Upper Albert Street, but you will find it hard to write an essay that runs about, or paint a grinning picture.

It used to be the hallmark of North American cities, even in my time, that they waspishly resented any breath of outside criticism, however light-hearted or good-natured. Sometimes I used to feel that the very act of describing them, even observing them, was resented. Those days have long gone—haven't they?—as Chicago and Vancouver, Chattanooga and Regina, have matured into sophistication. Certainly we may be sure that Toronto, that brave archetype of our times, will recognize in Michael Kluckner's words and paintings truths about itself, in the past and in the present, that could only be discerned by a visiting eye—if not from outer space, at least from across the Rockies.

Jan Morris,
January, 1988.

Preface

I first visited Toronto in the summer of 1966. It was my first time away from home alone; I was fifteen, and a contestant in the national diving championships, the tower portion of which was held at the Donald Summerville pool along the lakefront near the Greenwood Race Track. During the practice sessions, it was blazingly hot in the lee of any solid object, but nearly freezing in the wind which howled off the lake and across the pool deck. I soon found that, to land in the water in the centre of the diving pool, I had to fling myself off the ten-metre tower at a slight angle into the wind. During the descent of some forty feet from the top of my jump until I hit the water, the wind carried me back to the centre of the pool! Some of the dives which had to start from a handstand on the edge of the tower started rather abruptly. I remember standing on the tower, braced against the wind and shivering in a wet towel, watching the horses and trainers on the racetrack and the streetcars on Queen as they inched along toward the Beaches firehall. Today, although some of my recollections from that trip have become blurred and faded, I can still feel that wind.

In the two decades since then, I have spent a lot of time in Toronto but have never lived in the city. Jan Morris, in her introduction to this book, approves my status as an outsider—and in fact I am doubly so, for not only have I spent most of my life elsewhere, but most of the events I have written about happened before I was born. Thus, this is not a book of nostalgia—or at least not of *my* nostalgia—and it does not purport to be a comprehensive history of the city of Toronto.

Toronto The Way It Was presents a picture of the city in a collection of events and biographies, mainly of the period between about 1890 and 1950. The period before 1890 has been dealt with exhaustively by others—it would be difficult to glean new information or a new perspective from the original material available—and seems remote both socially and technologically to me; the period since 1950 is in most ways the present. The book is organized anecdotally, by neighbourhoods, and compared with normal historical treatments is something of a scrapbook—a collection of the things I would have known about, had I been there, in the sort of order I would have remembered them.

In the study of history, perhaps only chronological is logical, but I believe that human memory is much more anecdotal, and is triggered by recollections of people, places, and events, rather than by dates—for example, a few bars of a tune from a popular song elicit the memory of events which one can then pin to a certain year, whereas the date itself may elicit nothing. I am also mindful of Gilbert & Sullivan's *The Mikado*, and the Lord High Executioner's "little list" of people who would not be missed, including those "who are up on dates and bore you with them flat." The Australian writer and historian Patsy Adam-Smith said that "to know a country, you must know its memories"; the events and people within this book are, I hope, some of the memories of Toronto.

I have written about events which have a significance beyond their immediate place and time. Both the Toronto Transit Commission (pages 36-44) and Toronto Hydro (pages 80-83) were founded in a mood of "conspicuous collectivism" which, for the majority of Toronto citizens, was a radical departure from their previously held, unquestioned belief in unfettered free enterprise. The "Ne Temere" incident (pages 150-4) presents a different aspect of the shopworn Orange *vs*. Green strife which gave Toronto its nickname of "Little Belfast"—it started as typical "holier than thou" interdenominational bickering, escalated into what some felt to be a challenge to the nation's civil marriage laws, and ended as a jurisdictional dispute between two levels of government. Prohibition (pages 76-9) affected Torontonians as it did people elsewhere: one group in the community—which counted many of the most socially progressive, educated and "civilized" amongst its members—sallied forth to trample upon the civil rights of the rest. The controversial episodes of the Farmers Bank (pages 60-2), the Home Bank (pages 64-6), and the William Davies Company (pages 194-7) contrast strongly with the generally pleasant and progressive atmosphere and honest citizenship which otherwise pervaded the city. The Great War (pages 100-109) was a watershed in the history of Toronto. By comparison with the Boer War and the Northwest Rebellion, the two previous military episodes within the memories of those then living, World War One had a lot less glory and a lot more personal danger and self-sacrifice; a peculiar incident of that period was the free-speech dispute, involving the pro-German or neutralist opinions of a few professors at the University of Toronto (pages 96-7).

This is not a book about so-called great buildings—they have plenty of advocates, and many books devoted to their history. I am much more interested in the people who had the wherewithal to commission the fine buildings, and in the mores behind an "insignificant" building such as, say, the Women's Christian Temperance Union Building on Gerrard. Many of the structures illustrated here might be dismissed as mediocre architecture, but in their aggregate, when seen within the context of their neighbourhoods, or surrounded by fine trees or framed against a muggy sky, they seem very typical of Toronto.

To illustrate the book, I have chosen photographs mainly of people, and mainly by William James, which are part of the extraordinary James Collection in the City of Toronto Archives. It is extraordinary because it is such a fine portrait of the citizenry, not just the buildings or the nobs, of the period around the First World War. Most of them are news photographs, and I have tried to select ones which have not been reproduced elsewhere. Many of them are very grainy, without much depth of field, because they were shot with wide open lens apertures in order to freeze human action. By comparison, the James photograph of Bay Street on page 55 resembles a studio shot, probably taken with the camera on a tripod, with a small lens aperture (large "f-stop" number) and slow shutter speed; it is clear, glassy, and finely detailed throughout the foreground and background. The portrait photographs which line the margins are reproduced mainly from old books in my collection, and in some cases from newspaper clippings—for many of these people, there are no original photographic portraits in any public collections.

I undertook the paintings to recapture the atmosphere of old Toronto and the changing of its seasons—the deep green and brown shadows of summertime; the stark winter light which bleeds colour from trees and buildings, changing the tones from the fullness of summer and autumn to the contrast and bleakness of a *chiaroscuro* drawing; sometimes, there are summer skies and cumulus clouds, while at other times the light is flat under grey skies. Not surprisingly, very few old photographs capture the light and atmosphere of a specific season. I do not ordinarily paint scenes set in the past; the experience is, I suppose, not unlike that of directing or photographing a period film. All of the paintings are in watercolour, an ideal medium for this sort of thing as it allows one to paint quite spontaneously and quickly, and to add colours together as layers of *light*, the way nature does it; I hope they have the appearance of being done by someone who was alive at the time and painting the scene in front of him. The paintings on pages 230-1, 266-7, and 281 are contemporary scenes—I wonder at what point *they* will begin to look like period pieces.

In the various Toronto archives and collections, there are hundreds of thousands of black and white photographs; unfortunately, though, many interesting buildings and street scenes were never photographed—there is, for example, a paucity of photographs of the early days of Kensington Market. In other cases, if a photograph of a building or scene had been taken from a slightly different angle, it would have taken in a landmark in the distance, such as, say, Old City Hall. Some of the paintings were researched to give a more interesting view of an oft-photographed landmark, such as the North Toronto railway station painting on page 13; others were done because I found the buildings or scenes interesting, and could find no photographs of them in their heyday, such as the bus depot and view of Bay Street on page 43. In the appendix on pages 310 and 311, there is a list of historical sources for these paintings.

I find it difficult to imagine that Victorians would share our modern enthusiasm for black and white photography as an art form, although there was great interest in it for portraiture and as a documentary medium. Throughout the last half of the nineteenth century, the public enthused over J. M. W. Turner's "tinted steam," grew fascinated by the colour experiments of the Impressionists, read and were influenced by Goethe's thoughts on the psychological aspects of colour in his "Colour Theory," and bought houses decorated with multi-coloured brickwork. The populace also went wild for coloured postcards—about 80 of which are reproduced here; in their day, they were a legitimate and authentic art form capitalizing on a technological advance (see page 312).

I do all my own research; I find interesting and curious things to paint as a result of many long walks through the city streets. Much of the text in this book has been developed from gleanings of newspapers, especially the *Star*, the *Globe*, the *World*, and the *Telegram*, which have been preserved on microfilm rolls at the Metropolitan Toronto Reference Library and elsewhere; I found dates of events and obituaries—the key to relevant details within the dross of thousands of newspaper pages—and a contemporary sense of context in the remarkable *Canadian Annual Review of Public Affairs*, written and published between the turn of this century and the mid-1920s by John Castell Hopkins. The Goad's Fire and Property atlases in the Metropolitan Toronto Reference Library also provided an invaluable picture of street and building layouts which have since vanished; from them, the maps scattered throughout the book were developed.

Toronto's social history is particularly difficult to research as there is no comprehensive newspaper index. However, one splendid research tool in the Metropolitan Toronto Reference Library is a set of "biographical scrapbooks," composed of newspaper and magazine articles clipped by previous generations of librarians who acted on their own impulses as to what was important; they are cross-referenced to a card index, so that if one finds a name in a newspaper story, or on the deed of an interesting house, one can sometimes find more information. The *Who's Who* type of publication is also valuable.

I have not observed etiquette when referring to people with titles—I know that, for example, Sir Adam Beck should always be referred to as "Sir Adam," but I have usually called him "Beck" instead. As far as neighbourhoods are concerned, I have lumped together The Ward and Kensington, as the events moved so naturally between them; the Cabbagetown section takes in a lot of the area now called Little Trinity and the waterfront industrial area, as at that time it was more or less one neighbourhood.

Special credit is due to the following people: the staffs of the City of Toronto Archives, the Metropolitan Toronto Reference Library, and the city's branch libraries (especially Parkdale, Northern Districts, and Deer Park) who are imperturbable, tireless, polite and knowledgeable; Nick and Clare Rundall of Whitecap Books (Toronto) for their hospitality and remarkable faith; the Metro Toronto Police Museum; Michael and Anne Barstow; Angelo and Peter Vella; Arthur Keay; Frances Findlay; Mr. and Mrs. Anthony Adamson; Steven Otto; Mike Filey; The Ven. J.G. Morden; John O'Leary of Frontier College; Jack Ryrie; Dennis Yeomans; the manager and staff of the Rosedale Golf Club; my brother, Paul Kluckner, for sharing his knowledge and collection of obscure books on aviation; Keith Sacré and Sally Maulucci; at Whitecap Books in Vancouver, Michael Burch, Colleen Macmillan, and Elaine Jones; Margaret Baily of the Toronto Historical Board; and to my wife, Christine Allen, whose editing skills invariably make sense of my nonsense.

Looking south on Yonge Street from the corner of Alcorn Avenue in the 1920s. Increased traffic on Yonge had forced the Canadian Pacific Railway in 1913 to build overpasses for its railway line at Avenue Road and Yonge Street; concurrently the company, which was frustrated by the snail-like pace of construction on the new Union Station, demolished its old Yonge Street Station (which stood a couple of hundred yards to the west of Yonge Street) and built a grand new edifice at the Yonge Street crossing to give its railway passengers a suitable entry into the city. The old station's clock tower is still a landmark, although the building itself, its interior unrecognizable as a station hall, has been a liquor store since the early 1930s, when the CPR abandoned it after Union Station finally opened. The Rosedale Hotel building at the corner of Shaftesbury was known for a time as the Northgate and, before its recent demolition, as the Ports of Call nightclub; its site is now occupied by the Professional Engineers Building, while the coalyard across the street is now the Vickers and Benson Building. The area around the old station and tracks—nineteen acres of "unsightly railway land"—narrowly missed a complete razing and redevelopment in the late 1960s in a massive, multimillion-dollar scheme called "Summerhill Square," which was to include a 36-storey tower, several apartment blocks of four to fourteen storeys for about 3,000 tenants, two theatres, a tunnel for the trains, and a traffic ramp over Yonge Street which would have dumped cars into the adjoining residential streets. Nearby residents, led by the suddenly radicalized York University historian and Marlborough Avenue resident J. L. Granatstein, gathered support within the community and eventually at City Hall, and managed to get the project shelved.

Introduction

Even those people who claim to dislike Toronto or its preeminent status among Canadian cities concede that it has a superb location, that it deserves to be what it is because of where it is. However, its strategic site is not just a result of the settlement patterns and transportation methods of modern civilization. For thousands of years before the founding of the modern city, the site was the southern end of the "Toronto Trail" connecting Lake Ontario with Georgian Bay, used as a shortcut through the Great Lakes by travelling and trading Indians; the first whites to use it were fur-trading French explorers, who evidently knew about the portage around 1615—seven years after the founding of Quebec.

The main portage route was from the lakeshore northwards via the banks of the shallow, tangled, beaver-dammed Humber River; along there, archaeologists have discovered the litter of transient Indians, as well as the more substantial settlements of tribes such as the Iroquois of the village called Teiaiagon near the Humber's mouth. Both French and English traders passed through the area; to head the Indians off at the pass and prevent them from selling their furs to the English at Albany, the French established a storehouse near the mouth of the Humber in 1720.

Over the next thirty years, the competition for the spoils of the Ontario wilderness intensified between the British, ensconced in their prosperous American colonies, and the French in Quebec. The French had their big fort in the region at Niagara, but because of the great distances and poor communication, they built an outpost called Fort Rouillé at the Toronto site—on the grounds of the Canadian National Exhibition—in 1751. Three years later, the rivalry between Britain and France escalated into the so-called Fourth French and Indian War; at first, the English and their colonial comrades were repeatedly defeated by the French, but the tide turned in 1758. The following July, the British captured Fort Niagara, and the fleeing French burnt their Toronto fort; later that year, "Wolfe the dauntless hero came, and planted firm Britannia's flag on Canada's fair domain."

With the French defeated, and only one sovereign over the Canadian and American colonies, the Toronto site lapsed into remote obscurity, although fur traders still used the portage. Twenty-five years later, however, the outcome of the American Revolution placed an international boundary across the middle of Lake Ontario. Suddenly, Toronto's commanding position on the lake, its harbour tucked away behind the shelter of the sandbars which became the Island, and its command of the old trading route became strategically important.

Concurrently, a flood of Loyalists, displaced by the rampant republicanism to the south, surged into the wilderness west of the old French colony of Quebec, mainly along the northern shore of Lake Ontario around Kingston and on the temperate lands of the Niagara Peninsula. By 1791, there were 14,000 English-speaking immigrants in Ontario, so the British colonial officials created the province of Upper Canada, and distinguished it politically and by its legal system from French-speaking Lower Canada and the Maritimes.

The settlement of Ontario proceeded north from Niagara and west from

St Michael's Cathedral. Jarvis Street Baptist Church. St James' Cathedral.

PRINCIPAL CHURCHES TORONTO, ONT. CANADA.

St Andrew's Presbyterian Church Metropolitan Church.

Kingston; to prepare the Toronto area for the impending immigration, the colonial government in 1787 had made a £1,700 deal with the local Indians for the "Toronto Purchase"—a 28-mile-wide piece of land along the lakeshore from a point west of the Humber River all the way to the Scarborough Bluffs. In 1792, the new lieutenant governor of the province, Colonel John Graves Simcoe, arrived; after inspecting and rejecting both Kingston and Niagara as military bastions, he decided that Toronto was possessed of the ideal combination of features for a fortified, defendable provincial capital. Instead of choosing a name with local connotations, he called it York—thus currying favour with the Duke of York, George III's brother—but four decades later, when the fast-growing town incorporated itself, it reverted to the old name Toronto. In the two centuries since, the settlement along the lake has grown phenomenally, recently surpassing the much older Montreal to become Canada's most financially powerful city.

During its first half-century of existence, York-cum-Toronto was a parochial and fastidious place, inbred and gossip-prone, with a ruling clique whose fingers were in every pie from government through mercantilism. In the next half-century, from about 1850 until the turn of this century, Toronto grew and business thrived as railway lines opened up the fertile countryside and connected Toronto with the cities of Canada and the United States. The citizens built houses, banks, office buildings, and above all grand churches; the 1890s were the swan-song of the smug "Toronto The Good," where on the Sabbath it was against the law for

Canadian Winter Sports :
A Ladies Hockey Team, Toronto

men to play even sacred music in the parks or for children to play in the streets. In the third half-century, from 1900 until about 1950, automobiles took over the streets, and large office buildings—taller than the cathedral spires of a generation earlier—began to dot the skyline. The new secular city developed a character of its own, a brashness reflected in the razzle-dazzle of the *Star*, and a love for all things American, including movie stars, language, and everything connected with the automobile.

Still, its citizens hung on to the image of the "Queen City" as an outpost of England, with a cultural diversity little different from that of Great Britain. Writing in the city's official centennial history in 1934, Jesse Edgar Middleton opined that "it may be said in full confidence that if Toronto of today is a Tory city, it is so by inheritance more than by argument. Concentrate in one community the fierce loyalty of the Colonial exiles, the dour patriotism of Ulster, the placid conservatism of the English immigrant, the romantic feelings of the Scottish Highlander; intensify these emotions by neighbourhood to a Republic wherein demagogues continually raged against British institutions, a Republic which had sought twice to conquer Canada and had failed, though still cherishing hopes, and what else is to be expected?"

Was Toronto a British city, an American city, or a Canadian city? Perhaps it was a northern Irish city—a "Little Belfast" dominated by the Orange Order. Some of its respected and influential intellectuals, such as Goldwin Smith (page 145), and its institutions, such as the *Star* and the *Globe*, looked to free trade with America—even outright annexation—as

the best future for the city and the nation. Others, most publicly the "Toronto Eighteen" of 1911 (page 228), resisted suggestions of reciprocity with the republicans, and by so doing furthered the legend that the city's "big interests" wished to keep Toronto and southern Ontario as the biggest fish in the small pond of Canada.

Language and educational policy became an interesting aspect of the city's self-image during the early years of this century. In 1908, the "pro-England" members of the educational community sought to standardize in textbooks the retention of the vowel "u" in words such as honour and labour. The *Globe*, for one, attacked the proposal, arguing that convenience was more important than the old-fashioned England *vs.* America argument; John Castell Hopkins, a prominent local Conservative and writer, countered that "the people of the United States are developing what they boastfully call an American language," and asked the rhetorical question: "Why should Canada follow?" The disruptions of the First World War made the Imperialist members of the community even more prickly and defensive: in 1920, a Toronto-published textbook called the *History of Canada* by W. L. Grant, "a writer of culture and known Imperialism," was savaged in the press and in Orange circles for being "un-British in its records and biased in its attitude toward the French and Catholic part of Canadian annals"; a year later, the "Dominion Educator" incident provoked a similar tempest. An eight-volume encyclopaedia, edited by James Laughlin Hughes, the former chief inspector of Toronto schools and published for schoolchildren by the locally based P. D. Palmer & Company, it was discovered to be rife with "American bias"—48 pages on American history compared with sixteen on Canadian, lengthy articles on American states, statesmen, businessmen, explorers, and inventors, but precious little on Canadian ones. In the decades since these incidents, the Imperialistic aspect of Canadian society and history has diminished in importance; however, the Toronto-based literary and media community continues to caution against creeping Americanism, while the rest of Canada worries about creeping Torontoism.

* * *

The physical setting of the city—a flat plain, with only the escarpment (the shoreline of prehistoric Lake Iroquois) and the ravines as distinctive physical features—has allowed it to expand easily in the three directions away from the lakeshore. It received its dreary but functional grid system because of town planning philosophy at the time of its creation. Of the nineteenth-century neighbourhoods, only Rosedale departs significantly from this configuration. In 1891, the Rev. Henry Scadding—the son of Governor Simcoe's estate manager and the long-time rector of Holy Trinity Church, who was respected for his recollections of his youth called *Toronto of Old*—described why he felt Toronto had become such a successful city:

"Philadelphia, Washington, and other places in the United States have been laid out from the beginning in accordance with idealistic schemes....

Through the circumstances of their original development, Quebec, Montreal and even Kingston are all more or less affected in the direction and dimensions of their streets, and assessments for the needful straightenings and enlargements have been heavy. . . . Happily for Toronto, the town was from the first laid out, like Philadelphia and Washington, in accordance with the theories of the idealists, and it has had scarcely anything to correct in its general ground-plan, which was simply that of a parallelogram divided into parts by straight streets of about the same width, running north and south. Its site—a widely-extended, gently sloping plain—admitted of this, and, [in the years since,] . . . the germ-idea of the place has not been materially departed from. Unfavorable to the picturesque as is the parallelogram arrangement of streets in theory, in practice a good deal of impressiveness often results therefrom, and even beauty, so long as the roadways are wide and the building lots continue to be spacious. Fine vistas are secured, and in certain localities the array of comfortable residences coming in quick succession on both sides is a sight quite pleasant to see."

Lacking a dramatic natural setting, the city has created its own with fine buildings and trees. Unfortunately, many of the latter in the downtown area have been cut down, to make way for more cars. A few buildings have been placed in dramatic apposition to the city's biggest natural asset—the lake; the most stunning is the R. C. Harris water purification plant at the city's eastern limits, which stands on the bluff like a golden temple to the god of chlorine.

* * *

Late in the 1950s, following a decade of prosperity and non-British immigration, the Tory rectitude of old Toronto crumbled under the onslaught of loosened wallets and morals. Pierre Berton, in his book on Toronto called *The New City*, defined the recently deceased Hogtown as the place where the "Dullest Sundays in the World" were invented, and contrasted its residents with the new Toronto—Italians drinking wine and singing, people who lived in apartments, new immigrants who did not feel the need to rush about constantly on life's "eternal treadmill." In its new guise as "Metro," the city knitted together a vast sprawl of industry, towns, and bedroom suburbs into a cohesive metropolis. Metro built expressways, allowing the suburbs to spread almost over the horizon, and proving the adage that traffic will expand to fill all the available lanes. For a time, the old, inner-city Toronto of homeowners and brown houses looked as if it might disappear. Instead, in the 1960s and 1970s, the inner city began to rejuvenate itself, spurred on by people who looked disparagingly on both suburban and high-rise apartment living.

Because of their efforts, Toronto is still a city of neighbourhoods. However, these modern neighbourhoods are quite different from the ones in the old city, such as The Junction, Cabbagetown, The Danforth and Beaches, which were like distinct little towns, in which many families worked and worshipped within walking distance of their homes. People are still strongly attached to their neighbourhoods, but are today so much more mobile. Lucky ones can use the subway; elsewhere, the traffic whizzes and plugs in every direction, as inner-city residents fight to reach their workplaces in what were supposed to be bedroom suburbs outside the old city limits.

Since the 1950s, Toronto residents have become cosmopolitan, and proud of the city's buildings new and old, its history, social life, culture, and crime rate. In the popular phrase, Toronto is "the city that works," a short drive from a city like Detroit, which does not. *This* is the new Toronto, a city created by its residents which did not exist thirty-five years ago.

In old Toronto, King Street East was the main street. A tremendous fire in 1849 raged through the area, destroying the St. James church at King and Church, and levelling many of the wooden and brick buildings remaining from the city's modest, jerrybuilt beginnings. In the aftermath of the fire, civic pride and prosperity led to the erection of the lavish St. Lawrence Hall (on the left) at the corner of King and Jarvis, and a new, grand St. James Cathedral on the site of the old one (in the right middle-distance of the painting). After several decades of slow decay, St. Lawrence Hall was rescued by a public campaign and restored as the city's official Canada Centennial project in 1967.

Old York

"Muddy York" was the ten-block townsite on the edge of Toronto Bay bounded by Front, Berkeley, Adelaide, and George streets. The governor of Upper Canada, Colonel Simcoe, had chosen the site as his military headquarters and the provincial capital because of its strategic location and its well-protected, commodious, and easily defended harbour, but his opinion of the site's value was not shared by his superiors, who had instead opted for the older city of Kingston. Regardless, his Queen's Rangers built a log garrison near the western gap, at the mouth of Garrison Creek, laid out the townsite, cut Yonge Street through the forest to Lake Simcoe, and established a survey grid on the land beyond the town—plots of land for settlement and farming, the borders of which determined the locations of many of Toronto's main streets, including Bloor, Danforth, St. Clair, Eglinton, Bathurst, Dufferin, Keele, Bayview, and Leslie. Turning away from the site's traditional name of Toronto, Simcoe named his town York on August 27, 1793.

Less than a week later, the receiver general of Upper Canada, Peter Russell, wrote to his sister in the old provincial capital at Niagara, describing the new town: "The Governor and Mrs. Simcoe received me very graciously, but you can have no conception of the misery in which they live, the canvas house [a two-roomed tent which Simcoe had purchased from the estate of Captain Cook!] being their only residence; in one room of which they lie and see company, and in the other end, the nurse, children squawling, etc. An open bower covers us at dinner, and a tent with a small table and three chairs serves us as a Council room . . . . The town occupies a flat about fifty yards from the water. The situation I believe healthy as the ground is perfectly dry and consists for the present of four ranges of squares, each court containing five squares, and to each square two rows of houses, four in each row . . . . When this plan is to be carried into execution the Lord only knows, for no attempt has been yet made by any intended inhabitants except Mr. Robinson, who is making preparations."

Russell's perception of the healthy atmosphere of the place was proved wrong with each subsequent change of weather. After heavy rains, the Don's stagnant pools backed up and overflowed, sending rivulets through the flat ground at the eastern end of the townsite. Mosquitoes breeding in the marshes of the Don and Ashbridge's Bay visited the residents in the cool of the evening. The light soil had too much clay for decent drainage, and turned into a quagmire after only moderate amounts of rain. Spring breakup was an appalling mess.

In spite of its drawbacks, the town grew rapidly. The government erected brick parliament buildings at the foot of Berkeley Street, and government officials moved north from Niagara, some of them receiving hundred-acre park lots, stretching between what are now Queen and Bloor streets, in appreciation of their forbearance. The town expanded westward along the bay—Front Street was at the time waterfrontage, King Street became the commercial and shopping strip with a marketplace established in 1803 on the south side between Church and Jarvis, and an Anglican church in 1807 on the north side. By 1812, about 700 people had

made the little edge-of-the-forest hamlet their home.

In the gloomy observation of a temporary resident named Anna Jameson, which has often been quoted but bears repeating, Toronto was "a little, ill-built town, on low land, at the bottom of a frozen bay, with one very ugly church [the first St. James] without tower or steeple, some Government offices built of staring red brick in the most tasteless, vulgar style imaginable, three feet of snow all around and the grey, sullen wintry lake, and the dark gloom of the pine forest bounding the prospect; such seems Toronto to me now. I did not expect much but for this I was not prepared."

A more matter-of-fact description is volunteered by W.H. Pearson, in his *Recollections and Records of Toronto of Old*:

"There were no waterworks until about 1843, when they were established by Mr. Albert Furniss of Montreal. In most of the yards there were wells or pumps and rainwater was collected in underground tanks or in barrels; this was often frozen in the winter, when it was customary to melt snow as a substitute. As wood was the only fuel used for domestic purposes until 1854 [when coal became common in the city], the rainwater was quite satisfactory for washing purposes. When people ran short of water, it had to be carted up from the bay in barrels.

"The trenches for the gas supply were being dug in 1841. As coal oil was not discovered until about a quarter century later, and the price of gas was almost prohibitory, tallow candles were in general use for lighting. People had moulds and made their own candles. They were sold by the pound by the grocer and chandler, some six to the pound and some nine. It was also a common thing for people to make their own soap, utilizing the wood ashes [pouring boiling water through hardwood ashes produces a slurry of lye, which when cut with grease—to stop it from burning the skin—and scented, makes soap]. The soap and candle manufacturers used to send around to the residences for grease, for which they exchanged candles or soap. The streets were wretchedly paved, or not at all, and were generally in a very bad condition. All the sidewalks were of wood and in the principal streets were from eight to ten feet in width, the planks being laid cross-wise, and on many of the private streets not more than four planks (four feet) in width laid lengthwise. The nails frequently became loose, causing the ends to tilt, making it somewhat risky for pedestrians. These sidewalks had to be frequently renewed."

* * *

At the turn of the nineteenth century, York's economy grew slowly, dependent as it was on the salaries of its government workers. It was a government town—the political centre of Upper Canada—and drew to it a number of officials who made their mark on its development. Among them were William Jarvis, the registrar of Upper Canada, who was granted the park lot through which Jarvis Street now runs; Peter Russell, president and administrator of the province from 1796-1799, and a major

St. Lawrence Market, on the north side of Front Street East between Market and Jarvis streets, was built in 1850 and demolished in 1904. The buildings connected through to St. Lawrence Hall. The photograph looks northwest towards the spire of St. James Cathedral in the right background. Across Front Street is the old city hall, superseded by "Old City Hall" in the 1890s, then remodelled as a farmers' market when the buildings in this photograph were demolished.

St Lawrence Market.   Micklethwaite Photo.

land-holder; the surgeons Dr. William Warren Baldwin and Dr. James Macauley, the former the builder of the first "Spadina," the latter the namesake of Macauleytown, which was built on his old estate and later became the city slum better known as The Ward; and John Beverley Robinson, the future attorney general and chief justice, the dominant figure in the so-called Family Compact which effectively ran the province in the 1820s and 1830s. As well, there was the schoolmaster and Anglican cleric Dr. John Strachan, who had for a dozen years been a well-known figure in the colony due to his highly regarded schools in Kingston and Cornwall—he moved to York in 1812 to accept the appointment as rector. In addition to these official personages, there were a few merchants who traded in the town and bought their supplies from wholesalers in Montreal and New York.

The latter connection was abruptly severed in 1812 when Britain and the United States went to war. General Isaac Brock, the commander of British forces in Upper Canada, set out to fortify York. It became the naval base, and in its harbour the local shipwrights began to build a formidable schooner. Brock made plans for a new fort to replace the block-houses near the Western Gap, and got as far as digging the earthworks and installing a powder magazine and gun batteries to guard the harbour entrance. However, events overtook Brock's well-laid plans, for on April 27, 1813, an American force of 1,700 troops landed from a flotilla of fourteen ships, and moved quickly over the flat, lightly forested country towards the fort. Governor Simcoe's superior, Lord Dorchester, who had expressed the opinion that York could not easily be defended, was proved right. The Americans overran the several hundred troops defending the approaches, but as they charged into the incomplete fort, someone touched off the powder magazine. The explosion killed, among others, the American commanding general, enraging his troops, who swept on to inflict a modest sacking upon York, including looting and the burning of the parliament buildings. Although they had scarcely a military leg to

stand on, the residents found a champion in the indomitable Dr. Strachan, who negotiated a capitulation with honour. The troops withdrew in May, but returned briefly in the summer. The following year, British forces finally managed to complete their fort amidst the demolished bits of the incomplete garrison, six months before the declaration of peace.

All things considered, York had not fared so badly in the war. It had its own heroes, especially Dr. Strachan and John Beverley Robinson, who had fought under Brock; its merchants, notably William Allan and Joseph Cawthra, had prospered in the booming wartime economy; and it had developed a sense of community, hardened against the Yankees, and formed around a powerful oligarchy of wealthy government, religious and financial figures which became known as the Family Compact. The latter ran the city and province until its influence waned due to the rise of reformers such as William Lyon Mackenzie (page 74).

From the period of the Family Compact, a few buildings remain. The oldest is the house of Judge William Campbell, built around 1822 on Frederick Street at Adelaide, and moved in 1972 to a fine location opposite Osgoode Hall at Queen and University. In the same year as Campbell's house was built, the Bank of Upper Canada was founded—its surviving headquarters, at 252 Adelaide Street East, were erected a few years later. The Bank of Upper Canada was especially significant for two reasons. Firstly, it was an *Ontario* bank, established and controlled by members of the Family Compact, with a government-backed monopoly on financing and directing provincial economic development. Secondly, businessmen in Kingston, the largest town in the province, had received a charter for a bank in 1819 but dithered too long in getting it established; when they attempted to regain their charter, they found they had been outmanoeuvred by the wily Dr. Strachan and his associates. Through machinations such as these, Toronto tightened its grip over the towns and countryside of Ontario.

The corner of Yonge and Front streets, looking southwest. Visible are two of the symbols of Toronto's "foreign"—that is, Montreal and the Dominion—domination: the Bank of Montreal and the Dominion Public Building. The former, built in the 1880s in a lavish rococo style, was the Bank of Montreal's main Toronto branch until 1949. The latter, though built in the 1920s, uses Classical design precedents which seem to be both ancient Greek and republican American; it is Toronto's customs building. During the 1920s, Front Street became a grand boulevard: Union Station was finished, the Dominion Public Building and the Royal York Hotel were erected, and a curving motorway connected it with University Avenue. The corner of Yonge and Front was also a busy interchange for streetcars, including those of the Yonge, Bathurst, Dupont, Avenue Road, and Church lines.

Downtown

Much of the interesting visual clutter has disappeared from Toronto's downtown streets. In the financial heart of the city, the streets are cleaner, brighter and neater than they used to be; there is less dour brick and there are fewer smoking chimneys, but many of the streets are no longer lined with shops, and one must look west of University on Queen Street, or north of Queen on Yonge Street, to capture some of the visual flavour of old Toronto's downtown. The trams no longer run on Yonge, Bay or Front streets, most of the overhead wires have been buried, shop awnings are few and far between, and advertising signs no longer jumble and fight for airspace; replacing this hodge-podge are huge, sleek complexes with smooth, simplified designs, each bearing the mark of one single, cohesive style. Lining the streets are clean plazas and long, noble marble façades in hard, cold colours; interspersed among them are enormous, straight-sided towers like gravestones, set back from the streets. Today, the shops are underground in congruently designed, interconnected malls, linked with the subway and the vast foyers of office buildings.

By comparison, the old shops and houses that lined the downtown streets may have started out as, say, Georgian in style, to be modified by carpenters of later generations. Embellished with Art Deco typefaces or gewgaws, or advertising in styles such as Art Nouveau, they became an amalgam of the different owners' tastes or lack thereof, without the overbearing evidence of a central designing *authority*.

From its early days, Toronto's downtown grew as the city increasingly became a centre of finance and business. However, the most important industry—at least in terms of the numbers employed—was clothing, which at the turn of the century employed almost twice as many workers as the next biggest industry, iron and steel fabricating. Women did much of the dressmaking work, often under appalling conditions in "sweated subcontracts," working in lofts and back-alley sheds scattered through the downtown area. Early in the century, the factory system evolved, led by firms such as Eaton's, which built one of the early "high-rises"—a several-storey clothing factory in the midst of its multi-block retail and manufacturing complex northwest of Queen and Yonge. Before the catastrophic 1904 fire, the blocks along Front Street around the foot of Bay were occupied by a variety of such factories, and it was in a "neckwear factory" there that the fire started. Clothing stores lined the streets, their large advertisements filling page after page in the newspapers. King Fashion Tailors at 101 Yonge Street was "open evenings"; Tip Top Tailors at 245 Yonge Street offered made-to-measure suits for $19; Robinson's Upstairs Clothing Shop at Yonge and Shuter enticed customers with slogans, illustrated with drawings of Niagara, which declaimed: "The roar of the falls going over the precipice cannot be compared to the roar of the competition at my $25 values!", and "Niagara's waters have never swept aside obstacles as easily as I have swept aside competition!"

An astonishing variety of businesses and residences, in combinations

Government House occupied the eastern half of the block bounded by Simcoe, John, King, and Wellington. The one illustrated here was actually the second on the site; the first had been built about 1798 by the Elmsley family, and was bought by the government to replace the first-ever government house, which had been blown to smithereens in the War of 1812. This house was demolished in 1912, and the land used for Canadian Pacific Railway shops; the proceeds of the sale went towards the erection of the massive "Chorley Park" in Rosedale (page 245).

that would make a modern city planner weep, shared the streets. At the turn of the century, clothing factories, houses, sawmills, lumberyards, stables, a brush factory, hotels with stand-up bars, a billiard-table factory, churches, newspaper offices, printing plants and opera houses all stood shoulder-to-shoulder. On Temperance Street east of Bay, for instance, Dixon's Carriage Works adjoined the Ontario Veterinary College; two doors away was the Methodist Book Room, which was across the street from the Empire Burlesque theatre. Residents were obliged to endure the crowding and noise, the smoke from a thousand chimneys and the smell of a thousand horses. Very little of this old city remains: the Bank of Montreal at the corner of Yonge and Front (page 21), the warehouses along Yonge Street near Wellington, the Commercial Bank at 13-15 Wellington, and the Bank of British North America at the northeast corner of Yonge and Wellington are a significant few. Some of the last few old shops remaining on lower Yonge Street were demolished during the autumn of 1987 (pages 28-9).

The city's increasing influence as a financial and insurance centre, and the growth of companies, such as the Canadian Pacific Railway Company, prompted many of the demolitions in the old downtown. The office-space needs of these banks and corporations coincided with the development of

Toronto from St. James, TORONTO, Canada.

Looking northwest from St. James Cathedral across the rooftops of turn-of-the-century Toronto. In the centre of the postcard, at the corner of Richmond and Yonge, is the Confederation Life Building; visible past it is the City Hall clock tower.

the office tower (which the invention of the steel-frame building and the elevator had recently made feasible) in the United States. Following a protracted debate, city council agreed in 1905 to permit the Traders Bank to erect a fifteen-storey office building on Yonge Street near King. Within a decade, others had sprung up around that corner, creating the city's first "canyon" (page 32). In the 1920s and early 1930s, new skyscrapers went up on Bay Street and King Street West. But the "Manhattanization" of the skyline really began in the late 1960s, when Bay Street became a national synonym for financial power.

* * *

Long before the age of skyscrapers, the current Toronto downtown was known as "New Town," to distinguish it from the "Old Town" centred on King Street east of Jarvis. The city limits were Queen Street on the north and Peter Street on the west; beyond the former were the park lots given as tokens of esteem for services rendered to the colony by its early colonial officials, while beyond the latter was the Garrison Reserve, dating from the America versus Britain belligerency of the late eighteenth and early nineteenth centuries. The landmarks of New Town at the time

of Toronto's incorporation in 1834 included an official enclave on the streets between John and Simcoe: on the most southerly block, between Front and Wellington, were the parliament buildings; on the block between Wellington and King was Government House (see the postcard on page 22); further to the north, on the block bounded by King and Adelaide, was Upper Canada College. On John Street opposite Upper Canada College was the city's hospital. A number of fine houses of government officials and prominent merchants and citizens occupied the streets along the bay, which was reedy and breezy and unmarred by railway tracks and industry. On the site of the Royal York Hotel was the house of the colonial official William Powell; at 63 Wellington Street West was "Holland House," a battlemented little castle owned by the attorney general, H. J. Boulton; at the northeast corner of Front and Bay was the square brick home—with a twenty-five by ten foot wine cellar in the basement—of Dr. W. W. Baldwin; on Wellington near Yonge was the house of Frederick Capreol, the promoter of Toronto's first railway; and on the block bounded by York, Simcoe, Wellington and Front stood the grandest of them all, the house known as the "Palace" belonging to the powerful Rev. John Strachan.

With the coming of the railways in the 1850s, many of the residents of the fine houses along the waterfront moved to greener swards to the north and west; in their place came industry and hotels, both of which owed their prosperity to their proximity to the railways. One of the most famous hotels of the previous century was the Queen's Hotel, on the site of the equally renowned hotel of this century, the Royal York (page 118).

The government opened up the old military reserve to the west for settlement in the 1830s, and laid out Wellington Place, Clarence Square, and Victoria Square in what was hoped would become a fashionable address. However, the railway had the same effect on the area's desirability as it had previously had on the streets around the old parliament buildings. Instead of becoming a sought-after residential neighbourhood, it gradually evolved into part of the city's garment district, the home of clothing factories which in the 1920s fled the redeveloping downtown in search of less expensive land.

* * *

The general public has had few opportunities to pry off the protective case and examine the clocklike inner workings of so-called "big business." But not only business operated in mysterious ways—so too did the myriad fraternal organizations, to which most men belonged and whose rituals and proceedings rarely came into the public's purview. One of the rare occasions when outsiders got an inside look at both business and a fraternal organization occurred in 1906, when the insurance industry came under the magnifying glass of a Royal Commission, partially prompted by the thriving and controversial insurance business carried on by the Independent Order of Foresters.

The contemporary chronicler John Castell Hopkins summarized the Royal Commission's investigation: "A public inquiry into the detailed business and financial interests of Companies acting as trustees for nearly $400,000,000 of the people's money, or money expectations, and handling immense sums for yearly investment and profit could not but create a great stirring of dry bones—a cloud of dust in various circles which whirled around, settled down through the assistance of the press, and was brushed off or not as the case might be. All kinds of persons were involved in matters of evidence or discussion—politicians, officials, lawyers, financiers and even Judges. Some injustice was done and some reputations were improperly flecked with dust for a time, and it may be feared that the public conscience was not altogether benefited by the wholesale allegations of misdealing in what was called 'high finance.' "

Banks were not the only institutions to contribute to Toronto's prosperity and financial prestige; as well, there were the insurance companies, which expanded the city's business base and contributed to the growth of the province. In his 1891 *Toronto Old & New*, the chronicler G. Mercer Adam wrote that "of loan and investment companies, there are now twenty-five having their headquarters in Toronto with total assets of over $63 million. There is little need to say much here in commendation of those beneficent enterprises, which mark the provident character and the humanity of the age, the Life, Fire and Marine Insurance Companies. In their operations, aside from their practical benefit, they remove from the mind of the wage-earner, and all ranks of toil, a load of anxiety which would in many instances become an intolerable burden."

Many of the small insurance companies in Toronto were in fact fraternal organizations. Each of them had formed to promulgate a distinct set of beliefs, but they shared a common goal in that they operated to the mutual advantage of their members, who contributed a portion of their savings to a fund which assured them of financial aid in time of need and a decent burial at time of death. "Friendly societies" first organized in England as so-called "sick clubs," which evolved into fraternal insurance orders that collected premiums from members, made investments, paid insurance benefits and pensions, and in some cases maintained old age homes and asylums. At the turn of the century, the largest such organization in the world was the Independent Order of Odd Fellows; others included the Freemasons, the Order of the Eastern Star, the Modern Woodmen of America, the Knights of Pythias, the Loyal Order of Moose, the Improved Order of Red Men, the Elks, the Eagles, the Order of Owls, the Knights of Columbus, the Ancient Order of Hibernians, and the Independent Order of Foresters (which, although among the smallest, had a worldwide membership of nearly one-quarter of a million men in 1918). The most politically influential order in Toronto was the Grand Orange Lodge, which proclaimed its Protestant, pro-Ulster beliefs by clashing with the Catholic Greens, often to the point of fisticuffs, on July 12—the anniversary of the Battle of the Boyne. Its rabid proselytizing led to

Toronto's nickname of "Little Belfast," and Orange-backed candidates often dominated civic politics (the cartoon of Mayor Church on this page alludes to the political high-wire act he performed so well).

A St. Patrick's Day 1920 cartoon from the Star, hinting at the political juggling act performed by civic politicians; it was captioned: "Mayor Church a connoisseur of ties. He hesitated whether to wear a green one in the morning and an orange one in the afternoon, but finally compromises on a chameleon cravat."

The Stoodleigh Restaurant, "famous for excellent food served in an old English atmosphere," occupied part of the basement of the Star building, at 72 King Street West. Articles in the 1940s on what to do in the city invariably mentioned the Stoodleigh, noting the caricatures which then lined the walls and comparing its atmosphere favourably with that of the half-dozen other notable eateries—the Little Denmark, the Chicken Palace, the Winston Grill, and the roof restaurants at the King Edward and Park Plaza hotels.

Muirhead's Cafeterias offered "choice foods, in infinite variety, perfectly cooked, temptingly served" at three downtown locations—38 Adelaide Street West across from the Regent Theatre, 200 Bay Street, and the corner of Yonge and Shuter near Massey Hall. The company's president and managing director during the 1930s was chartered accountant Arthur Stanley Tindale (above), who started as a junior with the Royal Bank in his hometown of Arthur at age 18, in 1911. After war service, he moved to Toronto in 1920 and eventually entered the food business with the company's founder, R. J. Muirhead.

(Above) A postcard of King Street, looking west from Yonge, about 1910. The sign on the front of the tram advertises "Speedy—The World's Greatest High Diver," who was to perform at Scarboro Beach Park—an attraction operated by the street railway company. The tram is on the "Belt Line"—counterclockwise on the loop of King, Sherbourne, Bloor and Spadina. The white building with the classical façade at 8 King Street West, on the right of the picture, was the head office of the Home Bank, which in 1923 failed ignominiously (page 63). In the distance is the distinctive tower of the Mail & Empire building at the northwest corner of King and Bay, now the site of First Canadian Place. The retouchers who hand-coloured photographs for use as postcards usually eliminated much of the clutter typical of the streets. The dozens of power and telephone lines were in this instance removed from the sky, but remain visible across the buildings. (Below) Looking west along King Street West from a half block further west than the postcard above. This "night-time" view is a heavily retouched version of a daytime photograph which was also published by the company as a postcard—no camera or film of the period could freeze the motion of the cyclists with that amount of available light.

The Independent Order of Foresters was a branch of a fraternal organization founded in Newark, New Jersey in 1874. The local chapter erected one of the notable "modern" buildings in Toronto in the 1890s (pages 30-1). This building was one of the investments made by the I.O.F., which had several million dollars of members' insurance deposits by the turn of the century. The funds were administered by a Supreme Council composed of several businessmen and chaired by the I.O.F.'s Supreme Chief Ranger, Dr. Peter Oronhyatekha. In 1900, the I.O.F. decided to form its own Union Trust Company to invest in real estate and mortgages of all kinds, and engaged the Hon. George Eulas Foster, the minister of finance in the Conservative governments prior to 1896, as general manager. Foster had no connection with the I.O.F., and was not even a member, but was available for work as he had failed to be reelected in 1900. In 1904, however, he was elected to the House of Commons by the North Toronto riding and sat in opposition while continuing his duties as general manager of the I.O.F.'s trust company. Throughout this period, he invested the company's money skilfully and made some spectacular profits on land and timber deals in the west.

The Royal Commission on the insurance industry opened in March, 1906, and for several months heard generally dry, actuarial testimony. The investigation of many companies—even ones controlled by such well-known men as Senator Cox—failed to spark much interest from the public, although there were ample instances uncovered of "funds that had been used for investment in concerns and interests not contemplated by the Insurance Act," including several where directors had speculated in stocks and had made up the losses out of their own pockets.

Public interest suddenly increased when the Supreme Chief Ranger of the I.O.F., the mysterious Dr. Oronhyatekha, took the stand. He began his testimony on September 13, and continued daily until the twenty-fourth. He argued convincingly and colourfully for fraternal insurance, stating on one occasion that "we have money to burn, and we burn it for the good of the Order." Subsequent investigations of the I.O.F.'s affairs continued with few breaks until the middle of November. Spectators found the testimony doubly interesting because of the I.O.F.'s "aggressive and successful methods of acquiring business, its accumulation of funds and remarkable distribution of benefits, its large expenditure and picturesque management by Dr. Oronhyatekha, [and because] of the close connection of its investment agency—the Union Trust Company—with large schemes of speculation in land, stocks, and industrial projects which, however, had turned out profitably for the Order."

The involvement of Foster, a prominent front-bench member of the opposition and potential future prime minister, turned the proceedings into a political football match—the Liberal government had instigated the Royal Commission, and the prosecutor, at least according to one Tory newspaper, went on "a fishing expedition" to get at Foster. In one case in-

Yonge Street looking North, Toronto.

A view looking north on Yonge Street from King, probably—because of the Union Jacks and bicycles and the absence of automobiles—taken either during the celebrations in the spring of 1900 for the lifting of the siege of Ladysmith in South Africa during the Boer War, or during the 1901 visit of the Duke and Duchess of Cornwall and York (later King George V and Queen Mary). Faintly visible on the left is the Fairweather's Furs sign on the old Georgian-style shop at 84-6 Yonge Street, which was demolished at the end of the First World War and replaced by the building shown in the painting on page 28. In the distance, on the right-hand side of the street, are the distinctive towers of the Confederation Life Building, the tallest and most eyecatching structure in Toronto in the early 1890s. The Confederation Life Association felt that its fine, solid building exemplified the guiding principle of its founder, John Kay Macdonald: "Security and Stability and a Square Deal for All Policyholders." Macdonald was born in Edinburgh in 1837, grew up on his father's farm, received an education infused with Presbyterianism at Knox College, and evidently intended to join the ministry. However, he decided to enter the business world in 1863 as assistant treasurer to the counties of York and Peel, and eight years later he organized Confederation Life Association. He was one of the founders of the Toronto YMCA, president of the Children's Aid Society of Toronto, and a longtime director of the Upper Canada Religious and Tract Society and the Upper Canada Bible Society. His residence, called "Cona Lodge," was on Charles Street East. Often described as the "Dean of Canadian Life Insurance," he died in 1928, at the age of 90. Macdonald had been general manager of the company; he was succeeded in that position by his nephew, Colonel W. C. Macdonald (killed while on active service during the First World War), and his son, Charles Macdonald. The first president of Confederation Life Association was Sir Francis Hincks, who had been prime minister of the Province of Canada before, and minister of finance after, Confederation. As for the building itself, it survived a disastrous fire in 1981, and still stands amidst the enormous skyscrapers of downtown, though without its towers.

John Kay Macdonald

Dr. Peter Oronhyatekha (1841-1907), the Supreme Chief Ranger of the Independent Order of Foresters, was a Mohawk Indian born on the Six Nations Reserve. Determined to receive a western education, he became a fluent English speaker, and at the age of nineteen was invited to address the Prince of Wales during the latter's visit to the reserve in 1860. The Prince arranged for Oronhyatekha to study at Oxford University; subsequently, Oronhyatekha attended the University of Toronto and earned a degree in medicine, becoming the first native Indian to receive a degree from a Canadian university. Although hitherto open only to whites, the Independent Order of Foresters invited him to become a member, and in 1881 he was elected High Chief Ranger. Eight years later he retired from medicine and devoted his energies to I.O.F. work. He lived at 209 Carlton Street. The word Oronhyatekha means Burning Cloud.

volving a $55,000 discrepancy on a British Columbia timber deal the prosecutor gamely attempted to prove the existence of an illegal commission to an agent; in another case, Foster was accused of loaning I.O.F. money to a company, allegedly with Conservative party connections, which made such a fortune on C.P.R. settlement land-options that it was able to pay the I.O.F. six percent interest, plus an additional profit of "hundreds of thousands of dollars."

However, the Royal Commission found more smoke than fire; in the specific case of the I.O.F.'s affairs, it had the props cut out from beneath it when the I.O.F. decided to sell off a controlling interest in its Union Trust Company—largely, it was explained, because of United States laws pertaining to subsidiary companies. E. E. A. DuVernet, who later built the sprawling house in the centre of the circle in Wychwood Park, acquired slightly more than half the shares in the company for about one-and-one-half million dollars.

Both Foster and the I.O.F. survived the enquiry. The former returned to government in 1911 with the Conservatives of Robert Borden, received a knighthood in 1914, and served as minister of trade and commerce for nearly ten years until the Conservatives' defeat; he was elected a vice-president of the League of Nations in 1920.

* * *

The next Conservative minister of trade and commerce, Harry Stevens, chaired a much less sanguine public inquiry during the "Dirty Thirties" into business practices and conditions across the country. Stevens made a speech in Toronto in January, 1934, to a convention of retail shoe merchants, in which he charged that mass buying practices by department and chain stores were resulting in excessive prices on the one hand, and sweat-shop working conditions on the other. This speech was but one of Stevens's maverick outbursts, and was perceived by the prime minister, Conservative R.B. Bennett, as a provocation in defiance of government policy. After Bennett's rebuke, Stevens submitted his resignation; however, Bennett on second thought realized that Stevens had a reputation as a friend of "the little man"—a useful attribute in an upcoming election—and refused to accept it. Two weeks later, Bennett announced the formation of a special committee which was to "inquire into and investigate the causes of the large spread between the prices received for commodities by the producer thereof, and the price paid by the consumer therefore," as well as distribution methods of farm and other natural products. This Price Spreads Commission attracted tremendous attention over the next several months as it travelled the country; in Toronto, the activities of department stores and conditions in the textile and clothing industries drew the most attention.

The commission wasted little time in getting started—in Toronto on February 27 and 28 it heard detailed testimony by the welfare commissioner, the chairman of the Ontario Minimum Wage Board, and a University of Toronto professor named H.M. Cassidy, who "dealt exhaustively with sweat shop conditions, cut-price tactics and underpaid girls working in clothing factories." Early in March, the president of Canada Packers, J.S. McLean, was grilled on the marketing of livestock and meat. In June, the commission heard several days of testimony relating to Simpson's, the T. Eaton Company, and the Hudson's Bay Company, and returned to Toronto for several days in November to examine the business practices in chain grocery and meat stores. The evidence was sensational, and fully reported by the newspapers. Executive salaries and perquisites were contrasted with the pitiful wages and working conditions of tailors, packers and shop assistants. The vicious price-cutting tactics of chain-store buyers put small manufacturers into their thrall, but retail prices stayed high, and profits were alleged to be immense. According to the testimony at the commission, the Depression's effects had been somewhat selective.

Stevens developed an almost messianic zeal when dealing with some of his businessmen-witnesses, and sometimes adopted a harsh, accusatory manner of cross-examination. In the summer, a speech which he made ostensibly in confidence to a group of Conservative Members of Parliament was reprinted, evidently without his concurrence, in a pamphlet known as "the sweat shop booklet," which upon its circulation quickly became something of a manifesto. Before it was even published in the media, the prime minister received representations from "the president of one of the companies whose affairs were discussed in the pamphlet, the claim being made that the statements of Mr. Stevens were at variance with the facts." Bennett obtained a copy, and decided that it should be suppressed, but before he was able to act on this, he left the country for a meeting of the League of Nations in Geneva; while he was away, the Winnipeg *Free Press* published it.

Bennett returned in October, and at a cabinet meeting soon thereafter, he and some of his conservative colleagues attacked Stevens for his anti-business attitudes and crusading tactics. Stevens resigned, charging that Bennett had bowed to pressure from R. Y. Eaton and Charles Burton of Simpson's. On November 5, he told the national press that he was being followed by two Detroit private detectives who were reporting his moves to the Canadian financial establishment. Wealth, he said, "must be used in the interests of the people."

The following July, with a federal election in the offing, Stevens formed the Reconstruction Party which aimed "to defend the forgotten man against concentrated capital"; he castigated the government's legislation, proposed from the sanitized remnants of his Price Spreads Commission as "anaemic, inadequate and ineffective." A divided Bennett government walked meekly to the election gallows, and was reduced to a rump of 39 seats by Mackenzie King's Liberals; of the Reconstruction Party hopefuls, only Harry Stevens won a seat. The lid of Pandora's sweatshop box slammed shut.

The recently demolished buildings on the west side of Yonge Street, between King and Adelaide, were typical of the cluttered, visually interesting downtown of old Toronto. The painting shows the street as it appeared early in the 1920s. On the left, and much grander than the others, were the very elegant and expensive new premises of furrier Robert Fairweather; this building, erected after the First World War, replaced the southernmost two of three stores dating from several decades before. The remaining store, at 92 Yonge, housed Rathbone & Company Gentlemen's Furnishings, a competitor of the Dunfield & Company Men's Furnishings store at 102-4 Yonge—the mansard-roofed building to the right of the painting. Between these two bastions of sartorial splendour stood a row of old shops, with tenants including a photo shop, the Imperial Cigar Store, the Paris Kid Glove Shop, Hickey's Billiards, the Burgers Ltd. confectionary, and Ellis Brothers Jewellers. The Ellis brothers had prospered sufficiently by 1930 to buy and demolish the block of shops and erect a sleek and modern building in their place; only a few years later, however, with the wolf of Depression at their door, they amalgamated with Ryrie-Birks Jewellers (page 66). The Fairweather and Dunfield façades have been retained, and incorporated into new construction. In the foreground is the Star's roving radio station, an outlet for the broadcasting talents of a young sports reporter named Foster Hewitt, who in 1923 began to announce hockey games from the Mutual Street Arena, and for several decades thereafter was the voice of the Maple Leafs.

(Below) Looking north to Adelaide Street. At the head of the street, framed by the buildings on Toronto Street, stood the city's eighth post office, built in the Second Empire style in the years immediately following Canada's Confederation. It was demolished and replaced in 1960 by the hideous turquoise-coloured Adelaide Postal Station. On the extreme left of the photograph stands the Classical Greek-styled predecessor of the eighth Post Office, which provided comfortable living quarters for the postmaster on its second floor. Built in the 1850s, at the same time and by the same architects as St. James Cathedral, it subsequently had a chequered career including terms as a Bank of Canada outpost and customs office, before being restored for the offices of the Argus Corporation. (Right and next page) The Temple Building, erected in 1895 for the Independent Order of Foresters, stood at the northwest corner of Bay and Richmond. Visible above both little entrance-way balconies are carved mooseheads. The building, though similar in style to both the Confederation Life Building and Old City Hall, was significant architecturally as, according to historian Eric Arthur, it was the last tall office building to use cast iron for its frame (instead of steel), yet lavished attention on fireproofing. Its ten-storey height was certainly remarkable—the development of tall office buildings, made possible by the invention of the electric elevator, had repercussions throughout the cities of North America, not least in fire departments, which quickly purchased aerial ladder trucks and rebuilt their firehalls to store them. The photograph on the next page was taken during the First World War years from the front steps of Old City Hall, and shows the Temple Building standing proudly amidst the rabble and clutter of Bay Street and Queen. The Colonial Theatre, on the left of the photograph, had a strange façade including fluted columns with Corinthian capitals at street level; in 1919, it gained a cobbled-together second storey, assembled from bits of the demolished Second Empire-style Customs House at Yonge and Front (compare this photograph with the one on page 57). It was later known as the Bay Theatre, and has since been demolished; the Simpson's Tower now occupies the site.

Temple Building, Toronto

Toronto Street and Post Office, Toronto

Yonge Street looking North, Toronto

Three stages in the development of the Toronto skyline. (Left) A photograph taken before 1911, looking north on Yonge Street from just south of the corner of Wellington. The fifteen-storey skyscraper is the Traders Bank, built in 1905 following a landmark city council decision allowing tall buildings. The skyscrapers of the previous generation were the 1895 Temple Building (previous pages) and the 1890 Confederation Life building, clearly visible in the background. Around the Traders Bank were the mansard roofs, cornices, chimney pots, and awnings of the old city, with the woodblock-paved and horse-manure-strewn streets below. (Middle) Yonge Street looking north to King, about 1920. A fraction of the Traders Bank Building is visible on the extreme right. Next to it is the 1911 Canadian Pacific Building, and, across King Street, the 1914 Royal Bank, at 20 storeys then "the tallest building in the British Empire." On the left, the side wall of the Dominion Bank, built at the same time as the Royal Bank Building, completes the "canyon," at what was the most important and expensive corner in the First World War-era city. (Right) Reaction against the bulk and sheer walls of earlier skyscrapers, and the "canyons" they created, spurred the development of zoning restrictions, and a style which stepped buildings back from the streetline as they ascended into the dirty clouds. The Canadian Bank of Commerce Building at 25 King Street West, built on the eve of the Great Depression, is the best example of this new architecture. In contrast to these skyscraper styles, the nearby Bank of Montreal at the northwest corner of Yonge and Front (page 21), built in the 1880s, hearkens back to a more genteel time, when banks chose European—rather than American—design precedents to express their rock-solid permanence.

Hotel-keeper George Wright (right) lived at and owned the old Walker House Hotel at the corner of York and Front. Born in Glasgow in 1866, Wright joined the Royal Navy at the age of twelve, became a merchant seaman at nineteen, and lived in Japan before moving to Canada in 1887. He served for five years as president of the Toronto Hotelkeepers' Association, then was appointed as a commissioner first of Toronto Hydro and later of the T.T.C. He wrote that his only recreation was "the study of betterment of conditions in business." Walker House was one of the nearest hotels to the old Union Station; it advertised a fine view of Lake Ontario and a ventilation system consisting of exits at two opposite corners, securing coolness on summer days and making it "impossible for fire to cut off retreat." (Below) The King Edward Hotel, built in 1902 at the corner of King Street East and Toronto Street, was the grandest hotel in the city until the Royal York opened in 1929. It managed to keep its first-class clientele through the Great Depression, although it revised its room rates "in keeping with the times"—rooms with bath at $3.00, double room and bathroom at $4.50, and suites for as little as $8.00. In the restaurants at the "King Eddie," breakfast cost between 50 cents and 75 cents, lunch was 85 cents and a full dinner cost $1.50. The hotel advertised itself as the centre of the city's social whirl, with the renowned Romanelli 15-piece orchestra playing every night for the "Supper Dance in the Oak Room," and the cuisine of "the inimitable Claude Baujard, noted chef, who has been decorated by the French Government," presumably for his culinary skills. The tenth floor was reserved for women, with a private parlour for entertaining. (Left) A later arrival on the scene was The Ford Hotel, built uptown in 1929 at the northeast corner of Bay and Dundas (the site of a Red Indian-brand service station). Owned by Richard T. Ford of Rochester, the hotel was part of a chain which included the Lord Elgin Hotel in Ottawa, and others in Montreal, Buffalo, Rochester, and Erie. Its 750 rooms were "modern and fireproof," and convenient for the new generation of passengers coming to Toronto by bus, as the bus depot was almost directly across the street. The Ford Hotel was demolished in 1974; the "Atrium on Bay" now occupies the site.

King Edward Hotel, Toronto, Canada

Holt Renfrew and Company's store at Yonge and Adelaide was a familiar landmark to downtown shoppers; the drawing at left is from a 1934 company advertisement. Allan Edmund Renfrew was born in Quebec, but served as long-time manager of the Toronto branch before returning to Quebec and, in 1915, assuming the company's presidency. He resigned in 1919 and returned to Toronto.

Men's hats were a fashion necessity in the first half of the century, and Albert Walter Applegath sold them at four downtown locations—Queen and Victoria, King and Victoria, Yonge and Richmond, and the main store at Yonge and Trinity Square, now the middle of the Eaton Centre complex. His father, Llewellyn J. Applegath, moved from Hagersville to Toronto in 1885 to establish the business; Albert joined it at the age of eighteen, and took over the presidency following his father's death 33 years later.

An early entrant in the vanity industry was William Thomas Pember, who owned the W. T. Pember Hair & Beauty Stores at 127-9 and 272 Yonge Street, and a plant of the same name which manufactured hair dye. The photograph shows the former store, as it appeared in the 1890s. Born in Herefordshire, Pember worked for several years for the Midland Railway Company, before emigrating and starting his beauty business. By the 1930s, he was boasting that his company was "the most outstanding of its kind in the Dominion."

A fire wagon at full gallop, possibly on Bloor Street. Describing the Fire Brigade in his 1891 survey of the city, the writer G. Mercer Adam hyperbolized that it "vies in efficiency, and may we not say, in no objectionable sense, in the lust of manhood, with the city's other protecting arm, the Police Force." Adam noted that there were over 300 electric signal boxes throughout the city, and "the number of street hydrants is well-nigh legion, and very exceptional are now the circumstances that will permit a fire within the city limits to get a headway and do much damage." Such a circumstance nevertheless arose in the great fire of April, 1904, which devastated twenty acres of warehouses and manufactories in the area around Wellington and Front west of Bay Street, mainly because water pressure could not meet the demand. Mechanized fire trucks were introduced before 1910; the fire department sold off its over-the-hill horses, which often passed their final days before pasture or the knackery pulling delivery wagons around the city. An old caveat stated that one should never buy a retired fire department horse, as the sound of a bell or any commotion could trigger dim memories of a spirited youth, causing the old "hay-burner" to take off, with rider and cart careening behind, in search of an imagined fire.

Toronto Transportation Commission

Like Toronto Hydro, the Toronto Transit Commission is an example of the conspicuous collectivism evident in Ontario in the early years of this century. Unlike Hydro, which had a champion in Sir Adam Beck, the T.T.C. had no one individual who became identified with the cause of a publicly owned system; however, it did have a villain—the Toronto Railway Company, with its major shareholder Sir William Mackenzie, and its history, almost from the day it got its charter in 1891, of indifferent service to the populace.

The growth of the public transportation system parallels the development of what had been largely vacant land north of Queen Street. The first regular service predated even rails: it was a horsedrawn omnibus service, started in 1849 by a cabinetmaker named H.B. Williams, which connected the St. Lawrence Market with the Red Lion Hotel in the distant village of Yorkville. The buses ran every ten minutes along King Street and up Yonge Street to the hotel just beyond Bloor Street. For fifteen years, this little "Yorkville Bus Line" prospered, as the city it served doubled in population to 45,000 people.

The established cities of the American eastern seaboard—New York, Boston and Philadelphia—had experimented in the 1850s with horsedrawn *street railways*, which alleviated many of the problems, particularly those of mud, experienced by H.B. Williams-type omnibus operations. Early in 1861, a businessman named Alexander Easton approached Toronto City Council with a proposal to operate a street railway, and received a thirty-year franchise. That May, he incorporated the Toronto Street Railway Company, and undertook to operate his horsedrawn cars on Yonge Street from King to Bloor, on Queen Street from Yonge to 999 Queen Street West (the lunatic asylum), and on King Street from the Don River to Bathurst. The Village of Yorkville allowed the street railway access to its territory, to a terminus near the toll gate at Davenport and Yonge. The fare was five cents, and no transfers were issued. The old omnibus company started by Williams modified its carriages to fit over the new rails, and competed, like the jitneys of a half-century later, until they were bought out by the street railway. Such was progress that the city insisted that the cars not exceed six miles per hour, and that the service run for sixteen hours per day in the summer, fourteen in the winter; such was tradition that there was no service on Sundays; such was technology that in the winter the company spread a deep layer of straw on the floors of the horsecars for the passengers to warm their feet—the driver, who sat on an open platform at the front of the car, also had a box of pea straw for his feet. In deep snow, the company replaced its horsecars with sleighs, although it finally, in 1891, put into operation a snow sweeper, a huge contraption pulled by six pairs of horses. By then the company—actually a reorganization of the original because of a bankruptcy in 1868—had

grown from 11 cars to 262, and had a motive force of 1,372 horses pulling on 68 miles of track. The T.S.R.'s stables were scattered throughout the city, at locations such as the triangular park bounded by Dundas, Ritchie and Howard Park avenues, on Lansdowne between Paton and Wallace, and on King Street East at St. Lawrence and between Frederick and Sherbourne (the latter has been restored and converted to use as the Young People's Theatre). Around the stables were the sounds of buzzing flies and swishing horses' tails, all kept company by flocks of sparrows and veritable herds of rats. "Road apples"—the hockey pucks of winter—dotted the streets; their smell was everywhere, "sitting on your nose," according to artist and writer Emily Carr, "as comfortably as a pair of spectacles."

Even though the Toronto city limits expanded almost continually after 1891, the Toronto Railway Company refused to expand with it, and, as stipulated in its franchise, offered service only within the 1891 city limits—the shaded area on the map. Three other companies formed to attempt to serve the newly settled outskirts of the city. They charged separate fares, and commuters were forced to transfer onto the Toronto Railway Company's creaking system at points such as Danforth and Broadview, where huge crowds queued at morning rush hours.

Adapted from
"WHEELS OF PROGRESS"
Pub⁴ by the T.T.C.
1941

City Limit in 1921,
when T.T.C. was
formed

———— Toronto Railway C⁰
———— Toronto Civic Railway
– – – Toronto & York Radial R⁹
••••• Toronto Suburban Railway

1891 City Limit

When the Toronto Street Railway Company's franchise expired in May, 1891, the company's assets were taken over by the city for an arbitrated sum approaching one and a half million dollars. This plan for municipal ownership was ahead of its time, however, and a strong lobby of influential citizens urged the city again to grant a franchise to a private concern. Enter William Mackenzie.

Mackenzie had been born in Kirkfield, Ontario in 1849, and had started his working career as a rural public school teacher. Responding to the lure of business, he then ran a general store for a brief period, before a timely opportunity to enter the lumber business led him to try for some sectional contracts providing timber for the Toronto & Nipissing division of the Grand Trunk Railway. He acquired a reputation as an expert timber grader, and in 1884 followed the Canadian Pacific Railway westward, gathering construction contracts as he went. Hardworking and stubborn, yet kindhearted and considerate—at least according to his eulogizers—he had an extraordinary financial acumen, matched perhaps only by his ruthlessness. Like his future partner in the Canadian Northern Railway, Donald Mann, he was a large, physically strong man.

When the city called for tenders to operate its street railway, Mackenzie and three associates—George Washington Kiely of Toronto, Chauncey Clark Woodworth of Rochester, and Henry Agariah Everett of the East Cleveland Electric Railway Company—made the successful bid, obtained a thirty-year franchise, and then incorporated themselves as the Toronto Railway Company. Mackenzie owed one of his advantages over other bidders to his close association with Frederic Nicholls, whose Canadian General Electric Company had the technical expertise and hardware to electrify the system. Prompt electrification was one of the stipulations of the franchise.

Thus electric railway service arrived in Toronto. The idea was not new to the public, as a demonstration electric railway had been in service since 1884, connecting the Exhibition grounds with a point on Strachan Avenue just south of the steam railway crossing. Street railways all over North America were already going electric at a great rate—even Vancouver and Victoria had completely electric systems by the end of 1890. The first electric streetcar in Toronto ran on August 15, 1892, on Church Street, although the last horsecar remaining from the old Toronto Street Railway rumbled and clip-clopped along McCaul Street until the end of August, 1894.

The Toronto Railway Company's first custom-built electric streetcars, as distinct from converted horsecars, were built with interchangeable bodies—closed for winter, open-sided "toast-racks" or "Mexican cars" for summer—which fitted over a standardized truck and control set. Other innovations included coal stoves, which in the winter of 1891-2 re-

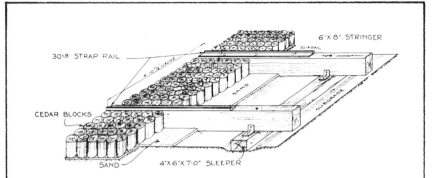

An example of horsecar-era track construction. The introduction of heavier electric streetcars in the early 1890s by the Toronto Street Railway Company forced a completely new style of track setting. Much heavier rails were used, laid over concrete slabs, and granite blocks were set against the rails to try to prevent them shifting. Even this type of construction deteriorated rapidly, and the T.T.C. in 1921 inherited an operational nightmare and had to replace most of the trackwork in the city. The illustration above shows cedar-block paving—in the last century, many of Toronto's streets were paved completely with cedar blocks, impregnated with salt or tar, embedded in sand, and coated with various types of bitumen and dustings of sand. The 1912 City Engineer's Road Surface Map catalogued an astonishing variety of road surfaces in Toronto, including woodblock, macadam, dirt, several types of stone, and brick. Most of the main streets downtown, and in areas such as the Annex and Rosedale, were asphalt-paved; some brick paving survived, for example on York Street between King and Queen, on Front Street east of George, on Hazelton Avenue and Prince Arthur Avenue in Yorkville, and on Bloor at Dovercourt, where the road looked almost cobbled (page 223). The rest of Bloor Street between Bathurst and Dufferin was cedar-block-paved. Davenport was gravel, with huge ruts and puddles in the spring. Queen Street East was unpaved east of Woodbine, and the only paved roads in the Beaches were near Kew Gardens. Most of West Toronto and Swansea were unpaved at that time, as was everything except Queen's Park Crescent on the University of Toronto campus.

placed the straw floor covering of the horsecars. The stove was affixed to a seat in the centre of the streetcar but there was no method of moving the heated air about. Copious quantities of cold air still found their way in, as the company did not see fit to install doors across the open front entranceway until about 1908.

Old-fashioned Torontonians saw in the electric street railway a fearsome vision of the future—much as a later generation was to regard the automobile—and lashed out against it. To allay fears of runaway cars menacing pedestrians, the company attached fishnet cowcatchers, which looked rather like children's homemade hockey nets, to the front of the cars; several fatal accidents later, new and more effective bumpers were developed, and the company finally settled on a fender which—according to a T.T.C. historical publication—dropped quickly to the ground after hitting something (presumably without pinning and flattening what had already been hit). The old friction brakes were gradually eliminated, be-

Sir William Mackenzie was 42 years old when he gained control of the Toronto street railway system. An extraordinarily ruthless financier, over the next 30 years he built a nationwide system of railways, land development, and utilities and was dubbed "The Emperor of the North" for his Canadian Northern Railway. One newspaper article on the hobbies of Canada's rich men noted that railroader Sir William Van Horne and banker Sir Edmund Walker collected art, but that Mackenzie was content to collect railway charters and municipal franchises. The collapse of the western Canadian economy in 1913 and the outbreak of war the following year dried up his London-based credit pool and eventually bankrupted his empire. Mackenzie died at "Benvenuto" on the Avenue Road hill in December, 1923, leaving three sons and six daughters.

ginning, in 1905, with the adoption of airbrakes on all of the new, larger, double-truck cars. The airbrakes were supplied with compressed air from a tank mounted on the car, which, as no compressors had been provided, the motorman refilled from large tanks located at points along his route.

Addressing another safety concern, a 1908 ruling by the Railway and Municipal Board ordered the gradual elimination of all the open-sided cars with running-boards—after the summer of 1915, open cars were banned from Toronto streets. On some routes during rush hours, passengers had packed onto the running-boards of the cars like bees onto a honeycomb, leading to accidents in which unfortunates were bunted or swept away by passing trucks and wagons.

The T.R.C. had to fight hardest against the constant charge that it wished to desecrate the Sabbath. It had entered into its franchise agreement with the city on the understanding that it would not, until so approved by a public referendum, operate streetcars on Sundays. Streetcars were only one object of disapproval—the campaign to keep Sunday sacred included denunciations of music in the parks, parades, and the goings-on at the Island. To promote the company's cause and obtain public approval for Sunday streetcar service, Frederic Nicholls of the Canadian General Electric Company (whose involvement with William Mackenzie and Henry Pellatt in the electric light system that sold the power to the streetcar company made him an interested party) bought control of a newspaper—the setting *Evening Star*. In addition to its trumpeting of Nicholls's favorite Toryisms, the *Evening Star* lobbied and cajoled and bullied for Sunday service. A referendum finally passed in 1897, after which Nicholls soon lost interest in his newspaper and sold it, in 1899, to

(Previous page) One of the echoes of the 1919 Winnipeg General Strike was a streetcar strike in Toronto. Local jitney operators—anybody with a truck or car and some spare time—found themselves swarmed upon by commuters; evidently, the "ladies-first" chivalry of genteel Toronto had not survived the hurly-burly of the First World War. Local attempts to organize a sympathetic general strike failed; the Street Railway Union had major grievances, though, and on June 22 voted 1,370 to 75 to strike, then stayed out until they won a new settlement on July 4. In Toronto, the real consequence of the Winnipeg General Strike occurred at the beginning of May, commencing with a strike of the Metal Trades Council. Sympathizers with the concept of One Big Union gathered to hear the speeches of labour leaders and socialists, such as James Simpson, later the mayor of Toronto. In a May Day address, Simpson declared, according to the Globe, *that "if working people organized, the Utopia of absolute freedom for all, plenty of the good things of life for the humblest workers, and the crushing of present-day 'democracy' would have arrived." In his speech he suggested that in Russia there had been real advances in Socialism, and that foreigners and aliens in Toronto were true brothers. About 5,000 workers in various trades were off the job with the metal workers; other workers joined in, while still others attempted to negotiate new contracts. There were rallies at Queen's Park, and deputations to city council and various employers' associations. A general committee formed to organize a "general sympathetic strike" for May 30; as they had promised that "no harm shall befall the general public," they excluded a motley cross-section of workers, including bakers, policemen, firefighters, sewage plant operators, theatrical stage employees, public school teachers, college professors, clergy, doctors, and hospital help! The strike fizzled, closing down no more than 230 factories and 50 shops.*

a Liberal syndicate. As late as March, 1905, the Lord's Day Alliance tried to revive the issue and attempted unsuccessfully to persuade the newly elected Conservative government to reinstate the ban. Although now running on the Sabbath, streetcars were forbidden to sound their gong within 200 feet of a place of worship, or pass one at more than four miles per hour.

The efforts of Mackenzie, Nicholls, and Pellatt, both in the street railway and the electric power fields, reflected their belief in unbounded liberalism and capitalism—in the individual's absolute rights, even when the liberties so taken conflicted with what the majority perceived to be the public interest. That had been the traditional Liberal view in Canadian political life; by contrast, Conservatives such as Adam Beck and Premier James Whitney advocated some public ownership, as did Liberals of Joseph Atkinson's ilk. But regardless of the reforming tendencies of some governments and the disgruntlement and criticism of the public, the empires of men like Mackenzie were still protected by the courts. Through much of the 30-year duration of the T.R.C's franchise, it was in litigation with the city.

Specifically, the company refused, as the city expanded, to extend its single-fare system beyond the seventeen square miles enclosed by the city limits in 1891—the time it was granted its franchise. (It even cut back its service into the Beach area, and turned over the operation of the shortened line to Scarboro Beach Park to the Toronto & York Radial Railway Company, making it an extra-fare service. In this instance, the Ontario Railway Board stepped in and ordered the T.R.C. to operate one-fare service as far east as Neville Street, but forced the city to rebuild the track to the T.R.C.'s specifications.) Three other railway systems, two of which also became part of the Mackenzie & Mann railway empire, were built to serve the new suburbs. The first of these was the Toronto & York Radial Railway, with three branches, one of which served points between the city limits on Yonge Street and Lake Simcoe, while the other two gave service up and down the lake as the Scarboro line and the Long Branch—Port Credit line. The second private line—the Toronto Suburban Railway—was an outgrowth of a service commenced in the 1890s by A.H. Royce to connect the Junction with Weston; it became part of the Canadian Northern Railway—a Mackenzie & Mann enterprise. The third line was the Toronto Civic Railway, inaugurated by the city in 1911 following repeated, fruitless attempts to budge the obdurate Toronto Street Railway; it established services into the east end, on Danforth and east of Greenwood on Gerrard Street, as well as along Bloor Street west of Dundas and on a portion of St. Clair from Yonge Street to Lansdowne. All of these pieces, operated by the four distinct companies, added up to nine separate branches, each collecting its own fares and (with one exception) permitting no transfers. A resident travelling between points within the city limits could pay from two to fifteen cents, and during rush hours had to endure interminable line-ups to board cars at the underserviced transfer points into the Toronto Railway Company's turf.

The city's legal attempts to bend the Toronto Railway Company and the affiliated Toronto Electric Light Company to its will were appealed all the way to the Privy Council in London, England—at the time, the last resort for aggrieved Canadian plaintiffs. The Privy Council's 1907 decision on the dispute declared that the control of Toronto's streets, at least in relation to the tracks and lines of the Toronto Railway Company, legally rested with that company. A bevy of skilled lawyers parried and fended off every thrust by the city to force the company to extend its services. Finally, in 1910, a bill passed in the provincial legislature banning the corporation from laying or ripping up tracks without the Ontario Railway Board's permission. The election of Mayor H. C. Hocken, whose public ownership stance had been strongly endorsed by his former employer, the *Star*, signalled the formation of the aforementioned Toronto Civic Railway; on December 18, 1912, the mayor inaugurated Toronto's first publicly owned tram.

While the city was debating how its public transit system should be run, the streets were becoming increasingly congested with automobiles. The war over the "devil waggons" on the roads was waged mainly between the newly formed Ontario Motor League and the Dominion Grange—the national branch of the organization which evolved into the United Farmers of Ontario. Women were too frightened to venture on the roads, it was said; windows had to be shut in the summertime because of the blowing dust. Motor vehicle legislation enacted in the years before the First World War indicated how complicated the rule of the road had suddenly become: if a horse appeared frightened the motorist must stop and, if the horse panicked, render assistance; upon meeting a funeral procession, a "motor" had to turn down a lane; a 1912 amendment prohibited motorcars from passing stationary streetcars—formerly, they had been allowed to pass at four miles per hour.

Early in 1913, Canada was in the midst of a serious depression. The still incomplete Canadian Northern Railway, the cornerstone of *Sir* William Mackenzie's financial holdings, increasingly was threatening to be a huge white elephant (with Donald Mann, Mackenzie had been knighted in 1910 in recognition for his railway work). On April 17, he announced that he was willing to sell to the city both the Toronto Railway Company and its distribution system, the Toronto Electric Light Company, which was in direct competition with Toronto Hydro (page 80). Enabling legislation was introduced at Queen's Park by W. K. McNaught, a member for the city. The asking price was said to be in the neighbourhood of $30 million, of which $22 million was for the street railway. City council, most of whom were in favour of the principle of public ownership, backed Mayor Hocken in the negotiations. However, a spanner, in the form of the Hon. Adam Beck—the minister responsible for the Hydro-Electric Commis-

sion—entered the works: he was alarmed at the prospect of civic ownership of both the street railway and the electric company, claiming that the two together purchased over three times the amount of power, from a Mackenzie-owned generating plant, as the publicly owned Toronto Hydro did from the provincially owned Hydro-Electric Commission. The competition would be deadly, implied Beck, both to the government commission and to government policy in general. Mackenzie, however, knew that he held the trump card, and insisted that both of his companies be purchased at once. In the discussion in the legislature of this McNaught Bill, Hocken and McNaught argued for the right to place a combined purchase before the electorate, but Beck held firm and successfully had the two referenda separated.

Regardless of these difficulties, reports prepared by expert consultants were generally in favour of the purchases, although the *Telegram*, a heavy influence on public opinion within the city, argued violently against it. But on November 26, 1913, the Harbour Commissioners, in a report from chairman Lionel Clarke, presented an alternative proposal for a system of "tubes," extensions to the Toronto Civic Railways, radial lines to the countryside along the waterfront, and new stations. The estimated cost was just under $15 million. So enchanting was the report's vision that, on the first day of December, city council about-faced and voted fifteen to nine against sending the Mackenzie-Hocken purchase proposal to the ratepayers.

During the years of the First World War, most of the Mackenzie & Mann railway empire collapsed into insolvency. Lest it drag down the Bank of Commerce and thousands of shareholders, the Canadian Northern Railway was nationalized in 1917. Mackenzie retained little interest in the Toronto Railway Company, seeming to view it as no more than a customer for electricity from his Niagara generating operations. The street railway's stagnation confined commercial and residential development within the city. At the end of the war, Mackenzie's emissaries approached the city in an attempt to get a raise on his five-cent fare, which had been set nearly thirty years before, but received little sympathy. A strike of 2,200 street railway employees on June 22, 1919, ostensibly in support of the Winnipeg General Strike, dragged on until the fourth of July, when the men were able to win new wages of 50 cents an hour, up nearly 60 percent from the old levels. Many people remembered the P.A.Y.E. riots of December, 1910, when Mackenzie, in an attempt to cut back on his payroll, had tried to introduce Pay As You Enter trams, thus dispensing with the need for conductors. The public had shown its disapproval by damaging several streetcars. Mayor Tommy Church, who had been city controller during the 1913 negotiations with the Toronto Railway Company, summed up the growing conviction that, when the latter's franchise expired, the city would take it over. "There will be no surrender to the railway," he said, "over the question of increased fares. The Company has been allowed to water its stock to the extent of six millions, and use it for the benefit of power and radial companies, instead of giving good service and paying its men." Describing the Toronto Railway Company stock, people said "it's mostly water!" Church also alleged that Mackenzie's shenanigans had damaged Toronto's credit rating.

On January 2, 1920, Toronto's ratepayers voted by nearly ten to one to run its street railway as a public enterprise. The Toronto Transportation Commission was formed with three commissioners, P. W. Ellis, George Wright, and Fred Miller, and a general manager, Herbert Couzens, who

The T.T.C. system during the Second World War. The company boasted that its one-fare system was arranged so that 87.5 percent of Toronto's citizens resided within 1,000 feet of services and 99.6 percent within 2,000 feet. In addition to its regular streetcar and bus services, the T.T.C. operated the Gray Line sightseeing tour network, a special students' service to Havergal College, Branksome Hall and several other schools, a ferry service to Toronto Islands, and motor launch tours of the harbour and the island lagoons.

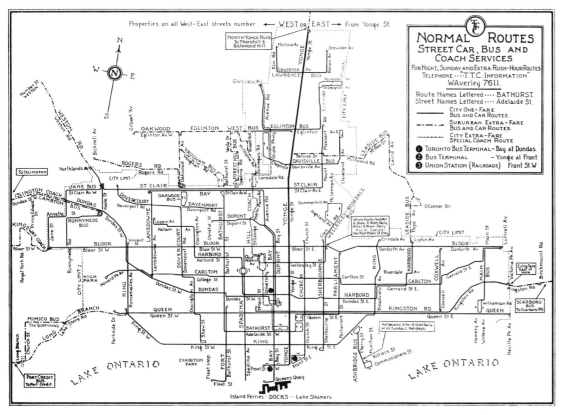

had been for several years previously the manager of Toronto Hydro. All were appointed in August, 1920, and in the year remaining until the expiry of the Toronto Railway Company's franchise, they reviewed the mess they were to inherit. Two major problems confronted them—the unification of the nine separate sections of railway into a single-fare system, and the replacement or rehabilitation of the track and streetcars. As part of the purchase deal negotiated with Mackenzie, the T.T.C. was also to fall heir to the Metropolitan, Mimico, and Scarboro divisions of the Toronto & York Radial Railway (although for a time, Ontario Hydro operated the portions of the lines outside city limits). In November, 1923, the T.T.C. also acquired the property of the Toronto Suburban Railway Company. By that time, the T.T.C. had extended its single-fare network to the city limits, adding many new pieces of track and a couple of bus routes through the newly annexed but still sparsely settled suburbs.

"While the achievements of the Commission in the unification and extension of Toronto's nine disconnected transportation systems were indeed noteworthy," noted the 1941 T.T.C. publication *Wheels of Progress*, "the accomplishments during the rehabilitation of the badly rundown facilities to which the Commission fell heir were truly spectacular." Most spectacular of all was the execution of all the work without serious interruptions either to transit service or to the city's traffic. In the first years of the T.T.C., it built 43 miles of new track, completely rebuilt 67 miles, did major repair work on 42 miles of old track, and reconstructed nearly every intersection in Toronto. Curves had to be realigned, as the T.T.C.'s newly ordered steel cars were too big to pass on the old, tighter-radius turns. In some cases, temporary track and overhead wires were rigged on the roadway beside the right of way while the latter was rebuilt with heavier rails and better ballasting. Many intersections, such as the one at Queen and Yonge, were completely overhauled in a single night; the remarkable "grand union" at the intersection of King, Queen, and Roncesvalles was prebuilt in the construction yard, then taken apart, transported to the site, and relaid in nine hours. Electric switches were installed at all the intersections, eliminating the motormen's tedious task of stepping down and manually moving the switches. To continue work through the dead of winter, workers sometimes burned tons of coal on the ground to keep it thawed.

The T.T.C. also paid attention to the new fashion of "riding on rubber"—it inaugurated bus services through areas still too rural to justify streetcars. The first route, employing four double-decker buses with solid tires, went into operation on September 20, 1921 between Dundas and Runnymede via Humberside, High Park, and Annette. Subsequent routes served Rosedale north of the Sherbourne streetcar loop, Merton Street, and Mount Pleasant Road.

In addition to using buses within the city, the T.T.C. transported the denizens of the surrounding countryside by motor coaches, which gradually superseded the old radial railways. Its exurban services were operated by a subsidiary called Gray Coach Lines; passengers flocked to the new buses, which offered such technological advances as four-wheel brakes, rear engines to reduce noise and vibration, reclining seats, hot-water heating, and weatherproof baggage compartments located under the floor instead of in a rack on the roof. In 1931, Gray Coach Lines erected a modern bus terminal at the corner of Bay and Dundas, which is still in use today.

A few modifications were also made to the T.T.C.'s "Peter Witt" streetcars. As an experiment, electric blast heaters replaced the old coal stoves beginning in 1934; as the Great Depression deepened, and the T.T.C. converted more of its streetcars to one-man operation, more of the so-called "Peter Smith" coal stoves were replaced, partly as the single operator could not both control the tram and tend the fire. Patronage declined, due to the Depression and—for those lucky enough to be able to afford one—the popularity of the automobile, so routes were shuffled and cut back. Ridership hit rock-bottom in 1933. Although a dozen years into its mandate, the T.T.C. was still operating some ancient T.R.C. equipment, and a lot of its own equipment still needed both a motorman and a conductor. Thus, in the spring of 1938, the T.T.C. ordered 140 of the new single-operator "PCC" streetcars, which had been developed by the Presidents' Conference Committee of North American streetcar companies. Many of this style of streamlined trams, in their various guises, are still in service today.

With the coming of the Second World War, motorists on the home front faced gas rationing and shortages of everything from tires to spare parts; the populace, having taken to their private automobiles like ducks to water, were now forced back into streetcars and buses. In common with other street railways in North America, the T.T.C. experienced its finest hour during the Second World War. Fortunately, the company had a lot of relatively new equipment. It responded to the acute manpower shortage by hiring its first woman bus driver in 1942, and its first woman conductor started work on the Yonge Street route the following year. The last of the wartime women employees were laid off in July, 1946.

As Toronto adjusted to peacetime, the T.T.C. modified its route layout. In January, 1947, the old Sherbourne streetcar route became a bus route, partly because the "devilstrip" on the old bridge across the Rosedale Valley could not accommodate any but the oldest, smallest trams. The Spadina line was likewise converted to buses the following year. Everywhere, the volume of traffic created problems. Throughout the downtown, on streets such as Jarvis, Sherbourne, and Carlton, the fine old boulevard trees which met in a leafy archway fifty feet above the centre line were cut down, and the streets widened. Bloor Street needed more than 30 street-

cars each way each hour during rush hours, but it was impossible to run that many through the bottlenecks and keep to any kind of schedule; the T.T.C. ordered 100 new PCC cars which could operate as two-car trains. Some form of rapid transit became inevitable.

As for the old radials, the Metropolitan line of the Toronto & York Radial Railway, which had had a mainline running north on Yonge Street from Glen Echo originally to Lake Simcoe and Sutton, was abandoned by 1930; subsequently, the segment between Richmond Hill and the Toronto city limits at Glen Echo loop went back into service, and operated until 1948. Like the other two divisions of the Toronto & York Radial Railway, which had connected to Port Credit and Scarboro, the Yonge Street radial was severely hampered by its lack of high-speed access into the city. The old Toronto Suburban Railway line from The Junction to Weston had likewise been abandoned, due to heavy losses, in August, 1931. Almost lost to memory were the grand plans of the Grand Valley Railway, a promotion of the Von Echa Company of Harrisburg, Pennsylvania, which had envisaged a network of electric interurbans between Detroit and Toronto, and had even built and operated some sections around Brantford, Paris and Galt before being put out of business by a snowstorm in 1912. Like all of the other pieces of Sir Adam Beck's radial railway puzzle, it had vanished due to the onslaught of the all-conquering automobile, fueled by the prosperity of the individual.

In the city, cars conquered the streets by strangling them; the T.T.C.'s solution was to go underground. Subways or "tubes" had been proposed before the First World War, and were a part of the Harbour Commission's 1913 report which scuttled the Hocken-Mackenzie agreement. The T.T.C. presented a plan to the city council in 1942, suggesting two major lines: a north-south one, from Union Station along Bay Street, angling northeastward across Ramsden Park to a Yonge Street stop at Roxborough, then north along Yonge to the old Belt Line right of way at Merton Street, where a future system could be extended without difficulty towards the grassy, subdividable fields of North York Township; and a crosstown one, from Trinity Park along Adelaide Street through downtown, under Queen Street east of Sherbourne to the Don, then north along a right of way on the present site of the Don Valley Parkway. City council rejected the proposal. Nevertheless, conditions in the city's centre soon demanded a prompt solution. Either the dozens of trailer-trains during rush-hours snarled the traffic, or else the traffic made it impossible to run the streetcars.

The desire for a Yonge Street subway was confirmed by the nine to one vote of ratepayers in a referendum on New Year's Day, 1946. The T.T.C.'s plans for this single line were quickly approved, and federal, provincial, civic, and T.T.C. officials, accompanied by the 48th Highlanders Band, held a groundbreaking ceremony on September 8, 1949, for the

(Next page) Providing "completely modern terminal facilities for motor coach travellers," the T.T.C.'s bus terminal opened in 1931 at the corner of Bay and Edward. The T.T.C.'s Gray Coach Lines, incorporated in 1927, used the terminal, as did Toronto Greyhound and the Colonial Coach Lines. Gray Coach Lines provided services throughout the region, as far north as North Bay (with special stops at Callander and the nearby Dafoe Hospital, famous for the Dionne Quintuplets), southwest to London, and south to Buffalo. The tall building partly visible on the extreme left of the painting is the Ford Hotel.

line's first phase. The public got its first glimpse of the new English-built subway cars at the C.N.E. in 1953. The following year, on March 30, the Yonge Street line—the first subway line in Canada—opened.

The year 1954 was a momentous one, not only for the inauguration of the subway, but also for the provincial government's creation of the revolutionary political entity of Metro Toronto. Included in that change was the expansion of the T.T.C.'s mandate to cover the 240 square miles of the new region, and a new name—the Toronto Transit Commission. Subsequently, both the Yonge and Bay streetcar lines ceased operation. The Church streetcar route became a bus route, due to increased electrical power consumption in the downtown area.

The first addition to the subway system was an extension of the Yonge Street subway, connecting Union Station with the corner of St. George and Bloor via University Avenue. The next, and more significant addition, the Bloor-Danforth, opened in February, 1966. Each extension triggered explosions of real estate speculation, and the creation of instant highrise cities. As the subway expanded, the T.T.C. abandoned several surface lines, and sold off dozens of its older PCC-model streetcars. One proposal, to sell thirty of them to an operation in Veracruz, Mexico, fell through; beginning in 1966, the Alexandria transit system in Egypt began to buy used T.T.C. trams, which were repainted in royal blue and cream with silver trim. Some of these were destroyed by bombing in the Six-Day War in June, 1967.

As Metro expanded over the horizon to the north, east, and west, both the T.T.C.'s operations and new highway construction attempted to keep up. The argument of private versus public transportation had its Waterloo when the Spadina expressway was cancelled by the provincial government in 1971 after a bitter wrangle. The Spadina extension to the subway system, connecting Bloor Street with Wilson Heights, was approved two years later.

As for the fate of the streetcars, the T.T.C. started work in 1967 on the elimination of streetcars, and their replacement by diesel and trolley buses and subways. By the time that a proposed Queen Street subway was to become operational in 1980, most of the downtown routes, including Bathurst, Queen, King, Dundas and Carlton, were to have been replaced with rubber-tired vehicles. However, the public supported the streetcars, and some tireless lobbyists, most particularly the group called Streetcars for Toronto, convinced a sympathetic "reform" city council in 1972 to retain the street railway. Now, almost precisely a century since the electric streetcars appeared on North American city streets, Toronto is one of the few cities where the evocative rumble of steel wheels on rails can still be heard.

Henry Herbert Couzens, an electrical engineer, became in 1920 the first general manager of the T.T.C. Born in Devonshire in 1877, he had first come to public notice in 1913, when he was appointed general manager of Toronto Hydro. He stayed in his post at the T.T.C. for less than four years, then accepted the general managership of the Brazilian Traction, Light and Power Company (now Brascan Ltd.) and moved to Rio de Janeiro. He was later knighted. In Toronto, he lived at the Selby Hotel on Sherbourne Street.

Eaton's

Looking north on Yonge Street, from Queen. The main entrance to the T. Eaton Company is on the left, beneath the square tower with gabled roof and flagpole, at 190 Yonge Street. Most of the buildings surrounding it were its own workshops, factories, and stables, but the company never owned the strategic northwest corner.

Slogans such as "Money Cheerfully Refunded If Goods Not Satisfactory" and "The Greatest Good to the Greatest Number" evoke the image of solid respectability and trustworthiness that helped the T. Eaton Company Limited to become the largest department store in Canada. However, it was to the legendary figure of Timothy Eaton that the store owed its extraordinary reputation. Eaton frowned on the selling of tobacco or liquor, and in keeping with his nineteenth century Methodist beliefs, decreed that all the store window-curtains be drawn to preserve the sanctity of the Sabbath, a policy retained by the firm until quite recently. Times have changed, and newer generations of Eatons have changed with them, ensuring that after almost 120 years of operation the store continues to thrive under direct family control. Indicative of the firm's sleek modern image is the Eaton Centre on Yonge between Queen and Dundas, supplanting the jumble of the firm's old stores, stables and factories. The Eaton Centre's ambience has become a tourist attraction in its own right.

Timothy Eaton was the fourth son and ninth child in his family; he was

The area north of Eaton's main store in the 1920s. The company's factories and storehouses surrounded the 1847 Church of the Holy Trinity, and spread over most of the land now occupied by the modern Eaton Centre. Eaton's also had a factory on the western half of the block bounded by Hayter, Bay, Buchanan, and Yonge streets (Buchanan was the one-block continuation, west of Yonge Street, of Ann [Granby] Street; Hayter Street east of Yonge became, after a jog, McGill Street). These factory buildings were levelled in the late 1920s for Eaton's College Park store.

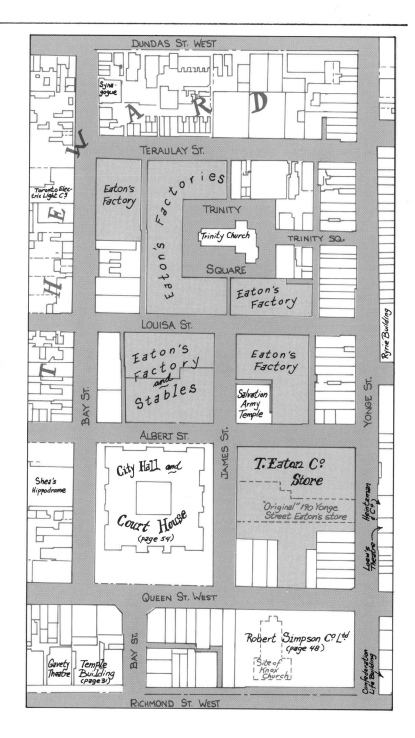

born in 1834 in impoverished rural Ireland, his family's circumstances doubly straitened by the death of the father before Timothy's birth. He apprenticed to a distant relative to learn shopkeeping and, following the death of his mother in 1848 and the privations of the concurrent potato famine, immigrated to Canada, settling in Georgetown with a number of his relatives. In 1860, with his brother James, he established a general store in the town of St. Mary's. While there, he met and married Margaret Beattie, a 21-year-old woman from Woodstock (page 229); at her behest, he converted to Methodism.

Eaton found that the operation of a country general store required too much dickering and bargaining, credit and bad debts for his taste. He set out for Toronto in 1869 with his wife, children, and savings, and established a store at the southwest corner of Queen and Yonge in "Britannia House," with 24 feet of frontage on Yonge, which he bought for $6,500. The first Eaton's owed its distinction to its being stocked with ticketed items that had cash prices.

King Street was the city's main shopping thoroughfare, but the efforts of Eaton and others expanded the fashionable shopping area northwards. In 1883, Eaton's moved north of Queen to the 190 Yonge Street location which became the core of the main store for nearly a century; the following year, Eaton's introduced its mail-order catalogue, and five years later illuminated its showrooms with electric lights. On the surrounding streets (see map), a warren of Eaton clothing factories grew up, employing about 1,200 workers and touted as the cleanest in the city; Eaton's soon had almost a monopoly in the women's clothing market in Canada, though a protracted strike by its tailors in 1912 against enforced, "sweated" overtime gathered a lot of public support and eventually diminished its dominance. Long before that time, however, the forthright and pious Timothy had become a Canadian institution, and Eaton's was promoting itself as "Canada's Greatest Store."

Timothy's eldest son, Edward Young Eaton, had joined the firm at the age of seventeen and was being groomed to inherit the presidency when he died of diabetes in 1900; his most lasting contribution to the company was the red, dark blue, and white colour scheme. There were four other children: two daughters, "Josie" and Margaret, and two sons, William Fletcher and John Craig. William Fletcher Eaton was a maverick who had no interest in the family firm, so the mantle fell to John Craig, who was named vice-president following his brother's death, and became president when his father died in 1907.

John Craig Eaton continued his father's business habits—he kept tobacco counters out of the store and continued to draw the drapes on Sundays—but added merchandising gimmicks such as the Santa Claus parade. He was an enthusiast for all the technological advances of the new century, including automobiles, telephones, and "the wireless." When he was 24, in 1898, he bought a Winton, probably the second automobile in Ontario and certainly the first in Toronto. His registration for a later, 1903-model Winton was Ontario License Number One—the license fee was $2, and the license plate was a leather pad with a metal number "1"

attached to it. Eaton's enthusiasm for motoring was quickly reflected in the merchandise at Eaton's. The cover of Eaton's fall-winter 1901 catalogue showed a couple driving in their tiller-steered Winton on fashionable Queen's Park Crescent; inside the catalogue were automobile coats—one of the ladies' was "made of good quality Preston cheviot, colors Oxford and medium grey, lined throughout with heavy black satin, box back is fastened with large pearl buttons, length 36 inches." The price was $12.

J. C. Eaton's philanthropy, evidenced most notably by the Timothy Eaton Memorial Church on St. Clair, the surgical wing in the new Toronto General Hospital (also named for his father), and, during the First World War, the Eaton Machine Gun Battery, earned him a knighthood in June, 1915. However, as was the case with his eldest brother, ill-health truncated his life and work—an attack of pneumonia following a bout of influenza killed him in March, 1922, a few weeks before his 46th birthday.

The two Eaton daughters were prominent in local society. Josephine married T. D. M. Burnside, who preferred to spend his life as an English squire; the couple separated and Josephine returned to Toronto, where she modified an old house on Clarendon Avenue (page 266), partly to hold her extensive art collection. Margaret married Charles Elbridge Burden, a Horatio Alger-like character whose Cabbagetown youth did not preclude a successful business career as a paint manufacturer; she served as national president of the Imperial Order Daughters of the Empire, and one of her daughters married the World War One flying ace Billy Bishop.

Following J. C. Eaton's death, the store presidency passed for an interim period to his cousin Robert Young Eaton (page 260) until, in 1942, the estate's executors determined that J. C. Eaton's son John David was ready to assume control. Near the end of his tenure as president, John David Eaton began the planning which led to the erection of the Eaton Centre in the mid-1970s.

Illustrations from an Eaton's advertisement of the early 1930s. The "new store" is College Park at College and Yonge, which was envisaged as an enormous 40-storey skyscraper. The depression and the Second World War intervened, with the result that the store never grew above seven storeys. Nevertheless, the College Street store stayed open until 1976; with the development of the Eaton Centre, the firm abandoned it; it has since been converted into chic shops.

Great enthusiasm—practically adulation—greeted the arrival of Lady Eaton, accompanied by her son John David, in spats, for the opening in 1928 of Eaton's College Street store.

Though comparatively youthful, the widowed Lady Eaton soon became something of a beloved dowager, appealing to crowds in the same way as does today's Queen Mother.

CTA JAMES 1641

Simpson's

The fine Robert Simpson Company emporium at the southwest corner of Queen and Yonge is cordially connected by a skywalk to its competitor, Eaton's, north of Queen Street. Until the Eaton Centre was built in the 1970s, Eaton's never had an impressive façade at Queen and Yonge—instead, it operated in the interconnected interiors of a number of storefronts. Robert Simpson, who started selling drygoods under his own name in 1872, moved to the corner of Yonge and Queen in 1881 and had a similar set-up to Eaton's—an original storefront at 7-11 Queen Street West, which interconnected as the business grew and expanded with three other buildings that wrapped around the old Knox Church on Queen Street. Simpson's business prospered and outgrew these premises, and early in the 1890s he demolished them and built a radically modern new store; it burned down in 1895, and was promptly rebuilt, but Simpson himself died in 1897, before he could taste the fruits of his labours.

The year after Simpson's death, Joseph Flavelle, A. E. Ames and Harris Henry Fudger purchased the store from the estate; Flavelle and Ames were investors, while Fudger was the drygoods expert, having already spent over 30 years in the business. Fudger was born in 1851 in a house on King Street between Yonge and Bay, and entered the business world as an office boy in the firm of Robert Wilkes, a wholesale fancy goods and jewellery dealer. Following Wilkes's death, Fudger started his own business, then formed the Goldsmiths Stock Company of Canada, later known as the Fancy Goods Company of Canada. In March, 1898, he became managing director and president of the newly purchased Robert Simpson Company. He remained as president for three decades. At the announcement of his death in 1930, Simpson's closed its doors and kept them shut until after the funeral; as a gesture of respect, Eaton's cancelled its regular advertising, substituted one of condolence, and closed its stores and mail-order office on the afternoon of the funeral.

Fudger's protégé and successor as president was Charles Luther Burton (1876-1961), who started *his* business career as an office boy, working for Fudger's Goldsmiths Stock Company in 1891. At the age of nineteen, he became Fudger's head bookkeeper, an unenviable position as the responsibility for keeping track of 6,000 accounts entailed considerable night work, for which the only recompense was supper money. Fudger amalgamated his personal business with Simpson's in 1911. Burton then joined Simpson's, and became president on Fudger's retirement; his son Allan, born in 1915, started work as a Simpson's stockboy, and spent 45 years with the firm, the last eleven as chairman. Simpson's is now a wholly owned subsidiary of another retail giant, the Hudson's Bay Company.

In the century since Robert Simpson established himself on the corner, the Simpson Company's buildings have gradually extended to cover the entire block. The nine-storey addition to the west of the main building went up in 1907; twenty years later, another addition was built at the corner of Richmond and Bay; the Simpson's Tower at Queen and Bay, built in 1971, occupies the site of a jumble of little buildings, including the curious Colonial Theatre (pages 31 and 57).

Robert Simpson

Harris Henry Fudger

Charles Luther Burton

Newspapers

In North America, where it is unusual for a city to have more than one daily newspaper, Toronto has three independent English papers, plus another daily which speaks the language of business. Nevertheless, it is still a far cry from earlier periods in the city's history; for example, at the turn of this century, there were six newspapers serving what was a much smaller market. But to compare today's newspapers with those of previous generations is to compare horses with camels—a newspaper was then a simple matter technologically, requiring comparatively little capital investment; nor did the electronic media offer competition.

In the early colonial days there was only the official government paper, *The Upper Canada Gazette*, which followed the government to Toronto from Niagara in 1798. Two decades later, the newly landed Francis Collins and William Lyon Mackenzie started their rabble-rousing, radical journals, which before long were afflicting the comfortable without spending too much time comforting the afflicted. Within a decade, there were seven newspapers in the newly incorporated city of Toronto: among them were Egerton Ryerson's *Christian Guardian*, a Methodist voice, and the three politically radical papers of Mackenzie, Collins and the Irish Catholic William O'Grady, in opposition to the Tory, Anglican elite which controlled the colony. Mackenzie's *Colonial Advocate*, founded in 1824, had the most lasting significance, as his trumpeting for social and political change spawned a political career that led to the 1837 rebellion and, eventually, lasting political reform.

Of the newspapers that survived more or less intact until recently, the *Globe* is the oldest, having been founded in 1844 by George Brown, a 26-year-old immigrant from Edinburgh. The *Globe* became the most influential voice for *laissez-faire* liberalism, Presbyterianism (or at least anti-Catholicism), and "Clear Grit" Liberal reformism, while Brown himself had a profound influence on Canada's confederation. His career was cut short in 1880 when a drunken former employee shot him in the leg, causing his death from gangrene six weeks later.

The second oldest paper, the *Telegram*, survived for nearly a century before its precipitate and controversial closure in 1971 by its owner, John Bassett. The *Telegram* was the great proponent of Imperialism, the Orange Order, and fiscal conservatism in the city; in its heyday—the half-century before the Second World War—it was the most powerful and influential voice in city politics, with a circulation considerably greater than any other paper's.

The *Telegram* was founded in 1876 by John Ross Robertson (1841-1918), a "notable and picturesque personality" whose many bequests to charity and sport have outlived his newspaper. Born in Toronto, Robertson was the son of a wholesale drygoods merchant; he showed little interest in his father's business, and while still a student at Upper Canada College he cobbled together, with a few fonts of type and a small press in the basement of his father's home on John Street, a newspaper called the *College Times* for his fellow students. When he finished school, he worked for a number of small papers, and briefly published a weekly satirical sheet called *The Grumbler*. At the age of 21, he became the city editor of *The Globe*, then quit three years later to start the short-lived *Daily Telegraph*. When the news broke in November of 1869 that some Metis on the prairies were revolting, Robertson and a *Globe* reporter named Robert Cunningham journeyed to the end of the railway line at St. Cloud, Minnesota, hired a two-horse sleigh, and travelled through snowstorms across 400 miles of prairie to Fort Garry; for their trouble, they were arrested and held for a week by Riel, before being more or less kicked out. Back in Toronto, Robertson worked as business manager for Goldwin Smith's *The Nation* in 1875, and after a conversation with the latter, decided to launch an independent daily newspaper. The *Telegram* became a feisty, prosperous little journal—today it would be called a tabloid—with classified advertisements occupying the first several pages, followed by terse and tightly written stories, in a style that was dispassionate for the time.

Sir John Willison was editorial writer for the Globe *from 1890 until 1902. It was he who hired Joseph Atkinson, the newspaper's best "human interest" yarn-spinner, as one of his reporters. Known as a superb editor, with a liberal, free-trading and possibly annexationist stance on the political issues of the day, Willison switched to the more conservative and imperialist* Toronto Daily News *in 1902. During the First World War, Prime Minister Sir Robert Borden offered titles to those influential newspaper editors who would back conscription and Unionist government: Joseph Atkinson, by then with the* Star, *came out in support, but refused a baronetcy; John Ross Robertson of the* Telegram *refused both a knighthood and a Senate seat, reportedly on the same day; Willison, however, took the proffered knighthood, as did Hugh Graham, the publisher of the Tory* Montreal Star, *who was made Lord Atholstan. Soon thereafter, Willison resigned his newspaper work in order to organize the Canadian Reconstruction Association, a national committee which sought to readjust Canadian industry to peacetime, improve industrial relations and the "economic understanding" between East and West, develop domestic and export trade through "the scientific utilization of natural resources," and help women become a permanent part of the labour force. He wrote several books on subjects such as the national railway questions of the day, Sir Wilfrid Laurier, and the relationships among Britain, the U.S., and Canada. Following the death of his first wife, he married the noted newspaperwoman Marjory MacMurchy (page 255).*

Robertson devoted his life to Toronto: he was a great collector of old photographs and art, and wrote and published the *Landmarks of Toronto* series, which have become standard reference works on the city's early buildings and residents; for 35 years he was chairman of the Board of Trustees of the Hospital for Sick Children, and gave over a half million dollars to it; each Christmas Eve, he dressed up as Santa Claus and delivered presents to every child unfortunate enough to be hospitalized; in addition, he built the Lakeside Home for Little Children at Lighthouse Point on the Island, a milk pasteurization plant on the hospital grounds, and a nurses' residence for the Hospital for Sick Children. A few days before he died, he cleared the latter's title with the presentation of a cheque for $111,000. (Not long before, he had remarked: "I will surprise everyone by the small amount of money I will leave.") Another of his passions was the Ontario Hockey Association—he was known as "the father of amateur hockey in Ontario," and is a member of the Hockey Hall of Fame. He was also the longest-serving and most prominent Mason in Canada, and the author of *The History of the Cryptic Rite*. His opposition to separate schools in Manitoba prompted him to enter federal politics in 1896—for one term, he served as Independent Conservative Member of Parliament for East Toronto. He claimed the unique distinction of refusing on the same day both a knighthood and a Senate seat—his newspaper had long argued against British titles for Canadians, and he could not picture himself as a Senator. "I declined them, I hope graciously and graciously," he explained.

Another story which appeared amongst the eulogies accompanying his obituary (in the *Star*) concerned an industrious office boy who had lost his $25 savings in the 1910 Farmers Bank collapse, and could no longer afford to attend night school. Robertson heard of the boy's plight, called him into his office, gave him five $5 bills, and told him to be more careful when selecting his bankers. Robertson died on May 31, 1918, at his home at 291 Sherbourne Street.

The third of the venerable Toronto newspapers is the *Star*, which under the direction and ownership of Joseph Atkinson grew to be the largest newspaper in the country. Originally the *Evening Star*, it was founded in 1893 by a group of printers who had been locked out by the owners of the Conservative *News*, and was supported by organized labour. It soon found itself in uncertain financial circumstances and was purchased by the schoolbook publisher and Conservative William Gage, who used it as a soapbox to attack the Liberal minister of education; Gage was also a mem-

ber of the Lord's Day Alliance, so the *Star* led the campaign against the public desire for Sunday streetcar operation. Having lost that campaign, Gage lost interest in his newspaper and sold it to Canadian General Electric president Frederic Nicholls, who insisted that his editors support his *laissez faire* ideals and tilt at fripperies, such as playgrounds attached to schools, and decry groups that resisted profitable and progressive civic improvements like Sunday streetcars. His staff, including former *Saturday Night* editor E. E. Sheppard, drifted away, and the paper lost circulation; Nicholls decided to sell it in 1899.

The *Star*'s meanderings through the ideological swamp were not unique, as many newspapers, responding to the journalistic styles of Hearst and Pulitzer in the United States, were, in effect, adopting a motto of "all the news that fits." The *World*, started as an independent in 1880, was at its most flamboyant and half-baked under the control of "Billie Bug Eyes" MacLean, and its reporters, including Conn Smythe's father, were given wide scope to explore the outer limits of any issue; if the newspaper adhered to any consistent philosophy, it was that of public ownership of utilities.

The other newspapers in the city at the turn of the century had staked out more solid ideological ground: foremost was the *Globe*, expertly edited by J. S. Willison, with a political bias in favour of the long-serving, corrupt provincial Liberal regime, and a free-trade stance which sometimes seemed to advocate annexation by the United States; the *Mail & Empire*, formed in 1895 from the merger of two Conservative party newspapers; and the *News*, an influential, conservative-minded paper founded in 1881 and bought in 1903 by J. S. Willison and the industrialist Joseph Flavelle.

Of these six newspapers, only one—the morning *Globe*—supported Wilfrid Laurier and the Liberal party. According to a story credited to John Willison, Laurier asked a group of wealthy Torontonians to find or found an evening paper which would carry the Liberal torch in Ontario. The group included William Mulock, the postmaster general and chief Liberal organizer in Ontario; Senator Cox of the Bank of Commerce; W. E. H. Massey and Lyman Jones of Massey-Harris; the railway contractor G. Plunkett Magann, who sought Liberal connections; Peter Larkin of the Salada Tea Company; and Timothy Eaton, said to be a great admirer of Laurier. Not all of these men had previously been identified with the Liberal cause; perhaps some, who had been nominally Conservatives, came on board because of disenchantment with the party following

The Toronto World *contained an odd assortment of rhetoric and religion, reflecting the opinions of one of its editors, Albert Ernest Stafford Smythe. An Irishman who had emigrated to Chicago in his early twenties, Smythe brought theosophy with him to Canada in 1889, and two years later founded the Toronto Theosophical Society and its mouthpiece,* The Lamp. *He was president of the Toronto Press Club in 1907, and from 1910-20 wrote a column called "Crusts and Crumbs" in the Toronto* Sunday World, *dealing with comparative religion, occultism, the esoteric basis of Christianity, the* Secret Doctrine, *and criticism of art, literature, music, and drama from an occult point of view. The Onondagas in Syracuse, New York, admitted him to their tribe with the name O-ake-wah-de-he. His son Conn had a remarkable career as the owner of the Maple Leafs (page 155). A. E. S. Smythe lived at 22 Glen Grove Avenue in North Toronto.*

its circus-like revolving-door performance before the 1896 election (following the death of Sir John A. Macdonald in 1891, a series of vacillating Conservative prime ministers grappled unsuccessfully with the problem of running the country, especially the question of separate schools in Manitoba).

The group bought out the *Evening Star*, and offered the editor's post to Joseph Atkinson, a capable former *Globe* reporter who at the time was editing the Montreal *Herald*, and had been dithering over an offer to join the Conservative Montreal *Star*. Atkinson was born in Newcastle in 1865, started his journalistic career in Port Hope when he was nineteen, and arrived in Toronto in 1888 to work for the *World*. He joined the *Globe* the following year, and became an expert writer of purple-prose, bleeding-heart human interest stories. In November, 1890, he joined the troupe of reporters witnessing the execution of the murderer J.R. Birchall at Woodstock Jail; whereas the other reporters were perhaps the stereotypical wise-cracking cynics, Atkinson was appalled by the gruesome spectacle, and at that point, according to his biographer Ross Harkness, became an abolitionist. Not surprisingly, his piety (he attended Bible classes given by Joseph Flavelle) and firm stand against liquor earned him the nickname "Holy Joe."

Atkinson accepted the Toronto *Star*'s offer. His pledge to support the Laurier Liberals caused him some grief in later years (partly as he came to believe in the need for conscription), but his refusal to turn the Toronto *Star* into a straight Liberal party organ allowed it to become a significant and successful newspaper. Neither the fact that the newspaper had changed hands nor the identity of the purchasing group was made public. A few other men, including railwayman and banker Michael Haney, bought *Star* stock; these men, plus the original purchasing group, and Atkinson were the only ones who owned common or voting stock in the newspaper from 1899 until the newspaper was sold in 1958. As the original owners put their shares up for sale, Atkinson bought them, and by 1913 he had a controlling interest in the *Star*. For example, he acquired Lyman Jones's shares in 1911, when Jones, identified as a sympathizer with the "Toronto Eighteen" (page 228), rebelled against the *Star*'s support of Laurier's reciprocity policy and dumped his *Star* stock. Another acquisition, recalled by Ross Harkness, was effected through John Craig Eaton's displeasure with the *Star*'s editorials: Eaton, who was the *Star*'s biggest advertiser, felt that it had been irresponsibly left-wing in its coverage of the 1919 Winnipeg General Strike and support of labour

unions, so after discussions with Atkinson, Eaton agreed to sell him his 11.7 percent holding in the newspaper. Following the conclusion of this deal, Eaton's in June, 1921, suddenly withdrew its advertising—the back-page "Eaton's Daily Store News" which had run since June, 1900. A year later, following John Eaton's sudden death, the flow of advertisements resumed.

Atkinson supported Laurier's "great vision" of the Canadian Northern Railway on the one hand, while on the other he lambasted the C.N.R.'s promoters, who in addition controlled the Toronto Street Railway Company. After Laurier's death, the *Star* enthusiastically welcomed the new Liberal leader, Atkinson's lifelong friend, the expedient chameleon William Lyon Mackenzie King—the two men shared a reformist, almost messianic, bent. Mackenzie King first came to prominence in 1897 as a labour reformer, writing a series of articles on "sweating" for the *Mail & Empire*; according to one story, he got his entry into the Dominion Department of Labour, which became his springboard to a political career, through an opportune suggestion by Atkinson to William Mulock.

In civic politics, the *Star* waged a ceaseless battle against the *Telegram*. The latter consistently maintained its readership of Tory, Protestant Imperialists by advocating low taxes and small government—through the 1920s, the votes of its readership dominated city politics. The *Telegram* was the only newspaper that espoused a blatant anti-Semitism; other papers, most notably the *Mail & Empire*, were positive towards the Jewish community, describing it as "thrifty," "enterprising," and "law-abiding"; the *Star* ran pictures and "puff" in its social section for prominent Jewish weddings, and extolled the achievements of Jews such as Sigmund Samuel.

The *Telegram* and the *Star* fought hammer and tong over issues such as the Mackenzie-Hocken street-railway purchase agreement (page 39*ff*.), which the *Telegram* opposed and "won," and Sir Adam Beck's "waterfront grab" (page 90), which the *Star* opposed and won. When there was no issue to be fought, the two papers sniped and carped at each other, concocting news to create more partisanship—an example was the "crooked lane" controversy (page 86).

With the exception of the *Globe*, which had a Liberal readership and influence of its own, the other newspapers struggled along in the shadow of these two giants. The *News*, which had been the only Toronto newspaper to support the granting of British titles for Canadians, collapsed in 1919 soon after the departure of *Sir* John Willison. The *World*, crippled finan-

In 1899, Joseph Atkinson was appointed by a Liberal syndicate as president of the Star, *which he piloted over the next four decades with skill, daring, and a flair for the dramatic. His moral rectitude earned him the nickname "Holy Joe." The Atkinson Charitable Foundation, which he established in 1942, a few years before his death, has given grants to a variety of educational and medical causes. He lived at 237 Warren Road in Forest Hill.*

cially due to the *Star Weekly*'s ascendancy over its *Sunday World*, went bankrupt in 1921; its owner, W.F. MacLean, sold it to the Douglas brothers, who merged it with their *Mail & Empire*. The latter's respectable, nonsensationalist outlook was reflected in its chief editor, Francis Drake Llewellyn Smith. The son of a clergyman, he took some legal training at Osgoode Hall, and before joining the *Mail & Empire* was chief editorial writer for both the *World* and the *News* (succeeding Sir John Willison). Throughout his career, he was a staunch Imperialist, one of a select group of Canadian editors that, during the Great War, toured the Grand Fleet and the Western Front as guests of the British and French governments. Even the *Mail & Empire* fell victim to the big-business economics of the Toronto newspaper market—in 1936, George McCullagh merged it with the *Globe*, creating the *Globe & Mail*.

The *Star* outgrew the others due to its preeminence in what it called "razzle-dazzle journalism." Almost anything could be turned into a promotion, a contest, or an event. The *Star* first used wireless in 1903, only two years after Marconi sent the first message across the Atlantic Ocean, to report the results of a Canada Cup race off Hanlan's Point to its office; later, it used radio demonstrations as part of its Canadian National Exhibition displays, and established station CFCA with reporter Foster Hewitt as an announcer. It began its regular radio reporting in June, 1922, and had a mobile studio which toured the city streets and visited local events (page 28). In addition, the newspaper featured a column by Hewitt on "radio tips," such as how to build a radio set. To experiment with the new art of merchandising, the *Star* offered a regular flood of premiums, including pictures of Queen Victoria and Lord Roberts, books and coupons. Always there were contests: in August, 1912, "Swat The Fly"; in October, 1918, a $10 prize for the best photo of mushrooms. As the years went on, the stunts, coordinated by promotion manager Main Johnson, became ever more crazy.

Early in the 1920s, Atkinson's son-in-law, Harry C. Hindmarsh, took over editorial duties, and became responsible for the *Star*'s dynamic and often controversial news style. Also hired at the time were reporters Gordon Sinclair and Gregory Clark, who "razzle-dazzled" readers with everything from serious pieces to hackneyed stunts such as frying an egg on the City Hall steps. The *Star*'s "flying squad" had staff cars gassed up and ready to tear off in any direction to scoop the competition. Also hired at that time was Ernest Hemingway, who wrote 67 articles for the *Star Weekly* before returning to Paris and writing *The Sun Also Rises*.

The *Star*'s flamboyance was in fact a carefully controlled balancing act, for looming over every reporter and editor was the figure of "Holy Joe." Although the *Star* (and to a lesser extent the other newspapers) felt it could create news and entertain readers as it saw fit, it managed to maintain a strongly moral tone throughout, even amidst the froth of the *Star Weekly*. All parts of the newspaper, according to Atkinson, should be suitable for all members of the family.

In the decades since the golden years of the 1930s, electronic media have become the eyewitnesses, and have witnessed the change in reporting away from the self-censorship of "family entertainment." Atkinson died in 1948; his family's control of the *Star* ended after Hindmarsh's death in the mid-1950s. The Bassett family closed down the *Telegram* in 1971, though its populist conservative readership was able to migrate to the new *Sun*. The *Globe & Mail* used satellite technology to publish a national edition simultaneously across the country, known jocularly as "Toronto's national newspaper." Today, newspapers are light-years removed from the primitive but effective soapboxes of William Lyon Mackenzie and his contemporaries.

F.D.L. Smith

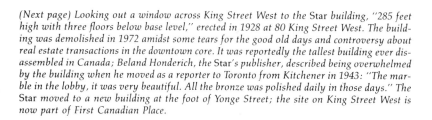

(Next page) Looking out a window across King Street West to the Star *building, "285 feet high with three floors below base level," erected in 1928 at 80 King Street West. The building was demolished in 1972 amidst some tears for the good old days and controversy about real estate transactions in the downtown core. It was reportedly the tallest building ever disassembled in Canada; Beland Honderich, the* Star's *publisher, described being overwhelmed by the building when he moved as a reporter to Toronto from Kitchener in 1943: "The marble in the lobby, it was very beautiful. All the bronze was polished daily in those days." The* Star *moved to a new building at the foot of Yonge Street; the site on King Street West is now part of First Canadian Place.*

City Hall

Old City Hall, built in the 1890s on the eastern side of Bay Street at Queen, replaced an 1844 edifice on the south side of Front Street East at Jarvis—now the South St. Lawrence Market. An 1891 touring guide noted that "the site is a central and convenient one, and when it is cleared of the old rookeries and other dilapidated relics of a bygone day, which at present occupy and surround it, the new and handsome pile will have an imposing appearance." Urban redevelopment, specifically the Eaton Centre and New City Hall in the late 1960s, cleared away most of the remaining tenements, but almost cleared away Old City Hall as well.

Old City Hall was built in a style called Richardsonian Romanesque after its promulgator, the American architect Henry Hobson Richardson. Described by the critic Willis Polk as "a Titanic inebriation in sandstone," the style reached its apogee in 1884 in Richardson's Allegheny County Courthouse, starting a craze which affected the design of public buildings all over North America. Each one in each city was slightly different; in Toronto, the architect E. J. Lennox, whose later contributions to the cityscape include the King Edward Hotel and "Casa Loma," produced a masterful interpretation of the original idea at the head of Bay Street (at that time, the continuation of Bay Street north of Queen was called Terauley Street).

In his assessment of Old City Hall, the architectural historian Eric Arthur conceded that "it is true that there are points of similarity in [Lennox's] scheme with the Pittsburgh Court House of 1884 by Richardson, of which Lennox was no doubt aware, but a comparison of the two would dismiss any suggestion of copying." In fact, Lennox's design bears a much more startling similarity, especially in its detailing and the asymmetrical placement of the clock tower, to the red sandstone Los Angeles County Courthouse by Curlett, Cuthbertson and Eisen (demolished in 1938), which was widely publicized in magazines such as the *California Architect & Building News* in June and August of 1888.

New City Hall, occupying a block which used to contain a jumble of buildings including Shea's Hippodrome, was the subject of an international design competition in the early 1960s. Its construction marked the beginning of the redevelopment of downtown, a time which saw the erection of the monumental towers at the crossroads of King and Bay, and the sophisticated galleria of Eaton Centre. Old City Hall and Union Station were two of the landmarks from earlier generations which, to the hard-nosed planners and developers of the time, had outlived their usefulness, but were nevertheless saved by citizen action.

Looking north on Bay Street to Queen, on a rainy Sunday in the 1920s. The "Bay" street-car ran north from Queen's Quay through the city to Davenport Road, then travelled up *Avenue Road to St. Clair and west to the loop at Lansdowne.*

Theatres

Even during those languid, long ago years of "Toronto the Good," when almost any form of entertainment risked being branded as sinful or salacious, one could see a wide variety of theatrical performances. For the half-century before 1910, when motion pictures began to triumph over live theatre, Toronto was a regular stop for all the theatrical and operatic companies which were now able to tour with a new-found ease, thanks to the ubiquitous railways.

From the prerailway days, a story survives of an American company that appeared in Toronto at the beginning of the winter of 1825. A sudden freeze-up forced them to stay in town; however, the company was practically insolvent, as audiences of their Shakespearean repertory had not exactly been plentiful, so a benefit performance of *Richard III* was organized for that New Year's Eve, to be attended by the town's well-lubricated politicians, merchants and military figures. The story, oft-repeated and probably improved with the telling, details how a Captain Matthews led the audience in the singing of "God Save the King" and then called out "Hats off for Rule Brittania!" Encouraged by an enthusiastic response, but without considering what emotions might have remained from the not-so-distant 1812 War, the Captain then called for a heads-bared rendition of "Yankee Doodle." When Philip Vankoughnet, later the minister of agriculture and chancellor of Upper Canada, refused to doff his hat, someone promptly knocked it off his head, precipitating a wild mêlée.

More typical of the performers in colonial-era Toronto was John Nickenson's stock company at the Royal Lyceum Theatre, located on the south side of King Street, between Bay and York. The Royal Lyceum was said to be the first real theatre in the city, superseding such improvised settings as the Theatre Royal of a Mr. Noah, which had been located at the northeast corner of King and York. (Naturally nicknamed "Noah's Ark," it presented such a tawdry season that newspaper editorialists called for the city to close it down and "abate the nuisance"; a timely fire in 1840 solved the problem once and for all.) The Royal Lyceum had "class"—J.E. Middleton, writing in the 1930s, noted that Nickenson had "established a sound stock company of which his four daughters were members, and in the fashion of the pre-railway times welcomed the travelling stars of the day and gave them adequate support." Charlotte Nickenson, the youngest of the daughters, had the longest career; much later, she leased the Grand Opera House, and in her old age "preserved many of the bodily graces of her youth, and her voice was still gracious and alluring."

The touring stock companies of the turn of the century presented all the possible variations of standard music hall fare, especially sweet-faced, rosy-cheeked girls with parasols, singing the popular love songs of

bicycles built for two, or the tried-and-true ante-bellum tunes of Stephen Foster; as well, there were usually melodramatists, buffoons, black-faced minstrels, and jugglers. At weak spots in the performance the audience would shout "23 Skidoo!" and pelt the performers with produce.

In 1912, the Star Burlesque Theatre (later known as the Empire), at 23 Temperance Street, crossed the boundary of contemporary taste with a risqué show called *The Darlings of Paris*. Allegedly a compilation of crude double entendres, the show prompted a complaint from the Rev. R. B. St. Clair, arrests by the police, and a lengthy and convoluted prosecution. The jury decided on January 13 of the following year that the theatre company was "not guilty of producing an immoral, indecent or obscene show," but added a rider that "such plays" should not be allowed, a decision which the judge felt to be "cowardly." So fervent was the Rev. St. Clair in his attempts to stir up public opinion against the show that he printed a circular "giving intimate descriptions of a vile performance," and was himself arrested and convicted of publishing obscene literature! St. Clair's conviction for "knowingly and without lawful justification selling and distributing certain obscene circulars tending to corrupt morals" was upheld on appeal the following month; one judge of the appellate court noted that "an ounce of ordinary everyday legal methods is far more effectual than a ton of hysterics." The original trial judge remained confused by the case, as "the man who drew the attention of the public to this and who described what took place in the theatre in a way that seems to be substantially undisputed has been convicted of publishing obscene literature, while those who produced the play have been, by the opinion of this jury, acquitted."

A more lofty standard of musical entertainment had been presented since 1851 at St. Lawrence Hall. Travelling opera companies frequented the Academy of Music at Church and Adelaide, and the aforementioned Royal Lyceum. The real boon to cultural life, however, was the opening in the 1890s of the Massey Music Hall, which allowed the Mendelssohn Choir and the Philharmonic Society to desert the "draughty firetrap" of the Horticultural building in Allan Gardens. Massey Hall became the venue for a sudden blossoming of ambitious choral and orchestral music, including performances of Beethoven's Ninth Symphony and the Verdi Requiem. Most of these early concerts were under the baton of Dr. F. H. Torrington, the organist of Metropolitan Methodist Church, and Dr. A. S. Vogt, who in 1894 founded the Mendelssohn Choir. The first performance in Toronto of Handel's *Messiah* had been a generation earlier—in 1857.

One of the main promoters of musical performances in Toronto was

Fred Jacob was literary and drama editor for the Mail and Empire *during the 1910s and 1920s. The son of an Elora barrister, he moved to Toronto after completing high school, clerked in various business offices, then joined the* Mail and Empire *in 1903 as editor of the young people's page, using the* nom de plume Tweedledum. *In 1910 he became the newspaper's drama editor, and began writing music critiques and poetry in his spare time. Twice he won poetry competitions, first with "The Departure of the Wild Geese," then in 1909 with "Laura Secord," which won the* Globe *Historical Poem Competition. He was a regular contributor of verse and prose to* Toronto Saturday Night, *and wrote two novels,* The Day Before Yesterday *and* P.V. *His other interest in life was lacrosse—he was president of the St. Simon's Lacrosse Club, which in 1920 won the Senior Lacrosse Championship of Ontario. During a dinner party at his home in 1928, he suffered a heart attack and died, though aged only 45.*

Augustus Bridle, the music editor of the *Star*. A former schoolteacher and choirleader who had helped organize the Arts & Letters Club in 1908, he had written several novels, including *Sons of Canada* and *Hansen*, the latter described as a novel of Canadianization. In January, 1922, with the cooperation of his newspaper, he organized a series of free "Good Music Concerts" in the city. Bridle also worked with Dr. Fricker—the successor to Dr. Vogt of the Mendelssohn Choir—to organize the Exhibition Chorus of 2,000 voices, which dominated the proceedings at Music Day at the C.N.E.

The grandest of the Toronto theatres was the Royal Alexandra at 260 King Street West, built in 1907 and saved from demolition and restored in the 1960s by the legendary "Honest Ed" Mirvish. The "Royal Alex" was built during what seemed as if it would be the last gasp of live theatre. By the end of the First World War, cinemas had been built in every neighbourhood, and were serving up a parade of newsreels and motion pictures to an insatiable audience. The theatre pages in the *Star* late in 1918 advertised only two theatres offering serious live performances: the Royal Alexandra, with seats at prices ranging from 50 cents to $1.50; and the Princess—the former Academy of Music building on King Street west of York. Featured at Shea's Hippodrome, on Bay Street directly opposite City Hall, was "The Suffragettes' Review," a music hall performance with a timely title but in the style of a previous generation.

Otherwise, Toronto's theatres were showing American movies (all of which, of course, were silent, with flashcard dialogue and usually a live piano accompaniment): at Loew's and the Winter Garden at Yonge and Queen, Mutt & Jeff cartoons preceded Theda Bara in *Soul of the Buddha*; the Oakwood, at Oakwood and St. Clair, featured Marguerite Clarke in *Uncle Tom's Cabin*; the Regent, at 27 Adelaide Street West, was showing Ethel Barrymore in *Our Mrs. McChesney*; the Madison, at Bloor and Bathurst, had Francis X. Bushman and Beverley Bayne in *A Pair of Cupids*; the invitingly named U-Kum at 962 College at Dovercourt featured Constance Talmadge in *Up The Road With Sallie* (there was also a Kum C Theatre, at 1288 Queen Street West); and the Allen Theatre at 19 Richmond Street East had the most sensational film—the talk of the town—D.W. Griffith's *The Great Love*, which was the only film playing in Toronto to acknowledge that there was a war on. "See the mighty air raid on London," read the advertisements, "foiled by a daring Canadian soldier." Griffith had by that time developed his own stock company, which included such luminaries as Lillian Gish; he had catapulted from fame to notoriety three years earlier with the release of *Birth of a Nation*, which stunned audiences with its cinematic brilliance, while its blatant,

"America's Sweetheart," Mary Pickford, was also Toronto's, as she had been born in a ramshackle little house on University Avenue. Her films always received star billing—here, at the Colonial Theatre on Queen Street opposite City Hall (see also pages 31 and 84), the billboards advertise her 1914 potboiler Tess of the Storm Country. *In two of her infrequent interviews, in 1934 and 1976, Pickford stated that the "Tess" character was her favorite, because "that girl was no goody-goody—I was praying one minute and hitting somebody the next." A local cinema, at the northwest corner of Queen and Spadina, was called the Mary Pickford Theatre from 1916 until 1947—it was later the Bargain Benny's discount department store (page 143).*

pro-Ku Klux Klan plot inflamed prejudices and provoked demonstrations (it had originally been released as *The Clansmen*). So all-pervading was the American influence that even the newsreels before the features showed only American troops—who had just entered the war the previous year—conquering everything in their path; nothing was seen of the British or Canadian exploits.

As the public was so enthusiastic for film, playwrights had a difficult time of it. A typical example was Merrill Denison, a Detroit native who made a living through a combination of playwriting, novel and magazine article writing, the art directorship of Hart House, and resort ownership. Two of his plays were *The Unheroic North* (1923) and *The Prize Winner* (1927); he published a set of humorous sketches entitled *Boobs in the Woods*, and wrote a series of articles for the *Star Weekly* on Ontario's back country. He also authored, in 1948, a history of Massey-Harris called *Harvest Triumphant*.

In the late 1940s, during one of Toronto's periodic bouts of self-examination, a spate of articles appeared in the press describing the entertainments available to visitor and resident alike. The articles, which recognized the Royal Alex and the cinemas, were evidently prompted by Mayor Saunders's campaign, launched in February, 1945, to "Make Toronto Popular." Lister Sinclair's radio play *We All Hate Toronto*, first broadcast on the Panorama series on CBC in January, 1946, added urgency to the quest to find something to love—more specifically, to find something live to watch, other than the floor show at the "King Eddie."

Noteworthy in the midst of the city's allegedly boring and moralistic quagmire was the Casino Burlesque Theatre at 87 Queen Street West—a block to the west of the Old City Hall, and now the site of the Sheraton Centre—where old-fashioned bump-and-grind was dished up four times daily.

The Casino was the big draw in the two especially sleazy blocks of Queen Street west of Bay, sharing the street with five "standard hotels," several restaurants smelling of fried onions and mustard, and a variety of pawnbrokers and discount clothing stores. The Casino could seat 1,100 people for the live striptease of stars such as Lizzi Cannon, who was reportedly paid $300 a week for 24 shows. The chorines who made up the rest of the show were rumoured to be $27.50-a-week girls in straitened circumstances from the city's dancing academies.

During the barren, entertainment- and liquor-free Sundays of Toronto in the forties and fifties, the Casino offered practically the only live Sunday theatre. But, on this one day of the week, the entertainment, starting at Sunday noon, was Chinese—traditional plays which ran without intermissions through the afternoon and into the evening.

Contralto Madonna Niles, though born in New York State in 1884, received much of her musical education at the Toronto Conservatory of Music, and was a regular performer at Canadian concerts. She married Carl Ahrens, an Ontario-born landscape painter who, in 1914, became the first Canadian artist to be invited by a foreign government to exhibit his works. Unfortunately for Ahrens, it was the Belgian government, which was invaded and went into exile before the exhibition took place.

Richard Stapells spent most of his working life as a manufacturer, though he excelled as a violinist. He was a member of the Toronto Philharmonic Orchestra, and played under the baton of Doctor Torrington at all of the big musical festivals held in Toronto in the 1890s. He was in the orchestra at Massey Hall on opening night. In addition, he was for seventeen years the baritone soloist and assistant choirmaster at the Church of the Messiah. He threw his organizing talents behind a wide range of causes, including the Savoyard Opera Company, the Ontario Musical Competition, the 1919 Navy League campaign which raised $165,000 in three days, the Toronto Publicity Bureau, the Dufferin School Old Boys' Association, and the Toronto Radial Association.

Few stories sold more newspapers during the twenties and thirties than that of the disappearance of Ambrose "Twinkletoes" Small. Born in Brantford in 1867, Small was the great theatrical impresario of World War One-era Toronto. With a New York office, the latest attractions from Europe, and control of a few dozen theatres, including the Grand Opera House and the Majestic Theatre, he was rich and famous. In December, 1919, shortly before his 53rd birthday, he simply vanished, never to be seen again. Many claimed to have seen him, and many impersonated him—each claim causing a flurry of interest. The gentleman pictured here was one Charles E. M. Churchill, who holds a certain distinction in that he twice claimed to be Small. The first time was in 1932, when he was an inmate of the Wisconsin Central Hospital for the criminally insane; in the second instance, in October, 1934, a news dispatch from Kalamazoo, Michigan, reported that this man, using the name Ambrose J. Small, was being held on a charge of illegally selling securities. Local lawyer A. J. Holmes, Small's nephew, talked with the man by phone, and was quickly convinced that he was an imposter.

Queen Street West, in the block west of Bay Street, is now the site on the right-hand side of the street of the Sheraton Centre, and on the left of Nathan Phillips Square and the new City Hall. This photograph, taken in the 1920s, shows its cluttered and somewhat sleazy former self. Occupied by pawnbrokers using the ancient sign of the three gilt balls, the street was dominated by the Vaudeville Theatre, in the middle distance, which was later the notorious Casino Burlesque. Visible in the centre background, facing Bay Street, are the domes of the Temple Building, more properly called the Independent Order of Foresters Building.

The Farmers Bank

Toronto the Good had its share of the bad. The numerous violations of liquor laws, which sullied the reputations of public servants, were all grist for the mills of reformers such as the controversial pamphleteer C. S. Clark. In his 1898 magnum opus "Of Toronto The Good," Clark seized on details from local newspapers to fuel his tirade against corrupt officials. An example is his reporting of a campaign rally to reelect mayor R. J. Fleming, later the manager of Toronto Railway Company. As Fleming declaimed " . . . I believe there is not another [police] force on this continent that will compare with ours," from the background, a heckler yelled: "At drinking lager!"

Elsewhere, referring to a statement from the Toronto *News*, Clark fulminated: "The burglar who escaped from the cells at Police Headquarters pried his way out with a crowbar, but the entire staff armed with crowbars could not pry the deputy chief from the well-paid job he fills so muchly that he overflows into judicial duties."

In the United States, it was the end of the era of the "robber barons"—magnates who controlled railroads, steel, coal and shipping with such an iron grasp that entire cities and state governments quaked in their thrall. In reaction, a generation of "muckrakers" arose there, whose most prominent target was John D. Rockefeller's Standard Oil trust. Journalist Ida Tarbell of *McClure*'s magazine wrote a sensational exposé of Standard Oil in an eighteen-installment series of articles, running from November, 1902 to April, 1904. The upshot was anti-combines legislation in the United States. This anti-big business sentiment spilled over into Canada.

During this period the extraordinary quasi-monopoly of Messrs. Mackenzie, Nicholls, and Pellatt was flourishing in Toronto. These three capitalists controlled a labyrinth of interlocking street railway, radial railway, power generation, transmission, and electrical distribution companies. They were able to operate quite free of restraint during a time when no government was willing to sally forth into the swamp of collectivism. Their business philosophy was ruthless and uncompromising; nevertheless, their combinations were legal, as long as they steered clear of any "conspiracies in restriction of trade."

The most widely publicized conspiracy trial of that period was prompted by the doubling of plumbing rates in the city, and involved the Master Plumbers & Steam Fitters Cooperative and the Central Supply Association, and their relationships with the large wholesale plumbing firm of James Robertson & Company. The criminal prosecution commenced on April 13, 1905, on the specific charge that James Robertson & Company had refused to sell supplies to a plumber who was not a member of the association. The company was alleged to have controlled the manufacture and set the supply and prices of plumbing supplies, thereby restricting

trade. The charge was dismissed on a technicality. Later that year, on November 14, eighteen master plumbers were arraigned on conspiracy charges, which had arisen because Toronto journeymen had threatened to strike if their employers did not join the Master Plumbers Association. In the course of the trial, conducted by crown counsel E. E. A. DuVernet, it transpired that a $20,000 rakeoff had been distributed among the members of the association. These charges held up; the Central Supply Association and the Master Plumbers' Association were each fined $5,000, and seven individual plumbers were fined between $250 and $500.

As the financial capital of Ontario, Toronto developed an elaborate banking and savings system whose success was due almost entirely to the credibility of its officials. By comparison with today, there was little government regulation; by comparison with the United States, there was an enormous amount of power concentrated and trust placed in a small group of bankers. The system worked well, although it was too conservative to encourage the sort of venture-capitalism that thrived in the United States. When the small banks got into trouble, they were in most cases absorbed into the larger ones—as was the case in 1906 when the Ontario Bank failed but was absorbed by the Bank of Montreal—with few people losing their shirts along the way. Three exceptions were, in order of increasing size, the York County Loan & Savings failure of 1906, the Farmers Bank collapse of 1910, and the Home Bank debacle of 1923 (page 63).

The case of the York County Loan & Savings Company first came to the public's attention on January 8, 1906, when its president, Joseph Phillips, was arrested on charges of conspiracy to defraud. The police magistrate, Lt. Col. George Denison III, reviewed the evidence before him and, fearing that Phillips might catch a train to Detroit, refused him bail and committed him to the county jail. The court's investigation delineated a web of interlocking companies and a veritable squadron of kited cheques; the companies involved included the Toronto Life Insurance Company, the Liszt Piano Company, and the Southern Light & Power Company, all of which "helped out" their affiliated loan company. Chronicler John Castell Hopkins noted that "features of the case included loose methods of management, extraordinary forgetfulness of witnesses, large payments to Phillips for unexplained purposes, and curious payments to employees." The court appointed an auditor, who reported in April that the company's assets, which were largely vacant land, could be valued at $1,319,064, while its liabilities were $4,112,632. It took nearly two years to liquidate the "assets," leaving the hapless creditors with about 40 cents on the dollar.

The Farmers Bank was a much larger scam. Incorporated in July, 1904, it was organized in Toronto by W. R. Travers and commenced operations

"Billie" Beattie Nesbitt was a medical doctor who always had a half-dozen business and political irons in the fire at any one time. He was the fourth generation of doctors in his family, and one Toronto doctor was quoted as saying that Nesbitt "has forgotten more than we ever knew"; regardless of his commitments, he usually arranged to spend his summers at Johns Hopkins hospital in Baltimore, immersed in bacteriological research. His business affairs included the publication of the Ontario Medical Journal *and the* Dominion Dental Journal, *the C.H. Hubbard Dental Manufacturing Company, a linen mill at Bracebridge, and a thread mill at Stratford, with plant erected and machinery started, for which investors "had nothing but experience to show for their trust." His recklessness culminated in the collapse of the Farmers Bank, and his arraignment on five charges including fraud and breach of trust.*

The head office of the Farmers Bank at the northeast corner of Bay and Adelaide, photographed in 1910. It was located in the Stair Building, on the site of the old Zion Congregational Church. The building on the left with the distinctive tower is Fire Hall Number One, located at the southeast corner of Bay and Temperance.

in 1906. Travers's associate in the venture was Dr. W. Beattie Nesbitt, the Conservative member of the legislature for North Toronto, who had earned a reputation as a distributor of patronage spoils—a party insider of the "Tammany Boss" variety.

William Beattie Nesbitt was born on a farm in Oxford County in 1865, and became the fourth generation doctor in his family. "Erratic, volatile and enthusiastic," he quickly earned a reputation for recklessness. Once, on a bet, he stripped naked and waded in the deep snow around the University College quadrangle; another time, someone bet him that he was not strong enough to throw his piano out his window—"Billie" won the bet when he managed to wrestle a corner of the instrument onto his window sill. On yet another occasion, he and a few friends managed to convince a cow to climb to the top of the University College tower; according to the story, it took university officials two days to get the animal down.

Nesbitt dabbled in a number of business ventures, ranging from the publication of *Ontario Medical Journal* to a linen mill in Bracebridge to a dental manufacturing company. Early in the 1890s, he helped to form the Young Conservative Association and was the leader of one faction within the party, while the writer John Castell Hopkins, the president of the Empire Club, led the other. Around the turn of the century, Nesbitt's faction was victorious: "thus, under the aegis of the ubiquitous doctor was banded together the little knot of men who for a long time dictated the policy and affairs of the Conservative party in Toronto." In everything he did, whether business or politics, Nesbitt acquired a reputation as something of an "operator."

After Conservative James Whitney was elected premier in 1905, Nesbitt expected a cabinet post, but Whitney, who evidently felt that Nesbitt could be irksome, shuffled him into the sinecure of registrar of West Toronto. Disillusioned, Nesbitt resigned his seat in the legislature early in 1906, to assume the presidency of the new Farmers Bank with his friend Travers as general manager. However, Nesbitt had not altogether given up politics—he ran unsuccessfully for mayor in 1908. Referring to the campaign, one "well-known gentleman" (the only appellation the news-paper gave) recalled: "He got a couple of hundred out of me but I knew what I was getting into, so he's welcome to the money."

From the beginning, the Farmers Bank's activities attracted suspicion. There was its willingness to gamble with its depositors' money on speculations such as the Keeley Mine—a concern probably quite distant from the ideals of the farmers who made up a substantial share of its clients. There was a deposit receipt suspiciously offered for sale in New York. But its balance sheet, as published in the official *Canada Gazette* at the end of the 1908 fiscal year, reflected a strong and stable organization; the Conservative provincial government was certainly impressed by its image, and more than once deposited public funds there.

Trading ceased suddenly at the Farmers Bank's head office at Bay and Adelaide on December 19, 1910. Travers was quickly arrested, and the provincial inspector of detectives caught the train to Muskoka, where Beattie Nesbitt had his home. Obviously tipped off a few hours before, the erstwhile banker fled, eluding the detective. A manhunt failed to locate him; soon, rumours surfaced that he had made it to the United States. The Toronto police issued handbills offering a $200 award for information leading to his arrest.

Both Nesbitt and Travers were charged with making false returns to the government. On January 16, 1911, Travers was sentenced to six years; his confession implicated several others, including Dr. John Ferguson and Alex Fraser of Toronto. They were picked up, but found not guilty of fraudulently obtaining commissions. In the unscrambling of its affairs, the bank was found to have assets of two million dollars and liabilities of two and a half million. Many of its small, unsecured depositors were ruined.

The police caught up with Beattie Nesbitt in Chicago on April 11, 1912. His trial on charges of forgery dragged on through January, 1913, by which time his health had collapsed. On the 31st, "one hour after his lawyer had succeeded in having the indictments quashed," Nesbitt died of Bright's disease (kidney failure), "aggravated by worry," at his home at 71 Grosvenor Street. He was only 48 years old.

The Home Bank

Michael John Haney, one-time president and director of the Home Bank of Canada, was born in Galway, Ireland, in 1854. He came to Canada at the age of nineteen, and worked as a farmhand before seeking more lucrative work with the railways. While still in his twenties, he was named superintendent of the Pembina branch of the CPR, then went to British Columbia as construction manager of the famed Onderdonk sections through the Fraser Canyon. His construction contracts, including parts of the Sault Ste. Marie canal, made him a fortune, and he became associated with a variety of companies, including shipyards, locomotive works, quarries, brick works, and the Canada Steamship Lines. Like most of the depositors and directors of the Home Bank, he was a Roman Catholic. He had resigned the presidency before the bank collapsed, but was still a director; although his questionable activities while president were the subject of a lot of testimony during the trial, conspiracy charges against him were dropped.

On the afternoon of August 17, 1923, customers wishing to enter the Home Bank were stopped by a locked door and a sign saying "Bank closed—payment suspended." That evening, people read in their newspapers that all 71 branches of the bank across the country, 47 of which were in Ontario, had closed after management was unable to convince either the Canadian Bankers' Association or another bank to take it over. Confusion followed the announcement, as it did not make clear how bad or permanent the situation might be. Editorialists were divided on how significant the situation was, and how culpable the government. The conservative *Mail & Empire* made the most sanguine, "stand-pat" assessment of the situation, drawing a comparison with the free-wheeling banking industry in the United States: "Canadians are now deploring the first Bank failure their country has had since the War, the first, indeed, since the Farmers' Bank went under. What other country has got off so well in the matter of Bank failures?" However, the bank's deposits were frozen, which in itself caused "great distress, as the depositors were in the main wage earners."

The Home Bank's depositors and senior executives were mostly Roman Catholics, and many Catholic institutions, including churches, school boards, the Knights of Columbus and the Catholic Order of Foresters, had kept their money there. This unusual situation resulted from the bank's founding, in 1854, as the Home Savings & Loan Company, an outgrowth of a charitable trust administered by a board of directors whose chairman was the Archbishop of Toronto. Changes to the Bank Act in 1905 required it to have shareholders and share capital, so in Toronto on June 6, 1905, the Home Bank held its first annual general meeting, at which the $3,500,000 deposits of the savings and loan company were taken over; the brewer Eugene O'Keefe was elected president; James Cooper Mason, who had been employed by the company since 1891, became manager of the Toronto branch; in addition, a board of directors, including E. G. Gooderham and Michael J. Haney, was elected. Following O'Keefe's death in 1913, the railwayman and contractor Haney became president. During the First World War, Herbert Daly joined the company as general manager and then became vice-president; Cooper Mason was promoted to assistant general manager and then became general manager. Early in the 1920s, Haney retired from the presidency but stayed on as a director, and Daly became president.

Before August, 1923, the Home Bank had seemed to be a solid and well-managed institution, and at the time of its collapse there was no public knowledge of any reverses. At its annual general meeting on June 26, 1923, the bank had presented a report to shareholders showing net profits of nearly a quarter of a million dollars, and the president, Daly, stated that "this institution has maintained its position in spite of the general adverse conditions" and that the bank's business "may be considered very satisfactory."

The main branch of the Home Bank on King Street West was one of seventy-one in Canada: forty-seven were in Ontario, three in Quebec, nine each in Saskatchewan and Manitoba, two in Alberta and one in British Columbia.

Early in August, Cooper Mason, who had become seriously ill, died, and his assistant, A. E. Calvert, assumed complete control. Within days the new general manager submitted a "bombshell" report to the bank's directors about "the bad and doubtful debts amongst the Assets of the Bank." The alarmed directors appealed to the Bankers' Association and other banks for assistance, but were rebuffed. No rearrangement of the bank's reserves could forestall the crisis. Soon after the collapse, the president of the Canadian Bankers' Association, Sir Frederick Williams-Taylor, issued a statement in Montreal which swept away any hope that Canada's banks would group together to shore up the Home Bank: "The association is not prepared to assume any such liability in this case or the case of any bank." Later, the association softened its position somewhat, and cooperated to allow a payment of 25 cents on the dollar to depositors, but by that time few thought that the bank's remaining assets would yield any more than another dime or so per dollar. By the winter, the full import of the crash was inescapable; in one parish, according to its priest, there were "widows and old men and women, sufferers from sickness, lack of employment and other causes, whose whole savings had been wiped out by the Bank's failure."

The Bankers' Association had some justification for its caution, as for a time the Home Bank calamity seemed to be a harbinger of an uncertain future. Both the Union and the Standard banks were forced to make readjustments to their capital and reserves; following months of falling deposits, the Bank of Hamilton successfully sought absorption by the Bank of Commerce; in Quebec, La Banque Nationale merged with the Bank of Hochelaga. The nearest thing to a panic afflicted the Dominion Bank, whose depositors in Toronto started a run on October 13 that was only halted when the Ontario government came to the rescue with a deposit of $1,500,000, and a reassuring speech by Premier Ferguson.

The run on the Dominion Bank started ten days after the sensational arrest, on the morning of October 3, of the Home Bank's president, vice-president, general manager, chief accountant, chief auditor, and directors. The accused were released on bail of between $50,000 and $100,000 each, while the public awaited the report of the government-appointed curator. On the morning of the thirteenth, the newspapers published a report stating that, in 1914 (by which time the western land speculation-based economy had collapsed), the western directors of the bank had been in touch with the federal minister of finance, Sir Thomas White, and requested an outside auditor, but "Sir Thomas was reassured, on enquiry, that conditions were becoming more satisfactory." The western manager had again complained to the minister of finance in 1918, at which time, according to White, he had done nothing because of the "grave consequence" and his "grave responsibility in time of War." (White had resigned as minister of finance in 1919, and taken a position as vice-president of the Canadian Bank of Commerce.)

Released late in the year, the curator's report detailed the Home Bank's probable losses on loans, including the following: to Sir Henry Pellatt, for three real-estate companies that had been dealing in land subdivisions near "Casa Loma" and elsewhere—an uncertain loss on loans of $1,700,000*; to the British Dominion Holding & Investment Corporation in Montreal, in advances through Home Bank director C. A. Barnard—a

loss of $1,100,000 on loans of $1,409,845; to A. C. Frost & Company of Chicago—an uncertain loss on loans of $1,856,301. As well, the curator listed losses on the Cooper Mason estate totalling $97,214, and a total loss on advances of $120,410 to the Arnprior Cabinet Company, which was owned by President Herbert Daly. On December 14, the court issued a winding-up order for the Bank; liquidators G. T. Clarkson and I. E. Weldon revised the loss estimates to a total of just under $5 million, including $50,000 out of $84,759 loaned to the president, and losses of $70,000 on loans to head-office staff. In addition to the already damning evidence against Daly, it was discovered that early in 1923 he had instructed his broker to sell his thousand shares in the bank. Later, it transpired that Cooper Mason's bad debts to the bank amounted to almost $400,000.

Although it was evident that the bank had come to grief because its officers and directors had not played by the rules, many commentators were also shocked at the size of the individual loans: the *Financial Times*, for instance, editorialized that "loans running into the millions, covered by a single risk, should have no place amongst the liabilities of any but the largest Banks," and characterized the standard shareholders' audit in all banks as "flimsy red tape"; the *Journal of the Canadian Bankers' Association* blamed the failure on the "extraordinary nature of the business transacted by the Bank." A consensus emerged that the government should tighten up its inspections. Geoffrey Clarkson's report noted that, in addition to its unusual lending habits, the Home Bank had never in its career been headed by a trained or experienced banker. Depositors formed organizations to lobby the federal government for a return of "one hundred cents on the dollar"; at one meeting, in Massey Hall in December, they justified their claim for full compensation on the grounds that "on more than one occasion the condition of the Home Bank had been brought to the attention of the Department of Finance and steps were not taken to see that proper precautions were provided."

The legal manoeuvring to bring the culprits to justice was well under way by the end of the year. The Crown wanted a trial before judge and jury, which the accused steadfastly resisted, appealing the rulings of minor courts all the way to the Privy Council. The latter decided, early in 1924, in favour of the accused, who then elected trial by Judge Emerson Coatsworth in County Court. Meanwhile, the liquidators had issued a writ against Daly and the directors, claiming $5 million damages for losses due to "misconduct, malfeasance and negligence." As well, they issued summonses to the bank's 1,800 shareholders, demanding they show cause why they should not immediately deliver the unpaid amounts on their shares, and double the amount in addition—the so-called "double liability." The shareholders appealed—in many cases, it was akin to the adage of getting blood from a stone—prompting the liquidators to suggest to one group of depositors that they would be lucky to receive 40 cents on their dollar. In June, after being "confined to his bed for two weeks," H. J. Daly died, reportedly from an "infection of the stomach" with which he had suffered for a year and a half.

Although two of the probable culprits—Daly and Cooper Mason—

The Home Bank's general manager was Lt. Col. James Cooper Mason, the son of Brigadier General and Senator James Mason. Born in Toronto in 1876 and educated at Toronto Collegiate Institute, he became an excellent oarsman—he won the Canadian junior and intermediate single sculls championship in 1899, and was one of the Argonaut "eight" who were champions of America in 1901. As a member of the Royal Canadian Rifles in South Africa during the Boer War, he was badly wounded, but several months later was able to rejoin his regiment, and served with such distinction that he won the Queen's South African medal with three clasps, presented to him personally by Queen Victoria at Windsor Castle. Like Michael Haney, Mason was a Roman Catholic; he lived at 268 St. George Street in the Annex. He died suddenly in August, 1923, a few days before the Home Bank suspended trading.

*In the decades since 1923, it has been implied that Pellatt's bad debts were solely responsible for the Home Bank's collapse; however, his loans were but a fraction of the total bad debt.

(Left) Major Albert E. Nash was the accountant who, during the Home Bank trials, untangled the web of capital, deposits, assets and debits. Born in Swansea, England, in 1881, he was educated as an accountant, but went to northern Alberta in 1907 and homesteaded for a year. He gave that up, joined a firm of accountants in Edmonton, then went overseas with the 19th Alberta Dragoons and won the Military Cross. Upon his return, he worked for a year for the MacLean Publishing Company, then joined Clarkson, Gordon & Dilworth (G. T. Clarkson was liquidator of the Home Bank). Nash's wife, the former Marie Yvonne Cauchon, was granddaughter of the first Speaker of the Canadian Senate after Confederation. They lived at 55 Donwoods Drive in York Mills.

Two of the Home Bank directors who were convicted of fraud and negligence, but had their convictions quashed by a majority decision of the Ontario Court of Appeal. James Frederick Martin Stewart (centre) had interests in boat-building, shipyards, paving and a locomotive works, usually in companies controlled by Michael Haney; he was also vice-president of the Michael J. Haney Real Estate Company Ltd. He lived at 7 Beaumont Road in Rosedale. (Right) Frank John Beddoe Russill was president of the Russill Hardware Company; he lived at 100 Maclennan Avenue.

Although only 41 years old in 1923, Herbert J. Daly was president of the Home Bank of Canada. A businessman with a wide range of experience, only some of which was in banking, Daly retained his interests in companies such as the Arnprior Cabinet Company, for which he approved generous loans. He was arrested on October 3, 1923, released on bail, and was facing criminal charges of fraud and misconduct, plus a $5 million civil suit, when he took to his bed the following May. He died two weeks later, "after an illness of over a year and a half," from an infection of the stomach. He lived at 72 Warren Road, Deer Park, and left a widow and five children.

were now deceased, the trial of the remaining officials and directors opened on September 9, 1924. D'Alton McCarthy was crown prosecutor; "an imposing array of legal men," including Newton Rowell, represented the accused. Sensational testimony kept spectators and readers riveted to the proceedings. Companies in which directors of the bank had interests had received $6 million in loans; in bank reports, $433,000 of bank assets described as buildings were in fact automobiles and other depreciating objects; Cooper Mason had fired the assistant manager of the Toronto branch when the latter refused to sign a bank statement which he considered incorrect; dividends had been paid from capital rather than from profits to conceal the bank's losses. The former president, Michael Haney, had fired his assistant in 1918—the latter had given Haney a draft of a letter, which he subsequently sent to the federal minister of finance complaining of conditions at the bank. (The draft letter, according to his testimony, stated that "Mr. Haney's policy was to endeavour to rehabilitate the bank by a series of speculative ventures, chiefly in steamship activities, and that the bank was loaning large sums of money and was to receive but a moiety of the expected profits," so perhaps his dismissal should not have been unexpected.) Haney, while president, had made large loans, including one of $206,651 to himself in 1919, without the directors' knowledge, and Daly's total indebtedness to the bank, according to final testimony, was $1,359,880; the Canadian *National* Railway (by this time a crown corporation) had, according to the Crown, deposited and then quickly withdrawn one million dollars in order to "pad the bank's statement" at the end of May, 1923.

The trials carried on for five months, concluding in January, 1925. Two officials, chief accountant Ocean G. Smith and auditor Sydney Jones, were found guilty of negligence. The former received a suspended sentence, the latter four months in the Ontario Reformatory. The vice-president, R. P. Gough, was convicted on six counts of fraud and sentenced to a year in the reformatory. Five directors were found guilty: Lt. Col. Clarence Smith of Montreal, guilty of negligence, six months; C. A. Barnard of Montreal, guilty of what was effectively fraud, eighteen months; J. F. M Stewart of Toronto, fraud, four months; S. Casey Wood, fraud, six months; F. J. B. Russill, negligence, sentence suspended.

The convictions of the directors were appealed to the First Divisional Court of Osgoode Hall, and at the end of June, 1925, were all quashed. At the same time, conspiracy charges against Michael Haney and the other directors were dropped. Gough's actions as vice-president, said Chief Justice Sir William Mulock, showed him to have been deceived by the president, but not guilty of negligence or fraud—in addition, he had not made any use of bank funds for his own purposes. The attorney general of Ontario subsequently declared that the government considered it to be useless to carry the case to higher court. The appeal court's decision limited the liability of the directors, as "they [had not been] ignorant because of their wilfully shutting their eyes to the facts before them." As well, the liquidators dropped their $5 million civil suit. The directors had been deceived, and the culprits were dead.

Ryrie Brothers

The name in jewellery in Toronto was Ryrie Brothers, a family company founded in 1854 with headquarters at "Diamond Hall" at the corner of Yonge and Adelaide. It was to jewellery in Toronto what Birks was in Montreal, and according to family recollection an agreement existed between the two firms that Ryrie Brothers would not open a store in Montreal if Birks stayed out of Toronto.

The two firms were similar in the quality of their merchandise and their pursuit of "the carriage trade." Ryrie Brothers published exceptionally lavish colour catalogues with embossed covers and tissue-paper inserts between the pages to ensure that the coloured inks did not offset and spoil the adjoining colour photographs; a few of these catalogues, published in the first decade of this century, survive in the collection of the Metropolitan Reference Library—other than that, little evidence of the firm survives.

Following Harry Ryrie's death in 1917 (page 260), brother James evidently struck an agreement to amalgamate with Birks. As the advertisement on this page shows, Ryrie-Birks then amalgamated, early in the 1930s, with another long-established Toronto jeweller, Ellis Brothers. In the decades since, both the Ryrie and the Ellis names have vanished from Birks's escutcheon.

Sharing in the growth of TORONTO

1854 1934

MAIN DOORWAY—1934

THE ROOTS of the Birks-Ellis-Ryrie business extend deep down into the early history of Toronto.

The oldest inhabitants may still remember the jewellery stores presided over by James Ryrie and James E. Ellis.

Upon the corner stone of CONFIDENCE these worthy merchants of the past built reputations which were of Dominion-wide repute; and it is upon this same corner stone that their descendants and successors are maintaining an ever-increasing business.

BIRKS-ELLIS-RYRIE
LIMITED
Uniting ELLIS BROS. Ltd. and RYRIE-BIRKS Ltd.
YONGE AND TEMPERANCE STREETS ● TORONTO

James Ryrie, a partner in Ryrie's Jewellers, was a prominent Baptist and one of the leading supporters of McMaster University on Bloor Street. He described his recreations as "golf and agriculture," and owned the enormous house at Number One Chestnut Park in Rosedale.

J. Earl Birks, born in Peoria, Illinois in 1876, was the nephew of Montreal jeweller Henry Birks. Having spent nearly thirty years in his uncle's firm, he moved to Toronto in June, 1923, to coordinate the changeover from Ryrie Bros. to Ryrie-Birks. An enthusiastic sportsman, he was a member of the Royal Canadian Yacht, York, Toronto Golf, Granite, and Badminton & Racquet clubs, and had four sons by his marriage to the splendidly named Selina Torrance Savage.

A Red Cross worker somewhere in the city about 1916.

(Above) One of Toronto's most memorable snowstorms commenced at 5:15 p.m. on the evening of December 11, 1944, and ended at nine o'clock the following evening. Nearly two feet of snow fell, creating huge drifts along streets and burying many cars. The photograph here shows the corner of College and Bay.

(Next page) The corner of Yonge and College, looking north. The building on the corner was built in the early 1890s for the Independent Order of Oddfellows, one of several well-organized and well-heeled men's clubs in the city. In the distance is the distinctive tower of the old Fire Hall Number Three, built in the 1870s. Apparently, it was never used for drying hoses, unlike the landmark tower on the almost contemporary "Number Eight" at College and Bellevue. The former tower is now a landmark for patrons of the St. Charles Tavern— the fire-hall ceased operation in the 1920s. The panel van in the foreground was one of the fleet of J. J. Sheedy's New Method Laundry Company (page 187).

Yonge Street

Anywhere in Canada, the name "Yonge Street" is instantly recognized as a Toronto place name. It can reasonably lay claim to being the longest "street" in the country, as in its original form it extended nearly 33 miles north to the Holland River. And, it is possibly among the narrowest—few major city crossroads in the world are as visually unprepossessing as the ones where Yonge meets Queen and Bloor.

Yonge Street owes its length and breadth to its original purpose, having been built as a military road to connect the fort and harbour at Toronto Bay with Lake Simcoe. Named for the British secretary of war, Sir George Yonge, it was cleared to the point of passability by the Queen's Rangers, the military corps of the province of Upper Canada. When completed early in 1796, it was a ribbon of stumps, roots, and muck passing through the forest to the lowest navigable point on the Holland River below Lake Simcoe. It had been cleared south as far as Queen Street, although the section between there and Bloor was swampy and impassable for much of the year.

Yonge Street had little connection with the original Town of York, which straddled King Street some distance to the east. As the city grew, however, Yonge Street became a major commercial thoroughfare. The fashionable part was south of Queen Street until Timothy Eaton built north of that corner. Shops spread north, gradually supplanting the residences. Some vestiges remain of the large houses which in the early years made Yonge Street a good address—one is the curious jog in Dundonald Street before it reaches Church Street, the result of the old layout of the block bounded by Gloucester, Church, Wellesley and Yonge. Before the turn of this century, a large house called "Dundonald," owned by drygoods merchant Donald Mackay, occupied the centre of the double block. By the time Mackay's house was demolished, it had been surrounded by smaller houses and shops facing outward onto the encircling streets, and Dundonald Street had to be fitted among them.

Alfred Alexander Walker was the president of Hudson-Essex Ltd., a motorcar dealership at 684 Yonge Street. The youngest son of Sir Edmund Walker, president of the Bank of Commerce, he had worked for Massey-Harris from 1913 to 1926. Sir Edmund's sons chose diverse careers—Alfred's brother, Edmund M. Walker, was a professor of invertebrate zoology at the University of Toronto and the author of over 50 publications, usually on entomology, with titles such as The Terminal Abdominal Structures of Orthopteroid Insects.

A postcard, made from a photograph taken for an 1898 Board of Trade publication, showing two of the buildings directly across Gerrard Street East from St. James Square (now Ryerson Polytechnic Institute), between Victoria and Church streets: on the right is the College of Pharmacy, on the left the St. James Square Presbyterian Church. Presbyterianism gained a toehold in Toronto partly due to the generosity of the tanner Jesse Ketchum, who in 1821 donated the site for a church. Ten years later, "The Kirk" was erected on Church Street near Adelaide. The pastor of St. James Square Presbyterian Church during the 1890s was the Rev. Samuel Kellogg, an American who spent several years in missionary work in India and wrote a grammar book of Hindustani dialects which became the official textbook of the Indian Civil Service. His other writings included books and articles comparing Buddhism, Judaism, and Christianity, and a work entitled From Death to Resurrection, A Scriptural Study of the Intermediate State.

Normal School, Toronto

Just east of Yonge Street, on the block which was then called St. James Square, bounded by Victoria, Gould, Church, and Gerrard Street East, stood the Toronto Normal School. Founded in 1847 as the teacher training institute for Canada West, it was the keystone in the provincial education system created by the Rev. Dr. Egerton Ryerson. "The work performed by the school is largely professional, the course of studies consisting of the History and Science of Education, the Principles and Practice of Teaching, School Organization and Management, together with instruction in English, Hygiene, Chemistry, Physics, Drawing, Vocal Music, Calisthenics, Drill, etc." Behind the Normal School was the Model School, where the trainees could practice their newly won skills.

By 1908, the proportion of women schoolteachers in Ontario had increased to 82 percent; during the same period, Toronto itself averaged about 600 teacher vacancies, evidently due to meagre salaries. The direction of education, like teachers' salaries, was often a controversial subject for the Toronto Board of Education: a 1910 resolution unanimously called for the total prohibition of French language instruction throughout the province; conversely, a denunciation of military training in schools by the board's new socialist chairman, the future mayor James Simpson, attracted few supporters.

After the Second World War, St. James Square was turned over to Ryerson Polytechnic Institute, and a new style of educational building grew up to surround the century-old, ivy-covered Normal School and Model School. Finally in 1963 the old buildings were demolished, except for a single wall which remains, like an imported Victorian-era "ruin," amidst the blackboard jungle atmosphere of the modern Ryerson campus.

Eugene O'Keefe

Eugene O'Keefe's "new" brewery at 11-17 Gould Street was the most modern and capacious in Toronto. Built in 1892, it employed a staff of 80 and replaced a much more primitive operation on the same site. O'Keefe (above) was one of the first to recognize that a large market existed for lager, and after 1879 he began to brew it in quantity, rather than producing mainly ale and porter. Born in Cork, in 1827, O'Keefe came to Canada at the age of five, and went into partnership with Patrick Cosgrave in 1862. His activities on behalf of the Catholic church led him to be dubbed "The Pope's Chamberlain"; in his obituary notice, the teetotalling Star concentrated on his devout Catholicism, and made almost no mention of his wide-ranging and profitable brewing business.

O'Keefe Lane, running between Shuter and Gerrard just east of Yonge Street, recalls the days of the old O'Keefe Brewery and its founder, Eugene O'Keefe, who lived almost next door to it in a house at 137 Bond Street. The brewery itself stood at 11-17 Gould Street, occupying the block bounded by Gould, O'Keefe Lane, Dundas, and Victoria streets.

O'Keefe was born in County Cork in 1827 and came to Toronto seven years later. His parents were relatively well-to-do, and owned property at the corner of Scott and Wellington. As a boy, he started work in the Toronto Savings Bank—the so-called "Bishop's Bank," a trust administered by a board whose chairman was the Archbishop of Toronto. However, at the age of 35, he decided to embark on an independent business career, and with a capitalist named George Hawke and a brewer named

Patrick Cosgrave purchased the 22-year-old Hanneth & Hart Brewery. They rebuilt the plant in 1862, renaming it O'Keefe & Company; Cosgrave quit the partnership a year later and started his own brewery on Queen Street West near Trinity University (page 220).

O'Keefe's clientele, like that of most breweries in Toronto, was used to drinking ale and porter, but O'Keefe recognized that a whole new market existed for lager beer, brewed in the light American style. In 1879, he erected a new plant on a vacant part of his Gould Street site to brew lager, and in the first year was rewarded for his perspicacity when he sold 5,000 barrels of it. Ten years later, he razed and rebuilt the old ale plant, and doubled the size of the lager plant, enabling the company to boast of being "second to none in the Dominion." An article in a trade journal in 1903 described O'Keefe as "one of the old-school brewers, who loves his art; though he has acquired a fortune in building up the large business which bears his name, he still takes an active interest in personally superintending and directing the brewing operations of his great plant."

His charitable activities centred on the Catholic church, and led to his being dubbed "The Pope's Chamberlain." He built St. Monica's Church, in North Toronto, and St. Augustine's Seminary, south of the Kingston Road at Brimley Road in Scarborough Township. Throughout his life, he remained involved with the "Bishop's Bank," which, because of amendments to the Bank Act, had to cease operating as a charitable trust and instead raise share capital. It became known as the Home Bank, but continued to be the repository for the savings of many individual Catholics; O'Keefe was its president until June, 1913, three months before his death. The loan company grew and expanded; in 1924, following several years of unorthodox loans, it collapsed (page 63).

The vicinity of the O'Keefe Brewery, in the early 1920s, played host to a mélange of buildings typical of old Toronto. As well as the brewery, there were schools, churches, a synagogue, and houses of various sizes; on the blocks to the south were the Loretto Convent, St. Michael's Cathedral, the sales office of the Tudhope Motor Company, and the back end of the Pantages Theatre. The Tudhopes of Orillia bought R. S. McLaughlin's Oshawa carriage business when the latter cemented his affiliation with W. C. Durant and started building McLaughlin-Buicks. Tudhope made some stylish vehicles, including a 1909 roadster which looked as sporty as a Stutz, and the Everett series of coupes and touring cars.

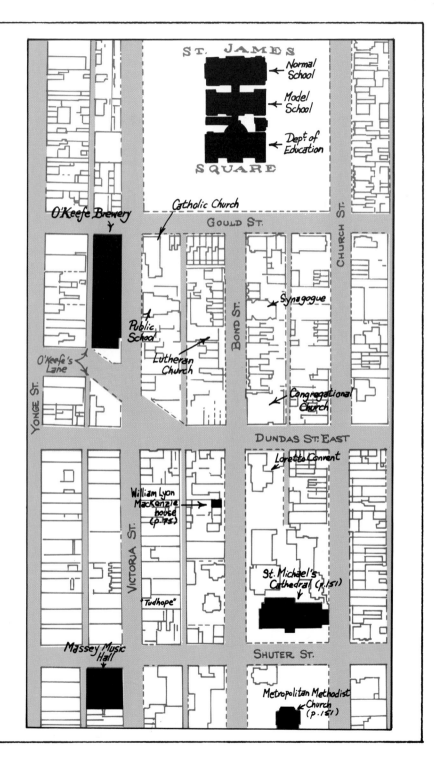

William Lyon Mackenzie

The complete story of the feisty rebel William Lyon Mackenzie has been told many times. A Scot who arrived in the colony in 1820, he started a newspaper called the *Colonial Advocate*. It soon became a thorn in the side of the smug Family Compact, which had run Upper Canada almost as a personal fiefdom. The reaction of Upper Canada's landed gentry pushed Mackenzie further down the path of agrarian reform and rebellion: in one instance, the "young bloods" of the town sacked his office and heaved his type fonts into the bay. Mackenzie soon became a lightning rod for the gathering storm of disaffection in the colony; he entered Parliament first in 1828, and was elected as Toronto's first mayor in 1834.

The reform group led by Mackenzie which ran the newly incorporated city soon passed from public favour; elections the following year went solidly Tory. However, a financial crisis prompted by the colony's depressed economy hit especially hard at Mackenzie's support base—the farmers—who staged a half-baked revolt in December, 1837. A group of rebels massed at the Montgomery Tavern on Yonge north of Eglinton, and marched on the city. However, this rag-tag band faced organized opposition, in the form of about 900 militiamen, and were dispersed. As the historian J. M. S. Careless wrote, "it was more a comedy of errors than an epic drama." Mackenzie fled to the United States, but many years later received a pardon and returned to Toronto to die.

The reality of Mackenzie's life and rebellion on the one hand, and the legend of it on the other, were often at odds. Subsequent generations have repeatedly analyzed his life and weighed his significance. In the case of one biography, written by the Royal Society of Canada president Dr. W. D. Le Sueur, the conflict between truth and legend was fought on the battlefield of the courts during 1911 and 1912.

W. D. Le Sueur was an unlikely figure of controversy—born in Quebec, he had joined the post office at the age of sixteen and devoted his career to that institution, retiring from it in 1902 at the age of 62. His biography of William Lyon Mackenzie was by no means his only work: he had in 1906 written a *Life of Frontenac*, which was published in the *Makers of Canada* series, as well as several philosophical works. His status within the community of letters was well recognized.

Le Sueur became involved with the Mackenzie biography when the publisher of the *Makers of Canada* series, the Morang Company, asked him to vet a manuscript on the subject written by one Dr. J. L. Hughes: as Le Sueur later explained, he criticized the Hughes manuscript not because it praised Mackenzie or because of supposed Liberal partisanship, but because of "the very flat, conventional, ready-made fashion in which

the praising was done." Morang then dismissed Hughes, and invited Le Sueur to provide them with a biography of Mackenzie; for ethical reasons, Le Sueur declined, but eventually agreed to write it once he realized that the Hughes volume would not be published in any case.

One of the major sources of material for Le Sueur's biography was a collection of private papers belonging to G.G.S. Lindsey, K.C., a grandson of William Lyon Mackenzie. Le Sueur claimed that his own opinions on Mackenzie were known to Lindsey, who knew that he was not antagonistic to the memory of Mackenzie, but only wished to treat the subject in a historical fashion, "according to the better models and standards of historical writing"; as well, during the research period Lindsey said nothing to Le Sueur about the way in which his grandfather should be treated.

In 1911, Le Sueur submitted the completed manuscript to Morang, and received a $500 advance. Morang, however, refused to publish it, evidently because of pressure from Mackenzie's descendants, notably Lindsey and future prime minister—then recently defeated minister of labour—William Lyon Mackenzie King (who, on the evidence of his diaries, showed throughout his life a tendency to idealize his ancestors). In order to regain possession of his manuscript, Le Sueur sent a cheque to Morang for the amount of the advance; when the publisher would not return the manuscript, Le Sueur sued Morang and eventually won. Lindsey then sued Le Sueur.

The contemporary chronicler John Castell Hopkins described the trial in his 1912 edition of the *Canadian Annual Review of Public Affairs* as "the most discussed literary incident of the year." Lindsey sought the return of extracts and copies compiled from his library, an injunction to restrain Le Sueur from publishing "any book containing such extracts," and damages for wrongful use of the material. The defence was hampered by lack of access to the necessary documents, and lost the case; Lindsey was granted "nominal damages, say $5." Le Sueur's appeal was dismissed by the Ontario appellate court in December, 1913. Castell Hopkins summed up the case: "Whatever the merits of these arguments, it would seem obvious that this judgement suppressed a book of much public interest."

(Next page) On Bond Street, south of Dundas, stood a three-house row at numbers 78, 80, and 82. The one furthest to the north (in the centre of the painting) today stands alone, preserved as a museum to William Lyon Mackenzie, Toronto's first mayor and most achievement-oriented rebel. Built in the 1850s, the house was Mackenzie's last, given to him by his friends in 1855 and occupied by him until his death in 1861. The Department of Street Cleaning truck is a right-hand drive, solid-tired Peerless model.

William Lyon Mackenzie's bad luck as a rebel rubbed off on one of his biographers—Dr. W. D. Le Sueur (above), the president of the Royal Society of Canada. Intense pressure from Mackenzie's grandson, the future Prime Minister William Lyon Mackenzie King, and a suit by another of Mackenzie's grandsons, G. G. S. Lindsey, charging that Le Sueur had used private documents to write an unsympathetic review of Mackenzie's career, dragged through the courts for much of 1913. Le Sueur died in 1917; his book, edited by A. B. McKillop, was eventually published by Macmillan in 1979.

G. G. S. Lindsey, K.C., who felt slighted by Le Sueur's biography of his grandfather, and filed suit to stop its publication.

Prohibition

Williard Hall, the Women's Christian Temperance Union building at 20 Gerrard Street East, is a reminder of the period when dozens of organizations in North America promoted the abolition of liquor. Of all the events which commanded attention during the violent social change of the early part of this century, Prohibition was certainly the strangest.

Advocates of Prohibition were motivated, they claimed, by the highest ideals. Banning the bar, ending the custom of treating (buying a round), and ridding society of the curse of drunkenness would, they felt, lead to a golden world where poverty, wife abuse, and child abandonment would be unknown. In their zeal, these advocates were willing to compromise the principle of individual liberty and ignore the moderation and common sense of the majority; in their patriotism, they claimed that only a sober nation, unbesotted by German beer, could beat the Germans; in their single-mindedness, some were even willing to look the other way when a crusading Methodist priest, who was a member of the Dry Squad, gunned down a hotelkeeper!

Like much of North America, Toronto during colonial days was a rather drunken place. Most people who came to North America in the nineteenth century found life there very hard; for some, grinding poverty begat escape with the all-too-available bottle, which begat further poverty. Drunkenness with its consequences was most prevalent among the working classes, whose income barely covered life's essentials and was often insufficient to keep them from indigency. Responding to this situation, a reform movement, urging better standards of public health, fair wages, good housing, temperance, and in some places outright Prohibition, began in both the United States and Canada. Described by the *Dominion Educator* school text as "one of the greatest moral and economic movements of modern times," the lobby for Prohibition arose in the United States concurrently with the antislavery agitation before the Civil War; Maine, in 1851, was the first state to become dry. An American federal Prohibition party formed in 1872, and two years later the W.C.T.U. was organized. The tide had turned against liquor by the turn of the century, due to the propaganda of these organizations and that of the Anti-Saloon League.

In Ontario, the new mood of temperance manifested itself in a "ban the bar" campaign, which by the turn of the century had become a political force to be reckoned with. James Whitney and the Conservative party were elected in 1905 to be the provincial government, partly because of their promises to end the abuses of the liquor trade and the scandal of the public bar. The new government promptly appointed a board of liquor licensing commissioners, headed by the Methodist teetotaller and businessman Joseph Flavelle. After only a month of meetings, Flavelle issued a statement that surprised few: many hotels, he said, were merely drinking places, or under the control of breweries and distillery wholesalers

through heavy mortgages; at least 25 places in Toronto alone were named as saloons and bars and nothing else, though there was no provision within the law for a drinking spot to operate without an attached hotel; the commission's inspectors described their difficulties in attempting to gain access to inspect some bars after 7 p.m. Saturday and on Sunday, due to the proprietors' efforts to hide the evidence.

After such a promising start, all three commissioners suddenly resigned, following the government's dismissal of inspector T. A. Hastings, which they claimed interfered with their right to hire unbiased local inspectors. Sympathetic voices alleged that the commissioners had refused to play the part of hired men, and that the government had caved in to the demands for spoils and boodles by party workers like the "Tammany Boss" member for North Toronto, Dr. William Beattie Nesbitt.

The "temperance wave," however, continued to make considerable progress. The government was pressured to pass Local Option legislation, which allowed districts to choose whether to be wet or dry; the number of liquor licenses in Ontario declined rapidly from 6,185 in 1875, to 2,691 in 1906. Toronto itself retained 150 licensed establishments for its population of 286,000, whereas in 1874 it had had 493 licenses for 68,000 people. In the city, the *News*, which ironically had been owned by Joseph Flavelle from 1903-8, was the main advocate of Moderation; the Drys were represented by the Ontario Alliance for Prohibition, the W.C.T.U., the Methodist clergy with its indomitable leader Rev. Samuel Chown, and a portion of the populace who sincerely felt that the bar, and the habit of treating for the assembled throng, was a terrible evil in society. Chown led an interdenominational congregation which believed more or less that intemperance, and even moderation, were inextricably linked with immorality.

The liquor interests rallied with a petition presented to the government in February, 1908, by James Haverson, K.C., containing nearly 38,000 signatures against further reductions in local liquor licenses. Three days earlier, another set of three liquor commissioners had resigned because city council had cancelled 34 licenses, even though in a civic referendum the previous month a majority had voted against further license reductions. But the wind was shifting direction—a bylaw sponsored by Alderman F. S. Spence, to reduce by one-third the number of Toronto licenses, passed the following January.

Perhaps the militancy of temperance supporters among the citizenry would have been appeased by the "ban the bar" movement, which over the next several years had a great influence over old habits and flagrant abuses. But by late 1915, with the war requiring ever greater economies from civilians and sacrifices from soldiers, the pendulum swung past voluntary temperance all the way to outright Prohibition. Everywhere, the public mood became one of greater self sacrifice. With G. A. Warburton

The Rev. Samuel Dwight Chown was, for 35 years, one of the strongest voices for temperance and Prohibition in Canada. Born in Kingston in 1853, he became a Methodist minister in 1879, and first came to Toronto in 1897 as chairman of the Toronto West District. He was secretary of Temperance, Prohibition and Moral Reform from 1902-10, and then general superintendent of the Methodist Church until 1925, when the Methodists, the Congregationalists, and most of the Presbyterians amalgamated to form the United Church of Canada.

as its chief organizer and chairman, a "Committee of 100" was formed in Toronto; soon, others formed across Ontario, and an advertising campaign commenced for province-wide Prohibition. It presented a variety of arguments, mixing moral and social ideals with straightforward appeals to Imperialism: Ontarians were spending $30 million a year on liquor, which if redirected could be a "silver bullet" for the war effort; France had abolished absinthe, and Russia vodka, and Britain had curtailed the sale and production of liquor; nineteen States in the U.S.A. had Prohibition in effect; even beer drinking, as chronicler John Castell Hopkins put it, "involved the consumption of much alcohol and other injurious products, leading to weakness of organs and grossness of body and brain, as in Germany." The campaign climaxed with a huge rally in Toronto on March 8, 1916; a procession of 10,000 believers from all over Ontario wound through the streets to Queen's Park, where a Prohibition petition containing 825,572 signatures was presented to the government. There were a multitude of banners, many brightly decorated automobiles, a chorus of students, and unfortunately a brawl, when a group of soldiers in the procession took umbrage at the number of young men in civvies in the crowd.

A variety of citizens worked for Moderation: in Toronto, the Personal Liberty League formed, primarily to urge the separation of evil whisky from "the poor man's beer," and to sponsor a number of advertisements to counter those of the "Committee of 100"; in London, Bishop Fallon campaigned against Prohibition, as he was "afraid of this orgy of collectivism"; Toronto hotelman F. W. Mossop wrote to the press that it wasn't British fair play to vote away his entire financial stake, after the government had taken thousands of dollars from him in license fees and made him spend money to improve his premises in compliance with what had been liquor law amendments; the Trades & Labour Council voted 78-25 against Prohibition, as it would throw unionists out of work and breed "dives and joints and contempt for the law."

But the government, feeling it was acting in the best interests of the war effort, introduced, on March 22, 1916, the Ontario Temperance Act (O.T.A.), which abolished all bars, clubs, and liquor stores, and made the sale of liquor legal only through drugstores by prescription for "medicinal, mechanical, scientific and sacramental purposes." Attorney General W. J. Hanna talked of holding a referendum on Prohibition three years hence. The O.T.A. came into effect on the first of September, following an orgy of liquor buying by the Wets—householders were allowed to keep liquor, provided it wasn't purchased in the province, so local liquor firms promptly opened branches in Montreal, but continued to advertise, solicit orders in, and ship to Ontario. Instead of beer drunks in the bars and on the streets, the problem became one of whisky drunks at home.

Three years had passed, and the war had ended, when Conservative Premier Hearst called an election. A referendum on the O.T.A. was included with the ballot. In the United States, an order of President Wilson had banned the manufacture of whisky; a week after the Armistice, he signed a food production stimulation bill containing a rider making the country completely dry after June 30, 1919, and continuing until the army was completely demobilized. Congress, reflecting the prohibitionist mood throughout the country, passed the Eighteenth Amendment to the Constitution—the notorious Volstead Act—which became effective in January, 1920. All of these events were widely reported in Canada; many English Canadians admired the Americans' forthrightness and felt that but for the political clout of Quebec—which alone among the Canadian provinces had enacted no wartime Prohibition laws—Canada might have a national Prohibition law, too. But in Ontario, where the Temperance Act was perceived to be honoured mainly in the breach, with reports of abuses regularly filling the newspapers, it was perhaps reasonable to assume that voters would opt for a return to prewar government and prewar drinking habits. Instead, there was a political upheaval, which upheld the O.T.A., defeated the Conservative government, threw out even stalwart ministers such as Premier Hearst and Sir Adam Beck, and elected in their place a motley minority ministry of the United Farmers of Ontario. The new premier, E. C. Drury, made it clear that he personally was in favour of temperance. Prohibition, it seemed, had come to stay.

The unbelievers amongst the populace continued to discover new ways to circumvent the O.T.A. For one thing, "native wines" were excluded from the act; this in itself did not offer much solace for beer or whisky drinkers—or perhaps even for wine drinkers—but it provided a loophole, according to legal opinions of John Ewart, K.C., and others, whereby Ontario did not fit the Dominion's definition as a province "in which there is at the present time a law in force prohibiting the sale of intoxicating liquor for beverage purposes." That being the case, Ontario residents could "short-circuit" the O.T.A. and the Dominion law banning importation of liquor from a wet province into a dry one, by ordering the stock from an agent, say, in Quebec, who provided it from stocks within Ontario kept ostensibly for export. The Ontario branch of the Dominion Alliance for Prohibition was determined to plug this loophole. Its secretary, the Rev. Ben Spence, was pledged to leave no stone unturned in his campaign to root out immorality. The previous April, he had been sentenced to four months in jail or a fine of $500 on the celebrated "parasite" charges, stemming from his defiance of a government ban during the war years by publishing a book called The Fiddlers, about the alleged drinking excesses of Englishmen and soldiers. Having heard the legal opinion of Ewart, Spence and his followers began to campaign for a more drastic O.T.A., which could, within the lawmaking ability of the province, restrict even the amount of liquor which any citizen could possess within his home. He fired his second barrel a month later, urging the removal from the O.T.A. of the native wines exemption, as a precursor to tighter Dominion regulations of interprovincial import and export. Attorney General Raney, though an advocate of temperance, turned down both requests on strictly legal grounds which included his desire to avoid costly litigation. At meetings, Spence hinted darkly that the government had backed down due to "influential representations"; in a speech, one Capt. The Rev. Sidney Lambert said that he "would rather Germany had won the war, than to see liquor dealers rule and damn the young men of Canada."

The public debate became ever more heated; some Prohibitionists attempted to convince the premier that mere possession of liquor should be illegal. Drury responded in what was his clearest statement about his own ideas on the limits of state-enforced temperance: "That the Province could undertake to forbid possession of liquor involves the transgression by the Government of private rights that every Englishman, every British subject, holds dear. I will set my face strongly against any legislation that would involve search of homes and spying upon the people and encourage a system of informers." But Drury did allow two resolutions, which he hoped would make the O.T.A. more enforceable. The first was the Sandy Act, named for its sponsor F. G. Sandy, which was to control the transportation and delivery of liquor within the province, and allow for the seizure of any contraband. The second was a resolution asking for a Dominion referendum on importation.

Meanwhile, a new enforcement problem had emerged—people had found sympathetic physicians and pharmacists to write liquor prescriptions for bogus medical reasons. The Chairman of the Board of License Commissioners had declared that 80 to 90 percent of the quarts of liquor prescribed for medical purposes were unnecessary, and that about 10 percent of the physicians in Ontario paid no attention at all to the O.T.A. He quoted figures that one physician had given 2,005 prescriptions in a month, for a fee of $2 from his regular patients and $3 from outsiders who had heard through the grapevine of the new service. Another physician had issued 487 prescriptions in a single day! Jail records showed that arrests for drunkenness had been climbing steadily, nearly doubling since 1918. A scuffle promptly broke out between the government and the College of Physicians over who had the right to discipline physicians whose judgement on medical matters was in question.

Some part of the populace was obviously becoming restive under the whip hand of the zealots, but few were willing to criticize the O.T.A. publicly. At a convention of the Citizens' Liberty League, formed in Toronto on February 17, 1920, to oppose the "hypocrisy, deceit, cant and lying" of enforced temperance, only the president, an ex-member of the provincial legislature named H. A. C. Machin, would speak to the reporters who had been banned from the convention's proceedings.

Everybody talked about the bootleggers, however, and their daring exploits in the Detroit-Windsor border area. Not only were the smugglers defying the O.T.A., they were also defying the Volstead Act in the dry United States. According to an article in the *Telegram* on the third of July, the Ontario side of the Detroit River was laced with caches of whisky, concealed in rowboats in marshes, in farmers' barns, and within hastily camouflaged blinds. Whisky was transported brazenly in trucks with forged manifests. To illustrate how ineffectual the O.T.A. had become, J. D. Flavelle pointed to the size of the bribes given to license inspectors, police and customs officers: "When you realize that a man who runs a carload of liquor across to Detroit is expected to make from 50 to 80 thousand dollars upon it, you will understand that he can afford to spend half that amount on bribes—$5,000 bribes are quite common." (At the time, the average annual salary for a working man was about $1,500.)

Late in May, the Rev. J. O. L. Spracklin, a Methodist minister at Sandwich on the Detroit River, went public against the local police and the owners of a local roadhouse called the Chappell Hotel, embellishing his charges with theatrical accounts of derring-do and gunfights between smugglers and the U.S. border patrol. A thousand cases of liquor a day were alleged to be illegally crossing the river. The license board decided to step up its enforcement along the border, and hired four new Special Officers for the licensing department. One was Spracklin, the noted authority on local conditions.

In his first enforcement operation in late July, Rev. Spracklin and his associates raided six roadhouses, "making two arrests and engaging in a free-for-all fight in which he showed considerable prowess." Throughout the summer, he continued with his unorthodox raids and, although his methods were controversial, he got results; the government provided him in October with the use of a fast motor launch. A few weeks later, in the early hours of the morning of the sixth of November, Spracklin and four fellow officers raided the notorious Chappell House in the early hours of the morning. In the ensuing brawl, Spracklin shot the hotel proprietor dead with an automatic pistol.

In Windsor Police Court, on the second of December, Spracklin was charged with manslaughter. Relatives and friends of Beverley Trumble, the late hotelkeeper, demanded that the charge be raised to murder. Elsewhere, many Methodist congregations passed resolutions supporting Spracklin; in Toronto, the Rev. T. A. Moore, head of that church's Department of Social Services, told the *Globe* that "we have sent assurance to Mr. Spracklin of our absolute confidence in his integrity." Other prohibitionist spokesmen expressed gratitude for the former license inspector's "courage and devotion." Spracklin had already been found

Rev. J. O. L. Spracklin of the Dry Squad.

78

Dour-looking Stewart McClenaghan, after a long career with the Retail Merchants Association and various Conservative organizations, became a commissioner of the newly formed Liquor Control Board of Ontario, in 1927.

guilty of another charge of wrongful entry following his search of a private yacht. For this, he was fined $500 in damages, which was paid by the attorney general's department. He was brought to trial in February, 1921, and acquitted.

Attention now shifted from the antics of the Dry Squad to the more sobering question of the upcoming Dominion Liquor Importation Referendum. According to an amendment to the tightened-up Canada Temperance Act, a province could ask Ottawa to hold a referendum which asked the question, "Should the importing of liquor into this province be banned?" If the referendum was approved, the Dominion government would then make importation, along with export from elsewhere into that province, illegal. Ontario itself could not pass laws to restrict interprovincial trade; that was a federal responsibility—thus the significance of the referendum. The "Sandy Bill" had been intended to dovetail with the prohibition on importation; according to the Prohibitionists, neither act was worthwhile without the other.

The opposing sides marshalled their forces in preparation for the eighteenth of April, 1921, which was to be Referendum Day. On the Wet or Moderate side, a diverse group gathered around the Citizens' Liberty League, with lawyer Isidore F. Hellmuth as chairman and, once again, a large number of supporters who preferred to remain anonymous. One of the few Moderates who went public was the provost of Trinity University, Dr. T. C. Street Macklem, who described *lack* of moderation as one of the great national evils, and said that a law which saved people from drunkenness but which produced spies and perjurers was not to be commended. The most famous advocate of Moderation was writer Stephen Leacock, who gave a resounding speech in Toronto on April Fool's Day, blasting the tyranny which the Temperance "fanatical minority" had forced upon society. But the most controversial Moderate, whose appearance did the most to weaken the cause, was the American orator Charles A. Windle, who was imported as a foil to the Prohibitionists' American champion—W. E. "Pussyfoot" Johnson. The problem with Windle lay with neither his oratory nor his witty metaphors, but with his war record of pro-German and anti-British sentiments, and the Drys dragged out a carload of damning evidence, including this statement published the previous month referring to England: "Was such a civilization worth saving? Is this heartless old hag clothed in the garments of lust, loot and murder, worthy the life of the humblest son of Columbia who died in France?" After that, all of Windle's clever inferences, including the one that Temperance was Christian and Abstinence Mohammedan, were lost in the clamour.

On the eighteenth, by a majority of 171,000, Ontario went solidly Dry. Even Toronto went decisively for what was, in effect, total Prohibition. Women in general and rural voters in particular had the most marked effect on the total vote. Attorney General W. E. Raney was quoted as saying that henceforth the O.T.A. would be easier to enforce. The *Pioneer*, the organ of the Prohibitionists, set out to cement its improved position with an attack on "the menace of the private cellar."

Raney, who had been asked to join Drury's government because there was not a lawyer among the United Farmers of Ontario MPPs, became the most dynamic advocate of Prohibition, the abolition of racetrack betting, and of social reform wherever he thought it needed. But by 1922, the year following the importation referendum, most commentators felt that public support for Prohibition had slipped; Raney threatened action against the "medical blind-pigger," as increasing numbers of citizens found sympathetic doctors to issue medicinal liquor prescriptions. A scandal broke over an alleged "farewell party" held in the legislature offices of a cabinet minister, the Hon. Peter Smith. Did a couple of young stenographers, who had been at work late, join in the celebration? Was liquor provided? Was it merely an innocent jollification? Investigations by all and sundry turned up little hard evidence and fewer witnesses, but resolutions of both the United Farmers of Ontario and Toronto City Council expressed doubts about the bland official attitude to what was said to be a gross violation of the O.T.A. Such incidents, along with newspaper reports of truckloads of whisky leaving the city for Windsor, and "organized defiance of constituted authority," tarnished the government's authority.

The pendulum swung back. Groups like the Moderation League gathered strength, while others like the Toronto Conservative Club passed resolutions recommending the sale of beer and wine under government control. The attacks in the legislature by the Conservative opposition against Raney and the government became more virulent, and ever more ludicrous. Howard Ferguson, who was soon to be premier, charged that the government, in order to get a conviction, had paid a fifteen-year-old boy to get drunk. In the 1923 election, Drury's U.F.O. government was swept from power, and virtually annihilated, by a Conservative tidal wave.

The Prohibition battle continued to be waged by public figures such as the newspaper publisher Joseph Atkinson, whose extreme views were reinforced by his dislike of the new premier, Howard Ferguson. Reporter Gordon Sinclair once described how the *Star*'s reporters kept the fervour alive by faking local stories of sordid blind pigs and liquor abuses, as well as crime and debauchery as far afield as British Columbia.

Late in 1926, Ferguson went to the people with a promise to introduce a government liquor board. During the campaign, the *Star* attacked Ferguson and his liquor policy, labelling him one of the "Canadian Mussolinis," the other being Mayor Foster. The Conservatives were reelected and introduced the Liquor Control Act on June 1, 1927.

Toronto Hydro

By 1933, when the Art Deco-style Toronto Hydro Building was erected on Carlton Street at Yonge, publicly owned and distributed hydroelectricity was no longer controversial. But for the first two decades of this century, the debate over public ownership—whether public utilities should replace the enterprise of capitalists—was anything but sanguine. For a time, two electrical systems, one private and one public, each with its own transmission lines, substations, and customers, served the residents and businesses of Toronto.

Before 1890, the primary use of electricity in the city was street-lighting. The first street lights had in fact been powered by coal gas, and went into service in 1842. Toronto at that time was about the 200th largest city in North America, but it was one of only eleven to have a street-lighting system. Some of the lamps had their own standards, while others were hung from brackets attached to the sides of buildings. Lamplighters made the rounds of the streets at dusk and at dawn, to turn the gas on and off. The gaslamps were replaced, beginning in 1884, when electrically powered carbon-arc lamps were introduced, the first being at the corner of King and Yonge. These lamps produced their light from the brilliant arc of electricity formed in the gap between two carbon "pencils." The positively charged one became gradually hollowed out and had to be replaced, so the lamps were suspended from ropes which ran through pulleys on iron brackets attached to wooden poles on the edge of the streets. An employee of the street-lighting system lowered them, cleaned the glass, and replaced the carbons. Modern tungsten lamps in "opal glass" cylinders were introduced to the city in 1911.

The early street-lighting system drew its power from dynamos powered by wood- and coal-fired steam boilers. Voltages were very low, so the lamps farthest away from the plant shed no more glow than fireflies. The system was quite adequate, however, to a populace whose houses were lighted simply with candles, gas lamps, and sometimes kerosene or acetylene lanterns. Other than street lights, there was no other widespread use of electricity until around 1890, when two new uses arose: street railways and home lighting, the latter becoming suddenly feasible due to Thomas Edison's invention of the incandescent light bulb. Seeking greater sources of power for the new demand, engineers studied the feasibility of tapping Ontario's rivers, especially at Niagara, and far-sighted capitalists organized to exploit the potential of this new "white coal."

In Toronto in 1883, the 24-year-old Henry Pellatt had organized the first electric street-lighting system, named the Toronto Electric Light Company. Six years later, to capitalize on Edison's new light bulb, an engineer named Frederic Nicholls organized the Toronto Incandescent Electric Light Company. They were acquaintances of a third man, the financier William Mackenzie, who in the early 1890s had obtained the Toronto street railway franchise with the promise that he would electrify the system. The three men bought shares in each other's companies and ploughed their profits into new capital investment. In 1896, Pellatt and Nicholls merged their two companies.

In 1894, some members of Toronto's city council had begun to lobby for the construction of a publicly owned electric light plant. They met resistance from influential individuals and from publications, such as *The Financial Post*, which felt that talk of public ownership would damage the city's reputation and credit. By the turn of the century, when city council adopted the resolution of Alderman F. S. Spence to distribute electricity in the city, the private system was well established.

Regardless, the city pressed on; its proposal to organize a public system went to the Private Bills Committee of the provincial legislature in 1902, where it was scuttled by a variety of interests, including the Toronto Electric Light Company. The pro-private enterprise Liberal provincial government had once again voted against Conservative Toronto. Not only Toronto was irked—so were most of the towns and cities between there and Niagara, including London, Brantford, Stratford, Woodstock, Ingersoll, Guelph, and Berlin (now Kitchener). The disaffected civic politicians held a convention in Berlin in June, 1902, to protest against the provincial government's bias in favour of the private interests; they feared that the private companies would sell power to the highest bidder, and probably commit a portion of the power from the Canadian side of the Falls to customers in the United States. At a subsequent meeting the following February, the politicians decided to study the possibilities of a joint municipal power system. The conclusion—that power could be transmitted and distributed at prices below those of the commercial competition—galvanized the Conservative opposition in the provincial legislature; led by Adam Beck, a member from London, they sallied forth with the banner of the public interest held high.

Sir Adam Beck championed publicly owned hydroelectricity in Ontario. His conflicts with the owners of the private power system in Toronto, including Henry Pellatt and William Mackenzie, came close at times to being personal vendettas; he was, like them, "a dominant personality of dictatorial tendencies." Beck was often vilified for his belief in public ownership, but in 1908 Premier Whitney applauded his determination, declaring that "we love him for the work he has done, and we love him for the enemies he has made." Born in Baden, Germany, in 1857, Beck worked for two years in his father's iron foundry and mill, then moved to Galt, where he prospered in a business which veneered lumber and manufactured boxes. He and Lady Beck, both accomplished equestrians, were internationally recognized for their thoroughbred horses, which they took to shows as far afield as London, England. A near-fatal bout of pneumonia in 1920 did not slow Beck down; five years later he died, in the words of one obituary, "utterly burnt out." His fine home, "Headley," is a prominent feature of Richmond Street in downtown London, Ontario.

Meanwhile, Henry Pellatt, Frederic Nicholls, and William Mackenzie had organized the Electrical Development Company, which received its provincial franchise to generate power at Niagara in 1903. Through an associate called the Toronto & Niagara Power Company, the E.D.C. brought power to Toronto on November 19, 1906, where it was distributed by its other affiliate, the Toronto Electric Light Company, to residential customers and still another affiliate—the Toronto Street Railway Company. Of the Electrical Development Company, Pellatt was president, Canadian General Electric owner Nicholls was general manager, and street railway owner Mackenzie was a director. Canadian General Electric provided the hardware and technical expertise. By early in 1906, the group had overcome tremendous technical difficulties and spent more than $9 million on their generating plant, and a further $1.6 million on transmission lines. The community was divided on the question of whether the capitalists were angels or devils: on the side of the "angels" were many influential individuals, especially Liberals, and several newspapers; opposing them were Adam Beck and his public commission, and newspapers including the *Globe*, the *News*, and the *World*.

The latter interests had gained ground early in 1905, when James Whitney's Conservatives took power from the provincial Liberals. Whitney invited Beck into the Cabinet, and made him chairman of a fact-finding commission on public power. On the fourth of April, 1906, Beck's commission made its report; in it, he argued strongly for municipal control, claiming that Toronto electrical users, including the street railway and street-lighting systems, would save $684,000 a year and that residential lighting costs would drop by forty percent to five cents per kilowatt hour. A month later, the legislature created the Hydro-Electric Power Commission of Ontario, and named Adam Beck as its chairman.

Meanwhile, the capitalists developed and further rationalized their power system—on St. Valentine's Day, 1908, in a juggling of the complicated arrangements among the companies, William Mackenzie amalgamated the Electrical Development Company (the producer of the power) and all of its contracts into an interlocking quasi-monopoly with himself as president, and Pellatt and Nicholls as directors. But public opinion had shifted to the point that most people were leaning towards Adam Beck's advocacy of public ownership, and chose to forget or to overlook the pioneering and risk-taking of Pellatt, Nicholls, and Mackenzie. On the third

of April, the Niagara Union of Western Municipalities, consisting of twelve cities including Toronto, signed an agreement with the publicly owned Hydro-Electric Commission to buy 100,000 horsepower, and to construct 293 miles of transmission lines linking the communities with Niagara. The *Financial Post* editorialized that the governments' decision was "a rapine of credit," and a direct attack upon the creditors of the Electrical Development Company, many of whom lived in England, and who had sunk a reported $15 million into Ontario's hydroelectric development.

Of all the ensuing civic controversies, Toronto's was the most turbulent. Should the city duplicate transmission lines, or use those of the Toronto & Niagara Power Company? Should the city set up its own distribution plant, or should it make a deal with the Toronto Electric Light Company? When a by-law authorized the city to spend $2 million to erect a distribution plant, the Toronto Electric Light Company promptly offered to sell out to the city. Premier Whitney, for his part, claimed that he could not negotiate with the private companies because of last-minute, secret arrangements made between the outgoing Ross government and the Electrical Development Company; regardless, the discussions between the Toronto Electric Light Company and the city ended in deadlock, as the former, represented by Pellatt, would not make public the details of its contract with *its* parent—the Electrical Development Company. Former Mayor Coatsworth wrote to Mayor Oliver and the press, detailing alleged technical difficulties with the civic scheme, and claiming that public power would cost exactly double what Adam Beck had promised. Finally, a shareholder in the private concerns, the leather merchant G. W. Beardmore, brought an action against Toronto to restrain it from proceeding with its contract with the Hydro-Electric Commission. In the press, there commenced a war of letters, amongst them that of Toronto Electric Light Company official J. J. Wright, who warned of the "grave danger to dwellings, barns and sheds from a high-voltage transmission line," and suggested that no rights of way be casually granted by farmers to the Hydro-Electric Commission.

All this was steamrollered by Adam Beck, who on November 18, 1908, turned the first sod of the public power line on the Exhibition Grounds in Toronto and declared that public power meant that Ontario would maintain "our supremacy as a manufacturing centre, and our independence of a foreign nation for our coal supply" (Toronto's coal came mainly from the United States, page 190). The absurd situation of duplicated electrical services was, however, soon seen more and more to be a personal duel between Adam Beck on the one hand, and Henry Pellatt and William Mackenzie on the other. Beck predicted that Toronto could be hooked up by the end of 1910; a legal action by a citizen named G. Plunkett Magan, who objected to the transmission tower in front of his house—"Thornhurst" in Parkdale (page 198)—delayed completion. Pellatt again suggested a deal to the city, offering it joint use of the Toronto Electric Light Company's power poles, as long as the city used its electricity only for waterworks, pumping stations, street lighting and illumination of municipal buildings. The city's response was another attempt to buy out the private system, which collapsed when no agreement could be reached on what was "a reasonable figure."

Accordingly, crowded streets and cheering crowds greeted the arrival of publicly owned power in Toronto. Throngs gathered in front of City Hall for the ceremony at nine o'clock that evening. Mayor Geary and Premier Whitney each made speeches, then Adam Beck stepped forward and pressed a button, illuminating a fabulous display on the façade of City Hall, and instantly, by means of glowing cluster lights stretching into the distance, lighting the city streets. Oohs, aahs, and murmurs of appreciation were heard. Not long thereafter, Toronto reduced its lighting rates, thereby gathering a number of new customers; the Toronto Electric Light Company soon followed suit.

The newly formed Toronto Hydro-Electric system was run by a board initially composed of P.W. Ellis, Henry Drayton, and Mayor Geary. Questions about the system's solvency prompted an audit of the work of the city auditor; the second audit claimed that the first was "marred by serious inaccuracies and confusion of thought evidently proceeding from insufficient inquiry into the facts." The upshot, at least according to Toronto Hydro's provincial overseer, was that the city system's rates were too high. Other problems surfaced in April, 1913, when acting general manager W. R. Sweany and ten of his associates sent a letter to the mayor describing Toronto Hydro as disorganized and demanding the retirement of Ellis. Sweany was immediately fired, as were the associates, including the chief engineer and the general superintendent, who had sent

in their resignations to demonstrate solidarity with their boss but were dismissed anyway. H. H. Couzens, an electrical engineer from Hampstead, England, was appointed general manager.

The city's increasingly acrimonious relationship with the Toronto Electric Light Company was exemplified by the so-called Playter Boulevard "Pole Case." In October, 1912, shortly after the private company had erected power poles on that quiet Riverdale street, the city came along and cut them all down. The company applied to the courts for an injunction against the city; in April, 1914, Mr. Justice Middleton ruled in favour of the company; the city appealed and won, so the company took appeals all the way to the Privy Council in London, England. The final resolution came on October 23, 1916, when the company's appeal was dismissed.

The Toronto Electric Light Company's relationship with the city was complicated by its association with the Toronto Railway Company, and the confrontation which was developing between the latter and the Toronto citizenry. Rumours in early 1913 that Sir William Mackenzie was willing to sell both the Toronto Electric Light Company and the Toronto Railway Company to the city were formalized in a speech on April 17—the asking price was to be roughly $22 million for the street railway, and a further $8 million for the electric light business. Negotiations commenced between the Mackenzie interests and the city, with Comptroller Tommy Church acting for the latter. Matters were further complicated when Church claimed that Adam Beck had strongly advised against the purchase of the electric light company, as it would mean the continuation of its supply contracts with Mackenzie's Electrical Development Company, thus doing serious damage to the publicly owned system, which was only consuming a third as much power in Toronto as were the combined street railway and private electric systems. Mackenzie naturally insisted that the city purchase both concerns at the same time; in this, he was supported by Mayor Hocken, but strongly opposed by Beck. Nevertheless, an agreement was drafted, apparently by Bank of Commerce vice-president Zebulon Lash, which was acceptable to both the mayor and Sir William Mackenzie. Over the next several months, discussion continued and support grew for the deal, and a by-law was prepared which was to be submitted to the city's voters on January 1, 1914. However, on Novem-

ber 26, the harbour commissioners' scheme of a more elaborate system of streetcars, "tubes," and radials was made public, and "fell as a bombshell into the councils of those who were urging the purchase agreement." A week later, city council voted not to submit the purchase agreement to the ratepayers; thus, the competition between the two power distribution systems continued (see also page 39*ff.*).

The hydroelectric empire of *Sir* Adam Beck (he was created a Knight Bachelor in 1914 by King George V) expanded to include electric railways. His desire to have a network of radial or interurban railways placed him, once again, squarely in competition with Sir William Mackenzie, who with Sir Donald Mann had been crisscrossing every available acre of Canadian soil with the tracks of their Canadian Northern Railway. Feeling that the C.N.R. was against his radials and fomenting unrest in the countryside, Beck by 1917 had launched an aggressive and personal attack on Mackenzie and Mann, and was hinting that their power system—the Electrical Development Company—was not doing its patriotic duty by giving priority to munitions plants. Following Beck's speech of the 20th of March, 1917, Mackenzie replied that he "would welcome legal action," and claimed that his system supplied over 60,000 horsepower to munitions plants. Beck, however, claimed that the public system was carrying 70 percent of the munitions load, and that the Mackenzie system was diverting power to customers in the United States.

By the winter of 1917, the power shortage in Toronto was acute. Brownouts during working hours were common. The Toronto Waterworks switched over to its old steam plant, releasing electricity for residential use. Lack of electricity in the munitions plants before Christmas was attributed to the stores' late hours and heavy trading, which made Beck practically apoplectic. A publicity campaign urged energy conservation. As most of the energy shortages were from 8:30 till noon, and from 1:00 till 4:30 in the afternoon, some suggested that the plants run at night; munitions plant officials responded that their preponderantly female work force would not work at night. The *Star* entered the controversy, castigating the Mackenzie system for not carrying "the patriotic load," and suggesting that the latter would not take on any munitions contracts, for fear of their collapse at the end of the war.

Sir William Mackenzie's empire had in fact begun to topple a few years before; with his and Mann's credit exhausted, and the western Canadian economy in a state of ruin, the collapse of their Canadian Northern Railway cleaned out thousands of investors. The battle of Mackenzie versus Beck, of capitalism versus public ownership in the Toronto electric market, was just a curious sideshow in the last few years of the First World War; the news then was dominated by the Dominion government's frantic efforts to bail out, or to take over, the bankrupt C.N.R. and its equally moribund boom-time transcontinental rival—the Grand Trunk.

Concurrently, the clamour in Toronto to take over the pathetic, Mackenzie-owned street railway system was coming to a climax. Mackenzie himself was getting old, and his franchise was to expire in 1921. On January 2, 1920, citizens voted overwhelmingly to run the system as a public utility. Finally, on December 5, 1920, after ten years of competition and two of negotiation, the Hydro-Electric Power Commission reached an agreement to purchase all of the Mackenzie interests, including the Toronto and York Radial Railways and the Toronto Electric Light Company, for $32,734,000. At a civic banquet three days later, Mayor Church presented Sir Adam Beck with a large, engraved silver loving cup. Triumphantly, the honoured guest declaimed that the agreement gave Ontario "the largest organic power system in the world—practically a public monopoly. Now, as never before, public ownership is on trial!"

Strangely enough, Adam Beck became the one on trial. The Conservative government had been defeated by the United Farmers of Ontario in the political upheaval in 1919, and even Beck had lost his seat. The U.F.O. were decisively in favour of public ownership, but felt that Beck—who retained the chairmanship of the Hydro-Electric Power Commission—was moving too fast and in a direction too favourable to Toronto (which had elected four Liberals, two Conservatives, and no farmers). Especially controversial were the cost and centralization of his radial scheme—even by the early 1920s, motor-truck hauling had become the preferred means of transportation for many farmers' goods. Increasingly, Beck was seen as a promoter, not as the unbiased manager of a public scheme. His influence declined, and he chose not to run for office again in the 1923 election. Lady Beck had died in 1921. Retiring to his palatial home in London, Ontario, he devoted himself to his thoroughbred horses, but died in 1925, a candle burned at both ends.

Mary Pickford

Gladys Smith, who left Toronto to pursue a stage and film career and became "America's Sweetheart," was born in 1893 in a small brick house on University Avenue not far from College. Her father died when she was four, after which her mother worked to support the family and single-mindedly pushed her into a stage career. She first appeared on Broadway in 1907, a year after changing her name to Mary Pickford.

She was one of the first true stars in the motion picture industry. Before her time, film pioneers like Bioscope had operated with stock companies and fended off attempts by leading lights and their fans to identify and idolize members of the cast, as they did not wish to duplicate the star system, with its attendant egos and salary demands, common to the stage. Pickford became famous, nevertheless, as much because the public saw in her the epitome of sweet, golden-haired innocence, as because, off the screen, she was a tough negotiator and an exceptionally shrewd businesswoman. She was rich before she was twenty, and with her first husband Douglas Fairbanks founded Pickfair Studios; later, they banded together with Charlie Chaplin and others to create the United Artists studio. Although her film business and production interests continued to grow and thrive, she herself retired from the screen at the peak of her fame before the end of the silent era and, her reputation and legend intact, lived in ever-increasing seclusion at her Hollywood mansion "Pickfair."

Mary Pickford returned only once to her birthplace, on May 9, 1934, "adding glamour to the Centennial Celebrations." Before her visit, the only equivalent demonstrations of popular adulation had been for the Prince of Wales in 1919, and the Catalina Island swimming champion George Young in 1927. Immense crowds gathered outside City Hall for the Pickford welcoming ceremony, packed three and four deep along King Street, and filled the lobby of the King Edward Hotel where a civic luncheon was given in her honour. In the afternoon, she visited every ward in the Christie Street Military Hospital, spoke to the crowds which gathered in front of the hospital, and waved to the throngs who lined Christie Street down to Dupont. On the way back to her hotel, her limousine drove past Queen's Park and down University Avenue, where the driver pulled over to the median strip opposite the little brick house. It was boarded up, awaiting demolition for hospital expansion; someone had written on the doorway in chalk that it was Mary Pickford's birthplace. Asked whether it should be saved or razed, she commented: "It looks sturdy enough."

Pickford's marriage to Douglas Fairbanks fell apart in 1935, and two years later she married Buddy Rogers. She was rarely seen in public thereafter and in 1976 when the Academy of Motion Picture Sciences presented her with a special Oscar, she refused to be filmed or photographed, choosing instead to accept by telephone. Not only did she wish to perpetuate the memory of her beautiful youth, but she also stipulated that

200,000 feet of her films be destroyed after her death, claiming that they would not stand the test of time—fortunately, her husband and friends convinced her to change her mind. She died in May, 1979, at the age of 86.

* * *

A few blocks away from Mary Pickford's birthplace is the Arts & Letters Club, on Elm Street near Yonge, a meeting place for artists, writers, musicians, playwrights and actors who wished to ply their trade in Canada. By contrast with Pickford, most of the members lived almost anonymous lives, usually supplementing their meagre artistic earnings with wages from teaching or other work.

The Arts & Letters Club was formed in March, 1908, following an invitation to about 70 members of the artistic community from the news-

Mary Pickford, speaking at the Christie Street Military Hospital during her whirlwind (and only) visit as a movie star to the city of her birth, in May, 1934. The odd white mark under her chin is probably due to the Globe photograph retoucher, who would have been trying to opaque the background around her, when his hand slipped—the letterpress newspapers of that period could not reproduce the tones in a photograph well enough to separate Mary Pickford's coat from the coats behind her.

CTA G&M 33301

paperman and critic Augustus Bridle to attend a meeting at the St. Charles Inn at Yonge and Melinda streets. The club's first permanent home was, appropriately for a group of artists, in a third-floor garret above the Brown Betty restaurant on King Street East, across from the King Edward Hotel. Ten months later the club received an eviction notice because, according to club legend, the landlord discovered Bridle making preparations to install a dumbwaiter which would deliver meals from the restaurant to the members. For the next ten years, the club occupied a second-floor room in the old County of York courthouse on Adelaide Street East.

In 1920, it was again forced to move; the architect Henry Sproatt, a member both of the Arts & Letters Club and the St. George's Society, arranged for the former to take over the latter's building at 14 Elm Street. The members contributed time, talent and money, renovating the building from top to bottom and creating a warm, leather-and-brown-wood atmosphere in the brown brick building. The style of the place—a combination of the warm comfort of a private club and the irreverent, self-mocking rituals of a group of clever people—was in part due to the artist J. E. H. MacDonald, who created mock-baronial coats-of-arms for the founding members and early presidents. Included in this group were Bridle, painters J. W. Beatty and E. Wyly Grier, architects Eden Smith and W. A. Langton, musicians Boris Hambourg and Richard Tattersal, novelist Alan Sullivan, librarian George Locke, Group of Seven patron and ophthalmologist J. E. MacCallum, and historian and industrialist Vincent Massey.

CTA SALMON 590

Under the spreading horse chestnut tree, St. George's Hall stands. The boulevard trees are long gone, but the building, built in 1891 at 14 Elm Street, is still home to the Arts and Letters Club, as it has been since 1920. Renovations supervised by architect and member Henry Sproatt added new windows, and a baronial fireplace to the main hall.

Hector Willoughby Charlesworth, an essayist and journalist who bore an oft-noted resemblance to King Edward VII, was for several decades a fixture on the local literary and cultural scene. He began his career at Saturday Night magazine at the age of nineteen, as a verse writer under Edmund E. Sheppard, and over the years sat in judgement over a wide range of both political events and musical and dramatic performances. His Candid Chronicles—Leaves from the Notebook of a Canadian Journalist, published in 1925, was so successful that he brought out a second volume, called More Candid Chronicles, three years later. Following the death of Frederick Paul in May, 1926, he assumed Saturday Night's editorship, a position he held until 1932, when he was appointed the first chairman of the Canadian Radio Broadcasting Commission (now the C.B.C.). He died at the age of 73 in December, 1945, "in harness" (as a eulogizer put it), while writing a review of a Toronto Symphony Orchestra "pops" concert for the Globe & Mail. Charlesworth lived at One Oriole Gardens.

University Avenue

University Avenue was originally a private road, running through open country north of Queen Street to the site of King's College, now the Ontario Parliament Buildings. It was one of two private roadways, the other being College Street, which approached the college in a suitably grand fashion. The city, annoyed by the existence of these private roads, built its own parallel roadway adjoining University Avenue on the east; this rather silly situation was resolved when the city expropriated the original University Avenue's right of way, but the upshot was a roadway nearly twice as wide as other Toronto streets.

The map shows the lower end of University Avenue in the early 1920s, before the connector was built linking Queen Street with Front Street. Of the several grand "motor boulevards" proposed in the city's 1929 plan, the University Avenue extension was the only one built. Originally, an impressive Parisian-style roundabout called Vimy Circle was planned for the intersection of University Avenue with Richmond Street West; to the west, a boulevard was to cut across streets and through buildings to the vicinity of Spadina and Wellington; a new boulevard between York and Bay, called Cambrai Avenue, was to connect Front Street with a plaza occupying the land between Osgoode Hall and City Hall (now Nathan Phillips Square); other boulevards were to extend north and east. Many automobile trips would be expedited, and many old buildings cleared away, leaving the city with several imposing streetscapes. Opposition to this vision sprang up immediately, led by the influential *Telegram*, which published bitter denunciations of the Cambrai "crooked lane"—especially bitter as its arch-rival, the *Star*, had just completed its new office building (page 53) at 80 King Street West, on land which would adjoin the new "crooked lane." Furthermore, the *Mail and Empire*, a half block to the east at Bay Street, also stood to benefit. Whatever its motives, the *Telegram*'s campaign was so effective that, although the plan had been endorsed by a variety of leading citizens, it was defeated in a referendum accompanying the 1929 election.

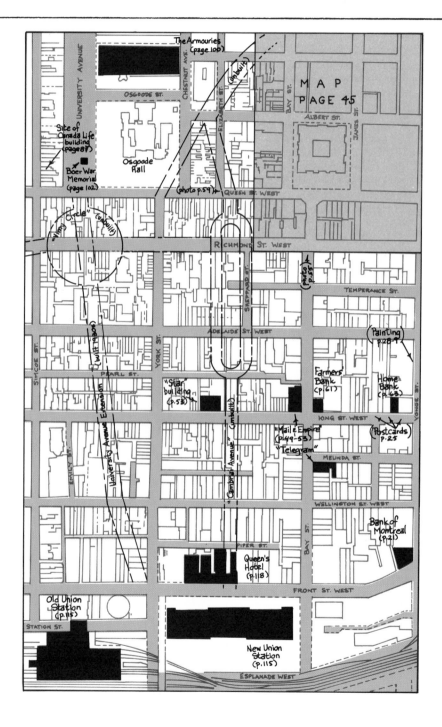

Alexandra Palace, Toronto, Canada

The Canada Life Assurance Company's building, erected at the beginning of the Great Depression, was intended to complement the vision of University Avenue as a grand boulevard. Founded in 1847 in Hamilton by Hugh Baker—who according to company legend could often be seen in the evenings in his rented office, writing insurance policies by the light of an oil lamp—Canada Life outgrew three head office buildings before erecting this one. Its previous building on King Street West had walls of Mexican onyx in its vestibule, and a "great corridor of old Roman mosaic tile."

The splendid Alexandra Palace Apartments stood on the west side of University Avenue south of Orde Street, on a portion of the street now lined with what architectural critic Eric Arthur has dubbed the "filing cabinet façades." It was a fashionable address, home to such pillars of society as Rufus Sawyer Hudson, a vice-president of the Canada Permanent Mortgage Corporation, and the Hon. James Vernall Teetzel, a judge of the Court of Common Pleas, Osgoode Hall.

Queen's Park

The parliament buildings in Queen's Park are the fourth in Toronto but the first on that site; they date from the late 1880s. The first provincial parliament buildings in the city were built in 1796 at the foot of Berkeley Street, just west of Parliament Street. The American invaders burned them in 1813, after which local parliamentarians met in a hotel on King Street between Berkeley and Princess, and then in the house of the chief justice at the corner of Wellington and York. In 1820, following the completion of new parliament buildings on the site of the old ones, the politicians moved back to the foot of Berkeley Street; their sojourn there lasted but four years, ended by a disastrous chimney fire.

Following five more years in undignified quarters—this time, the York Hospital—the parliamentarians moved to new buildings on Front Street between John and Peter, in the up-and-coming fashionable part of town. Adjacent were Government House and Upper Canada College. After 1841, when the provinces of Upper and Lower Canada united, the capital moved around, alighting for periods in Kingston and Montreal, and the parliament buildings saw duty as university buildings and even—in an ironic twist of fate—as an insane asylum. After 1849, they were again the seat of parliament for a period; following Confederation in 1867, they became the legislative buildings of the new province of Ontario.

Parliament buildings adjacent to the University of Toronto had been considered since the decision to "disenfranchise" King's College (page 91). The government held a competition for their design in 1880, but when it was unable to reach a decision, the matter lapsed for a few years. At that point, according to historian Eric Arthur, the American architect R. A. Waite obtained the commission by a fine bit of boodling—he had been one of three judges in the inconclusive design competition of 1880, and had subsequently been asked by the government to adjudicate the proposals of the two firms on the short list. In a unique move, he concluded that the judge was the only one capable of carrying out the work, and used his considerable talents at cronyism and poker to inveigle his way into the appointment. His design eventually cost two and a half times the tendered price of the cheapest Toronto firm.

* * *

Ontario voters have been intensely loyal not only to Queen and Country, but to incumbent governments as well. The province's political history has been quite straightforward—Liberal governments mainly led by

Two postcards showing the Ontario Parliament Buildings at Queen's Park, separated from the hustle and bustle of the metropolis by spreading trees and lawns—and also showing the wide range of colour indulged in by postcard colourists from different companies. The John A. Macdonald statue visible in both cards was sculpted by Walter Seymour Allward, born in Toronto in 1876. He began a study of architecture at the age of fifteen, but five years later abandoned it in favour of sculpture. Another of his many local commissions is the South African War Memorial at the opposite end of University Avenue. Allward lived at 76 Walker Avenue.

A polite, World War One-era version of the "press scrum," with newsreel photographers and reporters interviewing a group of politicians in front of the legislature buildings.

Sir Oliver Mowat from Confederation until 1905, Conservative governments of Sir James Whitney and others from then until the Great Depression, an experiment with Liberals led by the oddball Mitchell Hepburn until the Second World War, then four decades of continuous Conservative rule. The exception to this record of longevity was the curious and radical United Farmers of Ontario government at the end of the First World War.

By the end of the First World War, many Canadians, especially in rural areas, had graduated from a mere distrust of big-city, establishment-party provincial and federal politicians to an outright loathing; issues contributing to this shift included the failure of proposals for reciprocal trading with the United States, the failure of Dominion-wide Prohibition (blamed on the federal desire to kowtow to Quebec), and the establishment of conscription in 1917. They found their mouthpiece in the organized farmers movement, an American transplant of idealistic, radical tenor.

Farmers had begun to organize in 1867, when a meeting in Washington, D.C. gave birth to a nonpolitical, nonsectarian association called The Patrons of Husbandry. Its members split into branches, called Granges, and seven years later, the Dominion Grange organized itself in London, Ontario, stating its goals to be the elimination of middlemen and monopolies. By 1877, the Canadian organization had 31,000 members and had incorporated itself as The Grange in Canada. In 1891 in Toronto, Dr. Goldwin Smith (page 145) founded a newspaper called *The Farmers Sun* as a platform for his free-trading, anti-imperialist views; it soon became the unofficial organ of radical, politicized members of the Grange, who sought the nationalization of the telephone and electrical industries, abolition of the Canadian Senate, and a general simplification of laws and government. In addition, Grange members started their own cooperative commercial operations, including the United Farmers Co-operative stores, of which there were eight in Toronto, managed by the future grocery tycoon T. P. Loblaw.

At their 33rd annual convention, held in Toronto in December, 1917, the Grange decided upon more direct political involvement under the banner of the United Farmers of Ontario. Two years later, the U.F.O. joined with the Independent Labour Party to fight against the provincial Conservative government, although in the campaign leading to the October election that year, most metropolitan commentators felt that the Conservatives would be returned. To their immense surprise, there was "a political upheaval"—the U.F.O. won the most seats, and formed a government with E. C. Drury as premier; Toronto ridings elected four Liberals, two Conservatives, and no farmers. During the next four years, the U.F.O.

government presented a moral and upright face to the populace, especially on the issues of Prohibition (pages 76-9) and racetrack gambling (page 169).

On one issue their rural power-base came to the rescue of the city, helping to halt the juggernaut of Sir Adam Beck and the Ontario Hydro-Electric Power Commission. Beck, who as a Conservative government member had created the hydra-headed Hydro, planned a comprehensive network of electric railways radiating from Toronto. In 1916, he had won the approval of Toronto voters for a swath of railway tracks along the waterfront; however, because of the war nothing had been done, and when the U.F.O. government reviewed the scheme in 1920, it decided that its rural supporters preferred automobiles and truck-hauling to the centralized electric railway system. Although Beck—out of government but still the chairman of Ontario Hydro—won his greatest triumph that year when the private electricity and transit interests sold out to the public, the U.F.O. were cautious about expansionism and the radial railway scheme. At that time, the *Farmers' Sun* began to attack him for favouring industry over farmers; it had strange bed-fellows in conservative Toronto journals such as the *Financial Post*, which for decades had vehemently opposed the spread of public ownership.

That August, to ensure that the anti-Beck, anti-radial point of view was well understood by the public, the Ontario Hydro Information Association was organized in Toronto, with Lt. Col. J. Z. Frazer, a U.F.O. member, as president. The provincial government called a Royal Commission to examine the radial question, and heard "expert witnesses" describe Beck's radial scheme as extravagant. Highways and buses, they concluded, were the wave of the future. In Toronto, Mayor Church supported Beck and attacked the premier, hinting darkly that "certain interests," mooted to be Sir Joseph Flavelle and the Grand Trunk Railway, and the Canadian Pacific Railway management in Montreal, were trying to sabotage the scheme. City council persisted with its support of the radials; arrayed against it were the provincial government and newspapers such as the *Star*, which dubbed the plan "the waterfront grab." The anti-radial coalition carried the day in a referendum at the beginning of 1923, saving the waterfront from even more ribbons of tracks. (In the long run, however, the victory was a hollow one, for in the 1950s politicians agreed to build the Gardiner Expressway along the route which the radial railway was to have followed.)

Voters throughout the province soon tired of their flirtation with radical agrarianism—the U.F.O. had but one term in office, and were almost annihilated in the 1923 election.

Toronto was never more on the outside politically than during the period immediately following the First World War, when the United Farmers of Ontario, with its earnest leader Ernest Charles Drury (above), was elected in a rural landslide. Drury was born at Crown Hill in 1878, the son of the Hon. Charles Drury, the first minister of agriculture in Ontario. He was educated at the Ontario Agricultural College, and soon became prominently identified with farmers' interests, representing the Farmers' Association on the 1905 Tariff Commission, and becoming Master of the Ontario Grange in 1910; three years later, he became the first president of the United Farmers of Ontario. His Methodist beliefs and "simple ways" on matters like Prohibition made him, briefly, the people's favourite. The U.F.O was swept from power to near oblivion in the 1923 election, and replaced by the Conservative government of Howard Ferguson.

University of Toronto

Although the head of University Avenue is now occupied by the provincial parliament buildings, it was once the site of the main building of King's College, the forerunner of the University of Toronto. King's College was the Anglican institution which wore the mantle of higher education granted by an 1827 royal charter; as the ruling clique—the Family Compact—of Upper Canada was Anglican, so was the university, to the exclusion of other denominations. The King's College main building, three storeys tall with a Doric-columned façade, was built early in the 1840s, far to the northwest of the city centre on a quarter-section (160 acres) of grounds. Giving access to it were two private avenues, the pres-

ent University Avenue and College Street, separated from the city by toll-gates at Queen and Yonge streets.

King's College opened in 1843 and had only a half-dozen years in the sun before its charter was cut out from under it by the reformist Baldwin government. In 1849 the government decided to placate the members of other religious denominations by establishing a nondenominational university as the worthy future recipient of the province's educational largesse. Subsequently, new university buildings were erected west of the King's College building, and the miffed Anglicans led by Bishop Strachan built their own university on Queen Street West (page 219). Over the next half-century, colleges of the other denominations built on the university grounds and affiliated with the main university. As for the King's College site, it was expropriated by the province in 1849, at the time of the reconstitution of the provincial university; in the late 1880s the King's College building, which had served for a time as a lunatic asylum, was demolished and replaced by the provincial parliament buildings.

Old maps and photographs of the campus show a sylvan glade crossed by Taddle Creek, along which ran the Philosopher's Walk, similar in romantic intent to the *Philosophenweg* near the University of Heidelberg in Germany. Between the buildings were fine lawns and the "fussy Victorian flower beds" so despised by the architectural historian Eric Arthur. The imposing houses and large properties of some of the city's prominent old families adjoined the campus; on College Street west of University Avenue was the house of Sir John Beverly Robinson, BART; further west, between Beverley and Ross, resided Henry Cawthra; and Sir Oliver Mowat, the long-time premier of Ontario, lived on St. George Street north of the Knox College buildings.

On the Bloor Street edge of the campus, a world away from the sobriety of old family homes and interdenominational religious bickering, stands Varsity Stadium, the temple to the gods of college football and the coonskin coat (and, for a time, the Argonauts). Jesse Middleton described the popularity of the game in his 1934 history of the city: "Football is so essentially masculine that it has a natural fascination for the girls, especially for those in their late teens or their early twenties. Add to these a sufficient number of undergraduate esquires, a mob of alumni remembering the battles of their own and breathing the old song *Alma mater floreat quae nos educavit* ["May the old school flourish which educated us"], together with the vast company of folk who enjoy a fight of any kind and the total is imposing. It is no wonder that the University stadium is filled to the last limit for every important match."

A building boom on the campus started when the old colleges affiliated with the main university in the last years of the nineteenth century. Subsequently, the Massey family donated Hart House to the University as an undergraduate (men only) activity centre. It opened after the First World War and became one of the musical centres in Toronto. The Hart House Quartet was one of two chamber groups—the other being the Conserva-

John Cunningham McLennan, Professor of Physics, was one of the brightest stars in the galaxy of academic and research talent at the University of Toronto. During the First World War, McLennan and his assistants managed to operate a semicommercial helium plant, having worked out a method to extract it from natural gas. The announcement, in April, 1919, that McLennan had "perfected" helium offered the prospect of safe airship travel and was thus expected to guarantee Toronto's place "as the greatest aviation centre in America!" (The reports announcing MacLennan's discovery also speculated on the carnage which would have been visited upon London had the German Zeppelins in the recently completed Great War had the use of helium, instead of inflammable hydrogen; nearly two decades later, when the Hindenburg *exploded in New Jersey, the German airship industry still had not managed to fill its dirigibles with helium. The* Hindenburg *had been designed for helium, which at that time was manufactured only in the United States. It could not be exported without a government permit, which the German designers had failed to obtain.) MacLennan's worldwide reputation was cemented by his later discovery, in January, 1923, of a successful method to liquefy helium and other gases. He lived at 88 Prince Arthur Avenue in the Annex.*

Frederick Grant Banting's research into the causes of diabetes resulted in one of medicine's few "miracle cures"—the discovery of insulin. Born in Alliston, Ontario, Banting was educated at Victoria College and the University of Toronto before enlisting in the army. He served three years overseas, and won the Military Cross before being invalided home. Banting was co-winner of the 1923 Nobel prize with John James Rickard Macleod, a Scot who was a professor of physiology at the University of Toronto. Banting shared the cash value of his Nobel prize with Charles Herbert Best, a physiologist and his research assistant.

tory Quartet—prominent at the time; founded in 1924 by Hart Massey's grandson Vincent and sponsored for twenty years by him and his wife Alice, the Hart House Quartet originally consisted of Harry Adaskin and Milton Blackstone (violins), Geza de Kresz (viola) and Boris Hambourg (cello), all of whom were faculty members of Hart House.

University of Toronto faculty members dominated the musical scene elsewhere in Toronto, playing, as did the Hart House Quartet, in an auditorium built with Massey family money. This was Massey Hall on Shuter Street, where Dr. Ernest MacMillan's Toronto Symphony Orchestra played to overflow audiences. MacMillan, born in Mimico in 1893, was so enamoured of Wagner that he made a pilgrimage to Bayreuth in the summer of 1914, and ended up spending four years in a German prison camp. In 1926, he was named principal of the Toronto Conservatory of Music, and Dean of the Faculty of Music at the University of Toronto, succeeding the late Dr. A. S. Vogt, who in 1894 had founded the Mendelssohn Choir. Vogt's successor with the Mendelssohn Choir was Herbert Austin Fricker, an organist from Leeds who, in addition to lecturing and examining at the University's Faculty of Music, worked as choirmaster at Metropolitan Methodist Church. Fricker was an able composer, and well-known during the twenties as the conductor of the Exhibition Chorus at the C.N.E. Like a fellow composer, the organist Healey Willan, Fricker was an enthusiastic supporter of the Bach Revival, and added Bach repertoire to his church service programs.

* * *

An eccentric figure on the fringes of the gowned educational establishment was Alfred Fitzpatrick, who founded Frontier College. Fiztpatrick had first come to Toronto before the turn of the century, looking for an itinerant brother. His search took him through the workcamps of the boondocks, where he was appalled at the lack of stimulating recreation and education. Returning to civilization, he found a kindred spirit in George Grant, the principal of Queen's University, who was an early advocate of continuing education. They started in 1898 with the Reading Tent Association, run mainly by student volunteers. It evolved into Fron-

(Above) The Victoria College building, at 73 Queen's Park Crescent, was erected in 1892; however, Victoria College itself dates back to 1836, when it was founded by the Methodists of Upper Canada with a charter from King William IV. Located in Cobourg for its first half-century, it conferred the first earned degrees in Upper Canada. Its second principal was Egerton Ryerson. In 1881, it became Victoria University, with four faculties—Law, Medicine, Theology and Arts; eleven years later, it affiliated with the University of Toronto, a move prompted by the rise of experimental science, and the desire of Victoria University's governors to gain access for their students to the main university's facilities. The building shown here was erected to be the college's new home. Today, Victoria College is one of several colleges making up the Faculty of Arts and Sciences at the University of Toronto. After a century and a half of existence, it still retains its connection with the United Church, the successor to the Methodist church. The building itself, which used to be set amidst well-kept grounds and was easily visible from Queen's Park Crescent, is now hemmed in by modern buildings, including Northrop Frye Hall. (Below) The sylvan, peaceful campus—a view looking west from what is now the corner of Queen's Park Crescent and Wellesley Street West. The distinctive, asymmetrically turreted tower of University College looms in the background.

Victoria University, Toronto, Canada.

UNIVERSITY DRIVE, QUEEN'S PARK, TORONTO

McMaster University. Toronto, Canada.

Toronto from Parliament Buildings

(Above) Today's Royal Conservatory of Music, at 273 Bloor Street West, started life in the early 1880s as the Toronto Baptist College—one of several denominational colleges on the University of Toronto campus. Renamed McMaster University after a wealthy, philanthropic dry-goods merchant, it did not follow the example of St. Michael's, Trinity, St. Basil's, and Victoria colleges and affiliate with the main university. In the 1920s, its Baptist board of governors started looking for a new location; after receipt of an offer of land from Hamilton, the university moved there in 1930. (Below) Looking south along University Avenue towards the lake, at a time when many of the downtown streets were narrow and shaded from the summer sun by an arch of trees. The downtown skyline shows only the Confederation Life Building, City Hall, and the Temple Building, indicating that the photograph dates from before the 1905 erection of the Traders Bank Building on Yonge Street.

tier College, which finally received a federal charter in 1922, allowing the college to confer degrees in Arts. The college's graduates were sent out to mining, lumbering, railway and construction camps to work as labourers during the day, then to educate their fellow workers in the evening. Fitzpatrick was a heterodox figure in Canadian education, relentlessly agitating, in articles and pamphlets like the 1920 "University in Overalls," for the union of education with industry and agriculture. Born in rural Nova Scotia, he never lost his self-effacing rusticity, and twice turned down offers of honorary doctorates. His recreations were cabinetmaking and homesteading. Frontier College still survives, though the large labour camps do not. Today, the frontier is on the downtown streets, and the college pursues its goals in urban locations, attempting to open educational doors for the street people who fell through the cracks in the floor of establishment education.

Alfred Fitzpatrick   H. A. Fricker

A landmark on Spadina Crescent, on the northeast quadrant, was the City Dairy, with its large "milk bottle" on a scaffolding on the roof. The City Dairy property was initially the location of the home of Sir Adam Wilson—mayor of Toronto in 1859-60—and was adjacent to the Knox College buildings which still occupy the centre of the circle. Founded in 1901, City Dairy was a leader in the fight for unadulterated milk, and "in its early years fought ridicule. It formulated rules and regulations for farmers and dairymen. These rules were strange then—but by persistence and with the whole-hearted support of the medical profession and the Department of Health the sane, common sense of City Dairy's methods was acknowledged and commended." Much of the milk available for sale had been adulterated with water and colouring, or had been either improperly pasteurized or not pasteurized at all—in one test conducted in 1909, 40 percent of the samples did not make the grade. Many of the local milk suppliers operated from outside the city limits, and were thus out of reach of the Board of Health. A partial result was that Toronto's infant mortality rate was greater than that of London, New York, or Chicago—the public health advocate Dr. Helen MacMurchy (page 255) maintained that proper distribution of good milk could cut that rate in two. Another result, as reported by the chemist G. G. Nasmith (page 168), was that residents each year were buying one-quarter of a million dollars worth of water, at nine cents a quart. Milk depots opened on Edward Street in The Ward, and at the Fred Victor Mission at Jarvis and Queen. With the passage of the Ontario Milk Act in June 1911, the situation improved, but inspectors still had to be vigilant. A dramatic example, widely reported in the newspapers in the spring of 1912, was city inspectors dumping 900 gallons of milk into city sewers. Pasteurization became compulsory in 1914.

The fringes of the University of Toronto were fashionably residential, especially St. George Street, shown here in a postcard which looks north from Harbord Street to Hoskin Avenue and beyond. The zigzag from Hoskin to Harbord has since been smoothed; the odd-looking John P. Robarts Research Library now occupies the corner on the left of the postcard. The fine, turreted house on the right, at the northeast corner of Hoskin and St. George, was built in 1890 for the noted businessman Wilmot D. Matthews—it is now the Newman Centre.

St. George Street, Toronto

Knox College, on the circle of Spadina Avenue north of College Street, was established in 1875 as a Presbyterian seminary. It affiliated with the nearby University of Toronto in 1890; 25 years later, faculty and students moved to the building at 59 St. George Street, closer to the university campus. The old Knox College building became the Spadina Military Hospital, then the penicillin factory for Connaught Anti-Toxin Laboratories.

KNOX COLLEGE, TORONTO.

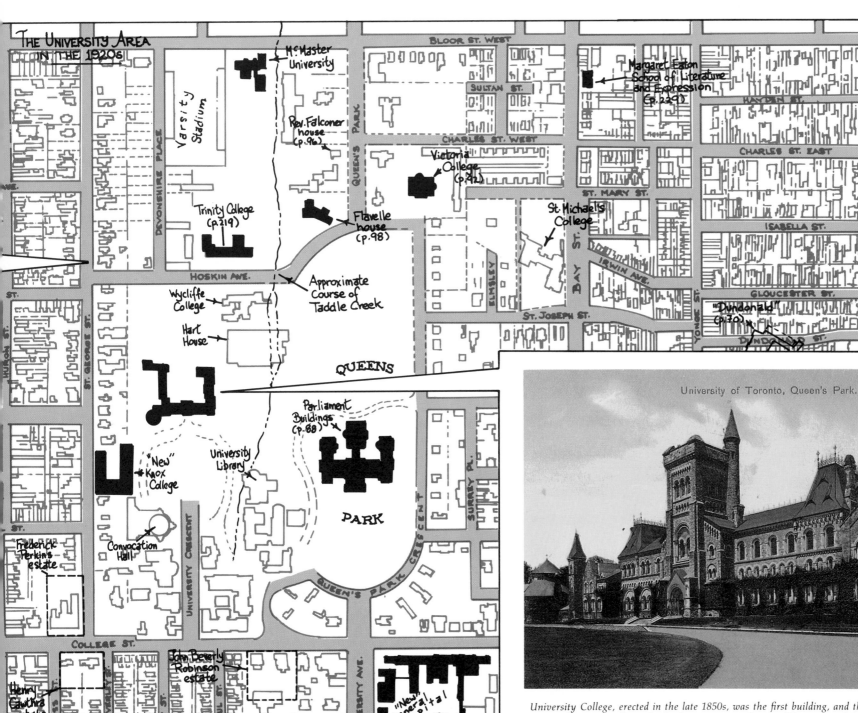

The University Area in the 1920s

McMaster University

Margaret Eaton School of Literature and Expression (p.229)

BLOOR ST. WEST

SULTAN ST.

HAYDEN ST.

Varsity Stadium

Rev. Falconer house (p.96)

CHARLES ST. WEST

CHARLES ST. EAST

DEVONSHIRE PLACE

QUEEN'S PARK

Victoria College (p.42)

ST. MARY ST.

ISABELLA ST.

Trinity College (p.219)

St. Michael's College

Flavelle house (p.98)

HOSKIN AVE.

Approximate Course of Taddle Creek

Wycliffe College

ST. JOSEPH ST.

GLOUCESTER ST.

"Dundonald" (p.70)

Hart House

ST. GEORGE ST.

HURON ST.

QUEENS

Parliament Buildings (p.88)

University Library

"New" Knox College

PARK

SURREY PL.

Convocation Hall

Frederick Perkins estate

UNIVERSITY CRESCENT

MCCAUL ST.

QUEEN'S PARK CRESCENT

COLLEGE ST.

John Beverly Robinson estate

UNIVERSITY AVE.

Henry Cawthra estate

ROSS ST.

BEVERLY ST.

HENRY ST.

"New" General Hospital

Alexandra Apartments (p.87)

CECIL ST.

MURRAY ST.

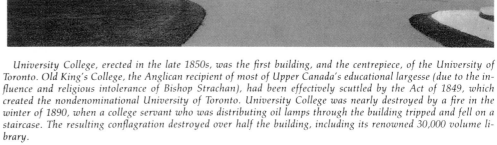

University of Toronto, Queen's Park.

University College, erected in the late 1850s, was the first building, and the centrepiece, of the University of Toronto. Old King's College, the Anglican recipient of most of Upper Canada's educational largesse (due to the influence and religious intolerance of Bishop Strachan), had been effectively scuttled by the Act of 1849, which created the nondenominational University of Toronto. University College was nearly destroyed by a fire in the winter of 1890, when a college servant who was distributing oil lamps through the building tripped and fell on a staircase. The resulting conflagration destroyed over half the building, including its renowned 30,000 volume library.

The Free Speech Dispute

Many episodes of the 1960s and 1970s saw the political beliefs of students and teachers pitted against those of the *status quo*—in the style of the time, the right to free speech was considered at least as important as the content of the speeches. The Rochdale College experiment of that period explored, in the guise of education, the outer limits of liberality and free speech; in the guise of creativity, they explored the possibilities of self-expression. Located in an eighteen-storey highrise at Bloor and Huron, the college was dubbed "the vertical Haight Ashbury" on account of its free-wheeling, drug-taking students; after several years of increasingly controversial funding by various levels of government, and increasingly outrageous behaviour, it was shut down, and its residents evicted.

Society was less tolerant a half-century earlier, at the beginning of the First World War, during a free-speech debate of sorts focussing on the pro-German opinions and affiliations of some University of Toronto professors. The other great universities of Canada, including Queen's and McGill, "held aloft a banner of Empire loyalty," but Toronto had chosen "to hold the view that education in the varied arts of peace was its sole mission, moral idealism its inspiration." In the months leading up to the outbreak of the war in August, 1914, the administration of the University of Toronto allowed its students to listen to views as varied as those of Henri Bourassa, the French Canadian nationalist opposed to all British Imperial commitments, and Lord Milner, a fervent advocate of British supremacy in South Africa; likewise, it did not proselytize for the formation of military associations or Empire Societies among its students. At the outbreak of the war, the university assumed an air of neutrality, provoking the *Globe* to ask rhetorically: "have the Presidents of Canada's great universities no national message for a great national occasion when the Nation is involved with the Empire in a life-and-death war of the world? What about the greatest Canadian University, the Provincial University, with its seat here in Toronto and its lines going out into all the earth?"

Early in September, following a speech "of the usual patriotic character" by the principal to the pupils at Toronto Collegiate Institute, two students protested against the characterization of the German people; their father, P. W. Mueller—an associate professor of German at the university—intervened in support of his sons; regardless, the two were suspended from school. Several of Mueller's colleagues joined him in a protest to the Toronto Board of Education, which was published in the press on September 18, and stated that "the undersigned, ratepayers of the City of Toronto" (all but one of whom were university lecturers in subjects ranging from Old Testament literature to chemistry, physiology, and French) wished to protest against the "outrageous conduct on the part of a teacher" in making "a harangue to his pupils on the war now raging in Europe, in which he said insulting things of the German people."

The contemporary chronicler John Castell Hopkins noted that "Whatever the personal opinions of these gentlemen were as to the War, or its causes, or the German people, this intervention in matters outside their sphere gave rise to much speculation and criticism and brought up the whole question of German employees of the institution—a subject which could not be discussed with academic calm and precision at such a juncture." A letters-to-the-editor war ensued, during which the issue of Mueller's citizenship was raised—though he had been in Canada for twenty years, he had not become a British subject. The Board of Education commended the collegiate institute's principal, issuing a unanimous resolution that he "did not use unduly strong language in denouncing the barbarism displayed by the Germans in this war but, on the contrary, he only did his duty in explaining to his pupils the causes of this war, and condemning the atrocious manner of carrying it on. The Board believes it is the duty of the Provincial Government and the Governors of this University to inquire into the conduct of these Professors, and to require them to retract publicly the language they have used."

Meanwhile, something of a witch-hunt had begun in the *World* and the *Telegram*. Both demanded the elimination of all German professors from the university staff, because, they claimed, it was wrong to pay public money to German subjects in time of war, their teachings "could not be patriotic and beneficial," and they could "send valuable information to the enemy via New York or by American sympathizers elsewhere" (America stayed neutral until 1917). The newspapers published the names of German nationals teaching at the university, including Mueller, a few German instructors, a philosophy professor, and a member of the department of forestry; the university's president, R.A. Falconer, wrote to the press on several occasions, defending the character of the individuals named and the patriotic action and attitude of the university itself.

Regardless of Falconer's justification, influential people within the community continued to demand action. One such was the president of the Imperial Bank of Canada, D. R. Wilkie, a copy of whose letter to Falconer was published early in December; in it, he recited a litany of complaints, including the university's reluctance to provide drill and military preparation. More partisans entered the fray, including a history professor with the unfortunate name of George M. Wrong, who described the

Rev. Sir Robert Alexander Falconer was president of the University of Toronto during the First World War years, and had to balance his love of Germany and of academic and intellectual freedom against the wartime mood which made every German a "Bosch," "Uhlan," or "Hun." The son of a clergyman, Falconer was born on Prince Edward Island, and educated in Trinidad, Scotland, Leipzig and Berlin. Although chiefly known as an authority on Greek and New Testament subjects, he wrote The German Tragedy and Its Meaning for Canada, *which expressed his dismay at the conflict between the philosophical and artistic ideals of traditional German culture and the militarism of Prussia.*

Cadet Full Dress Parade on University Campus, Toronto, Canada

Military drills were an unquestioned part of every young man's grade school educational curriculum. This postcard photograph was taken about 1900; within a decade, allegations of jingoism and militarism were being levelled at the practice of drilling, but only by a few, whose links either with socialism or with Germany made them easy to discredit.

it is only natural that German professors would have a pro-German influence . . . . None of the German professors are naturalized citizens—I cannot see why we should be paying Germans salaries here when thousands of young men of Britain are being killed by the Germans at the Front." In reply, Falconer described the university's policy as "British fair play," and the university made enquiries about the possibility of exchanging the controversial Germans for other professors of German in United States universities. Academics chose to tread no further in the issue, but the politicians rushed in. During his December mayoral campaign, Tommy Church said that he would "suspend the teaching of German throughout the province." A number of members of the provincial legislature demanded dismissal of the professors, and a thorough investigation of the university.

By the end of the year, the issue had died a quiet death: two of the four German nationals had left, one as he did not want to be paid for no work, the other by retirement when the idea of exchanging with the United States was abandoned; Dr. Mueller, whose protests at Toronto Collegiate had started the ruction, became a naturalized Canadian, and made a statement to the press on Christmas Eve that he hoped Great Britain would win the war.

In the meantime at the university, a variety of war-related activities developed: an Officer Training Corps comprised of 1,800 students and about 80 faculty members drilled two or three afternoons a week; 50 students were in uniform and training at Exhibition Park; another 100 former university students were at Salisbury Plains in England awaiting duty at the Front. University President Falconer sponsored a series of lectures on Germany and the causes of the war.

* * *

controversy as "absolute bosh" and declared that "any attack on the Faculty is an attack on the students," and the *Varsity* student newspaper, which protested against the persecution of professors, pointed out that the Prince of Wales had many German relatives, and opined that it was "puerile" to suggest that German professors might poison the minds of students.

At a meeting on the fourth of December, a committee of the Board of Governors reviewed the situation, and reached a compromise in which the three German professors of the German language were ordered to take paid leaves of absence. Dr. Falconer, the university president, had recommended no action at all, while the board, chaired by Sir Edmund Osler, had wanted to weed out all allegedly pro-German influence. Osler told the press on the seventh: "We have got to realize the influence of a teacher on the students. A teacher is no good unless he does influence the mind and

Several years later, in March, 1920, an echo of the war again stirred the ants' nest of free speech on the university campus. President Falconer had issued an invitation to the American pacifist, Jane Addams, to speak to students in the Social Service Department. The *Telegram* declaimed in its columns that she was in league with Bolsheviks; the newspaper implied that pacifism was a synonym for sedition. Falconer justified the invitation on the grounds that no one in Canada had any experience with that "phase" of postwar reconstruction—that is, no one had a pacifist outlook on the future. However, he decided to cancel the visit, as there was "a probability of disturbance which would make her visit unpleasant."

Sir Joseph Flavelle

"Holwood," the turn-of-the-century mansion at 78 Queen's Park Crescent now occupied by the University of Toronto's Faculty of Law, was home to the industrialist Sir Joseph Flavelle. Born in Peterborough, Flavelle came to Toronto as a packing-house manager when he was nineteen years old. A capable, cautious young man of deep religious principles, he practised his motto "moderation in all things" throughout his life, allowing only one exception—the making of money. One story recounted that the young Flavelle "brought with him a shaven lip above his beard," for his Methodism "had the truest Peterboro tinge."

Over the years, Flavelle owned or had a controlling interest in a number of important and influential businesses, including the *Toronto News*, the William Davies Company, and the Robert Simpson Company; for many years he was president of the National Trust Company, and he served as chairman of the Canadian Bank of Commerce, the Canadian Marconi Company, and the Grand Trunk Railway. More numerous still were his public and charitable activities, encompassing the University of Toronto, the Royal Ontario Museum, West China Union University, the Toronto Board of [Liquor] License Commissioners, the Victorian Order of Nurses, and the International Commission on Bovine Tuberculosis. He was chairman of the Board of Trustees of the Toronto General Hospital, and personally donated $100,000 towards the erection of the new (1913) buildings on University Avenue.

He was most in the public eye during the First World War, firstly because his unpaid chairmanship of the Imperial Munitions Board made a great contribution to the war effort, which was duly recognized in 1917 when the British government elevated him to the peerage with the title of baronet; secondly due to his controlling interest in the William Davies Company, a massive meat-packing operation, which allegedly benefited from the exigencies of wartime to such an extent that it provoked a profiteering scandal (pages 194-7). Flavelle's war work was said to be appreciated more in England than in Canada—in the former, he was a Canadian hero, while in the latter he was the focus of public anger about rising food prices. A typical comment was that of Liberal D. D. Mackenzie, speaking in the House of Commons on May 2, 1917: Flavelle and the William Davies Company, he said, were "grinding the faces of the poor and sucking the life-blood of the country." The Canadian government's response was to limit profits in the cold-storage and packing-house businesses. Flavelle himself became, to the general public, a symbol of why Canadians should not receive British titles.

Titles for Canadians had rarely been controversial during colonial and early Confederation times—for example, John Beverley Robinson, the leader of the Tory Family Compact in Toronto after the 1812 War, was created a baronet in recognition of his service as Upper Canada's attorney general; Canada's first prime minister, Conservative John A. Macdonald,

was likewise elevated to the peerage, as were the financiers of the Canadian Pacific Railway. Criticism of the practice began with members of Liberal governments in the 1870s and again at the turn of the century who felt they had no say in the distribution of honours; once they began to have a say, criticism began amongst the Canadian public. A movement started on the prairies against the granting of "tinpot titles," which rose to "a howl of indignation and disgust" in 1916 due to the elevation of the Canadian businessman Max Aitken to the peerage as Lord Beaverbrook.

In addition to hereditary titles, such as Aitken's and Flavelle's, there was the regular flock of knighthoods in the King's list of honours, such as the C.B.'s, C.M.G.'s and C.V.O.'s for achievements in literature, science, engineering, finance, and the military. These were different, as they were not hereditary, were given as a reward for service to one's community, and indicated that one was a person of consequence, not merely the son of a son or a person of wealth. A tremendous number of these were handed out at the behest of prime ministers—especially Sir Robert Borden during the First World War years; some nominated recipients, such as newspaper publishers Joseph Atkinson and John Ross Robertson, declined on principle, while many others, including the newspaperman John Willison, accepted.

As groups like the United Farmers of Ontario grew in influence, so the movement against titles grew. The U.F.O.'s official newspaper, *The Farmers' Sun*, refused to recognize any titles, and referred to individuals such as Sir Wilfrid Laurier and Sir Robert Borden as Mr. Laurier and Mr. Borden. Some of this opposition was analyzed as "an unconscious preference of American ways," but few could deny that unpopular recipients of hereditary titles such as the Montreal newspaper publisher Hugh Graham, who was created Lord Atholstan for his support of Borden, discredited the entire process. Flavelle was unpopular, too, but in his case the baronetcy was granted at the behest of the British government.

The parliamentary debate about the granting of titles started early in 1919, and opened a hornets' nest of acrimony, at the end of which the so-called Nickle Resolution was adopted, and submitted as an address to the king. It requested that no titles of honour or titular distinctions, whether hereditary or not, be conferred upon residents of Canada, and that hereditary titles or distinctions be extinguished upon the death of the holder if resident in Canada. This policy has remained in effect since, with the exception of the period from 1931-5, when the Conservatives under R.B. Bennett formed the Canadian government. When Bennett himself was elevated to the rank of viscount, he was immediately dubbed Lord Matchbox by his fellow countrymen, because he had owned the Eddy Match Company. (The Nickle Resolution was relaxed to allow Canadians to receive nontitular orders for their service in the Second World War.)

As for Flavelle, he outlasted the storms of the First World War and

Sir Joseph Flavelle, BART., was one of the most prosperous Toronto industrialists in the early part of the century. Although technically independent in politics, his high public profile and Methodist temperance made him an ideal commissioner to attempt to enforce the labyrinth of Ontario liquor licensing laws. Likewise, he was a logical choice for chairman of the Imperial Munitions Board during the First World War, a task he performed with such distinction that in 1917 the British government conferred on him the hereditary title of baronet. Concurrently, the public furore over the alleged war profiteering of one of his companies—the huge William Davies Company packing house near the mouth of the Don River—tarnished his reputation (page 194).

gave years more service to his businesses and favourite charities. He died at the age of 81, during a 1939 Palm Beach holiday, rich in more than years and respected for his lifetime's work.

"Holwood," Sir Joseph Flavelle's residence at 78 Queen's Park, is now the hub of the University of Toronto's Faculty of Law. In Flavelle's time, the university campus was little more than fields dotted with the buildings of the affiliated colleges—including Wycliffe, Knox, St. Michael's, and Victoria—and the large houses of people like university president Sir Robert Falconer, who lived just north of "Holwood" at number 86, and E. W. Wallace, the chancellor and president of Victoria College, who lived a stone's throw from the college itself in a house at 71 Queen's Park Crescent.

The Great War

The "test of strength" which occupied Europe from August, 1914 through the end of 1918 became a test of loyalty and mettle in the Dominions of the British Empire. After an initial year of great patriotism and enthusiasm, Canadians began to lose their sense of purpose and unified, directed action. Toronto was profoundly affected by the war: as citizens of the "Queen City," Torontonians felt that their patriotism should be a beacon for the rest for the country, but found recruiting to be as difficult as it was for other cities. Most eligible young men eventually went, and some returned—the carnage which overtook the others was reflected in displays of mourning in many streets in the city and photographs of smartly-dressed young men above brief obituaries in the newspapers. Munitions, aviation, clothing and food contracts made the city hum with activity, but allegations of war profiteering tarred the reputations of some of its prominent industrialists. With a need for greater self-sacrifice on the home front as its justification, the government legislated Prohibition, prompting a wave of law-breaking which had no precedent in the simple society of a few years earlier; later, the federal government's imposition of conscription—for like reasons—had a similar effect.

At Britain's side, Canada found itself at war, on August 4, 1914, to defend a European alliance. Suddenly, in the midst of an indolent summer, the call of king and country shook young men awake. A thrill of enthusiasm ran through the city: great crowds of would-be soldiers surrounded the Armouries on University Avenue; on the fifth of August, 250 private chauffeurs volunteered to serve in a mechanical transport division; members of the Ontario Motor League and their 800 cars formed a motor corps, with the aged automobile pioneer Dr. Perry Dolittle as commandant; thousands of volunteers who failed the medical examination were replaced by thousands more lining up to take it; the minister of militia, Sam Hughes, announced that no recruit would be accepted against the written protest of his wife or mother; at the University of Toronto, 50 students met on August 18 to form a Company of University Rifles, and a month later the university decided that any students who were enlisting for the War would be given "treatment of the utmost liberality" on supplemental examinations; on August 19, barely two weeks after the declaration, a contingent of 927 men left the city for the Valcartier mobilization camp.

As in every war since the beginning of history, prominent citizens used their personal wealth, and that of their companies, to help the cause. John Craig Eaton offered $100,000 to purchase and equip a battery of Vickers quick-firing machine guns mounted on armoured trucks; as well, he offered the use of his luxurious steam yacht *Florence* and his "Marconi station" to the authorities. The noted yachtsman Aemilius Jarvis had no trouble raising a contingent of 700 men with naval experience. More

The Armouries, on University Avenue just north of Osgoode Hall, were erected in 1891 and demolished in 1963. The site of numerous recruiting drives during both world wars, the Armouries were also a popular spot for huge banquets—although the building was 124 feet wide, its technologically advanced steel roof trusses gave a pillar-free interior. The site is now occupied by the Metropolitan Toronto Court House.

modestly, the president of Canadian General Electric, Frederic Nicholls, offered to raise, equip and pay a corps of 25 electricians. The Christie-Brown Company announced that it would pay the salaries of its employees at the front and guarantee them positions when they returned. The William Neilson Company presented the government with 65,000 bars of chocolate; the Cowan Company gave 5,000 pounds of chocolate. In Toronto, 81 physicians offered their services free to families of soldiers, and 62 druggists promised to give free prescriptions. Mrs. J. Kerr Osborne contributed a motor ambulance. Mrs. A. E. Gooderham, the president of the Imperial Order Daughters of the Empire, held an emergency meeting at "Deancroft" in Rosedale, at which members resolved to raise $100,000 to pay for a fully equipped hospital ship for the Admiralty; Miss Mary Plummer coordinated the fundraising, and on the first day she and her fellow clubwomen collected $32,000. The Women's Toronto Conservative Club met at the home of Mrs. Arthur Vankoughnet, and organized

Gertrude Vankoughnet was, by marriage, a member of an old Toronto family whose most illustrious antecedent was Philip Vankoughnet, the last chancellor of Upper Canada. With women such as Helen Bruce (page 182) and Julia Henshaw, she was active in the Imperial Order Daughters of the Empire, which coordinated the Soldiers' Comforts programs, sending millions of articles, such as socks, shirts and cigarettes overseas. She organized the Tag Day for the Amputations Association Club House, and helped wounded and maimed soldiers—common in wartime Toronto—to readjust to civilian life. Expressions of appreciation for her work include an illuminated address, signed by General Currie, from the Canadian Expeditionary Force, presented to her at the opening of the C.N.E. in 1923, and a tea set from the Amputations' Association. The Gertrude Vankoughnet chapter of the I.O.D.E. was formed in her honour. She was the first woman to give an address to the Empire Club.

themselves into a clothing factory, knitting socks and cutting out and sewing shirts—their "Soldiers' Comforts" efforts eventually produced 173,050 pairs of woollen socks! The American Aid Society of Toronto, composed of Americans living and working in Canada who were sympathetic to the Imperial cause, held a fundraising drive, including a public meeting and concert on September 10, which raised $100,000 for the Canadian Patriotic Fund.

There were few discordant notes amidst this symphony of common purpose. The newspapers made much of the alleged German sympathies of some faculty members at the University of Toronto (page 96). The Massey-Harris Company, hit by takeovers of their branches in Germany and Austria and claiming that over half their trade was with countries now at war, shut down its Toronto works on August 15; however, after "strong words" in the press and legislature, it took back 1,500 men, and was soon prospering with munitions work. Salada Tea raised its prices by ten cents a pound; prices of imported biscuits and jams went up by 25 percent. But for other businesses, the collapse of German trade created new opportunities—carpet manufacturers found there to be increased local demand, and the New Zealand piano market opened up.

Canadians were not in the majority in early enlistments; rather "the old country men rose quickly to the occasion." On August 10, whole columns in newspapers listed volunteers for regiments, of which the Mississauga Horse was typical, with an average of seven Englishmen for each Canadian recruit. The *Star* noted that only forty percent of the first local contingent to go to Valcartier were native-born; of the second contingent, only 18 of 120 were Canadian. Many Canadian men chose to bide their time and learn to shoot and drill as volunteers in part-time Home Guard groups, such as those formed at Osgoode Hall, the Arts & Letters Club, City Hall, the Toronto Electric Light Company, the Toronto Street Railway Company, and the University of Toronto. Major General Sir W. D. Otter, a hero of the 1885 Northwest Rebellion, was named colonel-in-chief of the Home Guard, and commented that the volunteers were very patriotic, but showed "a great lack of discipline and some unwillingness to accept it."

This casual, almost cavalier attitude to what was, after all, a physically remote war continued for most of the first year. Local recruiters had no difficulty finding enough volunteers, so less fervent men could find worthwhile tasks at home, and not feel that they were necessarily dodging their duty. However, the terrible battles of 1915 and the first half of 1916, including Ypres, Verdun and the Somme, wasted so many men that eligible recruits could no longer justify remaining on the home front, even in hitherto men-only jobs such as munitions manufacturing.

Recruiting officers and patriotic, ineligible-for-enlistment citizens be-

gan to beat the bushes looking for potential soldiers. A census of Toronto turned up 18,000 eligible men who had not enlisted. City council offered grants to aid recruiting: $1,000 each to a number of local battalions, and $500 each to corps of cyclists, guides, medics, and engineers, to name a few. Women, who had a reputation as very effective recruiters, went out and stopped young men on the streets. Films promoting enlistment accompanied regular motion picture showings—most of which were films of gay civilian life from the neutral United States—and their magic was most effective in raising recruits in rural areas. Some battalions resorted to novel methods to raise a contingent: the concept of a group of "pals"— the assurance that friends would not be split up—was put forward by one Colonel Chadwick, and attracted 1,000 men in twelve days; the 204th Beavers, under Lt. Col. J. A. Cooper, distributed cards inviting pledges and asking for names and particulars of eligible young men; Lt. Col. R. H. Greer raised a battalion in Toronto with a direct appeal to sportsmen; the 255th Queen's Own Rifles battalion urged the general public to "Give Us His Name." Even as recruiters became more zealous, the costs of recruiting continued to grow and to cause concern. At the beginning of 1916, it was estimated that it cost three dollars to recruit a soldier, but by the end of the year—after the news of the Somme and the return of many amputees and cripples to the city—that cost had jumped to between ten and twenty dollars. Recruiting departments found that one of their recurring expenses was the hiring of a brass band.

High wages in the local munitions factories drew fire as one of the temptations for men to remain at home. The munitions manufacturers were working at full speed to fulfil massive shell orders, as well as disabusing allegations of profiteering, noncompetitive bidding, and contracts handed out freely to the members of the Imperial Munitions Board. Massey-Harris reversed its original response to the war, entered the munitions business in a big way, installed a $300,000 plant in its Toronto works specifically to make eighteen-pounder shrapnel shells, and was sharply criticized for its profit of $400,000 on one contract for 100,000 shells. By contrast, there was the case of the Gooderham family in 1915, in which, according to a contemporary account, "the Imperial Munitions Board at Ottawa found itself facing a 75 percent increase in the already high prices of Acetone—a high explosive compound—supplied from the United States. They decided upon the manufacture in Canada and after investigation it was found that the Gooderham & Worts Distillery [on the waterfront near the foot of Parliament Street] at Toronto was the most suitable for the purpose. The Board thereupon offered to lease the buildings and plant from the company for the duration of the War, the rental to be based on the average net profits of Messrs. Gooderham & Worts for the past three years *plus* interest on their actual investment.

The offer (involving from $300,000 to $500,000) was refused and Colonel [A.E.] Gooderham, for his Company, asked the Munitions Board to accept the buildings and plant for the period named without charge or compensation and with any personal services that he and his son could render given upon the same basis."

Alternatives to military service which would still aid the war effort were proposed in a few quarters. *Saturday Night* magazine suggested that the best use for Canadian recruits was growing wheat and working in factories. The United Farmers of Ontario, which was gaining in political strength on the same "back-to-basics" wave that advocated Prohibition (page 76), met in Toronto on February 3, 1916, and resolved that no men should be pulled from farms for military service. Elsewhere, in sermons and street-corner conversations, people talked of the immorality of Paris and London, convincing some mothers to keep their boys at home—popular songs of the period had the refrains "How're you gonna keep 'em down on the farm, after they've seen Par-eeeeee?" and "You might forget the gas and shells, but you'll never forget the mademoiselles."

Concurrently, however, rallying stories were appearing in newspapers, such as the one in March, 1916, in the *Globe*, stating that City Hall was typical of Toronto office buildings in harbouring "about a hundred unmarried young fellows capable of service, who are not indispensable, and who have no one depending on them." Some commentators attributed the attitude of "slackers" not to a "yellow streak," but to a lack of the proper amount of Imperial education, leaving them susceptible to the attractions of dating girls, "baseball, football, hockey, lacrosse, movies, and the Orange Lodge."

Animosity between soldiers and eligible civilians took a variety of forms, from the subtle propaganda of the "What did *you* do in the Great War, Daddy" billboard at the base of the Boer War monument on University Avenue, to scathing graffiti and back-alley beatings. Soldiers were not, as a group, in favour of Prohibition, but during a demonstration at Queen's Park, some who were found themselves sharing the lawn with an enthusiastic group of young men in civilian clothes. A brawl broke out.

Few had any illusions, after the battle of the Somme in July, 1916, that the "test of strength" had become a fight to the finish; the quest to root out "slackers" and to maximize industrial production became more organized if not more effective. At the behest of the newly formed National Service Board—directed by future prime minister R. B. Bennett—the police undertook a military census of businesses, but once employers found out that it was not compulsory, many refused to give any information, and only 30 percent of the 70,000 cards issued were filled out; Sir John Eaton, for one, declined to allow the census, stating that 1,500 of his employees, whose wages he was still paying, had enlisted. In December, the munitions plants experienced a power shortage, as stores were staying

The "Daddy, what did you do in the Great War?" billboard, set at the base of the South African veterans' memorial on University Avenue opposite Osgoode Hall, was one of the more polite and subtle attempts to shame "slackers" into doing their Imperial duty. Recruiting drives featuring brass bands, rousing speeches, and pretty women were gradually supplemented with nasty graffiti, clandestine beatings, and fistfights when soldiers shared the same piece of ground with groups of nonuniformed men. The grand South African War Memorial bears witness to the adage that the smallest wars often have the biggest monuments. During successful recruiting drives, the queue of volunteers stretched back from the Armouries all the way to the memorial, but they were facing in the opposite direction from the glorious, godlike figures thereon.

open extra hours for the Christmas trade; Joseph Flavelle, the chairman of the Imperial Munitions Board, was enraged.

Women were the hitherto untapped labour force—a "silver bullet" for victory. On January 7, 1916, the Women's Emergency Corps had organized, with Mrs. Archibald Huestis as president, to register women who were willing to do men's work. Two months later, the English suffragette Emily Pankhurst visited Toronto and spoke fervently against men occupying factory jobs that could be held by women; she claimed that in England the ratio of women to men in munitions factories was three to one, and her aim was to make it six to one. At a meeting in June, women war workers rallied to the cause of the Women's Emergency Corps, and elected Mesdames Huestis, Gooderham and Adelaide Plumptre (wife of the rector of St. James Cathedral) to carry the torch for women in munitions factories. That summer, women began to work in banks, in the shipping departments of express offices, in seasonal berry-picking, as drivers of Red Cross vehicles (see the photograph on page 67), and in preparing relief packages. But factory owners were reluctant to hire women while men were still available—in August, although 800 women had registered for industrial work in Toronto, only 200 had been taken on. In September, 1916, a group of Toronto munitions manufacturers visited plants in Montreal which had pioneered the employment of women. At one factory which was producing the largest calibre shells, the visitors were impressed by the intricate work, all done by women "whose sensitive touch and reliability give best results."

As women came forward to work in the factories, one recruiting officer coined a new definition of a "slacker" as a man "who would rather make shells at $3.50 per day than shoot them at $1.10." A campaign sponsored by the Imperial Munitions Board and administered by a Miss Wiseman of the Y.W.C.A. improved sanitary conditions in the plants, so that by November a reported 4,000 women were employed making munitions in Toronto alone. Regardless of this increase, a survey that fall unearthed 14,700 men who were eligible for military service but were employed as munitions workers, postal employees, sales clerks, streetcar conductors, bookkeepers, tailors, chauffeurs, bank tellers or deliverers of bread and groceries—all positions which could theoretically have been filled by women.

By the end of 1916, a move was well underway to commence compulsory registration of eligible men. It merged gradually into a call for outright conscription. Organized labour was utterly against it. On November 16, the socialist leader, school board chairman and future mayor James Simpson spoke against it, and at the same time decried military training in schools, which he called "training little babies to fight on the battlefields of Europe." Five days later, the Toronto Local Council of

Herbert Horsfall was works manager for the Leaside Munitions plant. Born in Sheffield of a Montreal father, Horsfall came to Canada at the age of five and gained his manufacturing experience with wire and cable companies. He was a major in the 109th Regiment of the Canadian Militia.

Another highly successful munitions manufacturer was William Henry Banfield, whose Banfield & Sons metal factory on Pape Avenue thrived on the continuous orders for shells from the British government. Trained as a machinist in Quebec, he travelled from Omaha to California during the years 1864 to 1870, working in the machine shops of the Union Pacific Railroad, then under construction. He came to Toronto in 1877 to accept a position as die-maker for the Dominion Tin Stamping Company, and four years later started his own firm. The latter received orders for eighteen-pounder high-explosive shells from the Shell Committee (later the Munitions Board) in late 1914, at a time when few munitions had ever been manufactured in Canada. Banfield & Son branched out into shrapnel shells, powder cups, cartridge clips, percussion primers and time fuse parts, and at its peak in the war years employed about 1,500 men and women. A Methodist and a veteran of the Fenian Raids, Banfield lived at 219 Fern Avenue.

A not uncommon sight in Toronto during World War I— shell casings piled on the streets. The photograph looks east from Dufferin, on Liberty Street, a block south of King. The munitions factory, staffed mainly by women, operated in the building on the right, the former factory of the Sunbeam Incandescent Light Company and the Toronto Mazda Lamp Works, both firms controlled by Canadian General Electric chairman Frederick Nicholls. The low building on the left was then a components factory for the Russell Motor Car Company. In the left distance, on Mowat Avenue, the partly completed building is the factory of the Toronto Carpet Manufacturing Company. It has recently been converted to chic offices and studios, and is now called the Design Centre.

In the early months of World War One, soldiers were roundly cheered as they left, by the trainload, for the Valcartier mobilization camp and thence to the Western Front. The post-cards above reflect the sentiments of the times; the card on the right is part of a series of three, two of which feature girlfriends left behind, while the third has a vignetted picture and lyrics of "Mum" ("It's hard to find a pal that's true, that you can tell your troubles to, And when you send a letter home, your mother's voice rings in your ears"). Amusingly, the back of the postcard on the left is a letter from "Your loving wife M." to a soldier in France, and presumably within reach of the shops of Paris: "Have you picked me out a nice blouse of crêpe de chine yet. I wish you would send me one or two. I like them so much. I think they are lovely and they are much better than the ones you get out here, but dear, I hope I will get one from you. You know, dear, I am about 38 across the bust, so you can tell them that where you buy it. Pick me a nice mauve one. "

The war defied all predictions and refused to be over by the Christmas of 1914; as the months and years dragged on, casualty figures soared, recruiting became more difficult, and the new recruits and their families had few illusions about what lay ahead. Amputees and cripples were a common sight on the streets, "slackers" were hounded unmercifully and taunted by graffiti on hoardings and old buildings; brownouts became common as munitions plants cut into residential electricity supplies; recruiting officers railed at male munitions workers. The uncertainties of the time seem to be reflected on the faces of the little group on the next page, photographed by William James at the old Union Station.

107

Women voted for it. So grave was the crisis that in some quarters even the activities of local suffragettes were regarded as distracting people's attention away from recruiting and the war effort; on November 27, the Women's Patriotic League passed a resolution urging all women to forget about suffrage until the war was over (as it transpired, the Conservative federal government, in a ploy to ensure support for conscription, enfranchised Canadian women the following year).

In April, 1917, a month which included over 10,000 deaths in the battle of Vimy Ridge, fewer than 5,000 Canadians enlisted. The cow of selfless patriotism had been milked dry. City Police Magistrate George Taylor Denison III gave one Alex Auer a two-year prison sentence for declaring that if conscripted he would shoot the first British officer he met; Auer was released on appeal. Both Great Britain and New Zealand introduced conscription, and the United States, which entered the war the same month as the Canadians fought at Vimy Ridge, also had compulsory service. Bowing to what he perceived as the inevitable, Prime Minister Borden announced in May that he intended to introduce a Military Service Bill, and invited the Liberal leader of the opposition Sir Wilfrid Laurier to join him in a Unionist government. Laurier, who opposed conscription, declined the invitation, but both the Military Service Bill and a subsequent election in December went Borden's way. It was nevertheless apparent that neither the conscription legislation nor the new coalition government reflected any common purpose in the nation.

In Toronto, the nose-to-the-grindstone unity of the populace was further shaken by cost-of-living increases, power shortages, and the widely publicized charges of war profiteering directed against the William Davies Company (pages 194-7), whose president, Joseph Flavelle, had recently been created a baronet for his work as chairman of the Imperial Munitions Board. Supplies of coal in the early months of 1917 had been few and far

between, and families were reported to be burning their fences and furniture; as winter came around again, fuel shortages again became critical (page 190), exacerbated by blatant inequities such as the extravagant use of coal at the new Government House in Rosedale (page 245). The publisher W. J. Gage donated $100,000 to provide comfortable homes at nominal rentals for widows and children of deceased servicemen.

Amidst all the bleakness, one of the few local highlights was the arrival in the city of the 22-year-old aviator and Victoria Cross winner Major Billy Bishop—he was greeted by dense crowds at City Hall on September 27 and addressed an overflow crowd at Massey Hall on October 15. Two days later, he married Margaret Burden, a niece of Sir John Eaton, in a fairy-tale wedding at the jam-packed Timothy Eaton Memorial Church on St. Clair—photographs of the event show thousands of people, mainly women, overflowing from the sidewalk onto the street and straining between each other's hats to catch a glimpse of one of the few romantic heroes of the far-off war.

The final year, 1918, was the most bitter of all on the home front. The cost of living had continued to soar, prompting a number of strikes, including the first by Toronto letter carriers, who had had no increase since 1912, though the purchasing power of their wages had dropped by half: a weekly budget of staple foods for a family of five cost $13.54, compared with $7.92 in 1914. So demoralized was the country that a number of notables formed the Canadian Reconstruction Association in March, with the aim of bettering "the understanding between regions and classes, and easing the transition to peacetime." On Good Friday, anticonscription riots broke out in Quebec City. Farmers in rural Ontario had been placated by assurances that their sons would be exempt from conscription, but in April, when Borden reneged on this concession and lowered the draft age from twenty to nineteen years in response to the collapse of the

Jane Brown was organizer of the Women's Auxiliary, which, with over a thousand volunteer workers, operated in the Toronto Military Hospitals, the Rosedale Demobilization Camp, Exhibition Camp at the C.N.E., and Camp Borden. With Gertrude Vankoughnet, she directed the Tag Day for the Amputations Association's Club House; later, she arranged a series of banquets at the Armouries for returned soldiers and their families; she coordinated the Red Cross Society's aid to victims of the 1918 influenza epidemic, and five years later did the same thing during the Cochrane typhoid epidemic. The wife of wholesale stationer Albert Brown, she lived at 181 Crescent Road in Rosedale. One of her two sons, a captain in the 48th Highlanders, was killed at Passchendaele in 1917.

William Edward Turley used his war experiences on the Western Front as the grist for a series of stories entitled "Tales From The Trenches" which appeared in the Evening Telegram. An Englishman with seemingly little direction to his life, he married at twenty, then immigrated to Canada, where he held an astonishing variety of jobs, including machine operator, navvy, labourer, railroad worker, waiter, woodworker, fireman, and newspaper reporter. He was amateur bantamweight boxing champion of Canada, in 1907-8. Turley parlayed his interest in veterans' affairs into the secretaryship of the Great War Veterans Association, which organized and lobbied for protection of and assistance to widows and children of the dead, and helped returned soldiers; the G.W.V.A. evolved during the 1920s into the Canadian Legion.

Fifth British Army, the United Farmers of Ontario marched on the federal government in Ottawa. As if the privations of wartime were not enough, a flu epidemic started in Spain that summer, spread to Europe, and was carried all around the world by returning soldiers. Six million people died in three months; in Toronto, authorities closed schools and theatres, and suspended all meetings, but were unable to prevent 1,259 fatalities.

The event which best reflects the alienation of soldiers from the home front took place during the last summer of the war. The Great War Veterans Association held their national convention in the city starting on July 29. It was a fractious affair, with disputes on regional lines about resettlement policy and proportional voting, and carping about the maintenance of military discipline when delegates criticized their superior officers. On the evening of Thursday, the first of August, the owner of the White City Cafe at 433 Yonge Street ejected a returned soldier—one Private Cluderay of Dundonald Street. The following night, his mates avenged him against "the alien keepers and waiters" of a number of restaurants along Yonge and elsewhere. A crowd, led by soldiers in uniform, gathered at about six o'clock outside the Colonial Cafe at 349 Yonge Street; a small group of policemen attempted to block their entrance, but a fight broke out which quickly escalated into a pitched battle. Windows were smashed in a hail of rocks and bricks, and looters climbed through the broken windows and cleaned out the interior; the staff had beaten a hasty retreat through the back exit. According to reports, "the crowd was only pacified when they saw that no tobacco or cigars remained in the store." The police "were unable to take any prisoners."

A short time later, the mob reassembled at the corner of College and Yonge, and marched to the White City Cafe, which they utterly demolished. Soldiers threw tables through the windows, cheered on by a crowd of civilians which blocked traffic on Yonge. The mob, which had grown to a size estimated at somewhere between 200 and 400, then moved down Yonge Street, smashing and looting restaurants, most of which were owned by Greeks. Several of the owners and employees—who argued they were loyal and "had brothers fighting [the Turks] in Saloniki"— were compelled to salute the flag or face the consequences. Although the police had been reinforced by 100 soldiers from the Exhibition Camp, they chose not to intervene, "due to the size and temper of the mob."

Over the course of the next several hours, before the rioters disbanded at about 2:30 a.m., they demolished seven Yonge Street restaurants and the Klees butcher shop at number 504—probably because of its German-sounding name; they also smashed up the New London restaurant at 311 Queen Street West, the Alexander at 750 Queen Street West, and broke the windows of the Sunnyside restaurant at Roncesvalles and Queen.

When the rioters returned the following night, the police took to the fray with their batons, arresting ten and hauling away two dozen wounded, including a lieutenant colonel named A. T. Hunter. The following day, the third of August, the G.W.V.A. convention passed a resolution condemning the rioting, but two days later, on the fifth, it resumed. The next day, about 5,000 returned soldiers gathered in Queen's Park to protest alleged police brutality—especially of cripples— and some agitators attempted to restart the riot. The mayor read a warning proclamation, and 500 soldiers marched in to disperse the crowd. That touched off another brawl, during which several more participants were injured.

The Board of Police Commissioners published its report on the incidents on October 19. As a result, some members of the force were dismissed and others promoted. Less than a month later, the Armistice was signed.

Industry & The Waterfront

Not much remains of the old Toronto waterfront, largely because the shoreline keeps being moved. The Harbour Commission Building once stood proudly at the end of its own pier, on the water, sometimes with the commissioners' yacht *Bethalma* moored in front; today, the building is landlocked and surrounded by freeways and tall buildings. A century ago, boys swam from the Queen's Wharf, in plain view of the Queen's Hotel (now the Royal York site), and "a stately lady used to sit at her hotel window and survey the bathers through an opera or a field glass, until she made a complaint with the result that bathing without trunks was prohibited." Boathouses—allegedly the trysting places of the young (page 296)—lined the shore, and some of the finest houses in the city lined Front Street. The bay was relatively unpolluted, although by the turn of the century, when the main sewage outfall shared the bay with the drinking-water intake, the city experienced a number of typhoid fever outbreaks (page 168).

From the earliest days, the harbour was crowded with little boats, lake ships, steamers, and ferries which plied the bay to jetties on the Island. The arrival of the railways (page 115) threw a barrier between the lake and the citizens. The city had established, in 1850, a Harbour Trust, and appointed an aggressive harbourmaster who lobbied for changes such as the rebuilding of the Queen's Wharf, but there was little overall planning, the populace being more interested in roads and rails, so private companies added to their facilities along the harbour as they saw fit. The situation went from bad to worse in the 1870s and 1880s; a storm had broken through the Eastern Gap in 1858, and silt began to clog the channels. The Harbour Trust's business clique wanted to spend as little money as possible, and its neglect brought about a decline in the significance of the port. Ships had to be towed through the Western Gap. In the stagnant shallows between the wharves, rotting garbage shared the water with broken timbers from rotting wharves.

Reform came in 1911, when a spirited campaign championed by Toronto city council and supported by much of the press approved the founding of the Toronto Harbour Commission, and granted it power to borrow money, rebuild dock facilities, and reclaim land from the "1,300-acre swamp." By the 1950s, however, Queen's Quay was once again a derelict and dingy area of docks and sheds and places like the Electric Diner (page 114).

"Harbourfront" was to change all that. Touted in 1978 as "a unique opportunity to redevelop the prime waterfront lands as an extension of the urban fabric," it has had dubious success at making Toronto "once again a city which is built at the edge of the harbour." Some of the "narrow" buildings south of the Gardiner Expressway have, in the

The Harbour Commission Building, drawn in the 1930s by an unknown artist. The uncertain fate of the harbour in the early part of this century prompted the Board of Trade and other groups to lobby city council for a permanent commission which would administer and develop the waterfront. The result, in May, 1911, was the Toronto Harbour Commissioners' Act and the subsequent erection of the Harbour Commission Building. Initially, the building stood on the water's edge, but in the ensuing decades, as the commissioners fulfilled their mandate and filled the bay to provide more industrial and railroad land, the building became marooned and now sits on dry land a few hundred yards from the waterline.

measured words of a *Globe & Mail* editorial, "assumed forms and qualities that can only be described as cheap and ugly." The huge new domed stadium occupies some of the railway land east of Spadina. Toronto's best-known landmark, the C.N. Tower, occupies another piece of land there, and gives an unfortunate, albeit spectacular, view of the waterfront and the city, demonstrating conclusively how much of it is wind-blown concrete, and how much is devoted to the automobile.

Late in the 1870s, Alexander Keith and his brother George incorporated themselves as the Toronto-Hamilton Navigation Company and introduced cheap round-trip tickets—35 cents return from Toronto to Hamilton. Subsequently, they sold the business, and Keith returned to his father's company, which he reorganized as Keith's Ltd., selling plumbing, steam heating, refrigeration and automatic sprinkling equipment. He also developed an economical method of producing acetylene gas by automatically feeding granulated calcium carbide into water. This had considerable value, as during the early years of the automobile, headlights were usually powered by acetylene, fed from a tank on the running board; as well, much rural house lighting was by acetylene lamps. Keith was born in Toronto, and served in the Queen's Own Rifles. He lived at 199 Lyndhurst Avenue.

CTA JAMES 483

The Yonge Street wharf, about 1910.

111

The Harbour Master's house, with observation tower, at the Western Gap in the 1920s. The observation tower and lighthouse, built in 1861, still stands on a grassy little island surrounded by streetcar tracks and traffic, at what is now the intersection of Fleet Street and Lakeshore Boulevard, just west of Bathurst. In the distance, at the extreme left, is the Toronto Municipal Abattoir—the building with the square Italianate campaniles at its corners; the National Casket Company was at the southeast corner of Niagara and Tecumseh. Also visible are two large gasometers belonging to the Consumers' Gas Company. The Dominion Packing Company buildings in the middle distance block any view of Fort York.

CTA JAMES 1512

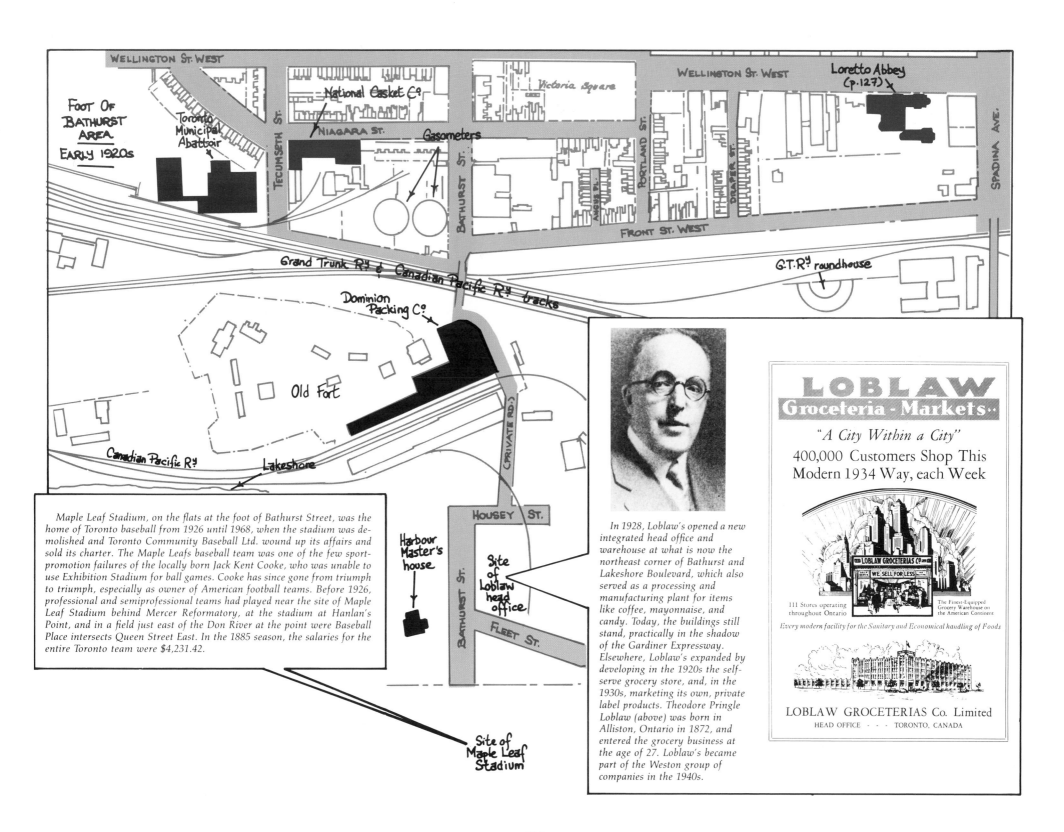

FOOT OF BATHURST AREA EARLY 1920s

WELLINGTON ST. WEST

National Casket Co.

Toronto Municipal Abattoir

Niagara St.

Gasometers

Tecumseth St.

Bathurst St.

Angus Pl.

Portland St.

Draper St.

Victoria Square

WELLINGTON ST. WEST

Loretto Abbey (p.127)

Spadina Ave.

FRONT ST. WEST

Grand Trunk R⁹ & Canadian Pacific R⁹ tracks

G.T.R⁹ roundhouse

Dominion Packing Co.

Old Fort

Canadian Pacific R⁹

Lakeshore

(PRIVATE RD.)

HOUSEY ST.

Harbour Master's house

Site of Loblaw head office

BATHURST ST.

FLEET ST.

Site of Maple Leaf Stadium

Maple Leaf Stadium, on the flats at the foot of Bathurst Street, was the home of Toronto baseball from 1926 until 1968, when the stadium was demolished and Toronto Community Baseball Ltd. wound up its affairs and sold its charter. The Maple Leafs baseball team was one of the few sport-promotion failures of the locally born Jack Kent Cooke, who was unable to use Exhibition Stadium for ball games. Cooke has since gone from triumph to triumph, especially as owner of American football teams. Before 1926, professional and semiprofessional teams had played near the site of Maple Leaf Stadium behind Mercer Reformatory, at the stadium at Hanlan's Point, and in a field just east of the Don River at the point were Baseball Place intersects Queen Street East. In the 1885 season, the salaries for the entire Toronto team were $4,231.42.

In 1928, Loblaw's opened a new integrated head office and warehouse at what is now the northeast corner of Bathurst and Lakeshore Boulevard, which also served as a processing and manufacturing plant for items like coffee, mayonnaise, and candy. Today, the buildings still stand, practically in the shadow of the Gardiner Expressway. Elsewhere, Loblaw's expanded by developing in the 1920s the self-serve grocery store, and, in the 1930s, marketing its own, private label products. Theodore Pringle Loblaw (above) was born in Alliston, Ontario in 1872, and entered the grocery business at the age of 27. Loblaw's became part of the Weston group of companies in the 1940s.

The Electric Diner Murder

On Queen's Quay, just east of the foot of York Street, stood the Electric Diner, a popular cafe and hangout in the late 1950s. The area, west of the old ferry docks at the foot of Bay Street, was sleazy and shabby. The Electric Diner itself had a reputation as a place where you could get a cheque cashed, or a small loan as an advance on a paycheque at a point or two above bank interest. It had two owners, Abe Rubinoff and Mike Orleski—the former made the loans and cashed the paycheques of truck drivers who could not get to the bank before it closed on Friday afternoons.

At the beginning of July, 1959, a 23-year-old convicted armed robber named Ronald Watts escaped from Kingston penitentiary and made his way to Toronto. Drifters often gravitated to the Jarvis Street area, where rooms were cheap and no one was very curious. Nearby, at the Reliance Club on Pembroke Street, Watts met the bouncer, 42-year-old George Burton. Burton had spent his childhood in Toronto, but moved to New York in his teens; there, he had had a dispute with a friend, which he settled by knocking him down and backing over him with his car. He was convicted of second-degree murder but was eventually paroled and deported; he drifted to Toronto and took a room on Pembroke Street near the club. Burton had been to the Electric Diner on a Friday afternoon, a payday, and had seen the owner take a truck driver's paycheque and squat down behind the till to get money. Figuring the cafe to be an easy target, Burton had stolen two .357 Magnums, and only needed a partner; Watts was willing. The following payday, July 16, 1959, a blazingly hot summer day, the pair stole a 1957 Dodge sedan from a parking lot on Dundas, and drove to the Electric Diner.

Meanwhile, Arthur Keay, a former policeman employed as a driver by Trans Canada Pipelines, had picked up some of his company's executives at the airport and delivered them to a launch which took them to a directors' meeting at the Royal Canadian Yacht Club on the Island. Ordinarily, the directors met at the company's offices at Wellington and Jordan, but as the building was being painted, and the smell in the boardroom was offensive in the heat, they had decided to meet on the Island; Keay, who would ordinarily have returned to duties, was told to wait around to meet the returning launch. Killing time, he went to the Electric Diner, sat down on a stool next to the cash register, and ordered a ginger-ale. Beneath a loose board in the floor below the till was $35,000 in cash.

The door opened, and there was a shout: "Everybody on the floor!" Before Keay had a chance to turn around or move, Watts rounded the counter and came up to the till. He pointed his gun at Keay, said "*You* get down on the floor," and stooped down below the counter. Thinking that the gunman was alone, Keay grabbed his ginger-ale bottle and clobbered him. Watts dropped the gun and Keay dived over the counter and wrestled with him. Burton ran up and hit Keay on the head with his gun butt. The gun accidentally fired, blowing a hole the size of a fist in Watts's head!

In a panic, Burton ran back to the Dodge and fled at high speed. A few blocks away, at Fleet Street, he broadsided a truck. Two policemen, unaware of the drama at the Electric Diner, drove up and were absolutely agape when Burton emerged from the wrecked car, holding the revolver in his limp hand and babbling "Is my partner okay?"

Keay recalled that he would never have jumped Watts if he had known that Burton was also there. Regardless, he was proclaimed a hero, and the owners of the Electric Diner gave him $500; the police also gave him $500 as well as a citation, and the insurance company gave him a valuable tea set—altogether a good payday, he felt. Burton was sentenced to hang, but the sentence was commuted and he died in prison. Keay spent another fifteen years with Trans Canada Pipelines before retiring; today, in his eighties, he is a well-known advocate and practitioner of racewalking.

Railways

The railway lines which stitch together the patchwork quilt of Toronto have been a mixed blessing: without them, there would have been little of the prosperity which created the modern city; with them, the waterfront has been cross-hatched with tracks which block access to Toronto's major natural amenity—the lake. Bird's-eye views of the harbour before the 1850s show a bustling port of docks and sheds, the harbour dotted with sailing ships, the streets with delivery carts, the warehouses and shops crowding up to the bay. Over the century and a quarter since, the harbour has been repeatedly filled to create more industrial land, and a no-man's land of tracks now isolates the city from the lake. The redevelopment of these railway and dock lands has been further confounded by the existence of the Gardiner Expressway, and the predilection of some developers, with the acquiescence of some politicians, to build lines of highrises along the waterfront.

In a land with a lot of winter, and difficult terrain at the best of times, railways permitted efficient year-round transportation in a manner only dreamed of by the earliest settlers. Toronto's first railway, the Ontario, Simcoe & Huron, revived the old "Toronto passage"—the *raison d'être* of the original Fort Toronto—and connected the city via Barrie with Collingwood on Georgian Bay. It was the vision of one Frederick Chase Capreol, a friend and associate of the Sir Allan McNab who had in 1845 incorporated the Great Western Railway, and of engineer Casimir Gzowski.

Capreol lived in a house at 24 Clarence Square, in the dining room of which hung a portrait of his grandfather, painted by Sir Joshua Reynolds—an indication of how venerable and influential his family had been. In May, 1847, he started serious preparations for his railway with the announcement of a lottery, the proceeds of which would purchase 100,000 acres of land. When sold, the land would pay for the construction of the railway. Writing in the 1890s in his *Landmarks of Toronto*, John Ross Robertson noted: "The plan was viewed with distrust by some, and condemned as immoral by others, and as a consequence fell through."

Undaunted, Capreol organized a company with a board of directors composed of eminent local businessmen. He used his influence to get a charter drawn up and passed by the legislature; when the governor general refused to approve it, the persistent Capreol went to England, "laid

Toronto's two Union Stations.(Above) The first one opened west of York Street (a block to the west of the current one) in 1873.(Below) The current Union Station, seen in a photograph probably taken about 1918 which looks east along Front Street. The children and basket-laden women crossing the street were probably going to the ferry docks, where they would board a ferry for the Island. In the distance is the tower of the old Union Station; on the right, the future location of the Royal York Hotel, built a decade later, at the end of the 1920s.

the bill at the foot of the throne and in the short space of seven weeks was back with the royal assent." Capreol renamed his project the Northern Railway, signed with a New York contractor, and ordered a silver spade and an ornamental oak wheelbarrow for the sod-turning ceremony at which Lady Elgin, wife of the governor general, was to do the honours. However, the railway's directors, "animated by jealousy," fired Capreol a few days before the ceremony! Robertson wrote: "At this time, the whole board which dismissed him so cavalierly had only £37 10s. at stake in the enterprise, while Mr. Capreol had spent out of his private means £12,350. To recompense him for his outlay he was voted by the directors bonds to the amount of £11,000, and beside this sum he never received a dollar from the company till [30-odd years later], when an annuity of $1,200 per year was granted him, which lapsed at the time of his death."

As Robertson described it, the sod-turning took place in fine weather on October 15, 1851, "in the presence of a great assemblage on the Esplanade, just west of Simcoe Street, opposite the parliament buildings. Lady Elgin pressed her dainty foot upon the richly ornamented spade, threw up a little dirt into the handsomely carved oak wheelbarrow which Mayor Bowes, who assisted in the ceremony, wheeled a short distance and then emptied. On this occasion Mayor Bowes was resplendent in a cocked hat, sword, knee breeches, silk stockings and shoes with silver buckles." Adding to the circus atmosphere were flags a-flying and banners with such apt slogans as "Never Despair" and "Perseverance Conquers."

The first train on the completed line pulled away from the wooden shed "which had been dignified by the name of station" opposite the Queen's Hotel (the Royal York site) on the morning of May 16, 1853; it consisted of the engine, a box car and a passenger car, and the first ticket was bought by a shoemaker named Maher, "who objected to paying a dollar to ride 30 miles." An indication of the railway's wild and woolly route, and its lightweight rolling stock, can be gleaned from an account of the line's first accident in July, 1853, between the city and Weston, when "the engine struck a cow, throwing off the rails the coach, which rolled down a steep embankment, totally wrecking the car and severely injuring an Irish passenger and two brakemen, who were its only occupants."

Two years later, the Great Western Railway, running between Niagara Falls and Sarnia via Hamilton, connected New York railways by a short cut with those of Michigan and beyond. A branch line from Hamilton entered Toronto with, as the historian J. M. S. Careless has pointed out, the intention of tying Toronto into a system whose hub was to be Hamilton. Instead, over the next few years, Hamilton and the rest of the province came increasingly under the shadow of Toronto, which had better lake connections and a larger population. In October, 1856, the eastern division of the Grand Trunk Railway from Montreal reached the city; construction was already near completion on a western section to Guelph, and soon thereafter the Grand Trunk reached Berlin (Kitchener) and finally Sarnia.

The first Grand Trunk Railway station was at the bridge near the mouth of the Don. In the early part of 1857, the railway company laid

tracks westward from that station, skirting the old jail at the foot of Berkeley Street and running along the south side of Front Street to the Northern Railway's depot at Bay Street. The following year, the three railways—the Northern, Great Western, and Grand Trunk—built the original Union Station, just west of the foot of York Street. A wooden building with a platform roof supported by posts with fancy scrollwork brackets, it had a ladies' waiting room, a refreshment room and a barber shop in addition to ticket, telegraph, and baggage offices.

The Esplanade, which had been deeded in trust by the province in 1818 for eventual development as a carriageway and promenade, became a right of way for the Grand Trunk Railway following a hotly contested po-

Sir Donald Mann, owner with Sir William Mackenzie of a controlling interest in the Canadian Northern Railway, was much less involved in Toronto utilities than was his partner (page 39). Born in Acton in 1867, he early abandoned farming for lumbering; through the latter, he met Mackenzie, and they embarked on their great railway-building adventure. Like Mackenzie, Mann was known for his great physical strength; one yarn recounts how, during a venture in China, the huge and muscular Mann was challenged to a duel by a Russian count. To Mann fell the choice of weapons; upon his choosing broadaxes, his adversary hastily withdrew. After the bankruptcy of the C.N.R., Mann lived quietly in Toronto in a house at 161 St. George Street. His splendid summer residence, built around 1905 at the southeast corner of Fallingbrook and Kingston Road in what was then semi-rural Birch Cliffe, burned down in the 1930s; the property became a golf course, though part of it is now the Toronto Hunt Club grounds. Mackenzie had died in 1923; Mann died at home in November, 1934, at the age of 81, almost a forgotten figure from an earlier generation. His death merited only modest attention in the newspapers.

In 1896, David Blythe Hanna was appointed by Messrs. Mackenzie and Mann as superintendent of their first piece of railway—the Lake Manitoba Railway & Canal Company. Over the next two decades, as the partnership of Mackenzie & Mann flourished with the Canadian Northern Railway and then foundered into bankruptcy, Hanna unerringly rose through the ranks. When the government in 1918 took over the system, renaming it the Canadian National Railway, Hanna was appointed president. The government stipulated that it wanted politics kept out of the new national railway, and Hanna took the admonition literally. Before the campaign leading to the December, 1921, election, Hanna issued an order forbidding any CNR employee participation, and subsequently fired three employees who had worked on the Liberal campaign. The Liberals defeated the incumbent Conservatives, and the new prime minister, W. L. Mackenzie-King, began to pry into the CNR's methods of operation in a way that challenged Hanna's independence. Hanna then issued a new order, banning any employees from nomination to any public post. One Manitoba railwayman, who wanted to run for the Liberals in the forthcoming provincial election, took his case to Mackenzie King, who overruled Hanna. The latter promptly retired. Several years later, he agreed to become the first chairman of the Ontario Liquor Control Board, a position he held briefly before resigning in favour of Sir Henry Drayton. His stories of his railway days, recounting the events of the early 1880s with the Grand Trunk and Sir Augustus Nanton, were collected into a 1924 book by Arthur Hawkes, published by Macmillan under the title Trains of Recollection. He lived at 37 Cluny Avenue.

At the foot of Bay Street, crowds of pedestrians crossed the railroad tracks to reach the Toronto Ferry Company wharves for the trip to the Island.

litical fight between the railway and its contractor Gzowski & Company on the one hand, and the city council on the other. In their pursuit of progress and industrialization, voters and politicians sacrificed the city's waterfront to the demands of the iron horse. What had been prime residential land deteriorated into weedy desolation, the air full of fly-ash from the constant shunting of wood-burning locomotives. In the period from the late 1860s through the early 1880s, three other main railway lines entered the city: the Toronto, Grey & Bruce Railway connected with both Teeswater and Owen Sound; the Credit Valley Railway went south-westwards through Woodstock to St. Thomas; the Toronto & Nipissing, a Gooderham family project, went north to Haliburton and elsewhere. These lines crowded together with the earlier ones along the waterfront.

In 1871, railway owners had agreed to feed their tangle of tracks on the waterfront into a new Union Station. The original one was demolished, and for two years passengers used a shed on the western side of Simcoe Street, while the grand new structure arose south of Front Street between York and Simcoe. A massive building and the largest station in Canada, it was nevertheless overcrowded almost from the day it opened in 1873. Further complications arose due to the fact that the Toronto, Grey & Bruce railway was a narrow-gauge line, and a third rail had to be added to permit its trains ingress to the station. An elevated iron walkway dubbed "The Bridge of Sighs" crossed the tracks, connecting the passenger areas with Simcoe Street; thousands of immigrants dragged their possessions along it, through the steam and smoke, to start new lives in the city.

It was an era which took railway building to excess, and the Ontario of 1880 found itself with too many miles of track trying to serve too few people in too uncertain an economic climate. With the creation of the Montreal-based Canadian Pacific Railway, competition for traffic in Ontario increased, forcing a number of amalgamations of little lines with the shark-like bigger ones. The Grand Trunk Railway absorbed the Great Western, the Northern, and the Toronto & Nipissing. The C.P.R. bought out the Credit Valley and the Toronto, Grey & Bruce railways, and although its main line ran a long distance to the north and bypassed Toronto completely, it ran a separate line from Montreal and Ottawa into the city—an 1892 bylaw gave it, too, a right of way along the Esplanade into Union Station. John Ross Robertson, in his *Landmarks of Toronto*, described the situation in the early 1890s: "When the present Union Station was built it was amply large for its purpose. Trains were small, consisting of from three to five cars, but now that trains are much larger and more frequent the building is found to be too small. If the two great companies occupying it [the C.P.R. and the Grand Trunk] come to an agreement the station will be torn down and a new and larger one erected on its site. Now the station is large enough for one road but not for both." Additions to Union Station put a new wing along Front Street (illustrated in the postcards on these pages), but provided no permanent solution.

The local situation was further complicated at the turn of the century by the development of the Canadian Northern Railway, a creation of the redoubtable local capitalists William Mackenzie and Donald Mann, with additional local direction from Zebulon Lash and Frederic Nicholls and financing from the Bank of Commerce and an English pool of capital managed by R. M. Horne-Payne. The Canadian Northern had been centred in Winnipeg, but harboured dreams of becoming a second transcontinental

The Queen's Hotel occupied the site of today's Royal York, on Front Street between York and Bay. In its heyday, before the turn of the century, it was reputed to offer an ideal combination of practicality and gentility, as well as a fine view of the scarcely polluted bay and Lake Ontario. Travelling royalty, including Grand Duke Alexis of Russia and the Duke and Duchess of Connaught (he the third son of Queen Victoria and later Canada's governor general), stayed there, as did Canada's vice-regals, and prominent politicians like Sir John A. Macdonald. "It has excellent cuisine and wine cellar," said an early account, "and the table-attendance and general management are such as give unbounded satisfaction."

line. The Grand Trunk Railway, with terminals in Maine and Chicago, had the same dream. In 1903, with the country's economy growing steadily, both railways went looking for a federal charter and either subsidies or bond guarantees. The Liberal government of Sir Wilfrid Laurier, rather than choosing between them or forcing them to amalgamate into one transcontinental system, saw more political benefits in chartering both.

In April, 1904, one of the worst fires in Toronto's history devastated the waterfront area, including the land east of Union Station, between York and Bay streets. The Canadian Pacific and the Grand Trunk agreed to collaborate on a new station, and in 1906 incorporated the Toronto Terminals Railway Company to build it. In the madcap atmosphere of the next several years, during which the Canadian Northern and the Grand Trunk both built towards different Pacific Coast termini, the new Union Station was one of the few projects which made little progress. Delay followed indecision until, in 1913, a design was finally approved. By that time, both the Grand Trunk and its arch-rival, the Canadian Northern, were tottering on the brink of bankruptcy, their credit more or less exhausted because of a depression, the collapse of the western land boom,

Both the Queen's Hotel and the Royal York have been inextricably linked with the railways and Union Station. This hotel postcard, published in the 1930s, noted on the back that all public rooms were air-conditioned, and advised users to affix a two-cent stamp for destinations in the British Empire, United States, and South America. By the late 1950s the hotel was in chronic danger of being overbooked. An addition was built to the east (right of the card) which, though it was faithful to the hotel's style, was glaringly white for several years compared with the grimy stone of the 30-year-old original. The Royal York had replaced the Queen's Hotel, which had in turn replaced the house of colonial official William Powell. Powell's house, built about 1800, looked out on the sand and reeds of breezy Toronto Bay, in the bucolic period before the waterfront became crowded with wharves, industries, railway tracks, and the Union Station. A Canadian Pacific Railways brochure of 1929-30 gave some advice for visitors: "the winters are just cold enough to make the air bracing and healthy, and although Toronto does not usually have much snow, conditions are such that ice skating and certain other forms of outdoor sport may be indulged in during the season." It went on to list taxicab rates to three representative locations—75 cents to North Toronto station (at Yonge and Shaftesbury), 50 cents to the steamship docks, and $1.50 to the Leaside airport.

and repeated war scares in Europe. In 1914, when war broke out in Europe, rail transportation to the west began to dry up. A year later, the Grand Trunk and its subsidiaries collapsed.

The Canadian Northern fared no better. In order to forestall its collapse and the resulting catastrophe for creditors—the most notable of which was the Bank of Commerce—the Canadian government had been forced to guarantee Canadian Northern Railway bonds though most felt them to be of little value. A Royal Commission of Inquiry recommended the nationalization of the Canadian Northern and the Grand Trunk and its subsidiaries. Out of the mess came the Canadian Northern Acquisition Bill of 1917, provoking a strange and vicious parliamentary debate in which the Conservative government found itself putting a value onto stock that was held by a bank and by former Canadian Northern directors such as Zebulon Lash, all of whom had torpedoed the Liberal party in the 1911 federal election (page 228). Was it a belated reward to the "Toronto Eighteen," or simply a responsible move by a Conservative government which had inherited a mess and was trying to save the country's credit? Regardless, the acquisition bill passed, heralding the birth of the Canadian National Railway. Mackenzie and Mann, the former multimillionaires, were each allowed to keep 100 shares, valued at $16.66 apiece.

Meanwhile, the construction of Union Station was still proceeding at a snail's pace. The Canadian Pacific Railway showed its disapproval by building a new North Toronto station (page 13) in 1916, which allowed its passengers a gracious entry into the city. The great hall of the new Union Station was completed in 1919, but the railways could not agree on how the tracks were to approach it. Five years later, they agreed to cooperate on the building of a viaduct, and completed it in time for the station's formal opening by the Prince of Wales during his 1927 Canadian tour. Four years later, with the building of the York Street underpass, the grand scheme of a generation earlier stood complete. A more modest, but more modern, transportation terminal opened the same year—the bus terminal on Bay at Edward.

After twenty-five years of planning and construction, the new Union Station had a heyday of only twenty years. Automobile and bus travel replaced many short-distance railway journeys, while airplanes replaced the longer ones. Travel fashions and destinations changed. The railways, especially the Canadian Pacific, did not stand to lose by this unexpected turn of technological events, as they held great quantities of land in potentially desirable locations. In the 1960s, Marathon Realty, the real-estate arm of the C.P.R., attempted a multimillion-dollar redevelopment of the North Toronto station area, and floated plans to demolish Union Station and redevelop "the railway lands" along the harbour. Both plans were vigorously opposed by citizen lobbies, fired by the same idealism which concurrently saved Old City Hall and the Holy Trinity Church from demolition for the Eaton Centre project. Union Station is today tied into the city's subway and commuter-train systems, and is a hub of activity, though the passenger trains operating under the Via Rail and Amtrak banners lack the prestige and elegance of those from the railways' golden age.

Grant Morden

A number of Canadians sought their fortunes or made their names in England. The most famous is probably Max Aitken (1879-1964), born in Ontario and raised in New Brunswick, who became a British Member of Parliament, newspaper owner, financier and, raised to the peerage as Lord Beaverbrook, a powerful force in British Empire political life through the Second World War years. More recently, there was Roy Thomson (1894-1976), a barber's son born in the rowhouse at 32 Monteith just east of Church Street, who made his fortune starting in the 1930s with radio stations and newspapers in northern Ontario. Like Aitken, he was elevated to the peerage, as Lord Thomson of Fleet. His son Kenneth, the second Lord Thomson, is a prominent resident of Toronto and reputed to be one of the richest men in Canada; both he and his father, unlike Lord Beaverbrook, have shown little interest in political power, preferring the greener pastures of business.

A contemporary of Lord Beaverbrook's, who founded Canada Steamship Lines and for a time operated in Beaverbrook's league of wealth and influence in England, was Walter Grant Morden. Born in Prince Edward County in 1880, he was "descended from United Empire Loyalist stock on both sides" and the son of the long-time captain of the steamer *Pictou*, which plied the Toronto-Port Dalhousie route. Grant Morden was educated at Toronto Collegiate Institute and took his first job selling furniture and pianos; he next became a representative of the Canadian Cabinet Company and Canadian Wood Manufacturing Company and travelled to England, where he made some influential financial contacts. In 1910, when he was 30 years old, he put together a scheme to amalgamate a number of the old Great Lakes shipping companies with which he was familiar from his boyhood; he was "a wizard with figures, an accountant to the 'nth' degree," and a man with "determination to succeed, grit physical and mental, and ambition." He gained the confidence of Lord Furness and Sir Trevor Dawson of Vickers and returned to Canada in 1912 with $15 million of financing, with which he formed Canada Steamship Lines. Over the next several months, he took over a number of companies, including the Richelieu & Ontario Navigation Company, the Quebec Steamships Company, the Niagara Navigation Company, the Northern Navigation Company, the Thousand Island Steamboat Company, the Chicago Steam Navigation Company, and the Century Coal Company; when the war broke out a year later, Canada Steamship Lines became a financial success, its ships and docks—in Toronto at the foot of Bay Street—a familiar sight throughout the Great Lakes. For years thereafter, one of the largest freighters in the C.S.L. fleet was a 14,000-tonner called the *W. Grant Morden*.

Morden did not stay in Canada, although he had investments trading on the Montreal Stock Exchange and maintained a residence on St. James Street there. In the early months of the Great War, he served as staff officer in England to the Canadian minister of militia, and became honorary lieutenant colonel of the Sixth Royal Canadian Hussars. However, he found the army atmosphere stifling and, gaining his leave, "adventured to Switzerland." There he got in touch with the brothers Dreyfus, whose formula for "doping" airplanes assured better performance in cold and wet weather (the cloth skins of airplanes needed to be treated or "doped" in order to make the skin smooth, strong, and impervious to wind and weather). He then evidently ventured into Germany, probably travelling as a neutral American businessman, and managed to obtain doping secrets from the Zeppelin Company. (Little information remains about these exploits, but Morden's son still has his father's Special Service medals.) Morden's interest in aviation translated into the chairmanship of the British Cellulose & Chemical Manufacturing Company, a postwar leader in supplies for the aviation industry, with a reputed capital of £6 million. Shares in the company jumped rapidly from sixpence to £14.10s, and by 1919 Morden was exceptionally wealthy, the owner of a huge estate called "Heatherden Hall" in Buckinghamshire on the outskirts of London.

His business contacts translated into political influence: he became an intimate of the Earl of Birkinhead, Viscount Long of Wraxall, and the Rt. Hon. Sir William Bull, all of whom gave him support when he ran successfully in 1918 for the Unionists in the Brentford-Chiswick riding (he later reverted to the Conservative party). At "Heatherden Hall," Walter Long and his colleagues agreed to join Lloyd George's first Unionist war cabinet; their discussions occurred on the same day that Lloyd George and Bonar Law were discussing cabinet matters at Lord Beaverbrook's house at Cherkley.

Morden returned to Toronto in 1920 and attended a banquet in his honour given in Ottawa by the Empire Parliamentary Association. The *Star Weekly* headlined its story: "Grant Morden Famous At Forty—Torontonian Has Done Big Things," and described him as "a financier and old Toronto boy." In his speech to the association, Morden described how the future of Canada was in steel, and announced the creation of the British Empire Steel Corporation.

Although Grant Morden started out modestly, selling furniture and pianos in Toronto, he had a knack for making influential financial and social contacts. In 1912, when he was 32 years old, he arranged the financing and amalgamated a number of Great Lakes steamship companies into the Canada Steamship Lines. By then, he was a permanent resident of England, and had a sensational rise to wealth and influence before the 1929 Wall Street crash wiped him out. The portrait above is by "Spy"—the caricaturist Leslie Ward—and depicts Morden as the Master of the Avon Vale Hunt.

If Your Holidays Come One Day at a Time

Spend the day on the lake. The restful comfort of the lake boats, the cool, fresh, lake-swept breezes will invigorate and refresh you.

Arrange to take one of the daily trips from Toronto to Niagara-on-the-Lake, Queenston, Lewiston, Hamilton or Grimsby.

There is a trip to fit in with whatever day or time you have at your disposal.

Information at any of our ticket offices. In Toronto Phone Adelaide 4200.

If you would have a real vacation of a week or more see description on opposite page of Canada's most wonderful boat trip.

CANADA STEAMSHIP LINES, LIMITED
Toronto Office: 46 Yonge Street

"NIAGARA TO THE SEA"

Canada's Wonder-Trip

The World's Most Famous Scenery

MILES of beautiful Lakes, Rivers and Rapids, including the Thousand Islands (the Venice of America). Quaint old Quebec (cradle of New France). The lower St. Lawrence (rivalling the fjords of Norway). The miracle-working shrine of Ste. Anne de Beaupre. The world-famous Saguenay River Canyon, compared with which the Rhine and the Danube are insignificant in grandeur. Murray Bay, with its duplication of the west coast of Scotland scenery, and the marvellous rapids, for which Europe has no counterpart. Spend a week—or a fortnight—on the lakes and rivers of Quebec, where the architecture and customs of the early French regime still survive.

From the moment you board a "Canada Steamship Lines" boat at Toronto, you will find each hour of the journey filled with new and surprising delights. The route is one of wondrous beauty—the boats are floating palaces, providing a new experience in travel de luxe.

Make your vacation a water trip this year—the kind of holiday that promotes health and refreshes the mind.

Send two cents postage for illustrated Booklet, Map and Guide. Address—John F. Pierce, Passenger Traffic Manager, Canada Steamship Lines, Limited, Montreal.

CANADA STEAMSHIP LINES, LIMITED
Head Office: VICTORIA SQUARE, MONTREAL

Two advertisements, published in 1919, directed at the Toronto market.

Morden was like a comet that burned brightly and quickly vanished. In January, 1932, he appeared in bankruptcy court in London. *The Times* reported that "his affairs became involved, and a receiving order was made against him in 1931. In his public examination, he attributed his difficulties to the depreciation in the value of his shareholdings which began in 1929." The Wall Street crash and subsequent depression wiped him out. His health collapsed and, almost blind, he died five months later, aged 51. His widow was reduced to living in a small flat in West Kensington and doing domestic work.

"Heatherden Hall" became a private club called "Heatherden"—one of its vice-presidents was W. D. Ross, the lieutenant governor of Ontario—but it could not survive the depression. In 1936, "Heatherden" was purchased by a motion-picture syndicate, which changed the name to Pinewood Studios and maintained its 150 acres of grounds. Interiors of the house can be seen in films such as *Sleuth*, and portions of the gardens in *The Prime of Miss Jean Brodie*.

* * *

As for Canada Steamship Lines, it grew and prospered, in spite of incidents such as the disaster of the *Noronic*, one of its steamers, which burned in Toronto Bay in 1949, killing more people than any other disaster in Toronto's history. Until recently, Canada Steamship Lines was part of the Power Corporation empire.

His wealth and influence continued through the 1920s; he was reelected as a Member of Parliament, and "Heatherden Hall" was the scene of many political "weekends" and lavish parties and the signing in 1921 of the Irish Free State treaty; his large interests included steel, shipping, airplanes and timber; a noted breeder of cattle and horses, he was the first Canadian to be master of foxhounds at an English hunt.

Another Torontonian who found the city too small for his ambitions was Sir Arthur Beverley Baxter (1890-1964) who, like Morden, got his first job as a piano salesman. He became a protégé of yet another Canadian who became an influential English financier—Max Aitken, the future Lord Beaverbrook. In 1922, Baxter became managing editor of Beaverbrook's Sunday Express and two years later took over the Daily Express as well. Known as "Bax with the Axe" for his sharp wit, his opinions of Canadian matters were solicited whenever he deigned to return to his native city; for 25 years he wrote the "London Letter" which appeared in MacLean's magazine. The photograph shows him and his wife visiting Toronto in the 1930s to promote his film interests. In addition, he wrote plays and novels, and sat for more than twenty years as a British Member of Parliament.

A regular feature of the Canadian National Exhibition, in a less sympathetic age, was the freak show on the midway.

A Scene at the Toronto Exhibition
Invincible Renovator Co., Limited, Electric Air Cleaners for Private and Public Buildings

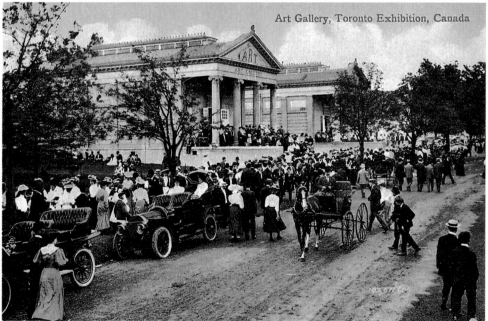

Art Gallery, Toronto Exhibition, Canada

For the past 110 years at the Exhibition Grounds along the lakeshore, the progress and paraphernalia of the industrial age have competed with produce, animals, amusements, and feats of sport and strength for the attentions of the flocking throngs. Since 1879, when city council advanced $75,000 for a set of exhibition buildings on the lakeshore, the annual exhibition has represented a sort of "rite of passage" between the freedom of summer and the responsibility and harvests of autumn.

Between 1858 and 1879, the Provincial Exhibition was held at the "Crystal Palace," a poor relation of the famous original in London, which occupied grounds bisected by the Grand Trunk Railway line directly south of 999 Queen Street West. Crystal Palace was modified and moved to the new Exhibition Grounds in 1879, where it stood near the Dufferin Street entrance until its destruction by fire.

The father of the exhibition was J. J. Withrow, its main promoter and first president in 1879, "in which year the Toronto affair had first become, in name at least, the Canadian National Exhibition." Following Withrow's retirement after twenty years as president, a variety of businessmen held the position, including George H. Gooderham from 1909-11.

The C.N.E. tried to appeal to a wide range of tastes with a combination of patriotism, entertainment, culture, moralism, sport, industry, technology, and profit. One exceptional year was 1912, dubbed "Imperial Year" in response to the European battleship scare. It was formally opened on August 25 by Queen Victoria's third son, the Canadian governor general, the Duke of Connaught, accompanied by his daughter Princess Patricia. The highlight that year was the Imperial Cadet Corps, "a large body of well-drilled youths from Australia, New Zealand, Newfoundland, and most of the provinces of Canada." Another year, an anonymous commentator noted that "the patriotic character of the displays given were particularly useful in illustrating to visitors the course of

(Above) A promotional postcard, published by Valentine & Sons for the Invincible Renovator Company. Patterson Ice Cream (page 126), had a concession in the tent on the left, competing for what would now be called the "junkfood market" with the likes of Coca Cola, Neilson's, O'Keefe's Dry ginger ale, Orange Mello, and numerous purveyors of Red Hots and French Fried Potatoes. On the back of this postcard, written in 1914 and addressed to "Mr. Robert Ewart, Esq., Edmonton, Albt."—no more detailed address was needed—these lines appear: "Hello Bob, How is things out in Edmonton. I was to the Ex it was the Same as other years the poultry building is was burnt down, They went over the million mark this year. I hope everybody is keeping fine out there. So long, Percy." (Below) A postcard which appears to show extraordinary enthusiasm for art. The Art Gallery stood on the northern part of the C.N.E. grounds, not far from the railway tracks and about equidistant from the Dufferin Gate and the Coliseum. Buildings for dogs, machinery, and agricultural implements surrounded it; today, it would be practically underneath the Gardiner Expressway. The Art Gallery was U-shaped—two wings at right angles from a backbone; both wings are visible in the postcard.

Canadian thought"; included were the late Queen Victoria's Jubilee (1897) gifts, displayed "to her Canadian people."

During the 1930s, the Canadian National Exhibition had in its general manager, Honeric William Waters, Ph.D., a man whose own experiences reflected the exhibition's diversity of goals. Waters was born in a small town in England and educated at public schools in Indianapolis, Indiana. Later, he served as secretary to Sir Herbert Austin of the Wolsely Tool & Motor Car Company in Birmingham. Moving to Toronto in 1904, he became secretary to Dr. J. O. Orr, general manager of the C.N.E., left to become an accountant for the MacLaren Imperial Cheese Company, and then returned to the C.N.E. to run the manufacturers' section during the years of the Great War. At the end of the war years, he went to the United States, where he obtained a doctorate in religious studies and entered the Baptist ministry with a pastorate in Tarrytown, N.Y.! He quickly tired of that and returned to Toronto, where he rejoined the C.N.E. organization and rose to the position of general manager in August, 1927.

Attendance at the Canadian National Exhibition first went over the million mark in 1913. Jesse Edgar Middleton described the setting in the city's 1934 official centennial history book: "The admission fee is twenty-five cents. All kinds of manufactured goods are brilliantly displayed. Visitors may see the best livestock in Canada, an automobile show of the first rank, a picture exhibition, an assembly of the finest agricultural and horticultural products . . . , exhibits illustrating farm and highway improvement, a railway show, a pageant and a night spectacle. The exhibition offers a conspectus of Canadian diligence, invention, industry and sport, and it is perfectly situated beside the blue lake in a spacious park which is a very paradise of flowers and velvet lawns. The buildings are of steel, brick and concrete, well designed and roomy. The roadways are of asphalt."

The Coliseum has seen many spectacles, but few of the scale and solemnity of the Service of Thanksgiving and Prayer for the city's hundredth birthday at 11 p.m. on March 5, 1934. Conducted by four ministers and a rabbi, it featured several hymns, two scripture lessons, a sermon, the "Hallelujah Chorus" from The Messiah, *and the national anthem. Dr. H. A. Fricker conducted his choir of 2,500 voices and the band of the Toronto Regiment, which together must have nearly raised the roof. The people in the left foreground of the postcard would be practically underneath the expressway; the lawns are now parking lots.*

Marathon swimmers at the C.N.E. in the 1920s, greased against the chill of Lake Ontario. Though hardly a spectator sport, marathon swimming was a popular feature over the years. The most famous marathon swim of all was that of sixteen-year-old Marilyn Bell in September, 1954. Her struggle in the waves and cold for 21 hours, as she swam the 32 miles from Youngstown, New York, to Toronto, has assumed legendary, almost mythic, propor-

tions. The city went wild with adulation for her; the only comparable outpourings were for the Prince of Wales in 1919, Mary Pickford in 1934, and for another swimmer, George Young, who won a $25,000 purse in January, 1927, by beating "the world's best" in a 22-mile race from Santa Catalina Island to the California mainland.

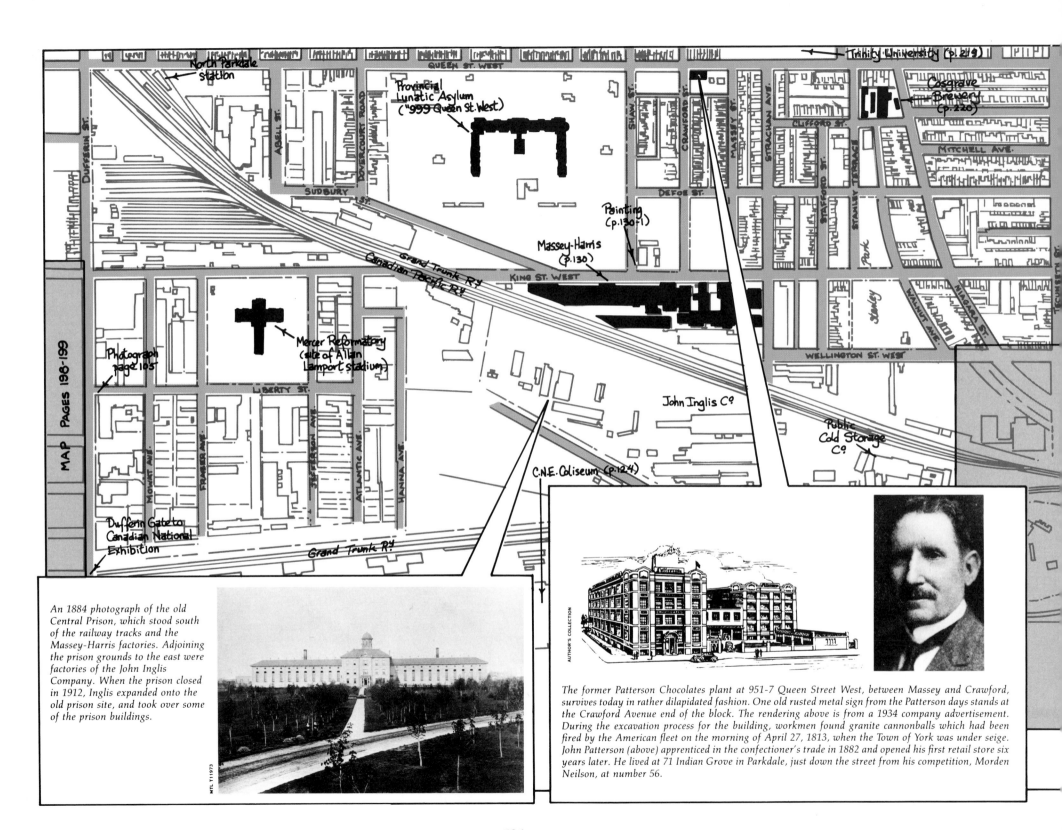

North Parkdale Station

Trinity University (p. 219)

Cosgrave Brewery (p. 220)

Provincial Lunatic Asylum ("999 Queen St. West)

QUEEN ST. WEST

SHAW ST.

CRAWFORD ST.

MASSEY ST.

STRACHAN AVE.

CLIFFORD ST.

MITCHELL AVE.

DUFFERIN ST.

ABELL ST.

DOVERCOURT ROAD

SUDBURY ST.

DEFOE ST.

STAFFORD ST.

STANLEY TERRACE

Painting (p. 130-1)

Massey-Harris (p. 130)

Canadian Pacific Ry.

Grand Trunk Ry.

KING ST. WEST

Stanley Park

WALNUT AVE.

NIAGARA ST.

TECUMSETH ST.

Photograph page 105

Mercer Reformatory (site of Allan Lamport stadium)

LIBERTY ST.

MOWAT AVE.

FRASER AVE.

JEFFERSON AVE.

ATLANTIC AVE.

HANNA AVE.

John Inglis Co.

WELLINGTON ST. WEST

Public Cold Storage Co.

C.N.E. Coliseum (p.124)

Dufferin Gate to Canadian National Exhibition

Grand Trunk Ry.

MAP PAGES 198-199

An 1884 photograph of the old Central Prison, which stood south of the railway tracks and the Massey-Harris factories. Adjoining the prison grounds to the east were factories of the John Inglis Company. When the prison closed in 1912, Inglis expanded onto the old prison site, and took over some of the prison buildings.

MTL T11973

AUTHOR'S COLLECTION

The former Patterson Chocolates plant at 951-7 Queen Street West, between Massey and Crawford, survives today in rather dilapidated fashion. One old rusted metal sign from the Patterson days stands at the Crawford Avenue end of the block. The rendering above is from a 1934 company advertisement. During the excavation process for the building, workmen found granite cannonballs which had been fired by the American fleet on the morning of April 27, 1813, when the Town of York was under seige. John Patterson (above) apprenticed in the confectioner's trade in 1882 and opened his first retail store six years later. He lived at 71 Indian Grove in Parkdale, just down the street from his competition, Morden Neilson, at number 56.

126

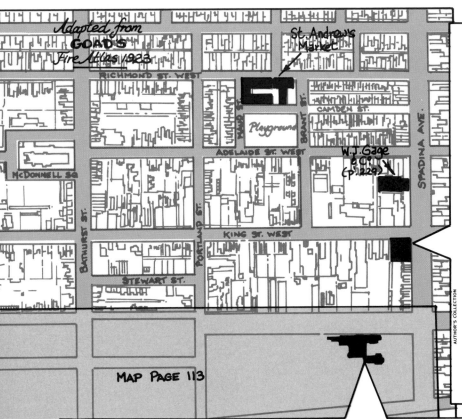

Adapted from
GOAD'S
Fire Atlas 1923

St. Andrew's Market

Playground

W.J. Gage
& Co.
(p. 229)

RICHMOND ST. WEST

CAMDEN ST.

ADELAIDE ST. WEST

KING ST. WEST

STEWART ST.

McDONNELL SQ.

BATHURST ST.

PORTLAND ST.

BRANT ST.

SPADINA AVE.

MAP PAGE 113

WARWICK BROS & RUTTER LIMITED
MANUFACTURING & IMPORTING STATIONERS
PRINTERS & BOOK-BINDERS

The printing firm Warwick Bros. & Rutter, at King and Spadina, printed books, magazines, catalogues, the postcard reproduced on page 241, and were the Canadian manufacturers of the Kalamazoo looseleaf binder.

Loretto Abbey, Toronto, Ont., Canada

Loretto Abbey, "a school for young ladies" on Wellington Street west of Spadina, shared the area with diverse businesses including knitting works, the Gurney Foundry & Stove Works a block to the north, several gasometers of the Consumers' Gas Company, the National Casket Company, and the Municipal Abattoir. The core of the Abbey was a house, "Lyndhurst," built in the 1830s by the Jameson family, he the one-time vice-chancellor of Upper Canada. The Sisters of Loretto bought the house in 1867, and expanded it by adding a five-storey wing with a dome, before moving in 1930 to more genteel surroundings in the Annex. The Telegram bought the land and demolished the Abbey in 1961; following the Telegram's demise, the Globe & Mail took over the property, and have since erected their own office building and printing plant there.

999 Queen Street West

The lunatic asylum at 999 Queen Street West was a daunting, prison-like edifice on 50 acres of grounds, an example of the type of building where design and scale have the connotations of an old-fashioned cautionary tale or a Franz Kafka novel, in which the fate of the nonconforming individual is utterly subsumed by the power of the state. The modern mental health buildings—which have been given the address 1001 Queen Street West in order to avoid even the local connotation of the old "999"—present a bland, indifferent façade to the street, expressing none of the powerful "bending of the will" of the old asylum.

In 1844 John Howard, the architect whose love of the pastoral found expression in his High Park estate and in landscape layouts at Osgoode Hall and St. James Cemetery, summoned the practicality necessary to win a £30 prize for design of the asylum. Under his supervision, the enormous stone and brick pile was built over the next few years, on what was a somewhat remote part of Queen Street. By 1890, the city had expanded beyond it, both Brockton and Parkdale having been annexed; the writer G. Mercer Adam, in a review of the city's progress, mentioned the lunatic asylum, which was "soon we believe to be removed out of town." The architectural historian Eric Arthur stated in the asylum's defence that, until 1900, it was considered to be the best ventilated in North America and refuted the old story that a furnace in the main central dome created a convection current which drew the stale air from the wards and expelled it above the roof.

The asylum at 999 Queen Street West was one of four large buildings in the area, buildings which dwarfed even the sprawling factories of the Massey-Harris Company. Due south of the asylum was the glass and iron Crystal Palace, a huge, hideous version of the famous original in Hyde Park in London; it was moved in 1879 to the Exhibition Grounds, near the current Dufferin Gate, and eventually burned. Nearby, on land and in buildings now occupied by the Inglis Limited factories, was the Central Prison, a low, spreading, brutal-looking place partly demolished in 1912. To the west, south of King Street between Jefferson and Fraser, was the Mercer Reformatory for women, now the site of Allan Lamport Stadium. In addition, to the west, were the Protestant Orphans' Home (page 203) and the Home for Incurables (now the site of the Queen Elizabeth Hospital), "and one or two other refuges for the city's sick and suffering, or the erring and the homeless."

The quality of care in the province's asylums was the lifelong concern of Dr. Charles Kirk Clarke (1857-1924), often considered "the father of Canadian psychiatry" and the namesake of the renowned Clarke Institute of Psychiatry. Born in Elora and educated at the University of Toronto,

Charles Kirk Clarke (1857-1924) was Dean of the Medical Faculty at the University of Toronto, and in the early part of the century was one of the more progressive figures in the treatment of the insane. He is the namesake of the Clarke Institute of Psychiatry.

Clarke began work at 999 Queen Street West in 1874 as a clinical assistant, during a period when psychiatry was "state medicine": institutional superintendents were political appointees, and patients were shut away with little chance of a cure. In 1880, Clarke accepted an appointment with the Hamilton Asylum, and the following year moved to the Rockwood Asylum in Kingston, joining his brother-in-law, Dr. William Metcalf, who was superintendent there. Over the next four years, they attempted to introduce innovations while placating the asylum's political masters; finally a frustrated Clarke tendered his resignation, exclaiming: "I love psychiatry but hate politics." The following day, as he and his brother-in-law were making their rounds, a patient rushed up to them and fatally stabbed Metcalf. Clarke withdrew his resignation and was appointed superintendent, "in order to protect several hundred defenseless creatures from a political hireling who might be pitch-forked into the position."

Clarke stopped using restraint on all but the most violent patients, and he introduced occupational therapy to the asylum, establishing shops where the patients made brushes and brooms. So successful was this cottage industry that the asylum was soon selling its wares to other institutions, and even on the open market, causing business and organized labour to complain, and the provincial government to order Clarke to cease. In 1887, Clarke established the first training school for psychiatric nurses and attendants.

In 1905, Clarke returned to Toronto to become superintendent of 999 Queen Street West. He visited Munich in 1907 at the behest of a royal commission, and returned with plans for a psychiatric outpatient clinic, which he established in 1909 at the corner of Chestnut and Christopher streets. He planned and lobbied for a psychiatric hospital, to be kept "absolutely free from political control"; a $5 million grant from the Rockefeller Foundation in 1919 provided the funds for this teaching and research facility which opened in 1925, a year after Clarke's death. A 1923 bequest from the Patterson family, for research into mental illness, became the seed money 40 years later for the Dr. C. K. Clarke Institute of Psychiatry, which opened in July, 1966, and superseded the Toronto Psychiatric Hospital.

Clarke himself had a variety of interests: he was a champion amateur tennis player, a violinist of some repute, and the president of the Canadian Society for the Protection of Birds. As well, he devoted time to establishing homes for tuberculosis patients. He lived at 34 Roxborough Street East.

The lunatic asylum, usually known as 999 Queen Street West, occupied most of the land bounded by Shaw, Dovercourt, King and Queen. The old asylum was demolished in 1977; the site has since been rebuilt as the Queen Street West Mental Health Centre, with a new address—1001 Queen Street West—both being attempts to distance the new facility from the bedlam-like connotations of the old asylum.

Massey-Harris

The abandoned Massey-Harris factories, a remnant of the smoky mills of the old industrial city, have until recently blighted King Street West; for years, their rusty skeletons bore witness to the power and prosperity of the firm when it was king of the agricultural implements industry. Recently, only the catastrophic state of the finances of its corporate successor, Massey-Ferguson Ltd., have brought it into the spotlight, but in its heyday it made its owner as rich as Croesus.

The firm owed its start to farmer Daniel Massey's fascination with newly invented American farming implements; a progressive individual with a bent for political reform, Massey saw the tools on visits to relatives in the United States, and in 1830 imported a clumsy mechanical thresher. At the forge in his shop, with the help of his eldest son Hart, Daniel Massey tinkered with and modified the primitive contraption. Late in the 1840s, he bought a bankrupt foundry in Newcastle, which he operated while Hart ran the family farm twenty miles away. Before long, their Massey Manufacturing Company had gained a sound local reputation, and in 1851 Hart joined his father at the foundry. The latter's health failed, however, and he died in 1856, at the age of 58, leaving the firm in his eldest son's exceptionally capable hands.

The genius of the Masseys was their ability to adapt other people's ideas to the rougher terrain of Canada and to sell the results around the world. When they found something in the United States which they liked, they purchased the patents. When they found an idea they could use, they borrowed it and modified it, and ended up competing directly against the machine's inventor—as in the case of the American-made implements of Walter Wood. When they found a successful company with which they could amalgamate, like the Harris Company of Brantford, or an impoverished company they could buy, like the Toronto Reaper & Mower Company, they did so without hesitation. Toronto Reaper & Mower had designed but been unable to market a twine binder which cut, bundled and tied grain, tripling productivity during the uncertain Canadian harvest. Massey-Harris products became well-known in Europe, dating from the 1867 Paris International Exhibition, when a Massey harvester won the grand prize for machines of its type.

The Masseys had a curious relationship with the United States, as on the one hand they lived, traded and had relatives there, while on the other they fought to keep Canadian tariff barriers high. Hart left his eldest son Charles in charge of the company, and moved his family to Cleveland in 1870. He became an American citizen a half-dozen years later, as did his son Chester, and they competed effectively in the American market. Meanwhile, back in Newcastle, Charles Massey proved himself an effective manager, guiding the company through depressions and bad harvests in the prerailway Canada of the 1870s. In 1878, Hart Massey and family returned to Ontario; four years later, they relocated to Toronto, and built a four-storey factory near the spot where old Grand Trunk and Canadian Pacific railway lines cross King Street West. When the Canadian Pacific

During the First World War, employees queued after their shifts for the "Dovercourt" streetcar, which "wyed" onto King Street at Shaw. After some initial hesitation, Massey-Harris threw itself wholeheartedly into the war effort—on August 15, 1914, barely ten days after the outbreak of the war, it suddenly closed down its works, throwing thousands of men onto the streets. The company argued the move was necessary as a large portion of its trade was with companies who were at war; however, after strong words in the press about Massey-Harris's great wealth and tariff protection from U.S. competition, the works reopened, and 1,500 men were taken back on. At the time, the Massey-Harris works covered an immense area—the triangle bounded by King Street, the railway tracks, and Stafford Street; now they are in the process of being demolished. A sign of the times is the fate of the weedy, windblown blocks to the north of the works—once vacant land in a derelict area, made doubly unattractive by their proximity to 999 Queen Street West, they have recently been redeveloped with "Victorian-style garden homes."

Railway opened settlement of the west, the Massey Manufacturing Company's fortunes soared. By 1890, the firm had 900 employees, plus "800 to 1,000 agents who earn the greater part of their living from the sale of the Massey machines."

The family was dominated by the stern, pious Methodism of its patriarch, Hart Massey. After his son Charles died of typhoid fever at the age of 36, in 1884, and Charles's widow made plans to remarry, Hart Massey intervened in an unsuccessful attempt to gain custody of the two youngest children. Hart's youngest son, Fred Victor, had a missionary streak in him which was nipped in the bud when he died at the age of 22; in his memory, his father built the Fred Victor Mission at Queen and Jarvis, for years one of the beacons for the indigent in the city's old Tenderloin. Hart Massey also generously endowed Victoria University in Cobourg, which he felt gave a proper Methodist education. He was a vigorous opponent of its desire to affiliate with the University of Toronto, which nevertheless occurred in 1892. Hart Massey died in February, 1896, at the age of 72, leaving an estate of over $2 million.

The Massey Company's amalgamation with the Harris Company in 1891, prompted by the latter's invention of an open-end binder which clearly beat the former at its own game, brought some new talent into the firm. Thomas Findley, J. N. Shenstone, and eventually Sir Lyman Melvin Jones helped to run the company during the period between Hart's death and 1926, when all family association with the company ended. Massey-Harris, through Sir Melvin Jones, was influential in turning Liberal support in Ontario away from Sir Wilfrid Laurier's trade reciprocity policy. The company had initially supported Laurier's low-tariff policies until it realized that made-in-U.S.A. agricultural machines were carving out a large share of the Canadian market. It then allegedly threatened to leave Canada if the Liberal free-trade policy became the law.

The company boomed in the period during and after the Second World War, increasing its sales five-fold. E. P. Taylor became the largest shareholder. The company became known as Massey-Harris-Ferguson Limited in 1953, when it acquired the industrial empire of the Irish inventor Harry Ferguson. Ferguson was for a time the largest shareholder, eventually ceding this position to the locally based Argus Corporation. Since 1958, it has been known as Massey-Ferguson Limited.

(Next page)The old Hart Massey house, usually called "Euclid Hall," at the northeast corner of Jarvis and Wellesley, is one of the few remaining that recall the grandness of turn-of-the-century Jarvis Street. Begun in the 1860s by Senator Arthur McMaster, it was extended and modified in the 1880s by Massey. Massey's son Chester Daniel built his own smaller house at number 519 (the left of the painting), on the northern quarter of his father's large lot. The size of the Massey property was not unique for Jarvis Street—that of Thomas Long at number 513, across Wellesley from Massey's, was the same size. As for "Euclid Hall," it was bought in the 1920s by the hotelier and inventor of five-pin bowling, Tommy Ryan, and used for years as a showroom for antiques and art; it has been first a coffee house, and then a restaurant, since the early 1960s. The property for the gas station which abuts the house on its south side was split off over half a century ago; in 1927, it became the first location of radio station C.F.R.B.

(Far left) Hart Almerrin Massey (1823-1896) left school at seventeen "to taste the sweets of independence" while working in a lumber camp. One contemporary biographer noted that, although he was "the son of a farmer, he early began to exhibit sound business instincts." So wealthy did the Masseys become, and so philanthropic, that they seemed like royalty, inspiring Saturday Night *editor B. K. Sandwell's oft-quoted couplet: "Toronto has no social classes / Only the Masseys and the masses." (Left) Vice-president Chester Daniel Massey, with his brother Walter Edward Hart Massey, the secretary-treasurer, assisted father Hart Massey in the operation of the Massey Manufacturing Company. C. D. became president in 1901, after brother Walter's death. He had two sons, Vincent and Raymond—the latter (1896-1983) became an actor, most famous for his portrayal of Abe Lincoln; Vincent was president of Massey-Harris until 1925, then embarked on a career in government service, culminating in his appointment, in 1952, as Canada's first native-born governor general. (Centre) Denton Massey was Chester Daniel's nephew—the son of W. E. H. Massey. Born in 1900, he attended Yale and the Massachusetts Institute of Technology, and joined Massey-Harris in 1924. Like his father, he married an American; like most of his family,*

he was a devout Methodist, and in his spare time he organized and led the York Bible Class for young men. Two of the non-Masseys in what had been a family business were Joseph Newton Shenstone (right) and Thomas Findley (far right). Shenstone, a Baptist born in 1855 in Brantford, had been for ten years the secretary of the A. Harris farm implement company when it amalgamated with the Massey Machinery Company. He became secretary of the new company, and later was named president following Vincent Massey's resignation in pursuit of a career in public service. Shenstone was also vice-president of C.C.M., and a director of the Russell Motor Car Company. At the time of his death, at the age of 78, he was still chairman of the board of Massey-Harris. Thomas Findley, born at Bond Lake in York County in 1870, started with Massey-Harris in 1891 as a telegraph operator, and was promoted to chief accountant four years later. He was president from 1917 until his death in 1921, during the time when Vincent Massey, just back from the war, was serving with the Government Repatriation Committee and considering whether to return to his old job as Lecturer in Modern History at the University of Toronto. Findley lived at 146 Warren Road in Forest Hill; Shenstone lived at 40 Walmer Road in the posh part of the Annex.

Neighbourhoods

The Ward & Kensington

The great slum of the old city spread like a rash north and west from the corner of Queen and Bay. Little frame cottages, junk wagons, pit privies, lean-tos in back lanes, open drains, the sweet smell of rotting plaster and manure, sweatshops, malnourished children, families crowded together—all were descriptive of The Ward. Today, the huge buildings of downtown have migrated northward, and those of the "hospital-town" southwards; the roads are wider and cleaner, and the traffic whizzes through, or circles blocks looking for parking, or disgorges shoppers and hotel guests. Only a few old houses and the vestiges of Chinatown survive, along streets like Dundas and Elizabeth.

Some contemporary descriptions evoke that vanished piece of the city.

An inspection report from the City Health Department, dated November 26, 1913: "In the rear of a store located at 142 Agnes Street were found living quarters consisting of three rooms, one of which was used as a storeroom for all kinds of rubbish. The bedroom contained four beds, used by father, mother and two children. The third room was a kitchen, which a daughter of about eleven used as a sleeping room. Under the bedroom was a cellar full of dirt, wood and rubbish. The cellar was inspected because a very decided dampness and strong odor was noticed when inspecting the bedroom. It was found that two tin or lead pipes which connected the sink of the kitchen with a tile drain pipe were overflowing."

Elsewhere, the same day: "The filth and disorder are not peculiar to this backyard. Similar conditions were seen in many properties in The Ward and in other localities throughout the city. It was learned that four months ago, two children were removed, owing to scarlet fever, to the isolation hospital from 128 Chestnut Street, the rear of which abuts this yard, and another child had just returned from the hospital, having had the same disease. In this yard, a very unsatisfactory toilet was found."

The Rev. H. S. Magee, writing in 1911: "the lanes, alleyways, and

Christian preachers, especially the bearded, Derby-hatted Henry Singer, gathered crowds about them whenever they attempted to convert Eastern European Jews in The Ward. Singer was a Polish former Jew who had come to The Ward from Boston in 1897 to take over the Toronto Jewish Mission on Centre Avenue. The early missions, which were non-denominational and supported by private donations, sought to help and convert the impoverished, culture-shocked Eastern Europeans with dollops of food and Christianity; Singer, though a charismatic preacher, had little impact. In later years, both the Presbyterian Church and Holy Trinity (Church of England) opened missions; itinerants preached on street corners and from the backs of wagons, some handing out gifts such as Christmas Eve dinner vouchers. Eventually tiring of the constant haranguing, the locals started to shout back and challenge the missionaries—at the corner of Agnes and Terauley, crowds spilled over into the street, and in June, 1911, began to brawl. The following year, Singer's mission was broken up; undaunted, he started to preach on Kensington Avenue, prompting barrages of rocks from the onlookers. Singer finally left for Detroit in 1919.

CTA JAMES 2348

backyards are strewn with refuse, houses behind houses, and in the yards between unsightly piles of ramshackle outhouses, some of these reeking with filth and stench. We are now told that in the midst of this these poor people pay $10 to $12 per month for these miserable rambling hovels." Sometimes, the houses became so cold that potatoes froze in their cupboards.

A Health Department report, from November, 1913, described 50 Terauley Street (the west side of Bay Street north of Albert—now the location of New City Hall; then, it was across the street from a T. Eaton Co. factory): "Two storey frame building, housing Polish people. In the second floor rear, two small rooms were providing shelter for six men. The health department had inspected these premises and had allowed, according to the cubical contents of the rooms, two men to sleep in the first room and one in the rear." Further north, at 154 Terauley, in the deep snow of an early winter: "Cottage, with cellar dwelling. Damp. Dark, ill-ventilated. Occupied by ten people. Closed." A further description of the "cellar dwelling" ensued: "In the half basement of a two-storey frame cottage were found living rooms in which three boarders besides husband, wife and two children were living. In the rear of the kitchen, which served as a dining room, was a toilet. In one of the corners of the toilet room were old clothes and kindling wood; in the other was a box containing vegetables and foodstuffs. The Health Department had taken action and closed these premises once, but due to the great demand for living facilities and lack of inspection facilities for a follow-up, tenants had again entered the premises . . . ."

The report of the city's medical health officer, Dr. Charles Hastings, was published on December 11, 1913. In it, he noted that at least 3,000 houses were each occupied by some two to six families. "As many as eight to ten families are today living in ordinary ten and twelve room houses."

* * *

The Ward was the old St. John's Ward of the city's 1880 electoral boundaries. It had another name, Macauleytown, from the Queen's Rangers' surgeon Dr. James Macauley, who for his services was granted one hundred acres in 1797, subdivided it into a little town considerably to the west of the settlement of York, and built himself a house called Terauley Cottage, on what was to become the site of Holy Trinity Church. By 1850, the area had assumed a distinctive character—a warren of streets and alleys lined with frame and stucco cottages in various states of repair.

From the waves of immigration—the "outscourings of the world"—which followed the 1848 rebellions, the potato famines in Ireland, and the pogroms and feudalisms of Eastern Europe and Russia, the poorest of the

Another proselytizer was Morris Zeidman (1894-1964), a former Jew converted to Presbyterianism, who took over the Elizabeth Street Presbyterian Mission. Born in Czestochawa, Poland, he came to Toronto in 1912, learned English, converted to Christianity, and studied at Knox College. The Presbyterian Mission, also known as the Christian Synagogue, evolved eventually into the Scott Mission, of which Zeidman remained as executive director until his death. When asked about alleged freeloaders at the Mission, Zeidman replied: "They can't cheat me of much. What can they take from me? A bowl of soup?" His anti-Catholic broadcasts on behalf of the Protestant Radio League, which he ran from his home at 307 Palmerston Boulevard, got him into trouble with the C.B.C. (page 154).

lot who arrived in Toronto gravitated to The Ward. Most notably foreign were the Eastern European Jews, who crowded together in an attempt to create some familiar surroundings as a bulwark against the hostile new country. Though not as extensive, degraded or teeming as, for instance, the tenements and slums of the Lower East Side of New York, it was truly a "rookery" of embarrassing proportions. The public purse offered little largesse to either the newly arrived or the downtrodden. Society's response was the private charity: the euphemistically named House of Industry—the poorhouse—was established at the corner of Elm and Chestnut in 1848 (the building, now called Laughlen Lodge, still survives). A different kind of industry developed on Centre Avenue—the best known red-light district in the city.

C. S. Clark, in his rabble-rousing *Of Toronto the Good—The Queen City As It Is*, published in 1898, is explicit about the good streets and the bad streets. Good ones were Jarvis, Bloor, Sherbourne, and Spadina, while bad ones were the east end around the Don, the west end east of Parkdale, and those in The Ward. On Centre Avenue, according to Clark, the girls stood in their doorways to solicit, and young boys could be persuaded to keep watch and spread the alarm when a policeman approached. Eighty-five babies—the issue of this commerce—were recorded abandoned to the Infants Home in a single year.

Coexisting with this disreputability was a growing Jewish community. By the time of the First World War, The Ward was more or less a self-contained Jewish neighbourhood—for the immigrant, impoverished, Eastern European Jews at least, as the more prosperous, better-educated Jews who had either emigrated from Britain or else been in the city for a long time were comparatively well assimilated, and worshipped at the Holy Blossom Synagogue on Bond Street. In The Ward, there were Jewish shops, cafes, theatres, synagogues for each persuasion, a seltzer factory on Chestnut Street, and the famed Dworkin's news agency on Elizabeth Street, which sold the latest Yiddish newspapers from New York. But always there were more immigrants flooding in, and no money to fix up the leaking roofs. Privies overflowed, the yards were full of slops and garbage and old wagons and piled junk; a single tap was sometimes the only water supply for an entire block, and the air carried a smell of privies and garbage and unwashed, crowded humanity.

Sharing the blocks with the little houses and shops were factories of every size and description. Those of the T. Eaton Company dominated the area, but there was scarcely a block that did not have some sort of tailoring enterprise, ranging from well-organized factories in lofts to the meanest, most pitiful sweatshops in grubby lean-tos in the back alleys. By 1911, 80 percent of Eaton's 1,200 factory employees were Jewish, and the clothing industry in Toronto employed about twice the number of people as the next most important industry—iron and steel. The majority of workers were women, eking out an existence doing piecework on "sweated subcontracts."

The 60-hour week was standard at the turn of the century; typically, for women in the textile industry, work began at 6:30 A.M. and continued till 6:15 P.M., with an hour off for lunch. This violated the ten-hour-per-day rule, but was preferable to many of the employees as it gave them a Saturday half-holiday. In order to hold their positions, many women had to take piecework home in the evenings, or accept illegal overtime. Some shops forced the workers to buy the thread and buttons they used; tailors often had to kick back a portion of their piecework earnings to the shop owner or foreman. Conditions were sordid and dangerous, and while amendments to the Factories Act in 1901 stipulated that the temperature should never drop below 60 degrees Fahrenheit, and that one privy should be supplied for each 25 workers, the factories were rarely inspected for compliance. For those men unfortunate enough to become unemployed, a small amount of charity was available at the House of Industry to any relief applicant who could prove that he was honestly willing to work: the work test was simple—the city provided stone, which the applicant had to break in front of city officials.

A series of articles on local sweatshops had appeared in the *Mail & Empire* in October, 1897, written by the social reformer and future prime minister, William Lyon Mackenzie King. Around that time, some employers began noticing that overall production did not in fact drop when employees worked fewer hours; the pressure of piecework, along with poor working conditions, inadequate ventilation, bad housing, and mediocre food, made employees less productive. This lack of productivity, rather than any apparent humanitarian concerns, prompted employers such as Massey-Harris to reduce working hours. By 1905, most construction workers and others in well-organized factories had eight-hour days, and a half-holiday on Saturday.

The Ward at times swarmed with the flies that thrived in the horse manure on the streets and in the pit privies; new awareness of how disease was transmitted, reflected in the statement that the fly "is no respecter of persons" and could spread pestilence to other districts of the city, resulted in a public health drive. *The Star*, in support, sponsored a "Swat The Fly" contest in August, 1912. People were warned that diseased tailors might infect the clothes which healthy people purchased.

These tiny steps towards reform had little impact in the small shops of The Ward, and did nothing to curb the abuse of child labour. As sociologist Michael Piva has pointed out in his book *The Condition of the Working Class in Toronto, 1900-1921*, in the first two decades of this century the few prosecutions over working conditions all involved Chinese laundries. The employment of children resulted in a few prosecutions, too, but the parents, not the employers, were summonsed. So close to ut-

Looking south on Elizabeth Street, from a point near Dundas, in the 1930s. At that time, most of the Jewish residents and businesses had left The Ward for Kensington and other points to the west and north, and newer generations of immigrants, including Chinese and Italians, had moved in. The building on the left, at 109-111 Elizabeth Street, contained a Chinese produce store in the left-hand shop, and the Markowvitz kosher bakery in the right-hand one. Its dilapidated and sagging condition drew the notice of the City Health Department, with the result that it was spruced up and painted white in 1937; 25 years later, its "classical pretensions" caught the eye of the architectural historian Eric Arthur. It has since been demolished.

A crusader for cleaning up The Ward's slums was medical health officer Dr. Charles John Colwell Orr Hastings. Born on a farm twenty miles north of Toronto and educated at the University of Toronto, Hastings devoted his career to public health concerns. In 1908, he organized the first Milk Commission in Canada; two years later, he was appointed the city's chief medical health officer. At the time, the over-all mortality rate in the city was 14.8 per 1,000; over the next decade, due partly to the improvements he made in sewers and water quality and the elimination of the notorious pit privies in many parts of the city, the rate declined to 11.8, which, as Hastings was wont to point out, meant 1,600 fewer funerals per year. Concurrently, the infant mortality rate was cut in half, saving the lives of over 1,100 infants a year, and giving Toronto "the enviable position of possessing the lowest general mortality and lowest infant mortality of any city of 300,000 or over in North America." Hastings served as president of the American Public Health Association and the Great Lakes International Pure Water Association. He lived at 252 Russell Hill Road.

(Above) A photograph by William James; its caption reads simply "Moving Day in the Slums." (Next page) Looking north along Kensington Avenue to Baldwin Street. By the 1920s, the area now known as Kensington Market was operating as a market: ground floors of houses were converted into little shops; produce and live animals in cages spilled out into the street; flies buzzed in manure piles on the pavements. The city directory listed shops— shoe repair, poultry, grocer, butcher, baker, and fruitseller—at most of the addresses on these streets. Few areas of the city have been so beloved by some members of the populace and so vilified by others. Recent controversies include a 1976 Planning Department report which sought to stop the expansion of the market further into residential areas, prompting a charge by some merchants of "Nazi-like tactics"; crackdowns on canopies and awnings occur regularly, as well. The "charming anachronism" of live animal sales has prompted even livelier controversies; only one campaign against livestock—a 1976 city campaign to treat all "wooden objects" in the market area for termites—received general approval.

ter penury were so many families that only the labour of their children kept the family going (see also pages 180ff). According to the law, children had to be fourteen years old before they could work in factories, though they could work in shops at the age of ten. In one case, a thirteen-year-old boy named Wellington Lawrence, who in April, 1902, applied for a job supposedly without his parents' knowledge, was given an age and consent form for his parents to fill out, but was sent in immediately to start work. Later that day, he was killed when an elevator gate crushed his head onto the floor. The factory inspector who investigated warned the owner to be sure to have the age forms filled out *first*.

Many of the poor, mainly Jewish immigrants in The Ward became peddlers and rag-pickers; they wandered outside the ghetto, crying a melancholy "rag-a-bo" to attract some custom. Beyond The Ward, they risked the scorn and abuse of young toughs, and it was not uncommon for a bearded, foreign-looking individual to be attacked. Examples from contemporary newspapers show that their fate met with little sympathy and on occasion proved a source of light entertainment, as in the following brief article from the *Telegram*, on September 25, 1913:

"Nearly Drowned A Peddler

"He Expected Pants

" 'Anything here for sale?' asked Joseph Rottenstein when he called at a house on Gerrard Street. 'Yes, come round to the back and we will sell you some pants,' someone is alleged to have said. As he was knocking at the back door, a deluge came. Someone had emptied a bucket of water on him from above. He ran for a policeman, who found Harold Hicks, and he yesterday appeared in the afternoon Police Court.

"Hicks denied having thrown the water, but as there was only himself and two girls in the house, he was found guilty. Magistrate Cohen told Hicks that he soaked the peddler, and in turn he must get soaked also: 'It will be in the shape of five dollars.' When plaintiff heard this, he told the magistrate that it took him two days to dry himself, and there should be some compensation. Nothing doing."

Not only were the Eastern European Jews visibly different, they were further distrusted in the years around the First World War as their patriotism was seen as open to question. The assimilated "British" Jews who congregated at Holy Blossom Synagogue were considered, both by themselves and by outsiders, to be gentlemen by comparison with the exotic, Yiddish-speaking, lower-class, possibly socialistic Jews of the teeming Ward. According to historian Stephen Speisman, there were definite social and ethnic barriers between the Holy Blossom Jews and the Eastern Europeans. One example he cited involved the Ladies' Montefiore Aid So-

The "Who's Who" type of publication has been most often a record of well-established Christian white male businessmen. Of the pre-Second World War editions of Who's Who & Why, *and its successor* Who's Who in Canada, *the largest number of Jews were listed in the early 1920s editions. By the 1930s, although the size of the book had more than doubled to over 2,000 pages, fewer Jews were listed. Below are three of the Jewish men from the 1921 edition.*

Leo Frankel operated the Frankel Brothers scrap metal and smelting plant on Eastern Avenue, which reprocessed and dealt in metals such as copper, brass, lead, zinc, tin, steel, and iron. Born in Biblis, Grand Duchy of Hesse, in 1864, Frankel came to Canada with his parents in 1881, and five years later started his metal business at the corner of Wellington and York streets. Frankel was president of the Toronto Hebrew Congregation at Holy Blossom synagogue on Bond Street, and lived nearby at 504 Jarvis with his wife and three sons.

Louis Michael Singer was a lawyer, a Conservative, and a member of the Holy Blossom congregation. Born in Jaworow, Austria, in 1885, he came to Toronto as a child and attended Jarvis Street Collegiate Institute and Osgoode Hall, from which he graduated in 1908 as a gold medallist. His election as an alderman for Ward Four in 1914 was the first victory for a Jew in city politics; he based his campaign on issues, whereas one of his opponents, also Jewish, appealed to the voters on ethnicity alone. Singer won a broad endorsement from progressive civic institutions including the Star. His success helped to lure other Jewish candidates into the electoral fray, including Nathan Phillips, who was elected as an alderman in 1924 and 31 years later became mayor. Singer's wife was the Toronto-born Dr. Bessie Thelma Pullan; they lived at 433 Palmerston.

Percy Hermant owned the Imperial Optical Company, operating from headquarters at the Hermant Building at 21 Dundas Street East. Born in Mogilev, Russia, in 1882, he was educated by a private tutor, and upon his arrival in Canada in 1897 became a travelling salesman. Three years later, he attended the Klein School of Optics in Boston, then established the Imperial Optical Company. He became the first large-scale optical lens manufacturer in Canada, opened branches of his company in cities all across Canada, married a shiksa, and was invited to join clubs and societies as diverse as the Empire and the Knights of Pythias. His Toronto home was 16 Cluny Crescent in Rosedale. His son Sydney continued the family business, and is remembered for his philanthropy and chairmanship until 1983 of the Royal Ontario Museum.

Bathurst Street at College, showing King Edward School, Toronto

ciety at Holy Blossom Synagogue, which dispensed aid to Eastern European immigrants with an arrogance and *noblesse oblige* little different from what had been standard aristocratic and bureaucratic practice in the empires of Europe and Russia.

The goings-on in the mysterious Ward were further feared and distrusted as support for Bolshevism began to grow there. The so-called "Arbeiter Ring," a working class mutual aid society which believed that only through socialism could Jews escape discrimination, came to Toronto in 1908 from its base in New York. Militantly unionist, it helped the garment workers defeat the T. Eaton Company in the landmark 1912 strike that broke the latter's stranglehold on the women's clothing industry. As well, the "Arbeiter Ring" was militantly anti-Zionist, while many in the outside community had developed some sympathy with the persecuted Jews—at least, with their desire to settle distant Palestine. To outsiders, the Zionist movement had the ring of a religious prophecy, and was all rather heroic. Would they succeed in cultivating Palestine? Further complicating the situation in The Ward were the events in Russia in October, 1917, which turned Russians, of whom there were said to be 10,000 in Toronto over sixteen years of age, into "enemy aliens." Said one preacher: "the alien is fattening on war prosperity" while European battles cleared Canada of its Anglo-Saxon stock. Mayor Church wanted to ban the German tongue from all educational establishments, and Yiddish sounded alarmingly like German.

* * *

Spadina Avenue and Knox College, Toronto

As The Ward became more crowded, those who could afford it moved away. Some of the prosperous Jews kept their shops and factories in The Ward, but moved their families west of University Avenue—the borderline of respectability—to streets such as Palmerston, Markham, and Spadina (the latter had previously been a "good" street for established Torontonians, as noted in the C. S. Clark quote above). The streets east of Spadina became very Jewish while retaining their respectability, with Beverley being the most fashionable and expensive—one resident of that street was the English supremacist D'Alton McCarthy, another was the leather merchant and master of foxhounds G. W. Beardmore, whose house "Chudleigh" is now the Italian consulate. The Ward maintained its strongly Jewish character, with its shops, theatres, and synagogues, until the 1920s, when it became dominated by the next wave of poor

(Above) The old King Edward public school, north of College Street on the east side of Bathurst, has been demolished and replaced by a smaller, boxlike school building, surrounded by spartan, paved grounds. The trees on the west side of the street have been removed, and the road widened. (Below) The corner is College Street; the old Bank of Commerce building there is gone, replaced by one in a sleeker, more modern style.

immigrants—the Italians; west of Spadina, in the narrow streets lined with cheap houses, a European-style market area—called a *shtetl*, according to historian Speisman—grew up and was well established by the end of the First World War. Long gone were the big estates of Bathurst Street, such as those of Sir Casimir Gzowski (now Alexandra Park) and James McDonald (now Toronto Western Hospital). "The Grange" survived, with a modicum of genteel open space, as the art gallery.

The move westwards to Kensington, and the Kensington Market area itself, represented a turning point in the life of the city's Jewish community. The time, about 1920, was one of considerable liberalism, social change, and optimism; many of the Jews who ceased to reside in The Ward became landlords, renting their old houses to poorer Jews. The community began to fragment over issues of prosperity and orthodoxy. Kensington Market became a picturesque curiosity to the outside secular community, and although it was too much like the old country for many of the newly prosperous Jews, it incurred the wrath of the ultraorthodox, who felt that those shopkeepers who succumbed to the opiate of modern convenience and stayed open Saturdays were desecrating the Sabbath. For many Jews, the humanism and secularism of the twenties, and even the demands of employers for a half day's work on Saturday, had more influence than religion.

Subsequently, all Jews suffered from a conservative, xenophobic backlash. For even the most "Canadian" of them, there were many closed doors. North of Bloor Street was almost out of bounds until the late thirties; some private clubs denied them membership; doctors and nurses found they could not train at major hospitals; families were unwelcome at summer resorts; some local newspapers, especially the *Telegram* and *Saturday Night*, remained staunchly anti-Semitic. In 1933, this genteel albeit overt racism shifted to outright violence, with the activities of the Balmy Beach Swastika Club (page 166) and the Christie Pits riot (page 224).

As for The Ward itself, it continued to house the poorest of each successive generation of immigrants, and served out its days before the urban renewal of the sixties as the local tenderloin. A 1942 article in *MacLean's* magazine, by Frederick Edwards, described the "Queen City Sideshow" within a quarter-mile of City Hall. Chinatown then stretched north along Elizabeth Street from Queen, with chop suey joints doubling as standard hotels, and grocery stores selling dried fish, lichee nuts and other exotica. The southern boundary of The Ward—Queen Street between Bay Street and Osgoode Hall, was lined with cigar stores, pawnbrokers, cafes venting the smells of mustard and onions, hotel beer parlours, and clothing stores offering 98 cent shirts and suits for $18.95. Two Chinese daily newspapers had their offices there—the *Shing Wah Daily News* on Queen Street, and the *Chinese Times* on Elizabeth—their walls often plastered with calligraphed bulletins and news headlines. Banks had Chinese signs in their windows. Three theatres competed for trade, two with a changing parade of second-run double-bills, the third with a regular striptease in a vast hall seating 1,100 people. Shea's, on Bay Street where New City Hall now stands, was still showing first-run motion pictures. A familiar sight was Bill, the open-air photographer, wearing a boater and a tie and taking pictures with his big box camera on a tripod, "while-u-wait." Each year, with the first snow, a dozen or more gypsy families moved into The Ward and set themselves up in vacant stores, advertising palmistry and crystal ball readings and other less intellectual delights. Women sat in the windows and beckoned; many a sucker was rolled.

The building boom of the 1960s, which saw both the new City Hall and the Eaton Centre erected on what had been a warren of cottages, shops and factories, consigned The Ward largely to memory. As for Kensington, the market became predominantly Portuguese for a while, and has since demonstrated resilience and flexibility and infinite cosmopolitanism. The Chinese community, having abandoned The Ward as well, has turned the crossroads of Dundas and Spadina into a great, glittering Oriental market.

From 1956-64, Bargain Benny's, at the northwest corner of Spadina and Queen, was a landmark exceeded in garishness only by Honest Ed's on Bloor Street. The lively paint job included slogans like "Everything From Suits to Nuts," "We Must Confess We Sell For Less," "Sure Our Floor Slants Down, So Do Our Prices," and even a Pig Yiddish "Du Findest den Billigtein Preis in Benny's." The business was later known as Little Scot's Close Out Marts, and the building has since been demolished. Built in 1910 as the John Griffin Theatre—probably little more lavish than a nickelodeon—it was renamed the Mary Pickford Theatre in 1916, and retained that name until 1947. Pickford's name persisted for a while in the late 1960s in the Pickfair Bargain Centre at 382 Queen Street West. ("Pickfair" was the Hollywood Studio and home of Pickford and her first husband, Douglas Fairbanks).

W.G. Weston

The George Weston Limited corporate empire started in turnovers and progressed into takeovers. To be more precise, George Weston started with the Model Bakery Company at the corner of Soho and Phoebe, just north of the Queen Street strip; in the apartment above the bakery, in 1898, was born Garfield Weston, who expanded his father's modest beginnings in the bread and cake business into a global food-processing and retailing operation.

George Weston was born in New York State of English parents, and came to Toronto at the age of fourteen, in 1868. His parents apprenticed him to a local baker, and at the age of eighteen he struck out on his own, first by purchasing a bread delivery route, then adding more routes, and finally purchasing bakeries. By 1898, Weston's Model Bakery was the largest in Toronto, with a capacity of 3,200 loaves daily and 40 employees. Weston was but one player in a highly competitive industry, one of the most organized and concentrated in Toronto: the 1911 census noted that the 39 wholesale bakeries in the city were all comparatively large shops, employing an average of 58 workers each. Weston sold his bakery to a consortium headed by Mark Bredin, a Dubliner whose Canada Bread Company in 1911 engineered a "large and lucrative" merger of several of the largest bakeries in the city.

Weston's deal with Bredin included an agreement that Weston would not make bread for ten years—instead, he confined himself to manufacturing only biscuits, cakes, and confections. In 1910, he built a modern biscuit factory at 134 Peter Street at Richmond, which prospered and made "Weston's" literally a household word.

Weston's eldest son Garfield attended Harbord Collegiate, joined the Canadian Engineers, and went overseas in 1917, serving mainly in France until the end of the war. However, he spent some time in England, where he shrewdly evaluated the traditional English bakery products. Upon returning to Canada, he joined his father's business, "working in every department" until he became vice-president in 1921 and general manager in 1922, at which point he introduced "English quality" biscuits to the Weston's line. Two years later, in April, 1924, his father died, and Garfield set out, according to a statement in the company's 1967 annual report, "to build a business that would never know completion, but advance continually to meet advancing conditions."

In 1928, he consolidated the family holdings into one company, raised capital through a public stock offering, and started an acquisition binge which continued for half a century, involving the takeover of at least 2,000 companies. George Weston Limited was a forerunner of the modern corporations that fulfil their objectives by swallowing other firms, rather than by innovating or by starting their own businesses. Weston's first purchases were local confectioneries, but he soon entered the American market, and within five years had invested in the English biscuit business, a move dubbed "taking coals to Newcastle." In 1935, he moved to the United Kingdom to expand his operations there and purchased firms including the world-famous Fortnum & Mason. Weston moved in the influential Tory circle of the expatriate Canadian Lord Beaverbrook, and in 1940 was elected to the British House of Commons.

Throughout that period, he had not neglected his Canadian base of operations—the 1937 purchase of McCormick's Limited of London, Ontario, made Weston's the largest biscuit and confectionery company in Canada. Other purchases included the Loblaw's supermarket chain in 1947, the William Neilson Ltd. confectionery in 1948, and the local Tamblyn's drugstore chain. A great believer in what came to be called "vertical integration," he told *Fortune* magazine in the 1950s: "all my life I've been looking for tied accounts—the kind you don't have to sell every day."

Many of his acquisitions were engineered by George Metcalf, a Manchester-born former William Neilson Ltd. employee who had met Weston in the early 1920s, when both were attempting to sell a food product line to Loblaw's. Following the death of Morden Neilson, Metcalf convinced the surviving family members to sell their company to Weston's; Metcalf then left Neilson's, became a vice-president of Loblaw's, and convinced Loblaw's president Milton Cork to sell a controlling interest in his company to Weston's. Metcalf's secretive acquisitions during the 1950s, including food processors and supermarket chains across the country, were not in some cases publicly announced until 1966. The legacy of this corporate Darwinism was a sprawling empire, controlled since Garfield Weston's 1978 death by his sons Garry and Galen, whose international activities—involving polo, fine houses, and well-publicized business manoeuvring—are avidly followed by both the business writers and the gossip columnists.

Willard Garfield Weston

Mark Bredin, born in Dublin in 1863, started a bread business in Toronto in the 1880s which grew into the Canada Bread Company; he purchased George Weston's Model Bakery in 1903 as part of an attempt to dominate the local market. A motoring and yachting enthusiast, Bredin also served a term as Ward Three alderman on Toronto city council.

Goldwin Smith

In 1875, Professor Goldwin Smith married the widow Boulton—the daughter-in-law of pioneer D'Arcy Boulton—and moved into her home called "The Grange," one of the oldest houses in Toronto. Built before 1820 in what was virtually wilderness, the house had over 100 acres of grounds, and was an oasis of gentility in colonial-era Toronto—even as late as Smith's death in 1910 it lent a graceful charm to the surrounding streets. It was willed as an art museum to the city, and has since been used as a gallery and offices. Now, after a complete restoration, it is a museum.

The death in June, 1910, of the intellectual and political writer Goldwin Smith was greeted with a reverence befitting the man one newspaper* called the "foremost citizen of Toronto." His health had been declining since one night the previous February, when he rose from his bed and moved to turn up the gas lamp. By mistake he turned it out and, unable to relight it in the pitch blackness, he fell, fracturing his leg. He was 87 years old.

Smith died at 3:20 on the afternoon of the seventh of June, a Tuesday. The *Star* scooped the other papers, and had an "Extra" on the streets by suppertime. The next day, amidst tributes from near and far, the newspapers reported that the noted sculptor W. S. Allward had been engaged to make a death mask, and that Smith's brain would not be sent to Cornell University as had been previously announced. On the Friday, Smith's body lay in state at "The Grange" for four hours in the afternoon, while "a steady stream of people passed without halt or pause up the long avenue, through the open door and wide hallway, and into the darkened drawing-room where the master of the beautiful old house lay sleeping

*The newspaper was the *Star*, which was especially effusive as the Liberal party had adopted a watered-down version of Smith's ideas on commercial union with the United States; the other local papers, which did not necessarily share the *Star*'s enthusiasm for the Liberals' then current free-trading stance, nonetheless shared the sentiment that he had been a remarkable man.

his last sleep among the green branches of the old trees he loved so well." An unusual aspect of the procession of mourning, wrote the reporter, was the number of members of the working classes, 600 of whom had entered by two o'clock, confirming Smith's reputation as "a friend of the working people." The *Star*'s anonymous reporter hyperbolized that "the beautiful drawing room with its two divisions had been transformed into a chamber of death. The blinds to the front were drawn, but the brilliant afternoon sun could not be denied its right of entry. Through the opened eastern door appeared a wide prospect of waving branches and sun-flooded lawns."

Professor Goldwin Smith's long, controversy-filled life began in Berkshire, in 1823. He attended Eton, then Magdalen College at Oxford University, where he became known as a radical and a free-trader. So great were his qualifications that he ascended to the chair of modern history at Oxford, from which he promulgated his belief in the vitality of the American political experiment, and championed the Union cause during the Civil War. He resigned in 1866, reportedly when he came into his patrimony (this, according to friends of Smith who eulogized him, was the custom of the time at Oxford). He then was urged to enter Parliament, but declined, either because his personal fortune was inadequate (Members of Parliament received no pay), or because he refused to ally himself with any political party (or vice-versa), or because of a mysterious "sad domestic duty" which occupied him for a year and a half.

In 1868, Smith met Andrew White, the first president of Cornell University, and was intrigued enough by its democratic and progressive ideals that he agreed to join it as professor of English and constitutional history; he set off for the campus at Ithaca, New York, leaving people at home in England to conjecture that he was "burying his brilliant gifts in an obscure American town." (Cornell University had been founded three years previously with a bequest from Ezra Cornell, the man who had originated the system of stringing telegraph wires onto poles, and subsequently made a fortune organizing telegraph companies. Cornell's wish was that "any person can find instruction in any study"; although he himself had little education and had started work as a mechanic, he had the idea, radical for his time, that people of ability, even if poor, should be able to get an advanced education.) On arrival at Ithaca, Smith took lodgings in a boarding house.

Smith first visited Toronto, where he had relatives, in 1871. Enamoured of the place and its Englishness, he bought a house in the Brockton suburb from G. T. Denison II; a confirmed bachelor, he lived there and wrote when not fulfilling his obligations at Cornell. A few years later, however, he met the widow Boulton, married her, and moved permanently to her estate "The Grange," a "bit of old England in new Canada." Smith's bride had been married to William Henry Boulton, twice Toronto mayor and the son of the D'Arcy Boulton Jr. who had built the

Goldwin Smith in his study at "The Grange," in 1909, the year before his death. At the time of the photograph, he was in his late eighties, though he was quite active and productive until a fall the following February. The writer Stephen Leacock told the following story to illustrate Smith's energetic manner: "One day, when he was over 80 years of age, I met him in one of the new skyscraper buildings of Toronto, about to start upstairs. 'Won't you take the elevator, Dr. Smith,' I asked. 'I haven't time to wait for it,' was his reply."

There were several outbuildings at "The Grange" before 1910, including three keepers' cottages, of which this one, near the northwest corner of the property, was occupied by the gardener Mr. Bullock.

house in 1817. Through the 35 years of his residence there, Smith made some modifications to the house and preserved its acres of fine grounds and gardens. From the peace and quiet of his library, he wrote some of the works that made him "the grand old man of letters in the English-speaking world," and a radical firebrand in Canadian political life.

His writings reflected his repugnance of militarism and imperialism (he was, for example, one of the few who opposed the Boer War), his belief in free trade and democracy, and his desire for union with the United States. In his 1893 opus *The United States: An Outline of Political History*, he described himself as "an Englishman who regards the American Com-

monwealth as the great achievement of his race, and looks forward to the voluntary reunion of the American branches of the race within its pale, yet desires to do justice to the mother country, and to render her the meed of gratitude which is her due." He was xenophobic, a trait expressed both in his anti-Semitism and in his feeling that the importation of African slaves into America was one of the great calamities of all time. Slavery, he wrote, was the chief molding force in American politics. Probably, the "Yankeeism" he experienced during his time at Cornell was not to his taste either.

As for Canada, Smith regarded it as a mistake both geographically and politically. In the first instance, he felt that Canada's regions had more in common with their counterparts in the United States than with each other; thus Canada's east-west union—the policy of Sir John A. Macdonald's Conservative governments, expressed through the creation of the Canadian Pacific Railway—was doomed to failure. In the second instance, he considered that sentimental ties to Britain and the existence of the parallel Québécois culture militated against Canadians achieving enough national feeling to make the country strong and unified. Absorption into the United States of America was for him the only logical and attractive future. In the 1890s, by which time the Liberal party had moved away from the "little Ontario" of Edward Blake, Smith's ideas of commercial union with the United States looked to the Liberals like the curate's egg—good in parts—and became the harbinger of their 1911 attempt at a free-trade agreement with the United States.

From "The Grange," Smith fired off salvoes of articles for magazines, including the *Canadian Monthly* and the political and literary journal *The Nation*. He established the influential *Bystander*, then *The Week*, for which he wrote under the pen name "A Bystander." Late in his life, he became identified with *The Farmers' Sun*, which after his death became the policy organ of the United Farmers of Ontario.

When he moved to Toronto in 1875, he was quickly appointed to the university Senate. Because of his "continental opinions" and lack of support for Britain on imperial questions such as the Boer War, he was denied an honorary degree, although this situation was corrected before his death.

His wife died in September, 1909. Smith bequeathed the house and its grounds to the city, for use as an art museum. It formally opened on June 5, 1913, featuring his collection of paintings and etchings, plus some others. A new gallery was built on the grounds in 1918, and "The Grange" became offices until its restoration as a museum in the 1970s.

Church Street

A butcher shop at the southeast corner of Church and Carlton in the 1870s. Recollections of the period invariably mention the aroma surrounding butchers and groceries. As there was no refrigeration, and few glass showcases, the meat hung on hooks and aged until succulent and tender. Meat was either cured in the traditional Scots or Irish way, or else killed fresh—say, on a Tuesday, and then hung to age for the Sunday supper. With luck a breeze blew through the shop, and made the flies work for their supper. The smells of wheels of cheese, barrels of sultanas and biscuits, and the gaslights all competed for attention. Families who were well-known to a shop's proprietor usually ran an almost unlimited line of credit, paying their large accounts at Christmas and receiving a free turkey in thanks.

(Next page) Looking south along Church Street from Shuter in the 1890s. The Metropolitan Methodist Church is on the right.

The first church at the corner of King and Church streets, now the site of dignified St. James Cathedral, was the modest "Church at York," opened in 1807. A map drawn a few years later shows the little community of York occupying the few tight blocks to the east of the church, from Jarvis to Ontario streets south of Duchess (now Richmond Street East). The church stood on the other side of the road from the schoolhouse at King and Jarvis; a trail ran from King Street in a northwesterly direction, passing the church and crossing fields to the house of the Hon. John McGill, the colonial commissioner of stores. Following his death, his 100-acre property was subdivided, and Church Street was cleared northwards. An 1842 map shows it extending to what is now College Street, although there were no buildings north of Shuter. Over the next few decades it was built up with houses, "somewhat less aristocratic" than either Jarvis or Sherbourne, but nonetheless a prestigious address due to its proximity to the street of cathedrals in the "city of churches."

M.KLUCKNER
©'87

The *Ne Temere* Incident

Church Street is the avenue of cathedrals in the midst of the "city of churches." No greater evidence remains of the power of religion in the nineteenth century than its Anglican, Roman Catholic, and Methodist cathedrals, whose spires dominated the skyline in an age before businessmen chose the height of *their* temples to express their power and influence. But the glory of the cathedrals masks the pettiness of interdenominational bickering: Anglicans dominated Ontario in Family Compact days, Methodists were "holier than thou" and led the fight against the sins of liquor, and everybody fought the Catholics. Everyone, of whatever persuasion, went to church—as C. S. Clark wrote in 1898, "the churches are pretty well filled, and there is a halo of respectability surrounding him who goes to church which nothing else can give."

Ontario was the headquarters of Orange, anti-Catholic sentiment in Canada. Beginning not long after 1791, when British North America was split into Upper (English) and Lower (French) Canada, English-speaking Canadians of the ilk of lawyer D'Alton McCarthy led crusades against what they said was the pernicious and growing influence of a separate, French-speaking Canadian culture. McCarthy was more than a bigot or a crackpot—the Jesuit Estates Bill, in which the Pope was to arbitrate a compensation settlement for lands seized from the Jesuits at the time of the conquest of Quebec, revealed McCarthy as an advocate of Canadian unity, which he saw as possible only within a unilingually English society. Later, he campaigned vigorously against separate schools, and his "McCarthyites" helped to split the vote in the 1896 election, ironically clearing the way for the Liberal government of the Catholic and separate school supporter Wilfrid Laurier.

The separate schools issue tore Manitoba apart, and in Ontario had the largest impact in Ottawa, where it dominated local politics during the First World War years. In Toronto, there were tirades from pulpits and rabble-rousing in the letters columns of the newspapers. Toronto had always been an Orange town, with members of the Orange Lodge usually dominating civic politics; a typical, if extreme, commentator was E. E. Sheppard, the founder of *Saturday Night* magazine, and for a time during the late 1890s the *de facto* proprietor of the *Evening Star*. His editorial pronouncements on religion were always virulently anti-Catholic, and his political opinions fervently pro-English, anti-French Canadian.

A typical year was 1905, when the separate schools issue dominated federal politics, and the cry of "Government by Rome" prompted angry public meetings and blizzards of letters to the newspapers. In Toronto, the Reverend Father Minehan championed the cause of the separate school, and defended Sir Wilfrid Laurier's Liberal government against the local Protestant clergy. In Quebec's opinion, according to *Le Soleil*, Toronto was "the hotbed of Toryism, Orangeism, of hypocrisy and of political stupidity—the City pretends to be the centre of intelligence in Canada, yet it is certainly the centre of fanaticism and bigotry."

St James' Cathedral, Toronto

Soaring over 300 feet into the sky, the spire of St. James Cathedral, at King and Church, dominated the surrounding city during a less secular age, much as the Anglican Bishop Strachan dominated the religious life of Family Compact-era Toronto (Strachan is buried in the chancel). Erected beginning in 1850, it is the fourth St. James on the site—its predecessor had burned, its spire like a torch, in the Great Fire of 1849. The postcard indicates fairly accurately the transition of brick colour in many Toronto buildings from the original bright ochre to the "pigeon grey" of presandblasted maturity.

"The Roman Catholic Church, though not a large or very influential body in Toronto, possesses a good deal of wealth, and within the sphere of its operations does much for religion and no less for charity." So wrote historian G. Mercer Adam in 1891, reflecting the popular feeling that, in Orange Toronto, Catholics were fish out of water. In the first two decades of the century, they accounted for less than fifteen percent of the population, and were mainly of Irish background. Acute resentment of Catholics, their schools, "their" province of Quebec, and the edicts of their popes and prelates continued until the end of the First World War, then simmered for decades thereafter. In the 1820s, Bishop Power had erected the first Catholic church in Toronto—St. Paul's on Power Street, south of the current (built 1887) St. Paul's on Queen Street. Bishop Power died in the cholera epidemic of 1847, by which time St. Michael's Cathedral on Church Street at Shuter was under construction. Bishop Power had to justify his decision to erect the cathedral in what was then practically bushland to the west of the city centre.

Six years later, a Papal decree practically set Ontario on its ear; it was not an issue which by any means was confined to Toronto, but, as with Prohibition five years later, it affected a tremendous number of individuals and brought the relationship between the Catholic and Protestant churches to a new low. This so-called *Ne Temere* Decree* had actually been promulgated in Rome in April, 1907, and came into effect a year later. Addressed to Catholics, it was intended to make the conducting of all Catholic marriages conform to the same set of rules, and was specifically aimed at resolving the dogmatic dispute of mixed marriages: it did

---

*Papal decrees are written in Latin and are identified by the first few words of their text. *Ne Temere* itself means "not heedlessly." The dogmatic inconsistencies of *Ne Temere* were corrected in *Matrimonia Mixta* in 1971.

The newest of the enormous churches on Church Street is Metropolitan United—called Metropolitan Methodist until the union of the Methodists with the Congregationalists and most of the Presbyterians in 1925. The large church behind it in the postcard is St. Michael's Cathedral. Along with the Presbyterians and numerous smaller denominations, the Methodists had had a bitter fight for recognition against the Church of England-dominated Upper Canada establishment. Methodism in Ontario was an outgrowth of the Methodist Episcopal church, which had been established in Baltimore in 1784. Outsiders applied the name to what founder John Wesley in England had called the United Society, because of the methodical way in which the believers ordered their lives. The main congregation in Ontario took the name of Wesleyan Methodist Church; it was especially notable in colonial days for its antislavery stance. By the beginning of this century, there were 34 Methodist congregations in Toronto.

not prohibit them, but held them to be invalid unless a special dispensation of the Archbishop had been obtained and they were performed by a Catholic priest. By way of justification, the Church explained that the Decree was only to prevent clandestine marriages. As it turned out, the Decree dovetailed very neatly with a clause in Quebec civil law which said that civil officials and priests who were authorized to perform marriages need not do so if something in their own creed stood in the way. Probably, most of the two million Catholics in Canada agreed in principle with the *Ne Temere* Decree, viewing marriage as a sacrament controlled by the Church.

The simplicity and logic of the issue—from the Catholic standpoint—was not apparent to the Protestants. Many Canadians felt that the validity of all civil laws—in this case, whether a marriage performed by a clergyman recognized as competent by the State could be declared invalid by some other body—was challenged by the Decree. All over Ontario, Orange orders spluttered their denunciations—Ontario and Manitoba were the centres of hostility, fanned by journals such as the *Orange Sentinel*. This strictly religious and racial aspect of the controversy added another dimension to several examples of real personal hardship, as the Decree, though promulgated only in 1908, could be applied retroactively. Many unfortunate couples, who thought they were legally married and in some cases had borne children, discovered that they were living in a state of sin, the Catholics among them risking excommunication and eternal damnation. In Toronto, there was a widespread rumour of the mixed marriage and subsequent difficulties of two members of well-known Toronto families. Urgency added to the general confusion, as in Ontario alone during 1910, 1,509 Catholics had married non-Catholics. Were they all living outside of wedlock?

In Montreal, three cases attracted national attention: the first, of a man married thirty years before who suddenly requested an annulment under church laws; the second, of a woman named Meunier who had her annulment request granted by the Archbishop; the third and most sensational, of two Catholics, Eugene Hébert and Marie Emma Clouatre, who had been married by a Protestant minister in 1908, had then had a child, and then—following Hébert's request to the Catholic church—had his marriage annulled, on the grounds that the ceremony was invalid according to the *Ne Temere* Decree. Mme. Hébert appealed to the Quebec courts, and lost when the ecclesiastical law was upheld. By this time, the case had become a *cause célèbre*, and its appeal in November, 1911, attracted a tremendous amount of interest, with two expensive and talented lawyers representing the litigants. Though Hébert withdrew for lack of funds, the judge ordered that the arguments should continue, which they did, through a tangle of precedents, treaties, history, and legislation, for two months. On January 21, 1912, the judge gave his decision in favour of the marriage as a legal contract.

During the year, the political aspects of the case had scarcely been ignored, but typically the issue was argued over which level of government had the jurisdiction, under the British North America Act, to regulate marriages. The federal minister of justice, Sir Allan Aylesworth, doubted that the Canadian Parliament could enact a national marriage law, doubted also that any province could declare who could or could not be married or could annul a marriage, but stated with some conviction that the provinces alone had the power to decide on the formalities of the wedding service. Soon thereafter, the Liberals lost the election to the Conservatives led by Robert Borden; nearly a year passed before the new minister of justice addressed the issue.

Meanwhile, a number of Protestants throughout the country were heaping abuse upon the Decree and Catholics in general. The *Christian Guardian*'s view was representative: "If a Roman Catholic now becomes married to a Protestant by a Protestant minister, although that marriage is perfectly legal, and is recorded as such in the proper Registry office, any Roman Catholic priest is compelled to advise him that, in spite of the fact that the law of the country declares him to be married, he is not really married and, if he would save his soul, he must refuse to live with his wife. Although the man has pledged himself to love and honour and cherish this woman, although he seems bound by laws of probity and honesty, and by the ties of manly honour, to be loyal to the woman whom he has chosen as his bride, his Church steps in and bids him, at the risk of eternal perdition, to abandon her." Concurrently, several local issues, unrelated directly to the *Ne Temere* Decree, seemed to lend credence to the *Christian Guardian*'s scenario of a future peopled with droves of abandoned wives and fatherless children: J. J. Kelso's highly publicized work as Superintendent of Neglected Children; Dr. Helen MacMurchy's reports on the relationship between working mothers and infant mortality; the number of baby farms, and reports in the press of an increase in wife desertions and the subsequent abandonment of children to orphanages. In addition, Canada was accepting large numbers of "Barnardo Boys"—children who were often but not necessarily abandoned from the meanest slums of England. These boys were brought to Canada as little more than indentured labourers and resettled with fami-

One of the most publicly active Anglicans in Toronto was Canon Henry John Cody, who at various times served as rector of St. Paul's church on Bloor Street at Jarvis, minister of education for the Province of Ontario, and president of the University of Toronto. He was elected bishop of Nova Scotia in 1904, but declined the office; in 1921, he was elected archbishop of Melbourne, Australia, but again decided to remain in Toronto. His other secular activities included trusteeships of the Royal Ontario Museum and the World Teacher's Federation, a membership in the Royal Canadian Yacht Club, and an honorary membership in the Commercial Travellers' Association. He lived at 603 Jarvis Street, a block from St. Paul's. Maurice Cody Memorial Hall there—the old or second St. Paul's Church—was named for his son.

lies, sometimes in the city, but usually in the country.

On the specific marriage issue raised by the Catholic Church's action, Protestants generally agreed that it would place young girls and women in peril at the hands of rakes and triflers. So strong was the grip of religion that few people saw indifference as a remedy; the *Globe*, however, hinted in its worldly way at that solution: "There is absolutely nothing in the Civil law requiring Catholics to be married by their own clergy. That is Church law only and of no legal effect. Two Catholics, or a Catholic and a Protestant, married by any properly ordained clergyman whatsoever, are husband and wife, and the Civil law will see to it that they discharge the legal obligations assumed by them under that contract."

These moderate statements and the genuine concern of many people for the unfortunate potential fate of the participants in mixed marriages, were only one side of the coin of Protestant opinion. The *Orange Sentinel* bombarded its largely Ontarian audience with a series of editorials which denounced the Roman Catholic hierarchy as arrogant, aggressive, intolerant, and insulting to every Protestant minister in Canada. In Toronto, a whirlwind of fire and brimstone emanated from the Broadway Tabernacle pulpit of the Methodist Rev. Dr. W. H. Hincks: "We denounce it as cruel, as arrogant, as an infringement on our Civil law, as immoral wherever applied, as the most bigoted piece of legislation attempted since the Reformation and, finally, as incompatible with the continued unity of this Canadian commonwealth." Joining him in these sentiments were local clergymen of the Congregationalist, Presbyterian, Baptist, and Anglican denominations. The Rev. Byron Stauffer of the Congregationalist Church asked: "Shall Roman Catholic wife deserters be allowed to hide behind the *Ne Temere* Decree, and be helped in so doing by our courts of law?" Many clergyman took particular offence because the gist of the Pope's decree, they felt, was that a marriage ceremony performed by a Protestant minister was no marriage ceremony at all. Father Minehan of Toronto, who had earlier attempted to defend Laurier and separate schools, tried to pour holy oil on the stormy waters: "Is it not time for respectable non-Catholics to take active steps to put down this devil's game? Are they not aware of the harm done to Christianity in every form by these successful appeals to ignorance and hatred?" He also, however, iterated his belief that one faith—that is, no mixed marriages without proper dispensation—was essential to make the "wondrous, mystical union of two individuals peaceful, pure and loving, with God at its centre."

By the following year, 1912, much of the heat had gone from the mat-

ter, except in Ontario, where the Rev. Hincks continued his polemic, and a Toronto Methodist minister, Rev. C. O. Johnston, stirred the ants' nest again by making an "absurd, filthy and criminal" anti-Protestant oath, purportedly used at some time in the past by the Jesuit Order, the subject of his text for a savage attack on the Roman Catholic church. But outside of Ontario, few people seemed concerned any longer. Also, it appeared that the *Ne Temere* Decree was no longer being applied retroactively— there were no repetitions of the *causes célèbres* which had led to the sensationalism of the previous year.

Regardless, ten days after Johnston's vituperative sermon, the Conservative Member of Parliament for Lincoln, E. A. Lancaster, introduced a private member's bill which would make all marriages performed by any legally authorized person valid throughout the country. His prime minister, Robert Borden, as well as the past and current ministers of justice and the deputy minister, said that because the word "solemnization" appeared in the section of the British North America Act pertaining to marriages, and that marriage had anyway been made a provincial jurisdiction, legislation such as proposed by Lancaster was not "within the legislative competence of the Parliament of Canada." Borden announced that the government had decided to send a test case to the Supreme Court, and thence to the Judicial Committee of the Privy Council in London, to determine who had the power to do what, when, and to whom. Thus a debate over marriage rites and rights became a secular constitutional issue.

Meanwhile, the central issue of the Catholic argument—that couples should not be able to marry in secret—was almost forgotten, and elopers and lovebirds of all denominations continued to steal away for "Detroit marriages" and to haunt the no-questions-asked honeymoon motels of Niagara Falls. As the Archbishop Bruchesi put it, "Have we ever seen a Catholic priest, even when urgently pressed, celebrate the marriage of two persons belonging to another religious congregation than the Catholic church? Such a thing will never be seen. If the Protestant ministers did accordingly, if they did not admit before them to receive their consent to marriage, imprudent and guilty Catholics, on the simple presentation of a civil permit, after neglecting to inquire their age and condition, we would not have these scandals that have caused so much trouble in society . . . ." The government's test case was readied for the Supreme Court, in what became an elaborate feast of fees for the selected King's Counsels. Two lawyers appeared for the Dominion government to argue that the Dominion had the power to pass the Lancaster bill; one appeared on behalf of

Ontario to argue that the Dominion should pass it; two appeared to oppose the right of the Dominion and were so appointed and remunerated by the Dominion; while a further two appeared for the Quebec government to argue that the Supreme Court had not "the requisite jurisdiction" even to hear the case.

The Ontario government's position was the most out of character, for it had never since Confederation—especially during the multi-decade stewardship of the Liberal premier Oliver Mowat—supported the Dominion in anything which could conceivably diminish provincial powers. Edward Bayley, K.C.—the lawyer appearing for Ontario—stated the province's case in a masterly convolution: "While of the opinion that it is difficult to give an unqualified yes or no to any one of the questions submitted in this case, and that the law on the subject is difficult to determine, the Province of Ontario favours a uniform general marriage law for the Dominion—if so framed that the Legislative authority of the Provinces in relation to the solemnization of marriage is not thereby violated; and the Province of Ontario adopts so much of the argument of Counsel for the Dominion as is consistent with the view above expressed, and no more. The Province of Ontario considers that an Act of Parliament which renders valid throughout the Dominion marriages performed in a Province by persons legally authorized by such Province would result in consolidating and perfecting Provincial authority throughout Canada, and, on this view, the passing of such an Act by the Dominion Parliament would enlarge rather than encroach upon Provincial jurisdiction."

The decision of the Supreme Court, made public on June 18, 1912, was appealed and sustained by the Privy Council in London. The latter's final verdict declared the Parliament of Canada unable to legislate a national marriage law. French Canadians appeared satisfied with that; the Orange school of thought concentrated in Ontario demanded an amendment to the British North America Act which would allow the Dominion that power; the Evangelical Alliance of Canada obtained 300,000 signatures on a petition for a national marriage law; elsewhere, there was indifference. So complicated had been the proceedings, and so muddied the issues, that the old allegations of the perils of fair maidens and the pernicious dogma of the pope were submerged in a constitutional tussle, with provincial rights declared victorious.

* * *

The *Ne Temere* Decree, and the vitriol it spawned, drove a broad wedge between Catholics and Protestants. Two years after the Judicial Committee of the Privy Council issued its decision, the First World War started, and the old fight between Catholics and Protestants shifted to the new battleground of whether French Canadians were as Imperialist as English Canadians. Near the end of the war, however, in one of the myriad charitable efforts sponsored by organizations in Toronto, the Catholic Army Huts Association set out to raise funds. Their campaign, at the beginning of October, 1918, lasted only three days, but even though war-weary Torontonians were tiring of tag-days, they contributed $300,000 *more* than the target sum. At a wind-up banquet on the fifth of October in the Pompeiian room at the King Edward Hotel, speakers described the feeling of fellowship, of unity, and of forgetting old differences, as "the greatest event in the history of Toronto." Sir Edmund Walker, a Presbyterian and the president of the Bank of Commerce, said that the greatest compliment ever offered him was being asked to be treasurer of the campaign. Two days later, the Catholic Army Huts Association placed a large advertisement in local papers under the banner "Toronto The Magnificent, We Thank You."

* * *

The social upheaval which led to the First World War also led inexorably to a decline in the relative importance of organized religion. New, less orthodox types of religion sprang up, often preached by evangelists such as the Rev. J. E. Hunter; some turned to new devices like radio to further their proselytizing.

Two of the most active Toronto radio priests in the 1930s—the era of the crypto-fascist Father Coughlin in the United States, the wacky Rev. Clem Davies on the west coast, and the transplanted Canadian Aimee Semple McPherson in Los Angeles—were the Rev. Morris Zeidman and the Rev. Charles Lanphier. Zeidman was a converted Jew who preached the Protestant gospel in The Ward, ran the Scott Mission, and operated the Protestant Radio League from his home at Palmerston and College (page 135). Lanphier was the Catholic cross-bearer: born in Toronto in 1901, he attended the De La Salle Institute, was ordained at St. Michael's Cathedral, and became the assistant at St. Paul's on Power Street. In May, 1933, he started the Radio League of St. Michael; his programs mixed religion with anti-Communism, and he was twice banned from the C.B.C. for his "active intervention" in municipal politics. Lanphier felt that Communist subversion was a greater menace to Canada than was Nazism. Throat cancer killed him in 1959.

The 1930s was the era of the radio priest. The Rev. Charles Lanphier, like Morris Zeidman, stirred up a cauldron of controversy whenever he stood up to a radio microphone. Born in Toronto and educated at the De La Salle Institute, he began his radio broadcasts in 1933, and was soon known as a fierce anti-Communist.

Maple Leaf Gardens

Maple Leaf Gardens, Toronto, Canada

The fourth cathedral on Church Street, dedicated to the gods of hockey and wrestling, was built in five months and twelve days—a day-and-night marathon culminating in the opening of the 1931 Maple Leafs' hockey season. With the building of Maple Leaf Gardens, acclaimed as the best arena in the world, hockey in Toronto came of age.

The Gardens' promoter, Conn Smythe, did nothing by half measures or without bravado. Born in Toronto in 1895 with the moniker Constantine Falkland Cary Smythe, he was the son of an oddball newspaper reporter and sometime mystic (page 50). Smythe was physically small but in all other ways was larger than life—he played amateur hockey, and made up for his lack of strength and talent by inspiring others to great performances; he enlisted early in the First World War, became a lieutenant in the 40th Battery, Canadian Field Artillery and won the Military Cross for a raiding action in February, 1917; his father wanted him to be an engineer, but when he returned to Toronto he started a gravel and cement business; he continued his interest in hockey, and in 1924 coached the University of Toronto team to win the Allan Cup; on the basis of that performance, the owners of the New York Rangers asked him to assemble a hockey team, but soon fired him for his impudence. Adjec-

tives used in "The Major's" obituaries to describe his personality include abrasive, bellicose, outspoken and outrageous; he was also ambitious, and a gambler.

He returned to Toronto and set out to build his own team. According to the legend, he took his savings to the racetrack and in short order doubled them to $20,000. He raised another $140,000, and purchased the old St. Patrick's Hockey Club, changing its name to the Maple Leafs. He was able to convince John Paris Bickell, a investor in the club, to transfer his allegiance to him, and to keep his investment with the team. Bickell agreed with Smythe that the draughty old firetrap on Mutual Street which had served as the "St. Pat's" home arena was a drawback to the growth of the new team, and provided the money, knowledge and management ability which made possible the building and running of Maple Leaf Gardens. In addition, Smythe took loans and made promises, and it is said that he personally convinced many of the workmen to accept low pay in return for stock in the Maple Leaf Gardens Corporation—a shrewd financial decision on their part.

Bickell remained involved with the team as president, and later as chairman of the board of Maple Leaf Gardens, until his death in 1951 (his photograph is on page 307). Smythe went from strength to strength. He gave up two players and $35,000 to lure "King" Clancy from Ottawa, to pair on defence with Hap Day, and was rewarded the following season when the Leafs won the Stanley Cup, in their first season in the Gardens. His promotional ability, and Foster Hewitt's whining radio voice, created a national spectacle every Saturday night.

Smythe never lost his quixotic sense of duty, and in 1941—like a romantic figure from the First World War—he raised an anti-aircraft battalion of noted athletic figures for overseas service. Stuck away from the front lines, he railed publicly at the authorities for not sending him into action, then after he was wounded in an attack on his battalion, railed again because he felt that all the Canadian soldiers were raw recruits.

The Leafs, with their unflappable goaltender Turk Broda, dominated hockey in the late 1940s, then again in the early 1960s. Smythe's chippy, aggressive attitude to hockey was reflected in the famous statement "If you can't lick 'em in the alley, you can't beat 'em on the ice," giving license to gladiators like Eddie Shack. He sold control of the Gardens in 1961 to his son Stafford, Harold Ballard, and John Bassett, but remained as a director until he disagreed with the 1965 decision to allow the draft-dodging heavyweight Cassius Clay to box in the Gardens. He was also known as a horse breeder, and continued his lifelong enthusiasm for the racetrack—two of his horses won the Queen's Plate. He died in 1980.

Sherbourne Street

Sherbourne is the easternmost of the three formerly fashionable residential streets which run from Bloor to Queen Street. The layout of these streets, as with the others running the mile and a quarter north to south between Bloor and Queen, dates from the 1790s, the time of Governor Simcoe and the establishment of the Town of York. Colonial officials received 100-acre strips of land, each one-eighth of a mile wide, called "park lots," between Bloor and Queen; a few of the officials established dignified residences and conducted themselves like landed gentry, while others subdivided, amalgamated, and traded their sinecures.

Sherbourne Street runs through the park lots of the postmaster, William Allan, and the surveyor-general, Thomas Ridout. The Ridout family birthplace was the town of Sherbourne in Dorset. Allan, who had a profound love of gardening, established the Allan Gardens between Carlton and Gerrard on Sherbourne. He turned them over to the Toronto Historical Society in 1861, and today they remain as a reminder of the street's genteel beginnings during the Victorian age, when a popular hobby was collecting exotic plants. By contrast, the land to the east is a different type of jungle—the 1960s highrise apartment development called St. James Town.

The painting looks south along Sherbourne Street to Howard Street in the 1930s. The boulevard and its trees were removed in the autumn of 1953 for the road widening which had earlier caused such a stunning change in the appearance of Jarvis Street. In the row on the left, there were originally four identical, modest houses, numbers 605 through 611—today, only 605 and 607 survive in a state of disrepair. The opposite side of Sherbourne Street was much more grand, especially the old Charles H. Gooderham house at number 592 (the Selby Hotel) and the James Cooper house at 582 (the Knights of Columbus clubhouse), which occupy the entire block between Selby and Linden. The former was a private residential hotel, like the nearby Isabella Hotel; its residents included Toronto Transportation Commission manager H. H. (later Sir Herbert) Couzens and publisher William Copp (right), whose father was the first president of the Copp, Clark Company. Number 582 Sherbourne became in 1905 the Keeley Institute for the treatment of drug and alcohol problems. For a brief period concurrent with the Keeley Institute's occupation of the building next door, the Selby Hotel building was the Branksome Hall Girls School—a situation similar to that of the Loretto Day School on Brunswick Avenue in the Annex, which shares the block with a group of houses serving as Salvation Army residences.

William Copp

The painting shows the house occupied by the Rosar-Morrison Funeral Home, at 467 Sherbourne Street. Built as a wedding present for a daughter of Senator George Cox, it was next door to Cox's residence—a large property immediately to the south called "Sherbourne Villa." The latter was built in 1857 for Thomas Ridout—the man who named Sherbourne Street—and was occupied by Cox from 1888 until his death in 1914. Two years later, Simpson's president H. H. Fudger bought it as a boarding house for his unmarried female employees from out of town. It was demolished in 1964, but the current building on the property—a senior citizens' home—is still called "Fudger House."

Undertaker Franz Rosar was an immigrant from Prussia who had been a wood moulder in Buffalo before coming to Toronto in 1853. He met and married Rosalia Solleder, the daughter of a Catholic undertaker; Rosar and John Solleder went into business together at the corner of King and Power Street, near St. Paul's church and the House of Providence. The business grew as funerals became more elaborate and embalming became the usual practice. Rosar died in 1903; his wife Rosalia carried on with the help of two of her nine children—Edward and John. They moved the business into a house at 180 Sherbourne, then bought this house at 467 Sherbourne. Later, Edward's son Bud managed it and brought up his four daughters in the apartment above the funeral parlour; one of them married Tom Morrison, who took the business over after Bud Rosar's death in 1965. In 1986, to celebrate the 125th anniversary of the family firm, Rosar-Morrison created a chapel by renovating the old coachhouse which faces Bleecker Street at the rear of the property. The house immediately to the north of the funeral home (in the centre of the painting), was used by the Catholic Children's Aid Society until it was removed in 1954 by Rosar-Morrison, which needed a parking lot after Sherbourne Street was widened.

The Ernescliffe Apartments in the background, facing onto Wellesley Street, were built on the eve of the First World War to replace an old house called "Ermeleigh." "Ernescliffe" was a modest but respectable address in a declining area. One of its tenants was the poet Wilson Macdonald (right), a bachelor and devotee of the Church of the Open Air. He had attempted during the 1920s to ply his trade surrounded by the mountain scenery of Vancouver, but returned to Toronto to be closer to his publishers. He was president of the Poetry Society of Canada, and had

Sherbourne Street, Toronto

books published by McClelland & Stewart, Ryerson Press, and Scribner's, amongst them such titles as *The Miracle Songs of Jesus* and *The Girl Behind the Man Behind The Gun*. In addition, he was the author-composer of a two-act musical comedy called *The Girl From Vagabondia*. His almost mystic attachment to the Indian poetess and chautauqua performer Pauline Johnson emerged through his etchings of her, and a maudlin poem called "Pauline Johnson's Grave"—"She sleeps betwixt the mountains and the sea / In that great Abbey of the setting sun / A Princess, Poet, Woman, three in one / And fine in every measure of the three"—published in 1926 by J. M. Dent & Sons in a school textbook entitled *The Voice of Canada*.

Wilson Macdonald

Jarvis Street

Jarvis Street got its name from William Jarvis, one of the government officials who came to York in the 1790s and, with others, such as Thomas Ridout, William Powell, John Beverley Robinson and Peter Russell, formed the colonial aristocracy. William Jarvis was a Loyalist during the American Revolution and served with the Queen's Rangers; after the flight to Upper Canada, he served as provincial secretary for a quarter-century and, like many of his colleagues, received for his travails a 100-acre "park lot" strip.

His son and heir, Samuel P. Jarvis, built a brick house on the family park lot amidst the rural scenery north of Queen Street; following the decline of his reputation and fortunes in the 1840s, he subdivided the property, creating city lots on either side of a long, straight avenue called Jarvis Street. By the 1880s, the northern part of Jarvis and its neighbour to the east, Sherbourne, were the most fashionable addresses in Toronto. On Jarvis Street lived political figures such as federal Leader of the Opposition Edward Blake (number 467), Liberal Member of Parliament William Mulock (number 518), Conservative Lieutenant Governor Thomas Thompson (at 471); and industrialists such as Hart Massey (515 Jarvis Street, see painting on page 133) and George H. Gooderham (504 Jarvis Street, see painting on page 2).

Most had moved on by the early years of this century, leaving Jarvis Street to slip into a decline. The process, which accelerated after the Second World War due to street-widening and land speculation as a precursor to apartment redevelopment, led to boarded-up old mansions, cheap rooming houses, and sleazy clubs on the side streets—the "Jarvis Street sin strip" of the 1950s.

Two of the institutions of Jarvis Street. (Above) The Jarvis Street Baptist Church at Gerrard Street East was erected in 1875 and renovated in the late 1930s (a few decades after this postcard was printed), most notably with the addition of doors on its west face. The Baptist faith in North America dates from 1639, when a church in Providence, R.I. chose to follow the practice of some English congregations wherein immersion—not the "pouring or sprinkling" of other Christian denominations—was considered to be the correct method of baptism. By the 1890s, the Baptist communion in Toronto had grown to the point that there were 16 congregations in the city. (Below) The old Jarvis Street Collegiate Institute stood south of Carlton Street at 361 Jarvis, next to the St. Andrews Church (now the Estonian and Latvian Lutheran Church). The Institute traces its lineage to the Home District Grammar School, established in 1807 by the first rector of York, George Okill Stuart, in his house at King and George streets. In 1812, following Stuart's death, the Rev. John Strachan took it over—along with York's other ecclesiastical responsibilities—and undertook to imbue its pupils with "strong religious principles and a rich and varied curriculum." The school moved in the 1920s to the current parapeted brick pile at Jarvis and Wellesley.

Sir William Mulock (1844-1944), the long-time chief justice of Ontario, lived at 518 Jarvis, in a house since demolished for an apartment building. The son of Mary Cawthra, he was born at Bondhead in 1844, educated in Toronto, and had a distinguished legal and political career including several terms as Member of Parliament for North York during the period 1882-1905. His government service included a time as postmaster-general—he helped to secure the adoption of penny postage throughout the Empire, and in his time eliminated the department's chronic annual deficit. Utterly devoted to Liberal politics, he was the chief political organizer for Ontario.

Sarah Trumbull Warren was the wife of the founder of the Gutta-Percha & Rubber Company Limited, one of the major manufacturers of automobile tires and rubber goods in the city (gutta-percha is a tree sap with many of the properties of india rubber, and was used mainly as a substitute for leather in shoes and as insulation on electrical wires). Her husband died before the First World War, and her eldest son was killed at Ypres, so she assumed the chairmanship of the board of directors of her family's company. She was a member of an astonishing variety of committees and charities in art, immigration, health and horticulture, and was named a Lady of Grace of the Order of the Hospital of St. John of Jerusalem for her war work. She lived in the house at 95 Wellesley Street East, more recently occupied by the Canadian Red Cross.

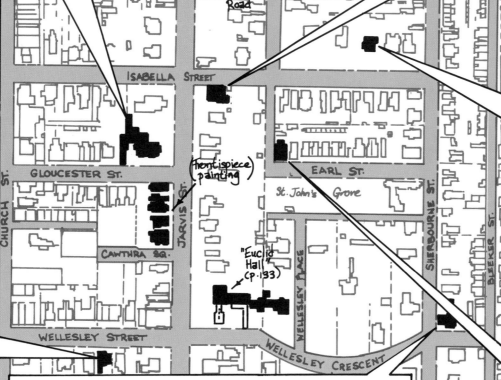

Adapted from GOAD'S Fire Atlas 1890

Robert Ross Bongard, a stockbroker who lived in the rambling house at 571 Jarvis, could trace his family back to William the Conqueror and the Doomsday Book. Generations of his ancestors bore titles ranging from seigneur to viscount. His great-grandfather settled in Philadelphia, but fled following the American revolution, and as a United Empire Loyalist received a tract of land in Prince Edward County.

Alfred Herbert Cox was the nephew of the powerful Senator George Cox, the influential Member of Parliament for West Toronto and president of the Dominion Bank, who lived on the property at 439 Sherbourne Street—now the site of "Fudger House." The former got his business training by managing the latter's affairs, and lived conveniently nearby, at 166 Isabella Street. A. H. Cox later became president of the Provident Investment Company.

Since demolished to make way for a highrise apartment, the house at 194 Wellesley Street East was in the 1920s a centre of Toronto musical education. Known as the Hambourg Conservatory of Music, it was studio and home for two members of the Hart House Quartet—cellist Boris Hambourg and violinist Harry Adaskin. Hambourg started his concert career in 1904, at the age of 20, with his brothers Mark and Jan; as the Hambourg Trio, they performed and toured all over North America. In 1911, with his "piano pedagogue" father, Boris founded the Hambourg Conservatory of Music. He played cello at the Canadian General Electric works for the Star's first radio demonstration, on March 28, 1922. Harry Adaskin, born in Latvia in 1901, joined the Toronto Symphony at the age of fifteen. He had a distinguished career as a composer and performer, and moved eventually to Vancouver, where he taught at the University of British Columbia.

In the house at the northeast corner of Earl and Huntley streets lived Arthur White, a consulting engineer who specialized in hydrology and hydroelectric power. After graduating from the University of Toronto, he collected data on power requirements for the fledgling Hydro-Electric Power Commission of Ontario, and became an expert on the power potential of Niagara. His study of Canada's dependence on coal and its practice of exporting electricity to the U.S. led him to advocate a nationalistic and independent energy policy. He married the granddaughter of Philo Remington, the manufacturer of firearms and typewriters.

The painting looks north along the west side of leafy, dappled, summertime Jarvis Street. In the years before 1947, when the road was widened, branches of the boulevard trees met in an arch high above the street, forming a canopy and a cool, shady tunnel. The buildings in the painting still exist, although now they are pressed against the sidewalk, as the sidewalk is against the street.

The building in the distance, at number 354, is now broadcast studios for the Canadian Broadcasting Corporation, but was built at the turn of the century for Havergal Girls College. The latter's principal, Ellen Mary Knox (right), the daughter of a Surrey clergyman, studied English and history at Cheltenham Ladies' College and Oxford University, played chess for recreation, and wrote three instructional books: *Bible Lessons for Schools* in 1908, and *The Girl of the New Day* and *A Girl's Week of Prayer* in 1920. Havergal moved to Avenue Road at Lawrence in the thirties; the old college building was used during the Second World War by the Royal Canadian Air Force, before being taken over by the C.B.C. The other local part of the C.B.C. establishment, the white house at 372 Jarvis Street, was the home for several years of Oliver Mowat, Liberal premier of Ontario from 1872-1896.

Ellen Mary Knox

A resident of the townhouses at 215-219 Jarvis was the bachelor William George Clysdale, the general organizer of the Conservative Association of Ontario. Born in Peterborough in 1875, he went to work for the Tories at age 31—the year after they gained power in Ontario for the first time since Confederation. Except for a two-year patronage stint as emigration inspector at the Port of Windsor, Clysdale was an Ontario Conservative party worker for three decades. His reputation was besmirched in 1934 by a judicial inquiry into a liquor "tollgate"—George Glover, the president of the Ward Four Conservative Association, testified before a government inquiry that he had written to the Stirling Bonding Company of Scotland, promising he would be able to get its products into liquor stores; he also confessed that he had paid Clysdale $50 a month to assist in popularizing "Gaelic Old Smuggler" brand.

Beaches

Though it has been nearly a lifetime since Beaches could legitimately claim to be simply a summer resort, it still *feels* like one, especially in the off-season when the privet hedges are bare of leaves and the lake and beach are windy, bleak and grey. It still gives the feeling, even though it is jammed along the shoreline between Toronto and Scarborough, of being "out past the city proper"—the sort of quiet little town to which people retire, and where the summer people board up their cottages at Labour Day or Thanksgiving and return to the city.

Beaches, or The Beach as some call it, was a resort community of cottages and canoe clubs where bare-legged girls and their beaux danced away the summertime Saturday nights at Balmy Beach. It was "small town living," especially as the lengthy ride on the Queen Street tram discouraged too much development dependent on daily access to the city. A portion of the now-famous boardwalk along the beach was built as long ago as the 1850s; as the years passed, and breezy little cottages were cobbled together along the shoreline, the boardwalk grew. What a place to spend a summer away from the oppressive city, with a canoe and a few friends and a screened front porch!

One of the first settlers to capitalize on these gentle surroundings was Joseph Williams, an Englishman who arrived in the early 1850s. His search for a farm led him to a wooded 20-acre property on the south side of Queen Street, east of Ashbridge's Bay. Here he cleared the almost flat land, leaving a few of the shade trees, and built a log cabin close to Queen Street. In his youth in London, Williams had been enamoured of the display gardens at Kew, where couples dallied amongst the dahlias, and crowds flocked to see the bananas ripening in Decimus Burton's Palm House. He named his little Beaches property Kew Farm, and even named his son Kew, as well. Resolved to have his own genteel pleasure park, he worked and scrimped and was finally able, on Queen Victoria's birthday in 1879, to open his own Kew Gardens.

Williams had been pipped at the post by an amusement ground further east called Victoria Park, on the site now occupied by the water purification plant. His, however, was a family park, closer to the city than its rival and offering tent rentals to families along the beach. He served breakfast and dinner, and was always willing to oblige the Victorians' passion for tiffin (or "elevenses"—impromptu meals, with tea, at other than mealtimes). The city expropriated Kew Gardens for a public park in 1907. The one remaining house, on Lee Avenue, was built by Kew Williams as a wedding present for his bride; it is now the caretaker's cottage.

There were other amusement parks in Beaches. The third to open, in 1898, was Munro, or Trolley, Park, on Queen Street between Nursewood and Silverbirch. The trolleys of Trolley Park were those of the Toronto Railway Company, which had established the park as a fare booster; a disagreement with the Munro family, which owned the land, and resistance from local residents who disliked the crowds and carny atmosphere, shortened its life to only a few years. The last amusement park

in the area—Scarboro Beach—opened in 1907. Five years later, the Toronto Railway Company purchased it, and ran it through the war years until its transit franchise expired in 1921. The postcard from the park reproduced on page 168 shows the "chutes lagoon" and its slide, more or less in the middle of the park. To the photographer's right was the Scarboro Inn cafe, and beyond that the seawall and sand beach. Visible in the right distance is the carousel, past which was the loading platform for a miniature steam railway whose track encircled a picnic area. To the left were formal flower beds, then a midway, and beyond that an athletic field and bleachers. Not a trace remains of the park today.

The amusement parks and pleasant beaches brought droves of strangers to the beach. In the twenties and early thirties, the beach became a popular picnic spot for Kensington residents, who could get there easily on the "Queen" streetcar. On Victoria Day, 1932, the city's "mile-long

The quirky and picturesque house of Kew Williams, built at the turn of the century in his father's Kew Gardens amusement park, was kept by the city when it expropriated the property in 1907 for a park. It still stands, at 30 Lee Avenue.

Gordon Tamblyn opened his first drugstore in 1904 at the corner of Queen and Lee—at that time on the edge of Walter Lee's estate and orchard. Born in Bellwood in 1878, Tamblyn attended high school in Markham and pharmaceutical college in Toronto and won the Robertson Scholarship and other awards of proficiency. In 1906, he took W. E. Corlett into partnership; four years later, Tamblyn's had expanded to five stores. The business was well patronized and profitable, and a number of companies including Loblaw's vied for its control. By the late 1920s there were 30 Tamblyn drugstores, mainly in the Toronto area. On every drugstore's window was the familiar slogan, "Tamblyn Saves You Money!" Tamblyn himself had to quit the business due to ill health and died in 1933, aged only 55.

park," taking in Kew, Scarborough, and Balmy beaches, opened to the public. Even more pleasure seekers flocked to the district, filled its picnic spots, and splashed and cavorted in the lake. Local louts in the Balmy Beach area who resented this influx took a cue from the fascist tactics so common in Quebec and Europe: they decided to take it out on anyone who they felt was "ethnic" and Jewish, and organized themselves in the summer of 1933 into the Balmy Beach Swastika Club. During July, and at the beginning of August, the louts displayed swastikas, harassed and bullied picnickers, and at a clubhouse dance fought with a crowd of Jewish boys who attempted to rip down the swastikas. A week later, at Christie Pits during a baseball game, there was a pitched battle between the louts and the Jews (page 224). Fortunately, the local fascists faded away with the summer season.

Winter storms and erosion have been the true menace to the preservation of the beach. In March, 1952, only twenty years after the proud opening of the eastern beaches, headlines in the *Globe* announced "Famous Strip of Beach Just A Memory Today." The article described how, in a storm the previous year, a refreshment booth had collapsed into the lake: "The walls began to bulge during a storm—then, within five hours, the roof fell in and the whole wooden structure disintegrated into the water. Only the ice box was saved. At the same time, the boardwalk had to be tied down with ropes to prevent it from being carried into the lake." The refreshment booth was rebuilt fifty feet further inland, but was almost immediately threatened by high water levels. Now, thirty-five years later, high water has returned to the Great Lakes system, but decades of erosion control work, including a breakwater, have limited the damage from winter storms.

* * *

The fine house at 10 Neville Park Boulevard was owned by Roland Caldwell Harris, commissioner of works and city engineer for Toronto, and the namesake of the R. C. Harris water purification plant at the foot of Victoria Park Avenue. Born in 1875 in Lansing, he grew up in Toronto; initially, he worked as a reporter for the Toronto *News*, then joined the city in 1901 as a clerk in the property department. Rising swiftly through the ranks, he became the head of the Parks Department, and commissioner of property and streets, before being named city engineer in 1912. His reputation for fairness made him a good choice for the controversial position of fuel administrator for Ontario during the last years of the First World War.

Harris's life spanned the period when Toronto had to get serious about its water supply. Before gas company pioneer Albert Furniss established the first waterworks in 1843, residents used rain barrels, cisterns and wells for their water supplies. In some cases, such as that of the house "Spadina," a windmill powered the water pump. During cold snaps and droughts, people had to melt snow or cart barrels of water from the bay.

Balmy Beach, Toronto, Canada

A recreation and summer resort area for city-dwellers seeking to escape the sultry heat, Balmy Beach was lined with cottages which, in the off-season, were regularly at the mercy of pounding waves and howling winds. In 1905, the Balmy Beach Club officially opened; its members held regular regattas against Kew Beach and the other local clubs; as well, it was a very fashionable dancing spot in the 1940s. A number of the cottages there were used only as summer cottages and were boarded up all winter. The one at 6 Balsam Avenue, since demolished, was owned by paint manufacturer Charles N. Haldenby, the president of Sanderson, Pearcy & Company. Commodore for a number of years of the Balmy Beach Sailing Club, Haldenby lived for the balance of the year with his wife, three sons, and four daughters at 92 Bloor Street West.

Furniss' waterworks were an improvement, but were undercapitalized from the beginning; he feuded constantly with the city, especially over the supply of water for the fire department—the city paid Furniss £250 a year, but usually found a lack of pressure whenever the fire bell tolled. In 1874, the city bought out the waterworks, and set about establishing a proper plant. For two decades, debate centred on whether Lake Ontario was a suitable source of supply for such a large city. In 1895, the city hired an English engineer named James Manserge to advise on the question; he concluded that lake water, properly filtered, was an excellent source.

But the city did nothing about a filtration plant. It continued to dump raw sewage directly into Toronto Bay, and draw its water from there, too. A laboratory test in 1906 found that fourteen percent of the water samples taken in the city were contaminated; in October, 1907, the city's medical

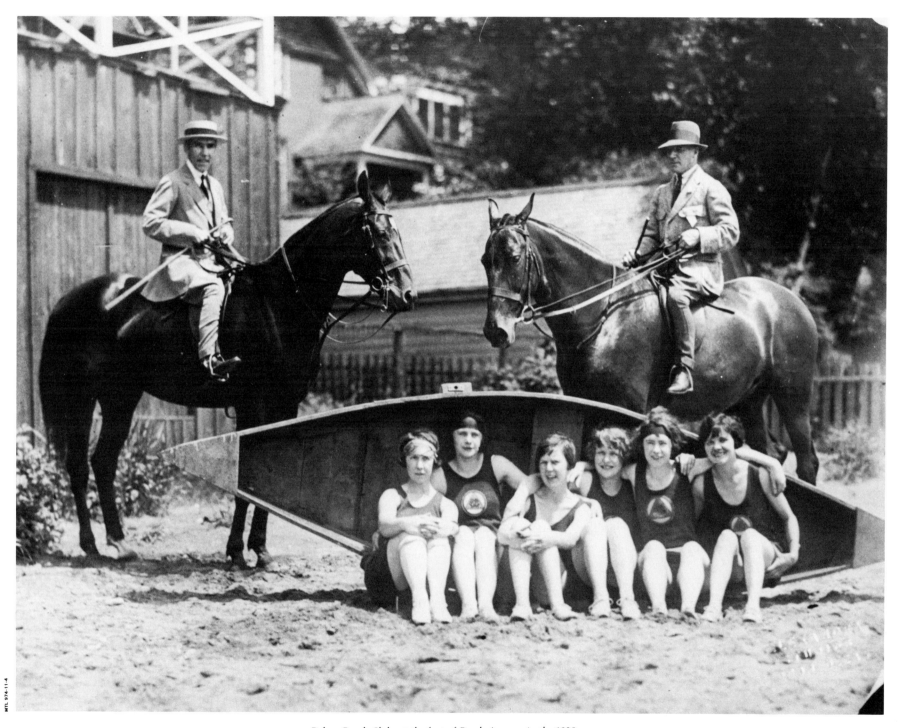

Balmy Beach Club, at the foot of Beech Avenue, in the 1920s.

health officer told city dwellers to boil their water until the city built a filtration plant. Slowly and ponderously, the city began to plan, and commenced the building of an outfall and sedimentation plant at the foot of Woodbine Avenue. Before it was finished, there was a typhoid outbreak in February, 1910. All the victims had been drinking city water. Finally, in 1911, the new sewage outfall opened, separating once and for all the intake from the exhaust. It did not, however, solve the problem of the purity of water at the intake, and Toronto Bay was, to say the least, very dirty.

The Toronto authority on purifying water was Dr. George Gallie Nasmith, a consulting engineer who was director of laboratories for the city's Department of Health. Born in Toronto, Nasmith began in his early twenties to conduct experiments on water and air pollution, during which he subjected rabbits to carbon monoxide and coal gas. His analyses of contaminated water samples led to the recommendation that the city introduce calcium hypochlorite into the water, and confirmed the need for filtration. At the outbreak of the Great War, he was put in charge of the water supply at Valcartier mobilization camp; a year later, at the Western Front, he developed the method of chlorinating and filtering water used by the British and Canadian troops. For his wartime contribution, he was made a Companion of St. Michael and St. George.

The R. C. Harris water purification plant at the foot of Victoria Park Avenue was part of a major improvement in the city's water supply undertaken in the early 1930s. Included in the work were a rock tunnel two miles out into the lake, the filtration plant, a supply tunnel seventy feet below street level stretching across the ten-mile front of the city, and a number of reservoirs. The plant itself is a golden, stunning edifice, low and long on the bank above the blue, blue lake, in an Art Deco form like a Mayan temple. On sunny days late in the winter, when the grass is free of snow and golden like the building, it is a scene of great tranquillity and beauty.

Scarboro Beach by night, Toronto, Canada.

"Rolly" Harris, the legendary works commissioner and namesake of the water purification plant at the foot of Victoria Park Avenue. His work was his pleasure, he said, and he thought nothing of putting in a ten-hour day. He liked the "mechanical and chemical aspects" of his one hobby, photography.

Scarboro Beach Park occupied the piece of land a block to the east of Kew Gardens. Bought and expanded soon after opening by the Toronto Railway Company—which used it as a weekend fare-booster like other amusement parks sponsored by street railways all over North America—it offered attractions ranging from slides and rides to shooting galleries, vaudeville acts, high dives, marathon bicycle races, and even unintentionally brief aviation demonstrations. The postcard—a daytime photograph skilfully tinted—shows, on the left, a pavilion devoted to the San Francisco Earthquake of 1906. Besides ogling photographs, patrons could witness the shaking of a tabletop diorama, and the subsequent cardboard carnage. In 1921, when the publicly owned Toronto Transportation Commission took over the street-railway system from the Toronto Railway Company, the former refused to include Scarboro Beach Park in the purchase deal. The Park limped along for a few years, but was superseded as an attraction by Sunnyside; the T.T.C. and the T.R.C. achieved a final settlement on the land in October, 1924; the old amusement park was subdivided and sold off for housing the following year.

George Gallie Nasmith

Woodbine

The horses from Albert Edward Dyment's Brookdale Stable won the King's Plate at Woodbine—now the Greenwood Race Track in Beaches—in 1903, 1904, 1912 and 1921. Dyment was born in 1869 in Wentworth County, at Lynden, where his father had a lumber business. Active in the northern mining boom early in the 1890s, he was elected from there to the House of Commons as a Liberal in the Laurier sweep of 1896, and only defeated in 1908, by which time his Dyment, Cassels & Company had a seat on the Toronto Stock Exchange. He became president of Canadian General Electric and the Ontario Jockey Club, and held directorships in a variety of companies, including several in the fledgling radio business. He lived at "The Dale" in Rosedale.

The Greenwood Race Track on Queen Street East in Beaches used to be called "Woodbine." Woodbine Race Track opened in 1874, seven years before the founding of the Ontario Jockey Club, moving in 1956 to a new location in Malton, north of the airport.

Other early race tracks in the city included "Runnymede," the estate on the Humber River of Captain John Scarlett, in the 1830s; the St. Leger Race Course southeast of Spadina and College on property owned by the Boulton family, appearing on an 1842 map; Charlie Gates's track near Danforth Avenue and Broadview; and the Carlton track, southwest of Dundas and Keele, used in the 1860s and 1870s.

Thoroughbred racing in Ontario gained prestige in 1859, when the Toronto Turf Club sent a petition to Queen Victoria, soliciting an annual prize for a sporting event. Queen Victoria responded with a purse of 50 guineas, and a decree that the "Queen's Plate" was to be run "at Toronto or such other place in Upper Canada as Her Majesty might appoint." For the first four years, Carlton Track hosted it; subsequently, Guelph, London, Hamilton, St. Catharines, Whitby, Kingston, Ottawa, Barrie, Woodstock, Prescott, and Picton were venues. In 1883, the Queen's Plate moved to Woodbine, where it has remained since as a social and sporting highlight of the month of May.

When this photograph was taken in 1929, Edward Plunket Taylor was only in his late twenties, but already was president and general manager of Carling Breweries. Born in Ottawa, he entered the investment firm of McLeod, Young, Weir & Company at age 22, was made a director six years later, but resigned to manage his brewery operations. He was president or vice-president of a large number of breweries—Carling's, Kuntz Brewery, British American Brewing, Dominion Brewery, Empire Brewing, Grant's Spring Brewery, Kiewel Brewing, Regal Brewing, and Brady's—most of which were "cottage" operations in the style of the previous century. In the 1930s, Taylor amalgamated his brewing interests into the giant Canadian Brewing Company and, in 1945, was one of the four partners who founded the Argus Corporation. His Windfield's Farm silks—teal blue with yellow coinspots and yellow cap—dominated the winner's circle at Woodbine. Probably his most famous horse was Northern Dancer, the 1964 Kentucky Derby winner, which finally retired from stud in 1987.

The writer Jesse Edgar Middleton, in the city's 1934 official centennial history, described the scene at what had become the King's Plate: "Always the governor-general attends, as representing His Majesty, and enters the park in a four-horse barouche with top-booted postillions before, and stately bewigged footmen in the dickey behind. The paddock is crowded with personages, male and female; top-hats being polished after the similitude of a palace, and ladies' costumes being all a-shimmer with the hues of the rainbow. The stands are black with people. Far beyond the rich lawns and the snow-white stables lies the lake, placid in the springtime sunlight, perhaps with two or three sailboats, white triangles on the blue." Before 1944, only Ontario-bred horses which had never won public money could enter. Notable records include the most visits by a royal (the Queen Mother, with five) and most wins in the first half-century at Woodbine (the Seagram stable, with twenty). In more recent years, the horses of E. P. Taylor's Windfield Farms dominated the affair.

Although the races attracted the *crème de la crème* of society, the Ontario Jockey Club was unable to escape allegations of moral turpitude in the righteous early 1920s. New provisions in the Dominion's Criminal Code limited the portion of the amount wagered which racing clubs could keep, and in May, 1921, Mounties took up positions at every race track in the country to ensure that the new rules were followed. W. E. Raney, the attorney general of the United Farmers of Ontario government, criticized the new provisions as being "along the German line of making the practice of vice cheaper and safer," and tilted "with much vigour" at the windmill of jockey clubs and race track betting. Claiming that race track wagering was placing Canada on the same level as Cuba and Mexico, and was in defiance of the will of 90 percent of the residents of Ontario, he attacked the shareholders of the Ontario Jockey Club. During the period from 1910-17, the club had, he said, turned an investment of $10,000 into profits of $100,000 per year, a profit of one thousand percent per year on the investment. The only thing holding Raney back from totally prohibiting race track betting was a lack of authority—the Dominion having the right of control; he had to content himself with a sudden, large increase in taxation. As well, he used the Ontario Temperance Act to attack the O.J.C.: two members were convicted and fined for drinking out of a flask on club premises during the spring races, and W. P. Fraser, the secretary of the club, was prosecuted and fined $1,000, evidently for lack of vigilance. The latter conviction was quashed on appeal.

The president of the Ontario Jockey Club, Colonel William Hendrie, fought back, disputing Raney's profit figures as wildly out of line; he claimed that the percentage of profit to the club's shareholders did not exceed five and that the large stock dividends were due to the increased value of the Woodbine property as the city expanded eastward. The 1921 assessment of the track was $715,040. As a public relations gesture, the O.J.C. decided at its annual meeting that November to distribute $200,000 to Ontario horsemen to develop thoroughbred horses, and Colonel Hendrie remarked that "the world would be a pleasanter place if we could eliminate those trying people who cannot endure the thought of others being happy in an occupation or entertainment that does not appeal to themselves." Nevertheless, the attorney general was not alone in his position; the *Star* and the *Globe* among local newspapers supported him, as did a number of church groups, most notably the Methodists who were the most consistent advocates of Prohibition. The following year, Raney continued with new taxation and legislation, but his attempts to abolish pari-mutuel betting, bookmaking, and the publication of race track news began to lose supporters, as the public drifted away from the same strident moralisms which had fueled the Prohibition argument. Raney went down to defeat when the United Farmers of Ontario were virtually annihilated in the 1923 provincial election. The new Conservative government of Howard Ferguson continued for a few years to support Prohibition, but ceased to harass the race tracks.

Bettors also pursued lady luck at three other tracks near the metropolitan area. The Dufferin Race Track (page 204) is now a shopping mall. Thorncliffe in Leaside is now an apartment development. Long Branch, at Brown's Line Road and Horner Avenue, has vanished.

The Seagram Racing Stable was one of the most famous on the Canadian turf. Founded by Joseph E. Seagram, it was later taken over by his sons Norman (right), Thomas and Edward. Norman Seagram was a partner with J. O. Buchanan in the stockbroking firm of Buchanan, Seagram & Company, but maintained his interests and directorships in the family's liquor business in Waterloo while living in Toronto on Castlefrank Road. Brother Thomas, eight years younger than Norman, lived in Waterloo, and had a distinguished military career during World War I as captain of the Fourth Machine Gun Battalion. The middle brother of the three, Edward Frowde Seagram, entered the liquor business with his father and eventually, in 1920, became president of Seagram's. By that time, the firm had taken a beating from Prohibition. Several years later, the more aggressive Bronfman family—who had found ways to sell liquor no matter what temperance legislation was in force—gained control of Seagram's, and merged it with their own Distillers Corporation.

William Edgar Raney, the attorney general for the United Farmers of Ontario provincial government in the early 1920s, was not content to tilt merely at the windmill of liquor consumption—he tried to shut down horseracing, too! Described in his 1933 obituary as "probably the most spectacular legal figure in Ontario in the past two decades," Raney was born near Aultsville in 1859, on a farm adjoining the birthplace of Sir James Whitney, the Conservative premier of Ontario in the first decade of this century. He became a country schoolteacher at the age of eighteen, then studied law, and gravitated towards politics as an Independent Liberal, helping the temperate Conservative Whitney in his first election campaign. After Whitney refused to legislate Prohibition, Raney became a Rowell Liberal, and ran unsuccessfully in Southwest Toronto on a "ban the bar" platform against the well-financed G. H. Gooderham. He finally made it into Parliament unopposed in a 1920 by-election, when Premier Drury, who had not a single lawyer amongst his U.F.O. caucus, picked him as the attorney general. Raney survived the U.F.O. defeat, and sat in opposition as the leader of the Progressive party, fighting against amendments to the Temperance Act which permitted stronger "4.4" beer. At one point in his career, he was invited by the teetotalling Joseph Atkinson to contribute an article to the Star Weekly, *resulting in the first successful libel suit against that paper in fifteen years. Raney was appointed to the Supreme Court of Ontario in 1927; he lived at 222 Forest Hill Road.*

Ontario Jockey Club meets at Woodbine were always spectacular fashion parades. Many of the women at this one, about 1912, were dressed to reflect the craze for "Turkish" fashions which had begun at the outlandish "1002nd Night" ball at the Paris mansion of the couturier Paul Poiret. A wave of pantaloons, turbans, hooped tunics, and other Orientalisms inundated fashionable society. The crinolined, elegant styles by the couturier Worth once thought so timeless seemed suddenly dowdy and exceptionally dated. What were people wearing? The World dispatched photographer William James to New York to photograph the Easter Sunday promenaders on Fifth Avenue. His photos were published on April 26, 1914, under the headline: "Are Women of Toronto Behind New Yorkers in Style?"

Riverdale & The Danforth

The Don River formed one of the few natural barriers to the expansion of the city of Toronto. Near the Don's mouth it was easily bridged, and the land to the east along Ashbridge's Bay, all the way to MacLean Avenue south of Queen Street, was quickly settled. This land was part of the original City of Toronto after 1834, and was called St. Lawrence's Ward. Further north, the broad valley of the Don made The Danforth more difficult to reach, and settlement proceeded slowly, only receiving a boost with the opening of the Bloor Street Viaduct in 1918.

Old maps show the southern part of Riverdale as a landscape dotted with little settlements. Ashbridge's Bay was a marshy, malarial inlet, protected from the lake by a sandbar extending southwest from the foot of Woodbine Avenue. A serpentine creek drained into it just east of Coxwell Avenue; between the creek and Woodbine Avenue was a horseracing track which developed into "Woodbine," now the Greenwood Race Track. Little settlements hugged the district's two major throughways, Queen Street and the Kingston Road: Leslieville, a brickmaking area named for a nurseryman and landowner, occupied the vicinity of Leslie and Greenwood avenues north of Queen; to the east of Leslieville, between Greenwood and Coxwell, was the Ashbridge Estate, of which the old family home still stands on Queen Street (page 177); the village of Berkeley was between Coxwell and Woodbine avenues, north of Kingston Road; Norway was another community, southeast of the corner of Woodbine and Kingston Road. From the earliest years, Queen Street and the Kingston Road were important strategically, and were kept open as toll roads: travellers paid at tollgates located at Don Mount at the river's mouth, Broadview Avenue, Leslieville at Leslie Street, and Norway at Woodbine Avenue.

Broadview, usually called the Mill Road or Don Mills Road, was another important artery, as it linked Queen Street with the lumber mills along the Don at the community which became Todmorden. Between Todmorden and the communities to the south ran Danforth Avenue, which, with Bloor Street, formed the first "concession line," dating from York's original survey, north of Queen Street. As was the case in the districts of Toronto between Queen and Bloor, the land between Queen and Danforth was divided into 200-acre lots; however, unlike the former, the Danforth Avenue lots were strips running east to west, not north to south, and, with their narrow frontage on the Don River, imitated the seigneuries along the St. Lawrence River in Quebec. This was advantageous for the industrial development of the Don River frontage, but as the lots had their long sides running along Danforth Avenue, development there was retarded. A bridge across the Don at Gerrard Street was built in 1856; from Broadview and Gerrard, a private toll road went north to Danforth, then east to Scarborough—one of its tollgates was at the

The meandering Don River rarely looked as idyllic as in this postcard, showing the artist Owen Staples (1866-1949), a Riverdale resident who wrote and illustrated a series of articles for his employer, The Telegram, on "How Spring Comes to the Don Valley." From 1906 to 1918, Staples devoted much of his time to illustrating the six volumes of Telegram publisher John Ross Robertson's Landmarks of Toronto. The most southerly, serpentine reaches of the Don, near its mouth, were dredged and straightened in 1886.

southwest corner of Broadview and Danforth. At the west end of Danforth, just north of its junction with Broadview, stood the village of Chester, sometimes called Doncaster, dating from the 1860s; a half mile north was Todmorden, the village for the lumber mills and brick plants in the Don Valley. At the other end of The Danforth was the village of Little York, centred at Dawes Road. In 1883, the area boomed when it gained a major employer—the Grand Trunk Railway, which located its railyards, roundhouse and York Station east of Main Street, south of Danforth. The 1890 Goad's Property Atlas marks the corner of Dawes Road and Danforth as "Coleman's Corner." Past Dawes Avenue is Dentonia Park, which originally was the country estate and model farm of the Massey family. Across the flat land between these communities, the wind sometimes blew so strongly in the winter that it piled snow into drifts that blocked the roads.

The house of Danforth pioneer John Lea Playter, built about 1875 at the head of the southern section of Playter Boulevard, which was then its driveway running north from Danforth. Its modern address is 28 Playter Crescent. This photograph was probably taken late in the 1890s, the era of leg o'mutton sleeves, safety bicycles, cribbage, and lawn croquet.

The opening of the Bloor Street Viaduct at the end of the First World War ended The Danforth's isolation and violated the tranquillity of the southeastern corner of Rosedale. Bloor Street had previously stopped at Sherbourne Street. The card above looks westward from the Danforth end of the viaduct. The card above on the right looks eastward along Danforth Avenue from the viaduct. The curious little "temple" on the right is a branch of the Bank of Nova Scotia, since demolished for the cloverleaf which carries cars down onto the Don Valley Parkway. (Next page) An extraordinary meeting and subsequent conflagration of a truck and streetcar on Danforth at the corner of Glebemount Avenue. Fortunately for the neighbourhood, the truck flipped rather than knocking over the curbside gas pump.

Much of the industrial activity east of the Don River came from the copious deposits of clay and sand, the former being quite free from the brickmakers' nemeses of organic matter, iron, and lime. The biggest clay deposits in the area were along Greenwood Avenue; they were depleted by the 1930s.

Another business, which by the 1930s was already into its third generation of family ownership was George Oakley & Sons, a stone and marble supplier at 355 Logan Avenue, "in handsome offices to which is connected a model stone and marble mill—unsurpassed anywhere in America—possessed with facilities for rendering an unexcelled service in fabricating and setting stone and marble of all kinds." The first two generations of Oakleys were both named George. George Jr., whose photograph appears on this page, was born in Toronto in 1877; after a three year apprenticeship in the study of stone in England and Scotland, he entered his father's business. In 1931, a dozen years after George Sr.'s death, George Jr.'s sons Sidney and Clifford entered the business, Some of their notable stonecutting contracts were the Union Station, the Royal York Hotel, and the *Star* building. George Oakley lived in the house at One Wroxeter, on the high ground east of Withrow Park, which allowed him a view of some of his completed downtown contracts. He was M.P.P. for Riverdale in the 1920s, and president of the Toronto Baseball & Athletic Club Ltd.

A business of a different sort was the W. Harris & Company knackery at Danforth and Coxwell. A handbill for its sprawling plant describes its wares: "Manufacturers and Cleaners of Sausage Casings, Dealers in Grease, Crackling, Hog & Horse Hair, Horns. Bones, &c." The historian Barbara Myrvold, in her book on the area, recounts the jocular reaction of new residents in the expanding area to the abattoir: when you paid your two-cent streetcar fare, you got your "scent" back. As urbanization overtook W. Harris & Company, it moved to Keating Street, on land since taken over by the Don Valley Parkway, and erected a huge plant with a railway siding and smoking, greasy chimneys—a glue factory in which many a horse met its maker. Part of its labour force of 150 to 200 men was recruited from the Don Jail, convicts who received day-parole for the duration of their sentences.

Much of industrial Toronto gravitated to the Don River and strung itself like dirty beads along the line of the Grand Trunk Railway. Typical was the area which is now Jimmy Simpson Park (named for the labour leader and mayor) north of Queen Street. Dundas Street East stopped at West Avenue, beyond which was a warren of mews, odd blocks, and dead ends lined with rowhouses and factories along the railway tracks. The now-famous Degrassi Street is there (the internationally acclaimed television series "The Kids of Degrassi Street" and "Degrassi Junior High" is produced from the curious, turreted house a few blocks away at 935 Queen Street East—the office of Playing With Time Inc.). Railway spur lines snaked among the blocks of houses, connecting factories like the Dunlop Tire and Rubber Goods Company at Queen and Booth, the International Varnish Company at Carlaw and Gerrard, the Canadian Chewing Gum Company at Logan and Dickens, and the Wrigley Chewing Gum Company on Carlaw Avenue, with the main line. Since then, Dundas East has smashed across the area, and many of the old rowhouses are gone, but pockets of it—for example, the corner of Busy and Verral—are still surrounded by smoking chimneys in a manner reminiscent of the novels of D. H. Lawrence or Charles Dickens.

The state of housing in this industrial area attracted the inspectors during the Physical Survey of the City of Toronto, in 1913. "Immediately east of the high-level bridge over the Don River is a row of apartment houses, 645-51 Queen. Certain rooms have been condemned by the Health Department for insufficient light and ventilation. There are some rooms with only one window opening into a light shaft. The same shaft provides the only means of ventilation for the toilet. Due to the fact that the Health Department have condemned one room as a living room, the tenants have vacated it, and had stored about a half-ton of coal and coke and a quantity of lumber in it. In case of fire, this would be a most dangerous hazard."

* * *

By the turn of the century, Queen Street was built up solidly all the way to The Beach; The Danforth, by contrast, was still like a country town. The march of the city's expansion had swallowed Riverdale and Leslieville—the area from Queen to Danforth, the Don to Greenwood—in 1884; it was called St. Matthew's Ward, and had a population of 3,350. Along Danforth Avenue roadsides were market gardens; the Playter family, whose farmhouse still stands at 28 Playter Crescent, its former driveway now Playter Boulevard, were typical gardeners. As the Grand Trunk Railway expanded, the area around Main and Gerrard grew, finally incorporating in 1888 as the village of East Toronto and swallowing nearby Little York in 1903—East Toronto and the adjoining lands all the

The house at 1444 Queen Street East, built in 1854, was occupied until the 1970s by the sisters Winifred and Dorothy Ashbridge, direct descendants of the original family who came from Pennsylvania in 1793 and settled along what became known as Ashbridge's Bay. The style of the house is so typical of the period and area that it is called the Ontario Cottage Style; the mansard roof, according to the architectural historian Eric Arthur, was added in 1900. The house and its fine grounds provide an oasis from a more sedate time, amidst the clanging of trolleys that screech in and out of the T.T.C. barns across the street.

George Oakley

way to Victoria Park Avenue (the modern city limits) had already been annexed into Toronto. A streetcar line opened on Broadview Avenue in 1889, connecting Danforth with downtown via the Queen Street bridge.

Toronto boomed at the turn of the century: between 1901 and 1921, the population of Riverdale and The Danforth soared from 4,500 to over 66,000. Thousands of immigrants, mainly from Britain and Ireland, swarmed into the area, filling up the subdivided former market gardens on streets south of Danforth Avenue. The area to the north had been subdivided and developed enough to be annexed to the city in 1910. The Toronto Railway Company's intransigence (page 39) forced the city to start its own streetcar line to the new area. Concurrently, the desire of both private and public interests to service the area was reflected in the Playter Street "pole case," a dispute which arose in October, 1912, when the privately owned Toronto Electric Light Company erected poles on Playter Boulevard to supply power to new customers in the area. The city, through Toronto Hydro, promptly cut them down! The T.E.L.C. applied to the courts for an injunction against the city, which was granted by Justice Middleton in April, 1914; the city then appealed and won; the T.E.L.C. then appealed to the Judicial Committee of the Privy Council in London, England, which on October 23, 1916, ruled in favour of the city. Today, concrete power poles line the streets.

The city's final annexations in the area took the city boundary only a few blocks north of Danforth Avenue, on a line along Milverton Boulevard and Fulton Avenue; included was the town of Chester, which had gone nowhere as it had not incorporated, and therefore could not tax in order to provide services which would attract residents. Todmorden slumbered along as part of East York Township until the post-Second World War boom.

The new residents of The Danforth demanded city services—Danforth Avenue was paved during 1912 and 1913, and ratepayers in a plebiscite in January, 1913, agreed to build the Bloor Street Viaduct. The latter opened late in 1918, stimulating yet another building boom which, by the 1920s, had completed The Danforth as a community. Gone was the isolated, rural quality of life there; replacing it was a solid, respectable, Conservative-voting, home-owning, xenophobic lifestyle, mainly of English and Irish workingmen and their families.

Recollections of life in The Danforth during the twenties and thirties note that most people both lived and worked in it, as if it were a self-contained, distinct town. As in Cabbagetown or The Junction, people did

Des jeunes sur l'herbe *at Riverdale Park; in the background, on the right, is the Don Jail, and on the left the Isolation Hospital. Prisoners did a lot of the work to maintain the grounds and fill in the humps and hollows of the park, which was 119 acres of the old Scadding estate, occupying both banks of the Don River. One remaining hillock was levelled in 1919—a group of unemployed returned servicemen were given seven dollars a day to dig it out, so as to give an unobstructed view to Broadview Avenue.*

not often venture elsewhere. Few could afford cars; even fewer took holidays in the modern Canadian sense of the word. However, mobility increased and attitudes changed dramatically with the prosperity which followed the Second World War. The cohesive old neighbourhood began to break up; into the breach came new immigrants, first Italian and later Greek. The opening of the cross-town subway in 1966 brought yet another influx, this time of middle-class commuters, to the affordable houses and new apartment buildings in the area. Danforth Avenue today is a lively, cosmopolitan street lined mainly with Greek shops.

Cabbagetown

Riverdale Park, Toronto, Canada.

CARLTON ST. LOOKING EAST, TORONTO.

"Cabbagetown" was of course a pejorative; most think of it as referring to the favoured crop grown in the yards of newly arrived, impoverished immigrants. During the nineteenth century, though, the word "cabbage" also had a number of other connotations in English slang, two of which could have contributed to the naming of the area: a "cabbage" was a tailor, and there were many in the area; the word also applied to the pieces of leftover cloth that dishonest tailors purloined after cutting out patterns. Thus, the word "cabbage" also came to mean the act of pilferage, of surreptitious appropriation.

Everyone has a different definition of the boundaries of Cabbagetown, especially as, in recent years, the name has come to symbolize affluent, desirable downtown living in renovated and restored historic buildings. For the purposes here, and fully aware of all the anomalies, Cabbagetown is defined as the area bounded by the bay, a line east of Sherbourne Street, the Don River, and Rosedale Valley. Before its recent transformation, it had large pockets of poverty, blocks of middle-class housing, a few grand piles in the north and the west, breweries, churches, and—the farther south one travelled—dirty industry, railyards, grubby streets and rowhouses. It was a complete city in itself, with a predominantly working-class tenor.

Although Parliament Street was named for the first provincial parliament buildings at its foot, it soon became the main street of an industrial area containing the small houses of workers and their workplaces along Front Street and the waterfront. Instead of a parliament, the foot of Parliament Street became the site of the Gooderham and Worts Distillery; to its west was one of the Elias Rogers & Company coalyards; at Front Street and Parliament were the gasworks and gasometers of the Consumers' Gas Company; east along the waterfront were Grand Trunk Railway yards, then the William Davies & Company meat packing house at the mouth of the Don; by the 1920s, the Canadian National Railway yards had filled up much of that corner of the neighbourhood.

(Above) Riverdale Park, around 1905. The Toronto Railway Company, whose "Winchester" car line brought visitors to the park, adorned it with the "Donnybrook" castle and the cannon. The postcard is coloured to emphasize the fashionable Victorian formal garden, featuring carpet-bedded geraniums, dahlias and carnations in the style of Queen Victoria's Osborne House on the Isle of Wight. The other attraction of the park was its zoo, complete with wolves that howled at night, and a polar bear that drank from a firehose. It closed in 1974, but today the park has a pleasant children's farmyard zoo and a replica farmhouse as attractions. Part of the ruined tower of the old "Donnybrook" still stands, surrounded by aimless, grazing cows. (Below) On Carlton Street, looking east, before the First World War. The part of the street east of Sherbourne began to be settled in the 1850s; by the 1870s, some fine, solid houses were being built in the area near Parliament Street, replacing the cottages and little shacks of the first settlers. The residential, sheltered look which characterized much of what is now downtown Toronto vanished when the boulevard trees were removed. Most of the street-widenings in the area took place in the decade after World War II, when traffic problems created by commuters from the suburbs overwhelmed the capacity of the old, narrow streets.

The Don River was a meandering, swampy little stream, until dredged and straightened in 1886. Its banks were a breeding ground for the dreaded rising damp; being so undesirable, the nearby area was the inevitable site for a workers' neighbourhood, and began to be settled with British and Irish immigrants late in the 1840s. Protestants generally settled north of Queen Street, and Catholics to the south ("Corktown," as the novelist Hugh Garner described it), leading to the well-known description of Cabbagetown, and Toronto, as "Little Belfast." Along Power Street, in front of St. Paul's Church and the House of Providence, the Protestant bands marched provocatively, practising for the 12th of July parade to commemorate the Battle of the Boyne. Every twist and turn of the Home Rule conflicts in Ireland—which continued unabated from the 1840s through the 1920s—was reflected in attitudes in Toronto, especially in the pronouncements of Orange Lodge leaders and like-minded politicians.

Block after block of little rowhouses, like those which survive today on the dog-legged Bright Street, St. Paul Street and Trinity Street (painting, page 181), housed workers and their families who lived in quite bleak poverty, verging in some cases on squalor. Workers' cottages, like the well-known Wellesley Cottages, were most common in the southern part of Cabbagetown, especially in what is now the Regent Park area, from Shuter to Gerrard east of Parliament Street. It was a scene not unlike the locale of D. H. Lawrence's *Sons & Lovers*: smoke filling the air and soot dirtying the snow; taverns that took the workers in, and gave solace to "the inner man" whether he could afford it or not. Children, when not on an endless search for coke or coal or firewood, played in the streets or along the Don. People worked, worshipped, and slept within their immediate few blocks. There was little incentive, and even less money, for a trip to downtown; few could afford to fritter cash on carfare, and to walk downtown was not worth the wear and tear on the Sunday-go-to-meetin' clothes and shoes. Electricity was a rarity until well into the 1930s; indoor bathtubs were a luxury, so people used the public bathhouses on Sackville and Parliament. Plumbing was outdoor, though the crusading city medical health officer, Dr. Charles Hastings, had eradicated much of that by the end of the First World War. To Hastings, the pit privy was "a relic of barbarism," the worst public health menace in the city. (Cabbagetown was not the only district cited in his 1911 report on city "slum conditions." Hastings named the area from Toronto Bay to Wilton and from Parliament to the Don, plus several other parts of the city: The Ward, the area from Bathurst to Bellwoods and from Queen to the bay, and the area bounded by Spadina to Bellwoods and Front to King. Typical of all of these areas, he said, were the privies—of which he estimated there to be 15,000 in the city—the filthy yards, poor water supply, dark unventilated rooms, and "back shops" in the alleys, which doubled as work places and housing.)

Several breweries in the area contributed to Ontario's respectable twelve-million-gallon-a-year (in 1898) output of lager and ale—nearly twice the amount produced in Quebec. Enoch Turner's brewery, later the East Toronto Brewery on Parliament Street at Derby, virtually adjoined

the Little Trinity church; his desire to see that local children received some education caused him to build the Trinity Street School, in 1848, behind the church. A few years later, following the introduction of free public education, the schoolhouse became a Sunday school. At the northeast corner of Queen and River Street stood the Davies Brewing & Malting Company, also called the Don Brewery. Thomas Davies had started brewing in Toronto in 1830, and established the Don Brewery in 1849; it was operated by his sons, Thomas and Robert. A block to the west was the Dominion Brewery, adjoining the still extant Dominion Hotel, at Queen and Sumach; it was founded in 1878 by Robert Davies and purchased by an English syndicate in 1889, after which time it brewed only ale. A fourth brewery was located farther north on River Street, at Blevins Avenue (now Mark Street): Lothar Reinhardt & Company, founded in 1887, brewed lager and later changed its name to the Salvador Brewery.

Most of the families who lived in the little houses nearby spent their lives in a constant struggle to keep ahead of indigence. At the turn of the century, a labourer typically earned $8 to $10 a week, and a modest house without electricity or indoor plumbing could be rented for about $15 a month. By the beginning of the 1920s, salaries had gone up somewhat, so that railway workers made about $26 a week ($1,200 per year), and even agricultural workers made about $18 a week. Despite the increases, food prices had skyrocketed (page 282), rents had more than kept pace, and chronic periods of unemployment dogged the workers and gnawed away at any pittance they might have saved. Few families whose breadwinner was a labourer or semiskilled worker could keep above the poverty line without a second income. Women's wages typically were much lower than men's—about $12 a week. Nevertheless, women slaved at piecework tailoring or took in laundry or cleaned, if they could get the work, and meanwhile raised their families, for "a man may work from sun to sun, but a woman's work is never done." Children found themselves under constant pressure to take a job, although their labour was truly exploited and conditions were dangerous. Depending on the availability of work and the health of the employable family members, some families found they had to double up, and they crowded together, several to a room, in the shabby little frame and brick rowhouses.

These unskilled workers were the last to be hired and the first to be gone whenever the economy "went on the skids." There were two short sharp shocks, in 1907 and 1913, and two longer depressions, a mild one

George Frank Beer was "Mr. Public Housing" in Toronto in the early part of this century. As the first president of the semipublic Toronto Housing Company, he was the prime mover behind the construction of the Spruce Court and Riverdale Court public housing experiments. Born on Prince Edward Island in 1864, Beer won a history scholarship at school, ran a general store, and operated a financial and real estate agency in Nelson, B.C.; later, he moved to Toronto, where he became treasurer of the Eclipse Whitewear clothing company. Over the next decade, he made himself an expert on housing and real-estate matters, and was asked to help draft the Model City Planning Bill for Canada—one of the first stabs at coordinated city planning.

(Next page) King Street East, at Trinity, in the heart of what the novelist Hugh Garner called "Corktown." From the historic "Little Trinity" Church (built in 1843), in the foreground, comes the common "Little Trinity" name for the area, which was once very much a part of working-class Cabbagetown, but is today separated from the area to the north by freeways and urban renewal projects. On Trinity Street, in the background of the painting, is the sidewall of the little schoolhouse paid for by the brewer Enoch Turner, who felt it unfair that local children whose parents were almost uniformly penurious could get no education—free education not being adopted until the early 1850s. The rowhousing across the street, built in the 1880s, was convenient to the numerous factories, breweries, churches, and taverns which made up the neighbourhood. A few years after he designed Little Trinity Church, the architect Henry Lane designed the Church of the Holy Trinity, a similarly modest (for its time) Anglican church in a similar unpretentious neighbourhood—The Ward.

immediately after the First World War and the Great Depression of the 1930s. During the former two, the economy of Ontario was not nearly so harshly crimped as was that of Western Canada, where people of nearly every social class and trade found themselves facing ruin; in Toronto, the consequences were visited mainly upon Cabbagetown and The Ward. In the winter of 1913-14, indigents and vagrants wandered the streets, slept in doorways, and overcrowded the meagre facilities of the missions. Rents went unpaid, though families could be thrown out onto the street. Few had any savings to tide them over.

The relief situation in the city was a slight improvement over that in the England of Charles Dickens. The attitude of influential citizens, which extended to the government, was that unemployment was usually the result of drinking and vice, and the government did not choose to help these "undeserving poor." This sincere belief, that drink led to much of unemployment and indigence, inspired the "ban the bar" movement and the subsequent social revolution of Prohibition. For the "deserving poor," society's deranged, wayward, and helpless, there were a number of private and public institutions, including the Mercer Reformatory for Women, the Protestant Orphans' Home, the Home for Incurables, the Infants' Home, and the Lunatic Asylum; in The Ward, there was the House of Industry—the workhouse or poorhouse; in Cabbagetown, on Power Street between King and Queen, there was the Catholic House of Providence. A primitive system of public welfare, for those who were not inmates of the above-named institutions, began at the House of Industry late in the nineteenth century; to ensure that it would not be abused by the "undeserving poor," relief applicants were required to break stone in front of city officials. The city provided some public money and some stone for the work test. The Salvation Army, whose headquarters were also in the The Ward at the corner of James and Albert (the Eaton Centre site), also received some public money. Accounts of the terrible privation of the winter of 1913-14 describe the long queues of relief applicants at the House of Industry, men so weak from hunger they could scarcely give the required information to the relief officials, and crowds gathering at the Fred Victor Mission and the Scott Mission seeking shelter from the cold.

The "noble pile" of the old Toronto General Hospital, on Gerrard Street East between Sackville and Sumach, was built in 1854, replacing an earlier building erected in 1817 at the corner of King and John. Old Toronto General was built at the beginning of a revolutionary period in the history of medicine: anaesthesia for surgical operations was first demonstrated using ether in 1846; the following year, the surgeon Semmelweis discovered the cause of childbed fever, which had made maternity wards in hospital often little more than morgues; nursing, through the teachings and example of Florence Nightingale, began during the Crimean War in the 1850s; in 1867, the antiseptic principle in surgery was introduced by Lister; Pasteur's discoveries of the bacterial causes of infection came soon thereafter. By the turn of the century, Toronto General had become too small and woefully out of date, and was itself replaced in 1913 by the current Toronto General Hospital on College Avenue. Old Toronto General was demolished several years later; its site was divided into 66 lots. The new subdivision was put onto the market in 1921, with "large quantities of second-hand building material for sale on the property."

(Next page) The Winchester Hotel, at the southeast corner of Winchester and Parliament, dates from 1888. Built as the Lakeview Hotel, it was reviewed in 1891 by writer G. Mercer Adam: "it is an excellent uptown hotel and is rapidly growing in favour as a resort for the travelling public and families. Electric bells and bathrooms are provided on every flat [floor]. There is a good lawn, telephone communication and convenient access to cars for all parts of the city. Iron and patent rope fire-escapes are placed in every apartment, so that guests are secure from danger of fire. This hotel is not far from the Horticultural Gardens and Riverdale Park. It is kept scrupulously neat and inviting throughout." Time has not been kind to the Winchester.

* * *

North of Gerrard Street East, on the higher ground, was a more prosperous neighbourhood, sometimes clumsily called in recent years the "East of Parliament," although named "Don Vale" by planners in the mid-1960s. Bordered on the north by the picturesque St. James Cemetery

Helen Rowsell Bruce lived at 37 Bleecker Street—a site now overrun with the huge apartments of the "South of St. Jamestown" era of the late 1960s and early 1970s. During the first decades of this century, she served with distinction in a number of women's organizations, including the national presidency of the Imperial Order Daughters of the Empire, presidency of the Women's Canadian Club, first presidency of the Toronto League of Women Voters, and organizing work for the 1914 Hospital Ship Fund and the Canadian War Contingent Association. After her education at Bishop Strachan school, she attended the London Musical Academy in England, and was long a supporter of and participant in the Women's Musical Club.

181

immediately after the First World War and the Great Depression of the 1930s. During the former two, the economy of Ontario was not nearly so harshly crimped as was that of Western Canada, where people of nearly every social class and trade found themselves facing ruin; in Toronto, the consequences were visited mainly upon Cabbagetown and The Ward. In the winter of 1913-14, indigents and vagrants wandered the streets, slept in doorways, and overcrowded the meagre facilities of the missions. Rents went unpaid, though families could be thrown out onto the street. Few had any savings to tide them over.

The relief situation in the city was a slight improvement over that in the England of Charles Dickens. The attitude of influential citizens, which extended to the government, was that unemployment was usually the result of drinking and vice, and the government did not choose to help these "undeserving poor." This sincere belief, that drink led to much of unemployment and indigence, inspired the "ban the bar" movement and the subsequent social revolution of Prohibition. For the "deserving poor," society's deranged, wayward, and helpless, there were a number of private and public institutions, including the Mercer Reformatory for Women, the Protestant Orphans' Home, the Home for Incurables, the Infants' Home, and the Lunatic Asylum; in The Ward, there was the House of Industry—the workhouse or poorhouse; in Cabbagetown, on Power Street between King and Queen, there was the Catholic House of Providence. A primitive system of public welfare, for those who were not inmates of the above-named institutions, began at the House of Industry late in the nineteenth century; to ensure that it would not be abused by the "undeserving poor," relief applicants were required to break stone in front of city officials. The city provided some public money and some stone for the work test. The Salvation Army, whose headquarters were also in the The Ward at the corner of James and Albert (the Eaton Centre site), also received some public money. Accounts of the terrible privation of the winter of 1913-14 describe the long queues of relief applicants at the House of Industry, men so weak from hunger they could scarcely give the required information to the relief officials, and crowds gathering at the Fred Victor Mission and the Scott Mission seeking shelter from the cold.

Helen Rowsell Bruce lived at 37 Bleecker Street—a site now overrun with the huge apartments of the "South of St. Jamestown" era of the late 1960s and early 1970s. During the first decades of this century, she served with distinction in a number of women's organizations, including the national presidency of the Imperial Order Daughters of the Empire, presidency of the Women's Canadian Club, first presidency of the Toronto League of Women Voters, and organizing work for the 1914 Hospital Ship Fund and the Canadian War Contingent Association. After her education at Bishop Strachan school, she attended the London Musical Academy in England, and was long a supporter of and participant in the Women's Musical Club.

The "noble pile" of the old Toronto General Hospital, on Gerrard Street East between Sackville and Sumach, was built in 1854, replacing an earlier building erected in 1817 at the corner of King and John. Old Toronto General was built at the beginning of a revolutionary period in the history of medicine: anaesthesia for surgical operations was first demonstrated using ether in 1846; the following year, the surgeon Semmelweis discovered the cause of childbed fever, which had made maternity wards in hospital often little more than morgues; nursing, through the teachings and example of Florence Nightingale, began during the Crimean War in the 1850s; in 1867, the antiseptic principle in surgery was introduced by Lister; Pasteur's discoveries of the bacterial causes of infection came soon thereafter. By the turn of the century, Toronto General had become too small and woefully out of date, and was itself replaced in 1913 by the current Toronto General Hospital on College Avenue. Old Toronto General was demolished several years later; its site was divided into 66 lots. The new subdivision was put onto the market in 1921, with "large quantities of second-hand building material for sale on the property."

(Next page) The Winchester Hotel, at the southeast corner of Winchester and Parliament, dates from 1888. Built as the Lakeview Hotel, it was reviewed in 1891 by writer G. Mercer Adam: "it is an excellent uptown hotel and is rapidly growing in favour as a resort for the travelling public and families. Electric bells and bathrooms are provided on every flat [floor]. There is a good lawn, telephone communication and convenient access to cars for all parts of the city. Iron and patent rope fire-escapes are placed in every apartment, so that guests are secure from danger of fire. This hotel is not far from the Horticultural Gardens and Riverdale Park. It is kept scrupulously neat and inviting throughout." Time has not been kind to the Winchester.

* * *

North of Gerrard Street East, on the higher ground, was a more prosperous neighbourhood, sometimes clumsily called in recent years the "East of Parliament," although named "Don Vale" by planners in the mid-1960s. Bordered on the north by the picturesque St. James Cemetery

with its fine chapel, it had on its eastern flank the malodorous animal rendering factory of Peter R. Lamb & Company. Lamb's son, Daniel, who built the gracious house at 156 Winchester Street, was an alderman for his ward, and contributed funds and effort to the creation of the Riverdale Park zoo just south of the Necropolis. This strange amalgam of boiling animals and "cities of the dead" did little for the area's reputation; however, the rendering factory burned down in 1888, and no other significant industry save bootlegging established itself in the area. There are still a few modest workers' houses—the Wellesley Cottages, little privately owned Alpha Avenue, and scattered other rows of bungalows—of the type once common in the southern part of Cabbagetown, which date from the 1880s. Otherwise, the houses are comparatively large and Victorian and well constructed—places that were built and owned by shopkeepers and people of some means. Now restored and embellished for an even more affluent generation, the houses and their streets have made the former pejorative "Cabbagetown" into a triumphant statement of taste.

During the mid-1960s, as other inner-city districts in Toronto braced themselves against the bulldozer onslaught, Cabbagetown came under the scrutiny of sociologists. One such was James Lorimer, who with his wife rented one of the little rowhouses on what he called Minster Lane—in fact, Alpha Avenue off Sackville Street. Over the next eighteen months, they conducted a "participant-observation" study of the working-class families who still lived in the area. Lorimer's time in the area, and his wife's photographs of it, were recorded in a book, *Working People*, published by James Lewis & Samuel in 1971. During the brief period they lived there, from late 1966 until the middle of 1968, most of the little two-storey cottages on his street were bought by middle-class, professional families. Lorimer noted that the house they rented was one of four which an architect had bought as an investment and renovated. It was truly a cottage, with no front yard and a minuscule backyard, about fourteen feet wide, with a half basement, a small livingroom, diningroom and kitchen on the main floor, and three small bedrooms above. Before the architect bought it and renovated it, two families had lived there: a family of five upstairs, one of ten down.

Elsewhere, he described the residents at the nearby Wellesley Cottages: "apart from Oracle Jones, who owns his little house, the six other families living in the one-storey, frame, attached houses on The Cottages are tenants of a single owner. Some of them have been there for years. One woman now in her eighties has lived on the street since she was seven. When she began renting her house, she paid $12 a month. Recently the landlord increased the rents for the four-room cottages from $47.50 to $75 a month, still something less than the usual rent in the neighbourhood for a small house of this kind."

A different fate overtook the other pieces of this diverse neighbourhood. In 1945, the project-oriented Robert Saunders became mayor and oversaw the clearing of the sprawling warren south of Gerrard Street. The grim Regent Park North housing project went up in 1947. Ten years later, the city built Regent Park South. These superblocks are the bastard children of an earlier effort at public housing—the Toronto Housing Company.

For the variety of reasons, some altruistic, some not, which gave society both Prohibition and better working conditions in factories, a movement for better housing gathered strength in the years before the First World War. The statement by its main proponent, the businessman Frank Beer, that "slums produce inefficiency," sums up the muddle of humanitarianism and practicality that led to the founding of the Toronto Housing Company. Initial support and financing came from local capitalists including Sir Edmund Osler, Joseph Flavelle, and Zebulon Lash; the governor general was patron, the lieutenant governor honorary president, and Beer the president.

The company built two housing projects. The first was on Bain Avenue in Riverdale; after nearby residents protested for reasons including the impending closure of Sparkhall and Bain Avenues, the company shifted its project north of Logan Avenue. There, the sod was turned on November 7, 1913, by the lieutenant governor. At the same time, a project began at 74-86 Spruce Street. Both were designed by the progressive residential architect Eden Smith.

The Toronto Housing Company had difficulty operating its new housing projects at competitive rents: a six-room "cottage flat" on Spruce Street rented in 1914 for $26.50, nearly fifteen percent more than an indoor-plumbing-equipped local house; the company had been set up to make a return on its investment—it was nicknamed the "Six Percent Corporation" by local labour leaders—and although it did not pay what the unions considered to be fair wages, it had paid too much for its land. The experiment in public housing ended there, with the two projects built and operating, though the cry continued for better housing.

Following years of agitation for some public action on low-cost rental housing, city council in 1945 approved the Regent Park North project. The resulting austere housing blocks, which would not have seemed out of place in postwar Germany, and the road widenings and demolitions in the area of the old House of Providence, eliminated much of what remained of old Cabbagetown. Later, private enterprise picked up the torch from the faltering city, and built the immense, hideous St. James Town project on the blocks north of Wellesley, between Sherbourne and Parliament. Completed in 1968, St. James Town was a watershed event in the city's history. Concurrently, citizens' groups were mobilizing to stop redevelopment both in "slums" and in stable residential areas along the newly opened Bloor Street subway line. In "boomtown," said a Central Mortgage and Housing Corporation report, housing had become almost a byproduct of the act of making money. A new generation of activists, including future mayor John Sewell, entered the public spotlight by joining residents in antidevelopment crusades at Trefann Court and the South of St. Jamestown area. Redevelopment was in many cases stopped, or at least had its wings clipped; the citizens' groups, which were commonly composed of low-income residents about to be evicted and their sympathizers, frequently won a Pyrrhic victory—through their efforts, the neighbourhoods were revitalized and restored, and have never looked back. Neither have the house prices.

The most modern—or at least most recently constructed—of the houses at the north end of Sackville Street is the curious single house at 450 Sackville, shown here from the lane running along its northern side. Built in 1910 and first occupied by Robert Simpson Company employee James Baxter, 450 Sackville is at least twenty years newer than its immediate neighbours, and occupies a piece of their deep back yards which was probably the earlier site of privies, sheds, and coops. This area of old Cabbagetown has some of the last workers' rowhousing remaining in Toronto—cottages, like the famous Wellesley Cottages further west along the lane ("behind the painter"), were more common in the area razed for the two Regent Park urban renewal projects.

Road relocations and traffic expediters have obliterated many of the old streets and buildings in the House of Providence area. The map shows the area as it appeared in the 1920s, when it was still intact—an old-fashioned working-class area of foundries, stables, breweries, a distillery, the gasworks, and railyards. Progress had by that time already razed an old residential area in the southeastern corner of "Little Trinity," around the Davies & Company packing houses—the sprawling railyards of the Canadian National and Grand Trunk Railway replaced blocks of houses east of Cherry Street and south of Eastern Avenue. Streets named Cypress, Olive, Vine and Water vanished.

"The care of the sick," wrote G.M. Adam in 1891, "has not been left entirely to the good offices of medical men." Private charities and the churches collaborated to care for society's jetsam. One institution for the poor was the House of Providence, also sometimes called the "House of Protestants," on Power Street north of King.

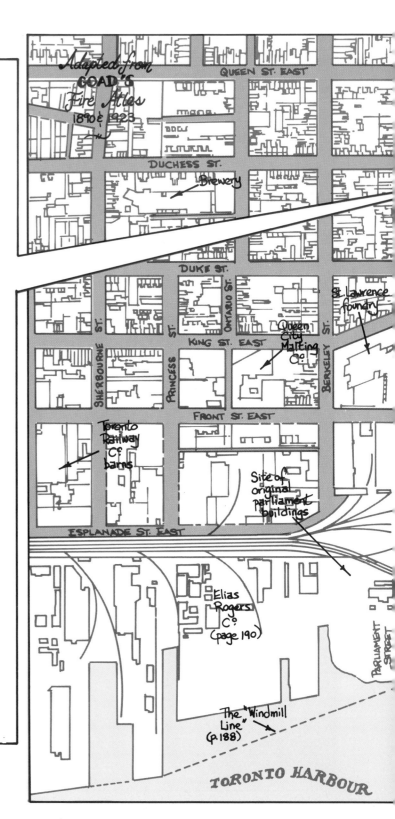

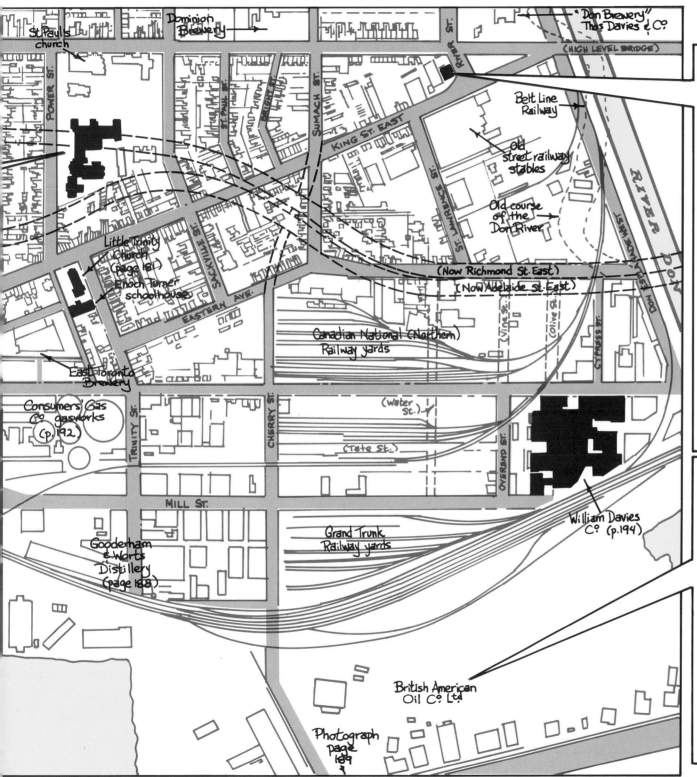

St Pauls church

Dominion Brewery →

"Don Brewery" Thos Davies & Co

(HIGH LEVEL BRIDGE)

RIVER ST.

KING ST. EAST

Belt Line Railway

Old street railway stables

Old course of the Don River

ST. LAWRENCE ST.

RIVER DON

POWER ST.

ST. PAUL ST.

PRINCESS ST.

SUMACH ST.

SACKVILLE ST.

ST. LAWRENCE ST.

EASTERN AVE.

Little Trinity Church (page 181)

Enoch Turner schoolhouse

(Now Richmond St. East)

(Now Adelaide St. East)

VINE ST.

OLIVE ST.

CYPRESS ST.

DON ESPLANADE

Canadian National (Northern) Railway yards

East Toronto Brewery

Consumers' Gas Co. gasworks (p. 192)

TRINITY ST.

CHERRY ST.

(Water St.)

(Tate St.)

OVEREND ST.

William Davies Co. (p.194)

MILL ST.

Grand Trunk Railway yards

Gooderham & Worts Distillery (page 188)

British American Oil Co. Ltd

Photograph page 189

John Joseph Sheedy's New Method Laundry Company trucks were a familiar sight on Toronto streets. Sheedy started his business in 1903 on Parliament Street, moved it a decade later to expanded premises at Number Two River Street, and, in 1929, at the corner of College and Crawford, built "one of the finest laundry plants on the North American continent, using exclusively the Miraclean (odorless) system" of drycleaning. Born in Toronto in 1873, Sheedy was a curler, golfer, Roman Catholic, and Knights of Columbus member; he lived at 176 Indian Road in Parkdale.

At the foot of Cherry Street, in 1906, the British American Oil Company Ltd. built its first Toronto plant on three acres of ground next to the factories of the National Iron Corporation. By the 1930s, "B.A." had expanded to over 40 acres and possessed two local refineries, other Canadian refineries in Montreal and Moose Jaw, a fleet of 481 tank cars, five lake tankers to supply crude to Toronto and return finished products to lake ports, seven ocean tankers, and oil wells in Oklahoma and Texas. Brand-name products at its many service stations were Nevr-Nox and Peerless Ethyl gasolines, and Autolene and Vulcan motor oils and lubricants. The company chairman and one of the founders was S. R. Parsons (above), who began his career in wholesale stationery in Winnipeg. Parsons was regularly appointed as a commissioner on government enquiries into labour and natural resources, and was a member of the postwar Canadian Reconstruction Association. He and his wife had three daughters, one of whom married Henry F. Gooderham. Parsons lived at 100 Forest Hill Road.

Gooderham & Worts

The Gooderham & Worts distillery on the waterfront dates from 1831, and the arrival in the colony from England of James Worts and his brother-in-law William Gooderham. They acquired the land to build a flour mill, and, rejecting the slow-moving Don River as a potential power source, they set out to erect a windmill with a tower 71 feet high at the foot of Parliament Street. This landmark, which was completed in November, 1831, became the eastern extremity of what surveyors called the Windmill Line, used to survey water lots along Toronto Bay (map, page 186).

When the winds, and thus the windmill, proved unreliable, the partners built a steam plant the following year. In addition to grinding wheat into flour and making hog food, they commenced to distil spirits. (If ever there was an example of a man's name determining his occupation, it must be James Worts, for a "wort" is the soluble, cooked mixture of grains to which yeast is added, creating the "mash" from which whisky is distilled.) Worts died soon after, and was succeeded in the business by his son, James Gooderham Worts; William Gooderham lived until 1882, and was succeeded by his son George (page 232). The distillery became effectively a money-making machine—by 1858, it was distilling 700 gallons of raw spirits daily, and in the 1870s produced one-third of all the spirits in Canada—providing a pool of capital for a variety of family enterprises, including the Bank of Toronto, Manufacturers Life, and the Toronto & Nipissing Railway.

The diversification of this wealth proved canny strategy when, beginning at the turn of the century, the public mood shifted towards moderation, then temperance, and finally Prohibition. In 1926, following ten years of provincial Prohibition, Gooderham & Worts Ltd. was purchased by its rival, the Hiram-Walker distillery; the following November, the name changed officially to Hiram-Walker Gooderham & Worts Ltd. Over the years since, the firm has purchased distilleries and wineries in Canada, Scotland, the United States, Argentina, France, and Mexico, becoming one of the largest liquor producers in the world. It amalgamated in 1980 with a subsidiary of its old Toronto waterfront neighbour—the Consumers' Gas Company—but continued in business under its own name. Some of the old distillery buildings, including a mill and malthouse from the 1860s, survive in the company complex on Mill Street at Trinity.

Colonel Albert Edward Gooderham was the second-oldest son of George Gooderham—the cofounder of Gooderham & Worts. He held directorships in several enterprises, including the Bank of Toronto in which the family long held an interest, and was named managing director of Gooderham & Worts in 1905 on the death of his father. Later, he became vice-president, and divided his time between the family firm and his military regiment, the 10th Royal Grenadiers, of which he was commanding officer. Gooderham's philanthropic activities included the establishment of The Preventorium on Sheldrake near Yonge Street, an institution that could accommodate up to 108 children with symptoms of tuberculosis; the University of Toronto's 50-acre Anti-Toxine farm, which supplied the serum needed by the Second British Army for the last two years of World War I; and a military hospital for the use of officers on Hyde Park Place in London. His residence—"Deancroft," near the north Glen Road bridge—was a Rosedale landmark (page 241).

William George Gooderham was the eldest son of the cofounder of Gooderham & Worts. Born in 1853, he was educated at Upper Canada College and became the supervisor of the family's financial interests, which included the Canada Permanent Mortgage Corporation, Canada Permanent Trust, the Bank of Toronto, and the Manufacturers Life Insurance Company—all of which he was president of. He was a member of a bewildering variety of clubs and societies, and lived at 42 Elm Avenue in Rosedale. Like his father, he sired a large family—his wife, the former Ella Hargraft, giving him nine sons and two daughters before her death, after 41 years of marriage, in 1916.

Harry Hatch was the first non-Gooderham to be president of Gooderham & Worts; he reorganized and became president of Gooderham & Worts in 1923; five years later, following the amalgamation of his company with Hiram Walker & Sons of Walkerville, he became chairman of the board. Born in Ameliasburg in 1884, he grew up in Deseronto, and worked with his father in the hotel business during the years of reduced licenses and the "ban the bar" movement. He started a liquor store at Whitby in 1911, then opened one in Toronto in 1916 with his brother. Forced out of the retail business by Prohibition, he moved to Montreal and ran a mail-order liquor business until 1921. A curler and yachtsman with three sons and a daughter, he lived at 38 Roxborough Drive.

Looking towards the city from the foot of Cherry Street, as it appeared in 1911 at the beginning of its redevelopment as industrial land.

Coal

The Toronto of the turn of the century ran largely on coal and hay; its homes were heated by coal furnaces, and lighted by coal gas, kerosene or acetylene lamps. A haze of coal smoke used to hang over the city in the wintertime; its sharp smell was as familiar in that season as the heady scent of horse manure on hot streets in the summertime. Soot darkened the snow and blackened the ruts on the streets. As electricity began to supersede coal gas for lighting during the first decade of this century, it came to be known as "white coal." The gradual acceptance of cooking with gas—and much later, electricity—eventually eliminated the cookstove from city houses and made the summer kitchen a relic of the past. But until that time, most of the stoves available on the market had duplex grates, so they could burn either wood or coal.

The coal business in Toronto was largely developed by men with business contacts in the United States, who dealt in Pennsylvania and Ohio coal. The largest operation was probably Elias Rogers & Company, which had coalyards and wharves on the Esplanade at Church and Berkeley, and at the foot of Bathurst Street. Rogers had been born in Ontario, but attended college in New York, and in his early twenties became interested in the export potential of coal mines at Reynoldsville, Pennsylvania. He found a wealthy partner and in 1876, when he was only 26, opened wholesale and retail business offices in Toronto. He was soon prosperous enough to become sole owner of the Reynoldsville bituminous mine and to build a grand home in Deer Park. His head office was on King Street West, in the North of Scotland Chambers Building (shown in the postcard on page 25).

Demand was so great for coal and wood in booming Toronto that the Ontario Coal Company, founded in 1889, was two years later doing business worth one million dollars a year. The firm shipped Lehigh Valley coal from the United States to its dock at the foot of Church Street, where two steam elevators and a variety of automatic appliances unloaded as much as 800 tons of it a day. Its deliveries in its second season included 115,000 tons of hard coal, 75,000 tons of soft coal, and 50,000 tons of wood. A business review published at that time noted that "if it is an iron age, it is also a coal age, and the industries are many and extensive to which the mining of coal has given birth." Referring to supply, the review continued: "Of bituminous coal, Canada has large deposits in Nova Scotia, and of anthracite coal she is understood to have plenty in British Columbia. But these provinces are both distant from Ontario and her [Ontario's] people have to be content in the main with the importation from nearer markets of domestic fuel."

The supply from those nearer, American mines seemed limitless in the early years of the First World War; although the munitions plants needed a tremendous quantity of energy—mainly electricity—which caused brownouts throughout residential Toronto, other big industrial users, including the Toronto Waterworks, could switch over to coal-fired steam, releasing thousands of horsepower for the use of factories such as the British Forgings Company. However, by early 1917, there was a serious coal shortage, stemming from the growth of American war-related industries, and the American entry into the war that April. The following winter, amongst poorer families, there was much privation; a cold snap early in February, 1918, resulted in coal being doled out in hundred-pound lots to long queues of people, while the newspapers reported instances of the burning of fences and furniture. Temporary relief came on February 18, when coal shipments arrived from the United States.

Elias Rogers

The dominion government's response to the crisis was the appointment of C. A. Magrath as fuel commissioner. Magrath was a land surveyor who, after a youth spent in the west, had settled in Toronto. He had gone as a surveyor when he was eighteen to what was then called the Canadian Northwest, and had developed irrigation projects in southern Alberta. He was a member of the Territorial Legislature and a Member of Parliament for Medicine Hat, and he became Lethbridge's first mayor when that city incorporated in 1901. Ontario Premier James Whitney appointed him to make recommendations on a comprehensive highway system for Ontario; later in his career, he became chairman of the Hydro-Electric Power Commission. He had been acknowledged as an authority on energy and Canadian sovereignty problems since publication of his 1910 book entitled *Canada's Growth and Some Problems Affecting It.*

To provide some direct control over local conditions, the Ontario government simultaneously appointed city works manager Roland Harris (page 168) as provincial fuel controller. The two government commissioners acted quickly, and by October had regulated all the charges and commissions of coal brokers, and threatened rationing.

Kenric Rud Marshall (above) and his father, Noel George Lambert Marshall, owned one of the biggest coal companies in Toronto—the Standard Fuel Company at 58 King Street East. The elder Lambert came to Toronto as a child with his parents and entered the coal business with George Chaffey Bros. in 1870. Ten years later, he purchased an interest in the C. J. Smith Coal Company, became an associate of William Mackenzie, and with the latter's help bought out the business in 1888 and changed its name to Standard Fuel. Coal was only one of his interests—he was president of the C.N.E., a director of the Sterling Bank and the Canadian Northern Prairie Lands Company (a Mackenzie & Mann colonization scheme), vice-president of the Hospital for Incurables, and an honorary lieutenant colonel of the Canadian militia during the First World War.

By December, the fuel shortage was critical. Small houses required five to seven tons of coal for the winter, while some houses, such as many in Rosedale, often needed over ten tons per person—at least forty to fifty tons per year. The *Star* charged that the existing system gave preference to the big customer, and reported that some families were being forced to double up, as they could not obtain enough fuel to heat their houses. Concurrently, the newspaper published the sensational fact that "Chorley Park," the new lieutenant governor's residence in Rosedale, required 965 tons of coal for the winter (the *Star* was simultaneously campaigning for the abolition of the office of lieutenant governor, page 245). Sir Henry Pellatt's "Casa Loma" required even more.

Heatless days were organized—many offices and stores voluntarily closed, as did some theatres and clubhouses. Petroleum shortages were also threatening, and although Magrath and Harris did not see fit to impose gas rationing, they banned all nonemergency sales of gasoline on Sundays, and promoted the idea of voluntary gasless Sundays. The latter idea was only partially successful—police, however, patriotically ticketed Sunday joy riders for minor infractions such as driving with an obliterated taillight. Suddenly, the statutory ten- or fifteen-mile-per-hour speed limit—depending on locale—was rigorously enforced. The most zealous of the law enforcers was Magistrate Douglas Davidson, who each Monday in his Mimico police court handed out dozens of fines for amounts up to $23.

Other orders from the fuel controller included a ban on the use of any gas or electricity for advertising or ornamental purposes. Musical instrument manufacturers, and other businesses considered nonessential, were cut back to 70 percent of their prewar coal supply. Meanwhile, a blizzard of posters, lantern slides in movie houses, and articles in newspapers promoted conservation. In the autumn of 1918, when the "Spanish flu" epidemic swept through Canada, the authorities asked churches to cut down on their fuel consumption; the churches refused, arguing that the danger of influenza increased in underheated buildings. Another order from Fuel Commissioner Magrath banned the use of any fuel of any description in any country, golf, canoe, or yacht club from December 15 to March 15. Most clubs polled by the newspapers said this presented no problem, as their memberships had shrunk as the war progressed. The Toronto Canoe Club, according to its president Charles Hoare, had had 174 active members at the outbreak of the war, but of those 119 had enlisted.

Then, in November, 1918, an armistice ended the war. All fuel control ceased the following March, and life—in fuel consumption, at least—quickly resumed its old ways. Gradually the Ontario hydroelectric power system developed, and more efficient use was made of other fuels including coal gas. But the problem remained of the source of coal—Ontario still received most of its supply from the United States.

In 1922, amidst enthusiastic press reports of great oil developments in Mesopotamia, coal miners in the United States went on strike. Suddenly, coal was once again scarce and expensive; Ontario was able to get only 40 percent of its usual supply of anthracite from Pennsylvania. The public's love of "King and Empire" was fired by an offer from a group of Welsh coal dealers to make up the shortage, but Toronto and Montreal coal dealers were said not to be interested—perhaps because so many of them, as had been the case with Elias Rogers & Company, owned coal mines in the United States. Two coal dealers in Ottawa filled some orders, and reported delightedly that the Welsh coal produced ten percent less ash and twenty percent more heat than the American anthracite. Only one Toronto coal dealer imported a shipload of Welsh coal, but no permanent arrangements were made.

That winter in Ontario was a period of acute distress due to the coal shortage. Local peat, said to be two-thirds as good as anthracite, was suggested as an alternative, although it was not available in commercial quantities. Despite rumours of profiteering, the price of imported anthracite was fixed at $15.50 a ton by the new Ontario fuel controller, J. A. Ellis. Tommy Church, the former mayor of Toronto who by this time was an M.P.P. for North Toronto, made many speeches urging that all American coal be replaced by Alberta anthracite, and called for cooperation to this end among all levels of government. His call was not heeded until several decades later, when the flow of natural gas from Alberta to the east became a significant and usually controversial fact of Canadian political life.

The Consumers' Gas Company

Toronto's oldest public utility, the Consumers' Gas Company, came into existence on March 23, 1848, by an act of the Ontario legislature. Nearly a century and a half later, two of the buildings of its Front Street gasworks survive, one being the old Station "A" at Berkeley and Front, the other the former purifying house at the northeast corner of Front and Parliament. Its operation sprawled across the site, at the foot of Berkeley Street, of a different sort of gasworks, the province's first parliament buildings.

The first gas company in North America was organized in Baltimore in 1816. Twenty-four years later, the appropriately named Albert Furniss introduced gas to Montreal; the following year, 1841, he did the same in Toronto, under the name of City of Toronto Gas, Light & Water Company.

From 1841 to the date of incorporation of the Consumers' Gas Company, the main use of gas was for street lighting. Albert Furniss owned the gasworks and the distribution system, and the first lamps were lit on December 28, 1841. Toronto was then a wild and woolly town, the streets in terrible shape, the plank sidewalks often with loosened boards, the nails snagging and tripping pedestrians. The little pools of light thrown by the gaslamps were small consolation to a pedestrian whose foot had just caught a warped board, or a teamster whose eye failed to discern a pothole.

Over the next few years, a number of businesses and homes decided to give up their candles and illuminate with gas. However, these consumers soon became disaffected with its high price, poor quality, and uncertainty of supply. At a meeting on September 17, 1847, they resolved to form a new company. Five weeks later, they again met; Charles Berczy, then the postmaster, became president, and a board of twelve directors, including a publisher, two druggists, a leather merchant, hotel keeper, four shopkeepers and a grocer, was elected.

As they proceeded to make arrangements to construct their own gasworks, it became evident that Furniss was willing to sell, "on advantageous terms to the stockholders and the Community at large." A deal was struck, and after the second year of operation, the directors were pleased to report that they had done so well that £670 had been set aside as a contingency fund. In 1851, they announced their intention to erect an office at 19 Toronto Street: "suffering inconvenience from not having a sufficiently roomy office, with a workshop attached thereto, and not find-

ing a house that answered the purpose in a proper situation, the Directors determined upon building one for the use of the Company which is now in course of erection in Toronto Street, where they will have their boardroom, office, showroom and a workshop, with a residence for the Manager above; the latter they consider of importance, that the Consumers and others should know where to apply in case of any emergency." The company expanded, literally over the horizon, as the Village of Yorkville requested gas service; an act of the legislature in May, 1853, permitted the company to lay its pipes between the Toronto city limits and those of Yorkville.

One of its few difficult periods came during the 1860s, when the introduction of the newly discoverd coal oil, and a general business depression throughout North America, pinched the gas company's pipes. To save money, Toronto city council voted, in April, 1861, to discontinue lighting about half the street lamps, and to keep the remainder extinguished "for eight nights per month during the time of moonlight." The company's receipts further dropped because the city reduced the number of tavern licenses. In 1862, the directors resolved to make the price of their gas more competitive with the popular coal oil, and reduced it by one-sixth. The following year, with the price of coal climbing due to the Civil War, they put theirs back up.

The company's gasworks occupied several acres along the Toronto waterfront. Scrap coal was delivered by rail or unloaded at the company's wharves, and crews of labourers packed it into large ovens. It was then cooked slowly, with a damped supply of air, over a steam coal fire, driving off the coal-gas fumes, which cooled as they passed along pipes into the purifying building. There the vapours condensed, releasing coal tar; then the gas was scrubbed of its napthalene, at which point it was a smoky brown colour. (The gas was considered a "miracle cure" for sufferers from catarrh and whooping cough. It was not unusual for asthmatics and consumptives to hang around a gasworks, and children were sometimes bundled up and taken to where a road-patching crew was at work, in order to breathe the tarry fumes.) Sulphur in the coal gas was then usually removed by passing the gas through tanks filled with a lattice of boards coated in lime and iron oxide. Continuing along, still driven by the pressure from the heated furnace, the now-pure gas was tested for quality. A number of ingenious contraptions were invented to measure its British Thermal Unit content; usually, as a final test, a measured beaker of water

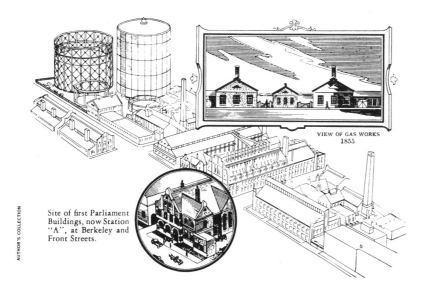

VIEW OF GAS WORKS
1855

Site of first Parliament
Buildings, now Station
"A", at Berkeley and
Front Streets.

was set to boil in a measured time. The process varied through the years, and in the late 1870s the company changed its works to use the patented "Lowe carburetted water gas process."

Through the years, the gasworks used gasometer-type storage tanks. As tall as a five-storey building, they consisted of huge, telescoping cylinders within a series of stabilizing tracks. As the gas entered from the bottom, it filled the gasometer and expanded its telescoping sides, pushing up on the "floating dome" atop. When full, the gasometer was connected to the distribution system, and the weight of the floating dome pushed the gas out at an appropriate pressure. In most gasworks systems, the problem of feeding the piped gas uphill was solved by smaller pipe sizes— this was not a problem in flat Toronto. Most of the early gas meters were water-filled, and froze solid in winter, cutting off the gas supply. The company advised its subscribers that draining the meter and refilling it with whisky assured an uninterrupted supply of gas. Nearly all of the technology of the coal gas industry—including the wet lime purifier, the gas meter, the gasometer, and the self-closing burner—had been invented by one man, Samuel Clegg, the assistant to the firm which had introduced gas street lights to London in 1806.

Everyone was sure they were courting disaster by permitting its use. As an anonymous chronicler of the industry's history put it: "Perhaps no invention ever received, during its period of initiation, quite as much abuse as did illuminating gas." Stories from around the world, many probably apocryphal, recount the sagas of misguided souls who, upon smelling gas, went looking for the leak with a candle.

Before 1879, the company had no authority to sell gas for anything other than illuminating purposes. The idea of using it for cooking and heating was not too popular, although Robert von Bunsen's gas burner, which made gas economical for heating, had been invented nearly twenty years before. The company, having successfully lobbied the legislature for the right to sell it for cooking, threw its resources into marketing this new use of gas, and in 1881 had induced local firms to manufacture gas cooking stoves and heating appliances. Their use caught on, and by 1905, according to company figures, there were nearly 9,000 gas stoves, and 11,500 gas rings, in use in the city. Many people retained their wood and coal stoves, but had a gas ring for the quick boiling of the kettle. Owning a gas cooking stove also eliminated the cook's standard summertime dilemma—whether to swelter in a 100-degree kitchen while cooking a meal, or try to set up a summer kitchen open to the breeze.

A great improvement in gas's lighting ability came with the invention, in 1885 by Carl von Welsbach, of the gas mantle burner, which survives today in Coleman-type lanterns. Concurrently, Edison invented the incandescent light bulb.

A company report in 1923 noted that it had taken 265,000 tons of bituminous coal, 120,000 tons of anthracite and coke, and 5,800,000 imperial gallons of gas-oil to generate the volume of gas needed to meet the city's demands that year. In the area served by the company, there were 645 miles of street mains. Gas for cooking and heating had become an indispensable part of modern city living.

In the years since, coal gas has been replaced with natural gas, the gasworks by tank farms and pipelines. The Consumers' Gas Company amalgamated with the Home Oil Company at the beginning of 1980. Four months later, this new firm amalgamated with the corporate successor of one of the gasworks' old neighbours on the Toronto waterfront—Hiram-Walker Gooderham & Worts Limited.

William Davies & Company

During the First World War, while young volunteers died in the trenches and civilians worked harder and dug ever deeper into their pockets to support the war effort, a spiral of price increases dug deeper still into the elusive wartime prosperity of full employment. By 1917, the tribulations and sacrifices on the home front found expression in resentment at the price of food, directing the cry of "War Profiteer!" against the William Davies Company Ltd., whose Toronto-area pork packing operations and related food businesses were doing an immense trade.

The William Davies Company was one of the earliest "vertically integrated" food companies in the country—it owned all aspects of the business from manufacturing through wholesaling to retailing, and its familiar food stores dotted the city streets. The company was founded in the 1850s by its namesake, a Berkshireman who came to Toronto in his early twenties. Capitalizing on Toronto's rapid expansion, he rose to prominence as a ham curer and sausage maker, and was the first to use ice on a large scale to provide cold storage and thus allow large-scale production. By the 1880s, he had developed both a retail trade, with dozens of stores throughout Ontario, and a large export business in meats and dairy products to Britain and the United States. Following Davies's death, the company became part of Joseph Flavelle's hydra-headed business empire. Flavelle was president and held slightly more than half of its shares, which in total were worth about $4 million. The William Davies Company also held 40 percent of the Harris Abattoir in Toronto, and 60 percent of another large meat company—Sheede-Thompson in London, England, which acted as its English agents. Flavelle (page 98), whose business ability was as legendary as his personal probity, was one of the wealthiest men in Toronto, and also one of the most public-spirited—his activities included support of the Methodist church and its charities, advocacy of Temperance, service on liquor licensing boards and committees, and involvement in public institutions such as the University of Toronto and the Toronto General Hospital, where he chaired the Board of Governors and to which he personally donated $100,000.

A typical William Davies & Company store interior from the First World War years. Hardwood floors, no refrigerated showcases, and an extraordinary mixture of aromas from aging meats and fermenting fruits and vegetables characterized grocery stores of the period.

Although the William Davies Company had greatly increased its business during the War, Flavelle had left it to its managers and had accepted the unpaid post of chairman of the Imperial Munitions Board, which coordinated, let contracts for, and supervised the manufacturing across the country of hundreds of millions of dollars worth of munitions. So exemplary was his work, in a country which had had meagre experience at manufacturing anything, let alone high explosives, that in June, 1917, the British government made him a baronet.

The inflationary spiral of food prices had predated the war years. The period from 1907 to 1912 witnessed unprecedented prosperity, with two new transcontinental railways under construction, new building projects everywhere, and a boom in spending on real estate and new technological playthings such as electric lights and automobiles. Along with the splurge came inflation, as supply could scarcely keep up with demand, and social change, especially in the cities, which further took life away from the simplicities and verities of Canada's rural past.

A speech by R. H. Coats, a staff member of the *Labour Gazette*, described some of the reasons for the fluctuations in prices. Tea had gone up in price, he said, as the United States had recently become a tea-drinking nation. As leather for upholstery and rubber for tires were in higher demand due to the expansion of the automobile industry, the price of workingmen's heavy shoes was increasing faster than that of dress shoes. By contrast, though, many of the old fuel companies had branched into gasoline sales, and many householders had converted to electricity for lighting, so the price of coal oil had dropped. In a similar fashion, because the vogue for fancy hats and frilly dresses was passing, the price of both silk and ribbon had dropped.

A committee of the Board of Trade, with members including Joseph Atkinson of the *Star* and Professor M. A. Mackenzie of the University of Toronto, came to the hardly revolutionary conclusion that Toronto was the most expensive city in Ontario in which to live. Cited as factors were the apparent disappearance of competition in the wholesaling of food supplies, the inferior shipping facilities for bringing produce into the city, and the absence of market facilities. The committee added, however, that there were also too many small retailers, resulting in inefficient and costly—though presumably highly competitive—distribution of goods. In the period from 1900 through 1911, the costs of meat, fish, and grain had each gone up by about 40 percent. Meanwhile, wages had doubled for domestic servants.

The city had changed, too. As land became more expensive, market gardens moved further away, making transportation of produce more expensive. More people lived on little lots and worked and played only as city dwellers—the back-yard chickens and cow, the orchard, and the kitchen garden became more scarce, eliminated in some cases by zoning, in others by a generation which had not been brought up to practise the frugality and industry of its parents. While most people accepted that there were several culprits for the inflation, they likely saw the middleman as bogeyman. One of the widely reported incidents that cemented this opinion involved a barrel of apples shipped to Winnipeg from Ontario. Hidden inside was a note from the farmer, saying: "I got 70 cents for this barrel of apples. What did you pay for it?" The purchaser had paid $5.25! Enquiries in Toronto amongst shippers and distributors indicated that it should have been offered for sale in Winnipeg for $3.00.

Thus, in 1917, after three years of war and ever more outrageous food price increases, the populace was searching for villains. Many felt that competition in the marketplace had ceased to exist because of the quasi-monopolistic combines created through mergers, and urged the establishment of a Dominion Food Tribunal to control prices. Wheat was a general target; in the west, it was sugar; others, noted by the Toronto Board of Control, were bread, milk, fuel, ice, dairy, and farm produce. The Imperial Order Daughters of the Empire and the War-Time Thrift Committee of Toronto campaigned for reduced prices and greater thrift among families, as "the present high price of foodstuffs is bearing heavily and especially upon the nourishment of children." In addition, there was widespread criticism of the rising price of meat—especially bacon—leading to the certainty, cobbled together from inference, innuendo and rumour, that the William Davies Company was holding back in cold storage massive quantities of pork, with the intention of driving prices up. A Member of Parliament named A. B. McCoig alleged that the Company had asked for bids to insure $2,800,000 worth of meats it was holding in cold storage. Was it holding these pending shipping or was it hoarding? Sir Joseph Flavelle was occupied elsewhere with the Munitions Board; the general manager of the Davies Company, E. C. Fox, dismissed the claim and said that it was necessary to carry some goods in storage in order to assure a "uniform and sufficient" public supply.

Fox's letter to the press was published on May 24, 1917, but the matter did not rest there. On July 9, W. F. O'Connor, the acting commissioner on the cost of living, made public his report on the cold storage business in Canada. In it, he dismissed most of the allegations that the various cold storage businesses had acted together as a combine, or had hoarded food to force up the prices. However, he did comment that, because a few of the companies were so large, efficient, and centralized (the Davies Company alone had exported 95 million pounds of bacon in 1916), they exercised a virtual monopoly. O'Connor submitted elaborate tables showing the volume of business conducted and the profits of the William Davies Company: an audit performed for the government by Clarkson, Gordon & Dilworth showed that profits had climbed from two million dollars in 1914 to five million in 1917 (according to E. C. Fox, profits in 1914 were only $373,350, and in 1917 $1,723,600)—much of the growth being due to the increased business from war orders; more ominously, a review of the company's sales showed that in the case of most of its products— butter, eggs, cheese, beef, ham and mutton—the margin of profit was around a few percent, but in its big seller, bacon, the company made a margin of nearly 25 percent. On nearly one hundred million pounds of bacon, that margin added up to nearly $20 million.

In conclusion, O'Connor wrote: "The food consumer has suffered as a result of war conditions. The food purveyor has not. He has seen to it that he has been well and sufficiently paid. Accordingly, while yielding well-deserved credit to the cold storage companies of Canada for the capable manner in which they have grappled with the problem of supplying the needs of the armies and people of Great Britain and the Allies, it will be well to remember that the performance has been upon strictly business and not upon patriotic lines. The consumer, who alone has suffered for his country in the process, is the patriot."

Sir Joseph Flavelle instantly became the public's whipping boy. Had he not been so forthright in his own denunciations of profiteers, and so pious about his personal behaviour, the battering ram of consumer bitterness might have dissipated itself on the brick wall of carefully worded statements from the William Davies Company. As it was, labour and consumers joined together in strident calls for prosecution of profiteering capitalists and manufacturers. A slowly building opposition to British titles for Canadians added heat to the debate.

Flavelle wired Prime Minister Borden with his opinion that the press comments and innuendo were "grotesquely untruthful in mass and in detail" and "a curious mixture of ignorance and malice." He went on to say that all the company's sales to the imperial government had been on the open market, and that O'Connor's alleged margin on bacon showed "a dangerous inability to coordinate figures," as operating costs, transportation, and insurance—which had skyrocketed on shipments to England, due to German submarine successes—effectively reduced the profit from the claimed five cents to less than a cent. The company itself fought back, publishing a full-page advertisement in newspapers across Canada in which it reviewed O'Connor's report, gave its own account of its business, and concluded that "this terminates all public statements of the Company—except at an official investigation." *Saturday Night* magazine responded with a series of articles by Gordon Waldron which dissected Flavelle and the company in scathing detail.

Agreed to was the mooted government accounting inquiry, which had been suggested by O'Connor in his report; it opened in Toronto under the

James William Bain, K.C., was one of an array of legal heavyweights on both sides of the bench during the lengthy enquiries instigated by the government to determine whether the William Davies Company was guilty of war profiteering. Bain was counsel for the government at the Royal Commission which commenced hearings in Toronto on September 18, 1917. A partner in the distinguished firm of Bain, Bicknell, White & Bristol, he was born in Toronto in 1872, the son of a Scottish Q.C.. His mother was the daughter of an Imperial army officer living in Ceylon. Bain was educated at Upper Canada College, the University of Toronto, and Osgoode Hall Law School, and became a director and general counsel for companies including Joseph E. Seagram & Sons, Distillers Corporation, and the Imperial Bank of Canada. He lived at 36 Forest Hill Road.

James Stanley McLean entered the meat business as a clerk in the Harris Abattoir Company when he was 25 years old; a quarter-century later, in 1927, he became the first president of Canada Packers Limited. His career was furthered by his marriage to Edith Flavelle, a niece of the president of the William Davies Company. Well-known as art collectors and in Toronto social circles, the McLeans occupied an enormous house on Bayview Avenue, now part of the Sunnybrook Hospital. McLean retained the presidency of Canada Packers Ltd. until his death in 1954.

chairmanship of Ottawa King's Counsel G. F. Henderson, with two accountants—Geoffrey Clarkson and Montrealer A. B. Brodie—as commissioners. Two King's Counsels represented the combatants: James W. Bain, a corporate lawyer, educated at Upper Canada College and Osgoode Hall, represented the government; Norman Tilley, an Osgoode Hall gold medallist who had specialized in railway law and had been special counsel for the Canadian Pacific Railway since 1913, represented the William Davies Company. Testimony dragged on for nearly a month until October 20, when the long-awaited star witness—Flavelle—took the stand. A formidable character who was used to speaking very directly and frankly, he agreed that his company would not have made the extra profits without the advent of the war and the increased demand for bacon, and he offered as justification that his company was in the business of business, rather than that of philanthropy. Startling profit figures were presented: the profit with interest on the Davies Company's sales had soared from 20 percent in 1914 to nearly 94 percent in 1916; Flavelle stated flatly that his profits on capital invested, which in 1917 came to 100 percent, gave him no "qualms of conscience."

Flavelle's forthrightness won him few admirers. Although there were no direct allegations that he had used his Imperial contacts either to aid his company in winning contracts, or to obtain spare shipping space on munitions ships for his bacon consignments, many were dismayed by his arrogant attitude. Most Liberal newspapers around the country took the opportunity to lambast the Borden government and Flavelle (who evidently usually supported the Conservative party), and to demand that he step down from the Munitions Board. The *Globe* on October 24 summed up its view of Flavelle: he had not applied to his own firm "the higher ethics of war contracts which he imposed upon munitions manufacturers." Flavelle continued to conduct himself as one who had done no wrong.

The hue and cry resulting from the so-called Henderson Report prompted the government to appoint N. W. Rowell, the former Ontario Liberal leader who was then a key Liberal figure in Borden's Union government, as chairman of a cabinet committee to delve into packing house

profits and to recommend ways of limiting future profits. In the immediate short term, the dominion food controller began to regulate all packing houses and cold storage plants. In the longer term, interest in the imperial government's questionable food procurement methods faded along with the end of the extraordinary conditions of wartime. But inflation did not—late in 1920, inflated prices of foodstuffs caused a consumer uprising, and investigations by the Ontario attorney general (page 282). But most of the criticism then was directed against an alleged grocers' combine, rather than the meat and cold storage business.

The William Davies Company merged in 1927 with Canadian Packing Company Ltd. (the former Geo. Matthews Company), Gunns Limited, and the Harris Abattoir Company, to form Canada Packers Limited. Its brand name, Maple Leaf Products, soon became a household word across the country. The first president of Canada Packers was James Stanley McLean, Sir Joseph Flavelle's nephew.

The Company's affairs again came under microscopic scrutiny in March, 1934, when McLean was grilled by the Stevens Commission into Price Spreads and Mass Buying. The unwelcome publicity concerning McLean's wealth and his lavish estate on Bayview Avenue probably prompted a kidnapping attempt that summer. On August 13, Frank Woods and the brothers Harry and James Leslie were committed for trial on a charge of conspiring to kidnap McLean. Police had discovered an excavation beneath a tourist camp at Mimico, where the victim was to be held supposedly for a ransom of $100,000. The accused were eventually dismissed. (The day after the McLean conspiracy case went to trial, John Labatt, of the London brewing family, was kidnapped from his automobile somewhere on the road between Sarnia and London. A note found in the automobile demanded $150,000 ransom. Three days later, Labatt was released, blindfolded, in a sparsely settled part of Forest Hill Village. It was not made clear whether the ransom had been paid, but the police soon had the perpetrator, David Meisner from Cincinnati, who was sentenced to fifteen years in prison.)

Parkdale

The Village of Parkdale, as described in 1881 by local booster John G. Scott, was "exceedingly picturesque, being surrounded by a landscape that possesses all the varying attractions afforded by beautiful Ontario, and the diversified scenery of an undulating expanse of fertile country, wooded, watered, cultivated, and adorned with attractive houses." Serious settlement of the area had begun only six years earlier, when the Toronto House Building Association purchased 50 acres, laid out roads and built sidewalks, surveyed it into lots, and sold them to the expanding city populace; earlier residents, such as Dr. William Gwynne (next page), had lived on what were effectively farms in a rural landscape. "The heat of summer," wrote Scott, "is tempered by the breezes from Lake Ontario which dispense a refreshing coolness that is lacking in the close and sultry city." Unlike the districts along the marshy Don River, "the place is not subject to malarial influences and is uncommonly healthy."

In January, 1879, the residents incorporated themselves into the Village of Parkdale. The story that a group of encamped gypsies were commandeered to vote as a makeweight—there being fewer than the required 1,000 permanent residents—is one of the enduring legends of the district. Ten municipal employees were hired, including three fence viewers, two constables, a road overseer, and a poundkeeper. Sensible local bylaws included a "very stringent" law to prevent cattle and hogs from running at large; "as a consequence, the trees do not require boxes around them— somewhat of a saving is thereby effected, as the boxes generally cost more than the trees."

Bowing to the inevitable, the community to the north of Parkdale, called Brockton, amalgamated with Toronto in 1884. Parkdale followed suit in 1889. Several of the city's institutions, including the Mercer Reformatory, the Protestant Orphans' Home, the Home for Incurables, and the lunatic asylum, had located in the area. At the turn of the century, its population stood at 22,000; it boomed in the next decade to 60,000. Although the area was an attractive one, as evidenced by its grand homes, many of its long-time residents had moved on by the 1950s; subsequently, Parkdale became a first harbour for many immigrants. Although much of the area has been beautified, and many of the houses renovated, there remain pockets which fit Parkdale's recent reputation as, in the words of one newspaper story, a "dumping ground for the city's social problems," exacerbated by halfway houses and the proximity of the mental health complex on Queen Street.

Looking east and southeast from the corner of Dunn and Springhurst. Traffic proceeding south on Dunn Avenue towards the vanished community along the lakeshore negotiated a level crossing at the Grand Trunk Railway tracks. The Dunn Avenue bridge and grade separation project were completed in 1911. The old Parkdale Station was a block and a half east of here, between Close and Jameson avenues. Today, a passerby looking east along Springhurst has a striking view of the C.N. Tower, framed by the houses lining the street, and of the Canadian National Exhibition.

"Sunnyside" page 205

Adapted from GOAD'S Fire Atlas 1923

Lawbook publisher Robert Carswell operated his business from the Equity Chambers at Adelaide and Victoria streets (the first office building in the city to be equipped with an elevator) and lived at "Bayview," his splendid pile on Dowling Avenue near the lake. Born in Colborne in 1838, he started to teach school at the age of eighteen, but moved to Toronto several years later to sell lawbooks. In 1879, he moved to Edinburgh and formed Carswell & Company. He prospered sufficiently to be able to return to Toronto, build the aforementioned office building and house, and settle down to a life of publishing, chess, card games, and worship at the Swedenborgian church. Later, he subdivided his Dowling Avenue property and moved to a more modest house at 1534 King Street West.

Frank Culver was a mine owner and self-styled gentleman farmer who lived in a house at 100 Jameson. Born in Buffalo, he was preparing to become a lawyer when his health deteriorated, and he was advised to seek a more active life in the open. He went to northern Ontario, where he worked as a teamster and endeared himself to the local capitalists by helping to avert a labour disruption. He was thus in a good position to purchase an interest in the Silver, Queen, Beaver, and Temiskaming mines. He became a "model" mine operator, and introduced safety features like the Red Flag Signal, which advised "illiterate foreigners" when they were in dangerous territory. Liquor was banned in all his camps, and entertainment societies provided moving picture shows and educational opportunities. "Don't capitalize your regrets!" and "Play Fair" were his mottos.

AUTHOR'S COLLECTION

"Thornhurst," sometimes known as "Thorncrest," was the home, at 19 Laburnam Avenue near the foot of Dowling Avenue, of George Plunkett Magann. Built in 1889 of Credit Valley stone, red brick, terracotta, and tile, the house was surrounded by extensive landscaping. Magann was a Dubliner who became a railway contractor and dealt in construction supplies; his objections to a transmission tower in front of his house, expressed in a lawsuit, delayed the arrival in Toronto of publicly owned electricity.

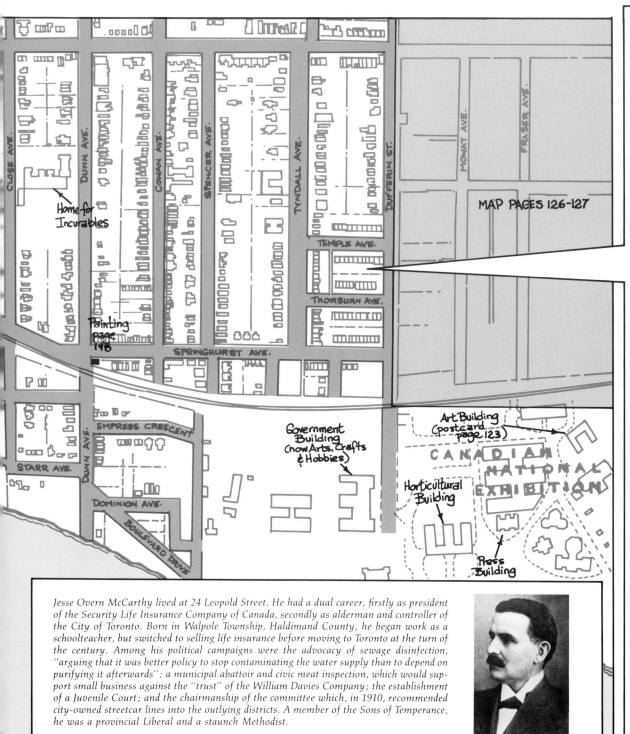

Home for Incurables

Painting page 198

MAP PAGES 126-127

Government Building (now Arts, Crafts & Hobbies)

Art Building (postcard page 123)

Horticultural Building

CANADIAN NATIONAL EXHIBITION

Press Building

The blurred photograph above purports to be the only one remaining of Nell Gwynne, standing in front of "Gwynne Cottage" on the west side of Dufferin Street between Temple and Thornburn streets, about 300 yards north of the lake. The land was settled and the house built following the 1835 marriage of Dr. William Gwynne, a surgeon and Nell's father. According to Robertson's *Landmarks of Toronto*, published in 1898, it was the last house of its type in the city: reminiscent of the bungalows in India of that time, it had foot-and-a-half-thick walls of clay bricks, insulated and finished with layers of straw, lath, and plaster on both sides. Iron plates inserted in the walls about half-way up made the building more solid; the hall was eighteen feet wide. Beds of old English cottage flowers were planted on either side of the front path, and, in 1910, it had the last hand-split rail snake fence in the city. Few verifiable facts are known about the family, but one story has been repeated often enough to become legend: beneath a large elm tree near the house, Nell Gwynne said good-bye to her lover and fiance, who went off and was killed in either the Crimean War or the U.S. Civil War (making Nell either about seventeen years old, or twenty-five). Heartbroken, she fenced off her "trysting tree," and chose the bedroom in the house which offered her a clear view of it through the French doors. She was an only child, never married, and died in 1910. The old Gwynne Estate was subdivided soon thereafter; first to go was the trysting tree, and the cottage was demolished in August, 1917. (It is curious that an educated man like William Gwynne would give his daughter the same name as one of the most famous prostitutes in English history—Nell Gwynne, the mistress of Charles II.)

Jesse Overn McCarthy lived at 24 Leopold Street. He had a dual career, firstly as president of the Security Life Insurance Company of Canada, secondly as alderman and controller of the City of Toronto. Born in Walpole Township, Haldimand County, he began work as a schoolteacher, but switched to selling life insurance before moving to Toronto at the turn of the century. Among his political campaigns were the advocacy of sewage disinfection, "arguing that it was better policy to stop contaminating the water supply than to depend on purifying it afterwards"; a municipal abattoir and civic meat inspection, which would support small business against the "trust" of the William Davies Company; the establishment of a Juvenile Court; and the chairmanship of the committee which, in 1910, recommended city-owned streetcar lines into the outlying districts. A member of the Sons of Temperance, he was a provincial Liberal and a staunch Methodist.

201

G.T. Denison III

Almost nothing remains of the old Denison estates which occupied most of the quadrilateral bounded by Dovercourt, Dundas, Dufferin and College streets, in what is now the *Rua Açores* section of Toronto. The Denison family were among the most haughty* and militaristic of the "old families" who came to Upper Canada in the early years. The house called "Rush Holme," built by George Taylor Denison II (a grandson of the original migrant), which is remembered in Rusholme Road, Drive, Park, and Crescent, stood at the bend of Rusholme Drive, on the western side, until its demolition in 1954. The house at 70-72 St. Ann's Road was the only one on the block to the north, which was also part of the "Rush Holme" estate. Today, it is surrounded by modest, boxlike infill housing.

The northeastern quarter of the quadrilateral was occupied by the house and property called "Heydon Villa," owned by Lt. Col. George Taylor Denison III. According to historian Lucy Booth Martyn, it was built as a replica of a Southern mansion with a neoclassical columned verandah, as Denison was a vociferous sympathizer with the ante-bellum South of the "Stars & Bars." In 1877, when he was 38 years old, Denison was appointed police magistrate, a position he held until he was well into his eighties. Descriptions of his judicial philosophy include the following, published late in the 1890s in the conservative *Telegram*, describing the fate of a "boy" who, on the promise of a pardon, was induced to plead guilty to a trumped-up charge of assault on a girl under fourteen years of age: "One of the worst of Colonel Denison's judgements was reversed yesterday by their Lordships . . . . Their decision set a boy at liberty after a confinement of more than five months and saved him from spending five years in the [Kingston] penitentiary and enduring fifteen lashes. Seldom has there been on record a case that better illustrated the inhumanity of some detectives and the off-hand methods of Col. Denison. Colonel Denison is generally right, but the case in point is proof that he is not above trifling away a prisoner's liberty and ruining his life in order that he can get through the day's work before eleven a.m." In another decision of the period Denison fined the bandmaster of the Queen's Own Rifles for "pursuing his worldly calling" by playing sacred music at Hanlan's Point on a Sunday afternoon, in violation of the Sabbath laws.

Denison died in 1925, and "Heydon Villa" was demolished four years later. His name survives in the Denison Armoury, on Dufferin Street in Downsview.

*Published descriptions of family members call them "aristocratic," though they were not members of any aristocracy.

CTA. JAMES 303

Denison Lodge, the gatehouse into Fred Denison's "Rush Holme" at Dundas and Rusholme Road. Now subdivided and covered with little brick boxes in the Rua Açores *section of Parkdale, the old estate grounds have utterly vanished. On the site of the gatehouse is a service station.*

George Taylor Denison III

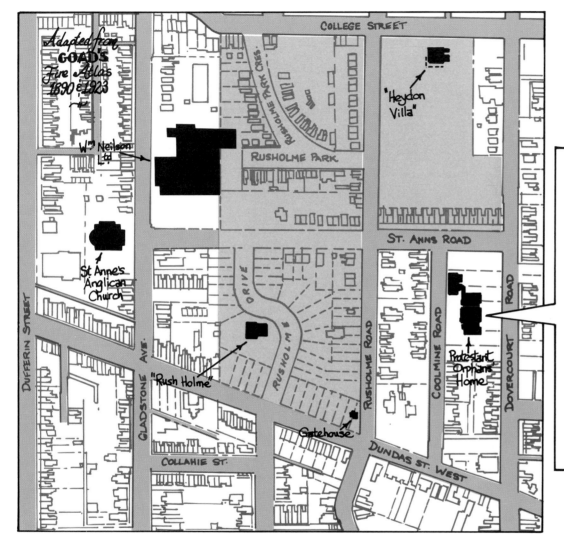

Adapted from GOAD'S Fire Atlas 1890 & 1923

COLLEGE STREET

"Heydon Villa"

RUSHOLME PARK CRES.

Wm Neilson Ltd

RUSHOLME PARK

ST. ANNS ROAD

St Anne's Anglican Church

DUFFERIN STREET

GLADSTONE AVE.

DRIVE

RUSHOLME

RUSHOLME ROAD

COOLMINE ROAD

DOVERCOURT ROAD

"Rush Holme"

Protestant Orphans Home

Gatehouse

DUNDAS ST. WEST

COLLAHIE ST.

One of the private charities in the city was the Protestant Orphans' Home (founded in 1851), which occupied a half block on Dovercourt Road just south of St. Ann's Road. The writer G. G. Adam described it as "surrounded by ample playgrounds, a model one, and by its comfort and cheerfulness tending to soften the asperities and brighten the outlook of its orphaned inmates." To benefit the charity, the famed soprano Jenny Lind donated the proceeds of a concert. (In 1850, three years after her Covent Garden debut, the 30-year-old "Swedish nightingale" travelled to America; thereafter, under the management of Phineas T. Barnum, she toured North America, and appeared locally at St. Lawrence Hall shortly after its completion. She was usually paid $1,000 a night.) The Orphans' Home was well supported by volunteers, especially Mrs. Matthew Vankoughnet, and housed between 150 and 200 unfortunates at any one time. The Protestant Orphans' Home was one of many private charities operating in the city, including the nearby Dunn Avenue Home for Incurables (on the site of Queen Elizabeth Hospital), the Sunnyside Children's Home, the Industrial Refuge for Girls (part of the Mercer Reformatory for Women behind 999 Queen Street West), and the House of Industry—the city's poorhouse on Elm Street in The Ward. The site of the Protestant Orphans' Home is now Heydon Park Secondary School.

Morden Neilson

The two grey quadrangles on the map were the extent, in 1890, of the old Denison estates—the one on the left that of Lieut. Col. Frederick C. Denison and the house called "Rush Holme," the one on the right that of Lieut. Col. Geo. T. Denison III and the house called "Heydon Villa." The map indicates the subdivision of the estate and the amount of building thereon in the early 1920s.

Almost next door to the Denison estates, at the corner of Gladstone and St. Ann's, stands the William Neilson ice cream and chocolate factory. A business started in 1893 by William Neilson and his son Morden (left), it was incorporated in 1908, but remained in the family's control. Morden Neilson ran the business until he died in 1947; he was a great contributor of time and money to "boys' work," most notably the

Y.M.C.A., and was president of the Ontario Motor League and an enthusiastic automobilist—an interest inherited by his son Harley, a noted collector of vintage cars. One of the firm's employees was George Metcalf, who had joined the firm at the age of fifteen. As a young man in the early 1920s, Metcalf had met Garfield Weston when both were attempting to sell food to Loblaw's. In 1947, Metcalf convinced the Neilson family to sell out to Weston's for $4.5 million; Metcalf then left Neilson's to become a vice-president of Loblaw's.

Across the street from the chocolate factory is the notable St. Anne's Anglican Church, the only Byzantine Cross church in Canada. Its interior decoration was supervised by the Group of Seven member J. E. H. MacDonald.

The Dufferin Race Track, on the west side of Dufferin Street between Muir and Awde. A row of houses and other buildings stretched along Dufferin Street, separating the street from the racetrack. A popular spot for the average wage-earner and wagerer, it had none of the panache of Woodbine, where fashion plates were attracted each May to the Queen's or King's Plate. The photograph shows a typical crowd—almost all men, puffs of cigar smoke wafting among them. Dufferin was one of four tracks in the Toronto area, the other three being Woodbine, Thorncliffe, and Long Branch. Enthusiasts could use the excellent radial railway and road system to journey to Hamilton, and even from there to Fort Erie and Buffalo, to test their skills at turf accountancy.

Across the street from the old racetrack is Dufferin Grove Park. When the skating rink there was under construction, in September, 1960, an electrician drilled through a retaining wall in order to correct a problem in the falsework, the day before the concrete for a wall was to be poured, and was greeted by a sickening odour. He enlisted the help of some other workers to knock down the wall. To their horror, they discovered a decomposing body wrapped in newspaper and bound with electrical cord. It was identified as that of a young woman by the name of Eva Blumberger. The following day, the twentieth of September, police arrested the resident of 163 Havelock Street—directly east across the park from the rink—and charged him with murder. Dezso Bakonyi was cousin, stepbrother, and lover of Eva. He had killed her in his apartment and dumped her body into the excavation. Had the concrete been poured, she would never have been found. Bakonyi, who had come close to committing the perfect crime, was sentenced to hang. The sentence was later commuted.

Sunnyside

The "Poor Man's Riviera" of Sunnyside was demolished about thirty years ago, after three decades as Parkdale's 130-acre "lakeside playground." A recitation of its attractions is a litany of the ephemera of a vanished era: Custer Cars, radio demonstrations, palmistry, dishwashing contests, Downyflake doughnuts, David Harem sundaes for 25 cents, "sterilized suits and towels," mountebanks and hucksters on the midway, "first aid room in charge of graduate nurse," an "entrée" of boiled ham with potato salad for 25 cents, dance gardens, and so on. Also in the style of the vanished era was the free "bathing car" service (all streetcars with both motorman and conductor, to control the unruly passengers), paid for by the city-owned transit system to reach the city-owned park, which allowed cooped-up city children some healthy supervised recreation.

The postcards on the left show the transition in bathing suit fashions. In the 1920s card above, the men are wearing singlets—several who doffed theirs during the July 1936 heat wave were arrested for indecent exposure—and the women, liberated from the tights, bloomers and parasols of their mothers' generation, sport voluminous singlets and knee-length shorts of wool flannel. In the 1950s card below, the chorines' swimsuits still have a vestige of a skirt, the lack of which would have been considered indecent.

Built on sand fill pumped from the lake bottom, Sunnyside opened in 1922 after years of planning which were interrupted by the First World War. Changing public tastes, and the prosperity and mobility which followed the Second World War, tarnished its lustre. It was demolished at the end of 1955, making way for the Gardiner Expressway.

Some residents of Parkdale.

(Top Row) Far Left: Donald Chadwick MacGregor, who lived at 891 Lansdowne, was Ward 6 alderman in the early 1920s, a director of the C.N.E., and a professional vocalist and certified teacher of singing ("exponent of Italian Bel Canto Method"). When not singing, teaching, touring, or politicking, he sold real estate.

Left: The writer and local historian Jesse Edgar Middleton lived at 427 Gladstone Avenue. Perhaps best remembered for his authorship of the city's official commemorative centennial history Toronto's 100 Years, he was a newspaperman and a sometime publicist for the Hydro-Electric Power Commission of Ontario. After a stint working for the Montreal Herald in Quebec, he moved to Toronto in 1903 as music critic for the Mail & Empire, then switched to the News and performed the same function until that newspaper folded in 1919. As a freelancer, he contributed articles to many of the Canadian and American magazines of the period, including Life, Judge, Munsey's, and The Smart Set. Other than his Toronto Centennial book, his major published work was a volume of wartime verse entitled Sea Dogs and Men at Arms.

Right and Far Right: Two other Parkdale-area writers were the brother and sister Archie McKishnie and Jean Blewett, who with their spouses shared the house at 353 Sunnyside Avenue. McKishnie wrote historical novels about pioneer life in Canada, including Gaff Linkum, Love of the Wild, Willow The Wisp, and Openway. His novels were used as textbooks in Alberta and Manitoba; a few were even translated into French. His Mates of the Tangle, a volume of nature stories, was "conceded by leading critics to equal the work of the world's greatest nature writers." In addition to writing, McKishnie taught at his Arts & Letters School at 481 Roncesvalles. His sister Jean wrote poetry, including two collections entitled Heartsongs and The Cornflower, and a work of prose called The Inn of the Open Door; she was also the editor of the Homemakers Department of the Globe. She married Bassett Blewett and raised a son and a daughter. Her poetry, an example of which is this quatrain from "Quebec," published in a textbook of Canadian literature, is of a type once familiar to every schoolchild: ". . . The doves are nesting in the cannon grim / The flowers bloom where once did run a tide / Of crimson when the moon rose pale and dim / Above a field of battle stretching wide."

(Bottom Row) Far Left: Lt. Col. Hon. William Herbert Price, K.C., an attorney general of Ontario, lived at 7 Indian Grove. He catapulted into the spotlight as solicitor for Andrew Miscambell, the M.P.P. in the Sault Election Trial in 1904; the disclosure therein of the "Minnie M" scandal contributed to the subsequent demise of the Liberal Ross government. Price practiced law with Conservative cabinet minister W. J. Hanna before entering politics himself, being elected in 1914 to represent Parkdale. Following the demise of the United Farmers of Ontario, Price became treasurer in the Ferguson Conservative government, then attorney general following the 1926 election. He was still attorney general in 1934, and introduced the "by-the-glass" amendments which allowed the drinking of beer and wine in hotel beverage rooms.

Left: At 50 Indian Trail lived Clara Humberston, who wrote magazine articles on scientific and natural history subjects. Born at Acton West in 1862, she was a schoolteacher before her marriage. In her forties, she began to write works such as "Why The Chameleon Changes Its Skin." Her chart of Birds of Canada demonstrated her knowledge and perception of the natural world; articles such as "Spiritism—the Hidden Secret in Einstein's Theory of Relativity," published in 1922, demonstrated her unorthodox taste in religion. She was a member of the Toronto Theosophical Society, and in 1924 she was appointed secretary for Cincinnati and Southern Ohio of the mysterious International Fixed Calendar League.

Right: William George Caulfield was the son of a Belfast Irishman who in 1888 founded Caulfield's Dairy at 45 Howard Park Avenue. In forty years, the company grew from a single delivery wagon to a fleet of 100.

Far Right: Frederick Zeidler served with distinction on the German side during the 1914 invasion of Belgium and won the Iron Cross. The son of a newspaper publisher, he was educated as a chemist in Germany and Boston—where he spent five years at Harvard—before starting work in chemical and fabric plants in 1912. He emigrated to Buenos Aires after the war, then came north and settled in Toronto, where he entered the business of dyeing and finishing textiles. Eventually, he became president of the Dickinson Dyeworks at 884 Dufferin. He had married a Chicago girl on June 30, 1914, a month before the First World War started. They lived at 60 High Park Boulevard.

(Next page) The area to the east of John Howard's estate, now High Park, was sparsely settled in 1890. A few roadways existed, like Indian Road which wound its way north and east over the rolling, wooded country; others, like Parkside Avenue, had been proposed but not cleared. At the junction of King, Queen, and Roncesvalles stood one of the few local landmarks, the hostelry of Thomas E. Scholes, later called the Ocean Hotel. The surrounding blocks were all but vacant; a hundred yards to the west, though, was a tollgate for travellers using the Lakeshore Road, and a little further along the Sacred Heart Orphanage, known as "Sunnyside." Scholes's Hotel still exists, minus its cupola and in disrepair, used as apartments and festooned with billboards.

The Junction

AUTHOR'S COLLECTION

Typical of the factories which proliferated in The Junction was the Wilkinson Plough Company, "manufacturers of garden barrows, railroad barrows, railroad and street ploughs, drag, wheel, and patent dump scrapers, and ploughs of all kinds." It was located at the junction of the Grand Trunk (C.N.R.) and C.P.R. rail lines, on Wiltshire Avenue.

Charles F. Wheaton's Dodge Manufacturing Company— originally called the Dodge Wood Split Pulley Company—was established in the 1880s at the corner of Osler and Pelham streets in The Junction. Over the next 30 years, it expanded into the manufacturing of power transmission, elevator, and conveyor equipment, and each year sold an impressive $1.5 million worth of manufactured goods. Wheaton was from Brantford and began his career as a clerk in a wholesale millinery company. He lived at 122 Bedford Road in the Annex.

Most recollections of old Toronto mention the isolated, self-contained nature of its neighbourhoods: people in Cabbagetown stayed in their own immediate few blocks; occasionally, in Riverdale, the residents went to the beach; and so on. Similarly, when one asks a West Toronto Junction old-timer where he grew up, the answer will probably be "The Junction," or "the west end," but not "Toronto."

Toronto Junction was a factory centre, an incorporated town with its own reeve and police and school board until the city swallowed it by annexation in 1909. "The Junction" itself was the crossroads of Dundas and Keele, where all the streetcars and railways and the Toronto & York Radial Railway line to Weston came together. To its residents it was a small Ontario town, with Dundas, from Keele to High Park Avenue, as the small town main street. Very quickly, in any direction, one came upon open fields at the edge of town, or to the south the rolling woods and glades of High Park. The city was distant and remote, at the end of interminable streetcar trips to Eaton's and Simpson's for Saturday shopping.

G. Mercer Adam's enthusiastic chronicle of progress, *Toronto Old & New*, published in 1891, reviewed the "Junction enterprises and their kinship to those of the city." Describing the city's recent expansion, he wrote: "True to the general law, the chief progress has been westward.

No sooner do Parkdale and Brockton blossom out into a new and populous Toronto, and in time come within the city's embrace, than still another civic extension appears and grows up to maturity like a gourd in the night. If the pace is maintained, we shall have ere long a continuous city, vocal with the sounds of industry, from the waterfront to Weston. A stroll through West Toronto Junction will astonish the Torontonian who rarely quits the beaten paths of the city proper. Here he will find manufactories and all manner of industries that have sought at the Junction room to expand freely, with exemption from city taxation. The suburb has a stir and life about it which mark it as an off-shoot of the city; and born of the same enterprise and energies that have made Toronto what it is."

Politically, the town was dominated by the Clendenan brothers, the namesakes of Clendenan Avenue. Daniel was a barrister, and was The Junction's first reeve. His brother, George Washington Clendenan, was a doctor, who held the positions of coroner, medical health officer, chairman of the school board, and president of the Mechanic's Institute (the library).

If low taxes were one inducement to industry, the availability of rail transport was certainly another. Multiple lines of the Canadian Pacific Railway and the Grand Trunk Railway laced the area, and spur lines were easily laid into every industrial nook and cranny. A tremendous concentration of industry soon dominated the community—the Theodore Heintzman Piano Company, the Nordheimer Piano Company, Comfort Soap Works, Toronto Stock Yards, Gurney Foundry, Fairbanks-Morse, the Canadian General Electric Company, the Dodge Manufacturing Company, Wilkinson Plough Company, and King Radiator, to name a few. Further north, along the railway line to Weston and beyond, were the sprawling factories of the Canadian Cycle & Motor Company.

C.C.M. was founded in September, 1899, at the peak of the safety-bicycle boom (the high-wheeled penny-ha'penny bicycles of previous decades had proved too dangerous and difficult for the general populace to ride). Much of the capital came from the bicycle branch of Massey-Harris; as was the case with much of Massey-Harris's growth in the agricultural implements field, it sought to amalgamate itself with its competition in order to dominate the market. Thus, C.C.M. was formed of five bicycle manufacturers—Massey-Harris, Welland Vale, Gendron, Cleveland, and Brantford—which had, before amalgamation, controlled over three-quarters of the Canadian bicycle market. Massey-Harris officials ran the company, with W. E. H. Massey as president, and J. N. Shenstone as general manager. However, within a few years the bicycle boom passed, and C.C.M. had to retrench and diversify.

Directed by its general manager, T. A. "Tommy" Russell, C.C.M. started to make sporting goods and soon came to dominate the winter-sports market; as well, it experimented in the infant automobile industry, initially with gasoline-powered quadricycles and tricycles, a few of which were purchased by the post office, and in 1902 with an electric runabout called the Ivanhoe. In 1905, the company introduced its Russell Model A, a real improvement over previous efforts, as "state of the art" as any vehicle in North America. With an advertising campaign which called it "the thoroughly Canadian car," built with "Canadian material, Canadian labor, Canadian capital," the Russell motorcar soon had carved out a niche for itself in the marketplace. Its Doctor's Runabout Model B, with sixteen horsepower and a price tag of $1,400, sold well.

By 1911, when the company changed its name to the Russell Motor Car Company, it had a well-earned reputation for quality, and offered no models in the low price range dominated by the Model T Ford. The company had sales offices in England, Australia and New Zealand. Russell cars used the "Silent Knight" sleeve-valve engine, an American invention which was used under license in Europe by the likes of Daimler and even Mercedes-Benz. Suddenly, however, a series of misfortunes caused the business to falter: in 1913, Russell's license on the American-built Knight engines expired, and its own designs, though incorporating many features of the Knights, had teething troubles and operating faults; concurrently, a serious depression wiped out many of its potential customers. Russell

staggered through the early years of the war, then decided to retool and devote a large portion of its factory to munitions work.

Before the end of the war, the Russell company was approached by John Willys, whose Willys-Overland automobile, based in Toledo, Ohio, was the second-biggest seller in the world. Willys wanted to open a factory in Canada and agreed to take over the Russell plant in Weston. During the 1920s, Willys-Overland in Weston made the "baby" Overland, and later the Whippet line. T. A. Russell himself served as president of Willys-Overland and became president of Massey-Harris for the decade before his death in 1940; as well, he served a term as president of the Canadian National Exhibition. Russell lived at 162 Walmer Road in the Annex. The Great Depression of the 1930s was too much for Willys-Overland—it ceased production at the end of 1933.

* * *

Another business which maintained close ties with the city was the Canadian Fishing & Sporting Association, which operated a notorious "poolroom" betting operation out of the Coffin Block, a modest flatiron at the corner of Dundas and what is now Old Weston Road. In 1904, an earlier West End betting operation, called the Toronto Junction Recreation Club, had lost its charter following a brief police investigation. The following March, the jolly clubmen regrouped and reopened their Junction operation, with a new name and a Dominion charter, which said they were to "provide and maintain outdoor recreation for members."

Earlier that year in the provincial election, there had been a landslide vote for the reform-minded Conservative government of James Whitney, which had waged a "crusade against public dishonour"—the corrupt antics of the Liberals who had been in power for 32 years, practically the duration of Ontario's provincial history. One day at the end of April, during question period in the legislature, the question of the poolroom came up. Premier Whitney ordered an investigation, and his new attorney general soon made plans to put it out of business.

At two o'clock on the afternoon of May 9, 1905, a party of police officers gathered in the attorney general's offices in the parliament buildings. There, Deputy Chief Stark and Provincial Inspector Greer reviewed the evidence gathered during the previous week by five operatives of the Noble Private Detective Agency. They then laid out plans for a raid on the poolroom. Soon, the several policemen, the head of the private detective agency, a magistrate, and Police Chief Royce of The Junction had piled into two hacks and were heading west along Dundas.

With catlike tread, they surrounded the Coffin Block. Then, they rushed the door, breaking it down and so surprising the lookouts that, inside, everything was in full swing when they appeared, their nightsticks

Theodore Heintzman, born in Berlin in 1817, started learning to manufacture pianos at the age of fourteen, four years after Beethoven's death, at a time when the modern piano had recently evolved from the knee-pedalled pianoforte of Mozart's day. With his four sons and a workforce of 150 at his Junction factory, he was by 1890 turning out some 800 pianos a year. His son, George Charles (above), took over the company and bought out the rival Nordheimer Piano Company, whose factory on the C.P.R. line east of Keele Street was within earshot of Heintzman's.

at the ready. Several of the club's patrons tried to rush the policemen at the door, but were repulsed. Two men got out of the window on a rope, though the second fell to the pavement below when it broke. Affixed to a wall in the room, there was a large blackboard, covered with the names of horses racing that day at Woodbine; as the police charged in, a man began frantically to wipe off the chalk, "but was hit across the hand by a thrown baton." Police gathered up evidence including a blackboard, a telegraph instrument, cards, and $389 from the club till.

That, anyway, was the *Star*'s account of the raid. The *Telegram*'s story said that police collected a "peach basket of evidence," including 200 yards of tickertape and "memoranda which had little to do with fishing." It also quoted club president Frank Baby of Jane Street, defiantly stating that there had been no locks on the doors, no lookouts, no betting pool, and no wagering. The ticker's wires, however, were soon traced to a similar operation downtown on Toronto Street. In a later story, the *Telegram* took the opportunity to get in a shot at the *Star* over whether two of the gamblers had escaped by rope from the window. Detective Forrest, according to the *Telegram*, denied the *Star*'s statement that the two had escaped the police's clutches. "We didn't move around like old women," he told the reporter.

In court, several men pleaded guilty, were convicted of keeping a gaming house, and were fined. Among them was Frank Baby, "the kingpin of the bunch of fishersports, who sidled in shortly after ten o'clock with a broad smile on his expansive countenance."

* * *

South of Dundas, especially south of Annette and west of Quebec, was a fairly grand district. North of Dundas, around Clendenan Avenue, between Dundas and the railway yards, was a different kettle of fish, considered by locals to be "the wrong side of the tracks"—the *streetcar tracks*. Typical of the families that moved there was that of Julio Vella, an immigrant from Malta. Vella had been a blacksmith in Malta, where he married and had three children, but there were few prospects for a young man; so Vella and five friends, who had heard about the enormous railway construction projects in Canada, decided to emigrate. By the time they did so, in 1913, Vella was about 25 years old. Unbeknownst to them, the boomtime in Canada was over, and both the Canadian Northern and the Grand Trunk railways were teetering on the verge of bankruptcy. There was little work.

Vella took a room downtown, somewhere near Spadina Avenue or The Ward, and began to look around. People said, "don't go out on the railroad—it's too tough," so he got his first job in a tailoring establishment. Later, he became a barber, then briefly took a job as a track

Travellers to and from Weston boarded a radial railway car at "The Junction"—the corner of Keele and Dundas. The line, running along Keele Street to Weston Road, and thence along Weston's Main Street as far as Humber Street (where the improved St. Phillips Road crosses Weston Road, just south of the 401 today), was jointly operated by the Toronto Transportation Commission and the Township of York Railways—thus, the cars carried two fareboxes, and passengers paid a second fare once they got beyond the city limits at Northlands loop. The painting shows the boarding practice that existed before an off-street terminus was built in 1940—the railway car, on the wrong side of the road, with both its doors open, loaded those passengers who had deftly managed to dodge the traffic. In the background is the Canadian Pacific Railway crossing, still extant today. The building on the right, on the south side of the tracks at the spot now occupied by a Canadian Tire outlet, was the Heintzman piano factory.

211

labourer for the Canadian Pacific Railway. Prosperity had more or less eluded him; then came his second disappointment: with the outbreak of the war, his plans to bring his family from Malta evaporated—with submarines attacking even American-flag liners, there was no safe way to cross the Atlantic. It was 1920 before he finally got them to Toronto.

Vella moved to The Junction about 1915, and spent the rest of his life there. Although he rarely bothered to go downtown, he liked to travel, and soon he had an old Ford in which he and a friend drove all the way to New York City. His neighbourhood was a railway area, and the railways hired English speakers for their operations; non-English-speaking immigrants could get work only as track labourers, or as packers at the huge abattoir and stockyards north of the railyards. When times were tough and there were few jobs, cardboard and tin shacktowns sprang up along the railway lines, mainly occupied by newly arrived immigrants. But Vella was lucky and got a job with Canadian Liquid Air in 1918; many years later, he retired after a career there as a foreman.

The Vellas lived on Clendenan Avenue, midway between Dundas and the railway yards, at its "T" junction with Maria Street. At the end of Clendenan, on the other side of a board fence, were the maintenance shops and roundhouse for the Canadian Pacific Railway; the constant smell of steam and oil, and the sounds of whistles and shunting trains, filled the air as they do today in what the street signs describe as the "Junction Gardens" area. The roads were dirt, few people had cars, and much of the traffic was door-to-door delivery carts or sleighs, bringing around everything from coal to milk to coffee beans. Also, there was the rag and bone peddler with his broken-down horse and wagon. In the surrounding houses were Italian, English, Jewish, Polish, and Maltese families; Maria Street was three-quarters Jewish; St. Paul the Apostle Church on Dundas had a Maltese congregation. Vella's son Angelo recalls the rabbi and the local monsignor walking together in the street and chatting.

In the 1920s, when Vella's children were still school-aged, his wife suddenly became ill. As she hovered between life and death, the neighbourhood mobilized to help him. One evening, there was a knock on the door. An Irish woman, a neighbour whom they hardly knew, was there; she said that Vella's children must come to her home every day after school and on weekends; she would make their meals, and ensure that they bathed and had clean clothes and did their schoolwork. Every night they returned home to sleep, but every day they stayed with the neighbour while their mother slowly regained her health and strength.

During the Great Depression, drifters often knocked on the door, looking for some work to do and a meal. As the Toronto-bound C.P.R. freight trains slowed for the Keele Street crossing, their unauthorized cargo of unemployed men jumped off. Some drifted to the shacktowns along the bush and scrublands of Keele Street north of St. Clair. Others hopped the fence and wandered down Clendenan. As for the local young men, there was little work, and even those with jobs were soon cut back from a full week's work to only a couple of days. According to Angelo Vella, when they weren't *playing* baseball, they took the streetcar all the way to

Maple Leaf stadium at Bathurst and Front Street to watch it. There was nothing else to do. Although regular admission was 75 cents, the team was so desperate for cash that a fan could get in and get a good seat for a quarter.

Now in his seventies, Angelo Vella is retired and lives in the Jane-Finch area. Has he ever spent time in other parts of the city? No, he's a westender. His son Peter, however, has lived all over the city, and travels the world as an airline employee.

* * *

In recent years, not too much has changed in the Clendenan Avenue area—the trains still shunt noisily through, and the blocks of little houses remain. There is even an example of that Toronto rarity, a midblock shop, Milan's butcher and delicatessen on Maria Street. Such was not the fate of the more expensive area to the south, adjoining High Park: being near the Bloor Street subway line, it was a prime target for redevelopment in the late 1960s. The huge Cadillac-Fairview Corporation began buying up houses in the Pacific-Glenlake and Quebec-Gothic areas, in the teeth of opposition from local residents. More often, in joint ventures with other developers such as Cemp Investments, Cadillac-Fairview had developed commercial buildings and residential subdivisions on the fringes of the city at locations like Erin Mills. In the ensuing brouhaha, many of the houses in Pacific-Glenlake were demolished; much the same happened on Quebec Avenue, directly north of the High Park subway station. The bitterly fought rezoning application soon went to city council, where the reform alderman and future mayor John Sewell exposed the conflict of interest of another alderman who had sold to the developers, for a tidy sum, two houses slated for rezoning. The urban activist and university professor James Lorimer, who was also deeply involved in antidevelopment campaigns in the "South of St. Jamestown" and "Don Vale" areas on the other side of the city, bought one share in the Cadillac Development Corporation, and with a few other like-minded single-shareholders attended that corporation's annual general meeting in June, 1972. Their attempt to get a local ratepayer leader named Mrs. Pat Adams elected to the Cadillac board of directors was defeated by a vote of six million to two. Pacific-Glenlake and Quebec Avenue are now solid forests of highrises. Curving, tidy Gothic Avenue, with its little houses, is still intact; at its southern end, the old High Park Sanitarium, at 32 Gothic Avenue, still dominates the hillside above Bloor Street.

Alexander James Anderson, K.C., ran a general legal practice at 2881 Dundas Street West, which became a local centre of Conservative politics. Anderson started his political career on the school board in The Junction in 1899, held office as an elected council member until 1902, then was appointed town solicitor, a post he held for the next seven years. After annexation, he served as Ward Seven alderman on Toronto City Council. He was nominated as a Conservative for the federal election in 1921, but withdrew in favour of Sir Henry Drayton and was rewarded by being named a King's Counsel that December. Four years later, he was nominated to run in High Park, and thereafter was elected repeatedly as Member of Parliament. He lived at 76 Evelyn Crescent.

(Next page) While parts of The Junction were poor and working-class, others were quite grand. The old St. Cecilia's convent, at 288 Annette Street at the corner of Laws, was originally Theodore Heintzman's house and had substantial grounds now occupied by townhouses. Annette Street was widened in 1935. At the corner of Evelyn Street, a block to the west, is the St. Cecilia's school. Annette Street was on the first local bus route, as the area was not settled densely enough to justify the expense of street railway service. Service commenced in September, 1921, using four solid-tired, double-decker buses on a route linking Dundas Street with Runnymede Road via Humberside, High Park Avenue, and Annette.

214

(Previous page) Looking west along Bloor Street West, at High Park. The tent and sign on the right mark the entrance to the "High Park Sanitarium Mineral Baths," a collection of tents, change rooms and swimming "tanks" below the High Park Sanitarium at 32 Gothic Avenue. The photograph above shows the facilities in the 1920s, after the infamous "sandy hill" on Bloor had been paved (the "sandy hill" was the scene of one of the Russell Model 30 motorcar's torture tests—while a crowd watched, the car climbed the hill from a standing start and reached the top without faltering). The High Park Sanitarium, at 32 Gothic Avenue, was the first house in the area, having been built in 1889 for the St. Leger family. Over the years, it served as a sanitarium, and as a private maternity hospital; it survived a demolition threat in the early 1970s, when much of the surrounding area was razed and rebuilt with highrise apartments.

Swansea

The Village of Swansea was like a little Ontario town, bordered by ponds and forests and rivers—in its case, Grenadier Pond, the forests of High Park, the lake and the Humber River. A 1950 newspaper article described it "slumbering along peacefully" with no worries except the rumours of an enforced amalgamation into what was to become Metro.

Swansea incorporated in the 1920s following a row with York Township over road repairs—a village incorporation reminiscent of Forest Hill's. Like Forest Hill Village, its municipal offices were regularly filled by acclamation; Reeve Dorothy Hague, who was also a champion at the Runnymede Lawn Bowling Club, was unopposed in five straight elections, and finally retired in 1982. Swansea had no secondary school, and in 1950 had the lowest per capita debt, $60.32, of the thirteen municipalities which eventually amalgamated into Metro. Its fire department had a ladder truck and pumper, and was staffed by 27 volunteers; it had no waterworks, choosing instead to buy 150 million gallons of water a year from Toronto at sixteen cents per thousand. Within its populace, there appeared to be little desire to redevelop or to grow.

It was not always so peaceful, as low taxes and proximity to Toronto in its York Township days made it an attractive place for several rather dirty industries. At the foot of Windermere Avenue was the Swansea Station of the Grand Trunk Railway. Nearby were factories of the Steel Company of Canada (formerly the Ontario Rolling Mill Company); an industrial belt-line branched from the railway mainline there, passing factories of the Dominion Sewer Pipe Company at Queen Street West, and the Indestructible Brick Company at Bay Street (now Ormskirk Avenue). Further to the east, Ellis Avenue was like a country road, with some large properties with substantial houses along the west side of Grenadier Pond. At the southern end of the pond, sitting just outside the city limits, was the Grenadier Ice House; ice was cut from the pond's surface during the winter, using horse-drawn saws, and stored deeply packed in sawdust for summertime home-delivery (electric refrigerators began to become popular in the 1920s). A traveller proceeding north along Ellis Avenue would see the plant's large "ICE" sign just past the C.N.R. bridge.

As befits a country road in what used to be called Muddy York, Ellis Avenue was so exceptionally muddy and rutted that motorists frequently needed the assistance of a horse to extricate their horseless carriages. Most of the roads in Swansea, The Junction and points west were unpaved. Partly due to this exigency, people embraced the Model T. The Ford Motor Company of Canada, founded in 1904 by a Walkerville carriagemaker named Gordon McGregor, had achieved only a modest success with its Model Cs. In 1908, it introduced the Model T; between then and 1927, when it was finally superseded, 750,000 were built in Windsor and sold to Canadians. Whereas most cars of the time had little low-end torque and stiff, solid-axled suspensions, the "Tin Lizzie" could practically pull stumps and loped across rough ground, its foot-high ground clearance avoiding all but the worst ruts. The key to its hill-climbing and mud-negotiating abilities was its complicated triple-banded planetary gearbox—a forerunner of the modern automatic transmission—which made driving it an unusual experience compared with most cars since. Instead of the now-standard arrangement of clutch, brake, accelerator, and gear lever, the T had a horizontal hand lever under the steering wheel which operated the accelerator, three pedals on the floor, and a vertical hand lever to the left of the steering wheel. When the latter lever was in the upright position, the transmission was in neutral; when pulled back, it engaged the emergency brake; when pushed forward, it engaged the high-speed range of the transmission. Of the three pedals, the right one was the brake, the centre one operated reverse, and the left one was the clutch. Light pressure on the left pedal engaged neutral, but full pressure engaged low gear. As the car picked up speed, a gradual release of that pedal changed the transmission to high gear. On a cold day, even when the car was in neutral, there was so much sluggish oil and there were so many gears in the transmission that many owners found they could not crank the engine over without turning over the back wheels at the same time; thus, they found it was easier to jack the rear of the car off the ground! The basic Model T was stripped to the point that windshield, headlamps, bumpers and temperature gauge were extra-cost options; all early models had to be started with a hand crank (the electric starter was introduced by Cadillac in 1912), and everyone was wary of the engine's notorious kickback, which could break the arm of a motorist who foolishly wrapped his thumb around the crank. Towards the end of its life as Ford's flagship, the Model T sold for $395, with electric starter an $85 option. Henry Ford's classic adage that his cars were available "in any colour you want, as long as it's black" resulted from his inability to find paints other than a "japan black" enamel which would dry fast enough not to slow down the assembly line. The Model T was one of the first cars anywhere in the world with its steering wheel on the left—Ontario, like the United States, always drove on the right, but early cars had steering wheels on the right-hand side so that the motorists could avoid tipping into ditches, a more frequent occurrence than a meeting with an oncoming car.

High Park

Few cities in North America have benefited from private generosity more than Toronto. Examples of the largesse of individuals include that of the Masseys, represented by Massey Hall and Hart House, and Joseph Flavelle's donations to Toronto General Hospital and the University of Toronto. In a class of its own is John Howard's bequest of his High Park estate, for it is the largest park in a city which has not always valued its open spaces.

John George Howard arrived in Toronto in 1832, just before his thirtieth birthday and two years before Toronto's incorporation. He developed a private architectural practice while working as drawing master at Upper Canada College, then became city surveyor. With his savings from this industriousness, he purchased 165 acres in the west end of the city at one pound sterling per acre, and thereon built his own house, "Colborne Lodge"—in honour of his patron Sir John Colborne, a lieutenant governor and founder of Upper Canada College—in 1836. Over the ensuing decades, he engaged a tenant wheat farmer, built a house called "Sunnyside" near the shore as a speculation, worked as a landscape designer on the grounds of Osgoode Hall and St. James Cemetery, and was an architect.

When he turned 70 years old, in 1873, he made arrangements to bequeath his estate to the city as a park, in return for a modest pension. He lived for another seventeen years, after which his house stood abandoned and derelict until its restoration in the 1920s. Subsequent purchases added land to High Park on the east and the west, so that today it occupies about 400 acres.

Trinity

Trinity College, Toronto, Canada

Old Trinity College, "in the pointed style of English architecture," sat "with a background of romantic beauty" in a 20-acre park. Losing its raison d'être when the new college buildings—a copy of these—opened on Hoskin Avenue in 1925, old Trinity College was finally demolished in 1956, over a century after its construction. Only the gates stand today; inscribed "Academia Collegii Sacrosanctae Trinitatis" and acknowledging Bishop John Strachan as Johannes Strachan, they mark the entrance to what is now Trinity-Bellwoods Park.

The Trinity neighbourhood has a few major landmarks, and many long straight blocks of quite ordinary houses. Its name* comes from the old Trinity University, which stood on the north side of Queen Street, in what is now Trinity-Bellwoods Park.

The park lot bounded roughly by Queen, Bloor, Ossington and Dovercourt was purchased for £200 by John Denison, a friend of Governor Simcoe who had arrived in Upper Canada in 1792. His home was "Brookfield

*"Trinity" is the name which the Metropolitan Toronto Reference Library uses for the area bounded by Queen, Bathurst, College, Spadina, Bloor, and Dovercourt. In such an amorphous area, the boundaries are difficult to define. The city's old St. Stephen's Ward was bounded by Dufferin, Bloor, Bathurst, and Queen. The boundaries of Ward Five in the old "strip ward" system valid before 1969 were the waterfront, Bathurst, the C.P.R. tracks, and Dovercourt. The current "block" Ward Four has boundaries of the waterfront, Palmerston, Bloor, and Dufferin.

House," at the northwest corner of Queen and Ossington. With the construction in the late 1840s of 999 Queen Street West—the lunatic asylum—the area lost some of its desirability. However, due to the political vagaries of the time, the "establishment" university of Canada West located nearby.

Before the spring of 1849, the city's university was King's College, a strictly Anglican institution dominated by Bishop Strachan, which was located at the top of University Avenue on the site of the current legislative buildings. As the city and future province grew and attracted a population from a wider spectrum of creeds and cultures, pressure began to be applied on politicians who until that time had not questioned the control of publicly funded university education by one denomination. The provincial government responded on May 30, 1849, by creating the University of Toronto, in which "there shall be no Faculty of Divinity."

The septuagenarian Bishop Strachan responded to this "calamity" by setting out for England with a petition to the queen, seeking a royal charter to incorporate a new Anglican university, to be called Trinity. During the two years it took for the British government to assent, a fund raising campaign in Toronto came up with land and donations of $32,000, enough to build a fine, picturesque edifice in the midst of twenty parklike acres on Queen Street West. Professor Goldwin Smith's observation that "no place in Canada so forcibly reminds me of Oxford as does Trinity" acknowledged the success with which its indefatigable founder had pursued his goal. In later, more tolerant times (1904), Trinity University decided to affiliate with the University of Toronto; a new college building, a copy of the old, was built on Hoskin Avenue in 1925. Old Trinity College was demolished in 1956.

The grounds were the lower part of a property called Gore Vale. Just east of the college building, a stream wound through the lawns, crossing Queen Street at Gore Vale Avenue. At the northwest corner on a steep mound stood a blockhouse, remaining from the days when the entrance to York might have needed defending. Directly across Queen Street from the college gates, which are the only relic remaining today, is the top of Strachan Avenue, named for the Bishop. The stream crossed a coal and wood yard on the south side of Queen Street, then meandered past the West Toronto brewery, providing both water and power for the latter.

Near Trinity University, the streets were cluttered with a hodgepodge of houses and little factories. Two notable examples of the latter were the Newcombe Pianoforte company on Bellwoods Avenue and the brewery on Niagara Street.

Unlike the German Jews T. A. Heintzman and the Nordheimer brothers, Octavius Newcombe was an Englishman from Devon who had not apprenticed as a piano builder. His family moved to Toronto in the late 1840s, when he was barely shorn of his baby curls. Octavius—the eighth child—studied medicine briefly at Victoria College, became a surgeon's clerk, then a bank clerk, then a bank accountant, before joining an Ottawa lumber company. In 1871, he was offered a partnership in a piano manufactory, which opened with showrooms downtown at 107-109 Church Street and a factory on Bellwoods Avenue north of Robinson Street. Newcombe pianofortes gained an excellent reputation, being used by composers of the stature of Sir Arthur Sullivan. Newcombe died in Toronto on February 8, 1905.

The Cosgrave Brewery, now the site of an apartment building, occupied the land between Niagara Avenue and Walnut Avenue just south of Queen Street. Patrick Cosgrave (1814-1881) arrived in Toronto in 1849 and went into the brewing business with fellow Irishman Eugene O'Keefe. In 1863, he decided to strike out on his own and purchased the old West Toronto Brewery on this site. Two of his sons entered the business, and in 1895 changed the name to the Cosgrave Brewing Company of Toronto. As business expanded, the brothers erected what became a massive complex, the main building of which "is six storeys in height and comprises a large bottling department, to which the ale and porter are pumped from the racking cellars. A four-storey addition to the malthouse was erected in 1902, increasing the annual malting capacity to 75,000 bushels. The main stock cellar, for ale and porter in casks, is 150 feet long, 18 feet high and 35 feet wide and is capable of holding 150,000 gallons. This cellar extends under the brewery yard, leading to still another which is located under the ice-house, wherein is stored, on the average, one thousand tons of ice. This burden is supported by an iron and steel framework, resting on stone foundations and passing through walls three feet thick."

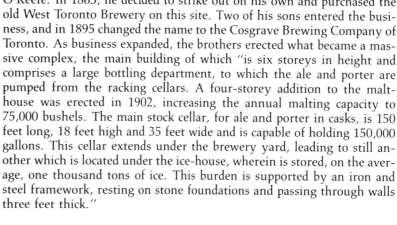

Brewer Patrick Cosgrave

Octavius Newcombe and the pianoforte factory on Bellwoods Avenue north of Robinson Street, near old Trinity College.

Dr. Caroline Brown, a physician, lived at the house at 601 Ossington Avenue, at the corner of Harbord (next page). Born in Derry West, Peel County, she started working as a teacher at schools in Halton County and, later, Toronto. While at Alexander Muir school, she decided to study medicine and graduated in 1900 from Women's Medical College and Trinity University. After further education at the College of Physicians and Surgeons, she became house surgeon at Watertown City Hospital, then embarked on a quest for postgraduate study which took her to hospitals in Dublin, London, Birmingham, and Paris. An active proponent of women in politics, she was president for three years of the Ward Five Women's Liberal-Conservative Association; she was first elected to the Board of Education in 1915, became its first woman chairman in 1918, and headed the polls in elections through the 1920s. However, her attempt to enter federal politics in the 1925 election was unsuccessful. (The painting shows the old "Harbord" streetcar, which gave access to the downtown area via Spadina and Adelaide streets—later, via Spadina and Dundas.)

The painting shows the southwest corner of Bloor and Dovercourt; in the 1920s, that section of Bloor Street was still paved with cobblestones. Just west of the corner, at 991 Bloor, was the jewelry and optical business of Eleanor Taylor, the first woman to graduate from the Canadian Horological Institute, and reputed to be the "first and only lady to make a watch" in Canada. She lived with her husband Donald in an apartment above the store, and was vice-president of the Canadian Business Women's Club. The Canadian Horological Institute (left) on King Street East, established in 1890 by H. R. Playtner, aimed "to impart a thorough practical and scientific training in all departments of watchmaking, and is the only school of its kind in Canada."

Eleanor Taylor

On the east side of the block of Westmoreland immediately north of Bloor Street, there is a double and a triple house in the pointed gable style so popular with Toronto builders in the last part of the nineteenth century. In the 1920s, in the small bungalow to the south of this row, at 17 Westmoreland Avenue, lived a curious character named Joseph Hunt Stanford, an architect who specialized in designing apartments, including Hampton Court, King Edward apartments, and St. Charles Court.

Born in Staffordshire in 1871, Stanford could trace his lineage to ancestors who fought with Cromwell, and he had a number of engineers in his immediate past, including one who worked with George Stephenson on the "Rocket" locomotive. Stanford apprenticed as an architect in London in 1889, came to Canada in 1902, and started his Toronto practice two years later. He had for his time unorthodox extracurricular activities and beliefs: the authorship of *Miriam and Other Poems*, published in 1906; membership in the Toronto Theosophical Society; the vice-presidency of the Toronto Dickens Fellowship; the presidency of the mysterious Boz Club of Toronto; an unsuccessful run for office with the Board of Education in Ward Six; distinguished service, including mentions in dispatches, with the 20th Canadian Mobile Artillery and Railway troops on the Western Front during the First World War; membership in the Conservative party; and, according to his "Who's Who" listing, he claimed to be a Buddhist.

J. H. Stanford

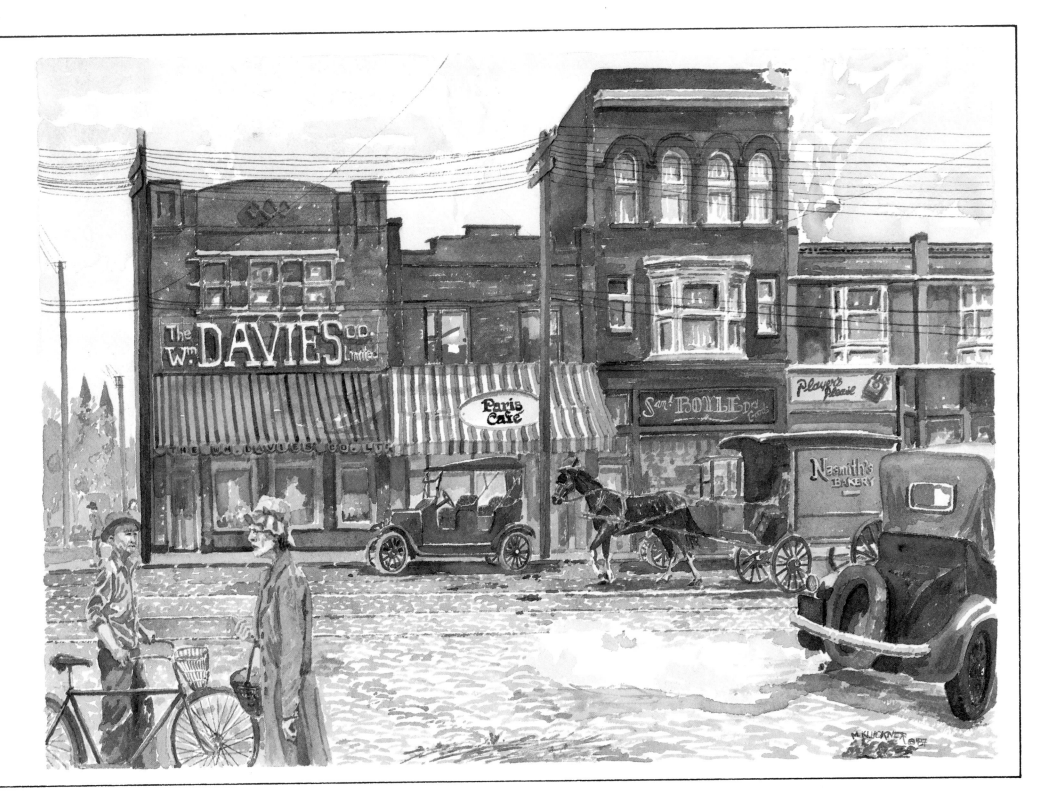

The Christie Pits, also known as the Ossington Avenue dump, was a former sandpit much beloved by local waders for whom there were few other recreational opportunities. Old maps show the Christie Street Sand Pits extending east of Christie Street; a small creek ran through from north to south, creating the "dangerous waterhole" shown in the photograph. The Holtby Brothers mined the sand and gravel there, and one 1907 photograph shows their small office-shack sporting a sign saying "The Gold Mine of Toronto." The area north of College Street around Shaw was known as "The Brick Fields," as the clay there was of a suitable consistency for brickmaking. In 1909, the city filled the waterhole at the Christie Pits and created Willowvale Park, though the old name has stuck to it till this day; after planting the grass, the city found it necessary to post signs stating that "Persons dis-
turbing the turf in search of mushrooms will be prosecuted." The park has always been popular for baseball games. It is on the edge of Kensington, which in the early 1930s was the Jewish district in Toronto. At a baseball game between a Jewish and a non-Jewish team, before 10,000 spectators, on the night of August 17, 1933, a local Nazi group waved a swastika and repeatedly shouted "Heil Hitler!" In no time, fistfights started and rapidly escalated in violence as bats, truncheons, and pieces of pipe were introduced by other participants. Rumours of the impending provocation had obviously circulated throughout Kensington, as truckloads of young Jews from the local social clubs quickly arrived. Six hours later, at two o'clock in the morning, the fighting finally stopped (see also page 166).

The Annex

Simeon Janes had ancestors in the New World dating back to the Pilgrims. Although he had studied law, he sought a commercial career, and after a number of years in the drygoods business saw the opportunities available for large-scale real-estate development in areas served by public transit. His purchase and subdivision of the Annex area, bounded by Bloor, Dupont, Bathurst, and Bedford, was a shrewd and daring move for its time. Like Professor Goldwin Smith, Janes was something of a radical Liberal with a penchant for free trade.

CTA JAMES 328A

"Benvenuto," S. H. Janes's house on the Avenue Road hill, was built on a five-and-one-half-acre property originally owned by Senator McMaster. Like several of the large houses in nineteenth-century Toronto, it was built just outside the city limits, for obvious tax reasons. G. Mercer Adam described it in 1891 as "pure Norman, the massiveness of the huge grey stone of which it is built being relieved by the maroon tiling of the roof and the rather quaint continental design of its corner towers. The building is in the form of an L, and is approached by a winding drive from the massive lodge, with its beautiful gates and curved stone wall that flank the grounds on Avenue Road. It is a splendid piece of masonry, which puts to shame the flimsy ephemeral edifices, with their stuccos and veneers, of modern house construction." Most of the Annex was indeed, by comparison, flimsy and ephemeral and veneered. The architect of "Benvenuto" was the famed Stanford White of Madison Square Gardens, who is more often remembered for his seduction of the teenaged "girl in the red velvet swing"—Evelyn Nesbitt—and his subsequent murder by her other lover, the psychopathic steelman Harry Thaw. The house itself is often remembered because of a later occupant, the financier Sir William Mackenzie (page 39).

The painting is of the northwest corner of Bedford Road and Bloor Street, looking north, in the 1940s. Like most of the streets in the area, Bedford was quiet and two-laned; cars parked on the west side, under the canopy of the boulevard trees, as the road was too narrow to permit parking on both curbs. Bedford Road was the eastern boundary of the Annex. Although it is today something of a drag strip, it used to be a fashionable street, when such traffic as there was followed the streetcars on Avenue Road. It changed irrevocably in the spring of 1948, when the city cut down the boulevard trees and widened the road.

Zoning restrictions, lot sizes, prices, and nearby transit made the Annex attractive to the moderately prosperous merchants, bankers, brokers, and university professors of the city. There were few extremes, either of wealth or personal fame. The four individuals below lived on the eastern boundary of the Annex in the twenties and thirties.

(Far left) John Murray Clark, K.C., lived at 70 Tranby Avenue, at the corner of Bedford Road. One of the bright stars at the University of Toronto in the early 1880s, he won the Young Prize in Logic, the Blake Scholarship in Constitutional Law, Economics and Jurisprudence, the McMurrich medal in natural sciences, the Gold Medal in mathematics and physics, and a prize for his essay on proportional representation. Although called to the Ontario bar (with, naturally, the Law Society's Gold Medal) in 1886, he chose to be mathematics master at St. Mary's Collegiate Institute, and in his spare time was an examiner in physics for the university, and president of the Royal Canadian Institute. He was sometimes called upon to explain the significance of great scientific discoveries to the common folk—one such instance occurred when Professor MacLennan's work with helium was announced (page 91). (Left) Major William Walter Pope, the secretary of the Hydro-Electric Power Commission, lived at 117 Bedford Road. A descendant of United Empire Loyalists who settled in Quebec, he took part in the Fenian Raid of 1866; later, he was a railway company solicitor and a Belleville alderman before moving to Toronto. (Right) Lt. Col. Le Grand Reed lived, in the early 1920s, at 23 Bedford Road—one of the last houses still standing near Bloor Street. He had a successful insurance career with Reed, Shaw & McNaught; he was prominent in military affairs, commanded the Toronto Mobilization Centre during the First World War, and was gazetted to the rank of lieutenant colonel to mobilize the 170th Overseas Battalion of the Canadian Expeditionary Force. He was considered to be one of Canada's experts on bunting and flag signals and their proper use and display. (Far right) Charles Herbert Easson, the general manager of the Standard Bank of Canada, lived at 23 Bedford Road in the early 1930s. Other residents of Bedford Road during that period were Gertrude Vankoughnet (page 101) at number 141, and insulin codiscoverer F.G. Banting at number 46, a house since demolished for Taddle Creek Park, in an area now redeveloped with highrises.

Zebulon Lash

It does not disparage the memory of Zebulon Aiton Lash, K.C., to describe him as a "backroom boy" of business and Liberal politics during the early years of the century. His influence was evident in many of the enterprises of that time, although he always stood a pace back in the shadows. A resident of the Annex, he lived in the house at 59 Admiral Road.

Zebulon Lash was born at St. John's, in the crown colony of Newfoundland, in 1846, but grew up in Ontario and attended the University of Toronto, from which he graduated in law at the age of 22. He first worked as a junior partner in the firm Vankoughnet & Lash, then became federal deputy minister of justice in 1876, during the Liberal administration of Alexander Mackenzie. He resigned in 1882, returned to Toronto, and formed Blake, Lash, Anglin & Cassels. Over the next thirty years, he became one of the best-known members of the Canadian bar, and the legal mind behind the Bank of Commerce, the Canadian Northern Railway, and numerous other corporations.

According to a story told by one of Lash's friends—quoted in his obituary—Lash introduced the railway promoters William Mackenzie and Donald Mann at a Board of Trade banquet in Toronto. Along with Frederic Nicholls and the English financier Robert Horne-Payne, he became a director of the Canadian Northern Railway, its chief counsel, and a vice-president of the Bank of Commerce. As well, he was vice-president of several threads of the web of Latin American power and street-railway companies owned by Mackenzie, Nicholls, Senator Cox, and Henry Pellatt. It evidently was his shrewd assessment of the legal meaning of the term "riparian rights" which gained the Canadian Northern Railway its most elusive prize—a downtown terminus in Vancouver, something which had been utterly opposed by the Canadian Pacific Railway. His legal skills were again in evidence during the Manitoba graft trials of 1915, when he argued for the right of a telegraph company to destroy telegrams between individuals instead of letting them fall into the hands of a Royal Commission.

Lash was a member of the "Toronto Eighteen"—the group of wealthy Liberals who turned on Sir Wilfrid Laurier and his reciprocity policy in the 1911 election campaign. Their manifesto, published on February 20, was a several-hundred-word refutation of Laurier's proposal for a limited free-trade agreement with the United States. The signatories included Lash, described as an eminent lawyer and capitalist; Sir Edmund Walker, president of the Bank of Commerce; Wilmot Matthews, vice-president of the Dominion Bank; Sir Mortimer Clark, a former lieutenant governor of Ontario; John Eaton, president of the T. Eaton Company; R. J. Christie of Christie, Brown & Company; various financiers and a director of the *Globe*, "the chief Ontario organ of the Liberal party." Several members of this group were prominent at an antireciprocity rally held at Massey Hall on March 9, featuring many imperialistic and anti-American speeches. The Laurier loyalists responded to the manifesto by denouncing the "Toronto Eighteen" as representative of the "big interests" of finance and manufacturing. The *Star*, which under Joseph Atkinson's leadership always backed Laurier to the hilt, supported reciprocity; its head office window revealed a giant display of goods purchased in Toronto and in Buffalo, purporting to show how much money reciprocity would save the average Canadian. The election was closely fought, and opinion at the time credits the influence and prestige of the "Eighteen" with swinging voters in Ontario to the Conservatives. Laurier's defeat ushered in an era of Conservative governments under Robert Borden and Arthur Meighen.

Lash's best friend and constant fishing companion was Edmund Walker of the Bank of Commerce. Lash was the camp cook, and on their fishing trips carried a black bag full of odds and ends with which he could repair any fishing pole. Said Walker, "he could supply the cord, gum and other material which would save a man's day on the Godbout River." Lash made his own fishing poles and flies in a workshop behind his house on Admiral Road. He was widely known as an elocutionist and storyteller, his recitations an attraction at many fashionable social affairs.

Lash died, at the age of 73, in January, 1920.

Zebulon Lash, the Liberal backroom boy and lawyer of the Laurier years, lived at 59 Admiral Road. His son, Miller Lash, lived nearby at 60 Lowther, now the Society of Friends (Quaker) house, and he continued his father's close association with the Liberal party, and was president of the Brazilian Traction, Light & Power Company (now Brascan). Born in Toronto in 1873, Miller Lash was educated at Upper Canada College and the University of Toronto. He was made a K.C. in 1921 by the first Mackenzie King government. Miller was his mother's maiden name.

The western half of the Annex was built up later than the eastern half. It was planned to be a little more posh than the eastern Annex, especially along winding Walmer Road. As the decades passed, and the original set of owners died off, the district underwent a genteel decay, the old houses being converted into apartments. The advent of the cross-town Bloor Street subway in the early 1960s spurred a number of demolitions and the construction of several highrises.

One of the few surviving houses on lower Walmer Road is at number 21, formerly occupied by Senator Sir Allen Aylesworth, a very active Liberal and lawyer, who is perhaps best remembered for his refusal, as Canadian commissioner, to sign the Alaska Boundary award which gave the Alaska panhandle to the United States. His political career began badly when he failed to be elected in 1904 to represent the Durham riding; regardless, Sir Wilfrid Laurier invited him into the Cabinet as postmaster general, and arranged a resignation and subsequent by-election in the safe North York seat. Six months later, Aylesworth became minister of justice, a position he retained until Laurier's ultimate defeat several years

later. He was one of a party of three Canadians who officially represented the Dominion at the funeral of King Edward VII.

At the northeast corner of Bloor and Walmer Road was the residence of the publisher Sir William Gage (1849-1921). Born in Brampton, Gage had attempted unsuccessfully to become a medical doctor, and subsequently taught school, before joining the stationery and publishing firm of Adam Miller & Company. He became a partner in the business, and after Miller's death changed the name to W. J. Gage & Co. The firm became a giant in paper and stationery manufacturing and in educational publishing. One of Gage's sidelines was his ownership of the *Evening Star*, from which platform he attacked the Liberal government and especially its minister of education, the future premier G. W. Ross. Gage, a member of the Lord's Day Alliance, also campaigned through the *Star* to keep streetcars banned on Sundays. He sold the *Star* in the mid-1890s to Canadian General Electric president Frederick Nicholls. Gage received his knighthood for his philanthropies: he had made the cure of tuberculosis his personal crusade, and after his medical career was nipped in the bud, he devoted

(Far Left) Sir John Aird (1855-1938), who lived at 39 Madison Avenue, had an exceptionally long career with the Bank of Commerce. Following education at the Toronto Normal School, he was for a few years "engaged in railway work," then joined the Bank of Commerce at the age of 23. Forty-six years later, he became president, and remained in the office until he was well into his seventies. His Aird Commission in 1928 recommended publicly owned radio broadcasting, the harbinger of the Canadian Broadcasting Corporation. (Left) Surgeon Abraham Isaac Willinsky was born in Omaha, Nebraska, but moved to Toronto as a child, where he went to Jarvis Collegiate and studied medicine at the University of Toronto, winning the 1908 George Brown Memorial Scholarship. Studies followed in Dublin and Vienna, before he established his practice at 569 Spadina. (Centre) When not exploring and developing mining properties, Harry Cyril Boydell lived at 273 St. George Street. He worked all over the world, spending years in New Zealand, Australia, the gold mining areas of Randfontein in South Africa, the Gold Coast Colony in West Africa, and various copper, tin and gold mines in Nevada, New Mexico and California. In 1928, when he turned 50, he decided to settle permanently in Canada, and indulge in the game of his Berkshire boyhood—cricket. (Right) Architect Frank Darling was the son of the long-time

rector of Holy Trinity Church. With various partners including J.A. Pearson, Darling designed most of the bank head offices in Toronto, including the old Commerce, the Dominion, the Union, the Standard, and the Nova Scotia; the Royal Ontario Museum; the CPR building; and, several of the buildings on the University campus. He lived at 11 Walmer Road, just above Bloor Street, until his death on May 19, 1923. (Far Right) Margaret Wilson Eaton was wife and, for nearly three decades, widow of Timothy Eaton, the founder of the department store chain. Born in 1842, she married at twenty, and like her widowed daughter-in-law Lady Eaton, lived into her nineties. She was interested in literature and dramatic arts, and she founded the curious Margaret Eaton School of Literature and Expression, housing it in a drab neoclassical temple on what was then called North Street—now Bay Street—just south of Bloor. The girls who enrolled wore a sort of Girl Guides' uniform, and learned deportment while performing gymnastics, massed calisthenics, theatricals and what were called "dramalogues." She lived at 182 Lowther Avenue at Spadina; following her death in 1933, the house was given to the Imperial Order Daughters of the Empire. It was torn down in 1965. A portion of its encircling wall survives, though a highrise now occupies the site.

energy and money to supporting tuberculosis research, and established and maintained several local sanitariums, including the Toronto Free Hospital for Consumptives.

Another interesting character who lived in the Annex was the Rev. John Gibson Inkster, minister of the Knox Presbyterian Church. A widely travelled man who had apprenticed in the dry goods business on the Orkney Islands in Scotland—his birthplace—he moved to Ontario and farmed in the 1880s, then taught school, and finally, when in his late twenties, studied for the Presbyterian ministry. An outspoken man who railed against the "heathenism" of secular grade-school education, he devoted his own off-duty hours to managing the University of Toronto rugby team and was the first president of the Intercollegiate Rugby Union. As well, he served as chaplain to the 75th Regiment, Toronto Scottish, during the First World War, and wrote the book *The Menace of Bolshevism* in 1921. Following his retirement, he went on a visit to New Zealand in 1940; on the return voyage, his ship, the *Niagara*, was torpedoed and sunk. Inkster was one of the survivors. Six years later, when he was 79 years old, he was run over and killed by a car as he was trying to cross Bloor Street. He lived at 407 Brunswick Avenue, next door to the set of houses which are now hostel and offices of the Salvation Army.

The opening of the cross-town "Bloor" subway line in 1966, and the expansion and subsequent demands for housing of the nearby University of Toronto, turned the Annex into a battlefield. Neighbourhood advocates fought rooming-house operators and developers. A rejuvenated Annex Ratepayers Association, which had been founded in 1923 but had languished until repeatedly prodded by the neighbourhood's rapid deterioration and change, set out to catalogue all of the houses built before 1910. Publicity quickly followed rediscoveries such as the house at 12 Admiral Road, where future prime minister Lester Pearson and family had lived from 1923–8, during the time when he was studying at the University. In 1973, city council made a definite move to save the neighbourhood, allotting $800,000 to buy nine houses on Huron Street and Madison Avenue simply to save them from developers. Today, the Annex is still a mix of the stable and the not-so—an incident in 1983, involving an estimated 90 rowdy youths in an 84-unit rooming house at 93 Madison, was compared by disapproving neighbours with the notorious Rochdale College episode. The building at 93 Madison, like much of the now-fashionable Annex, has since been renovated.

The painting looks north past St. Alban's Square. The Church of St. Alban-the-Martyr was finished in the early 1890s—as finished as it ever became, though attempts continued for 40 years to make it into a full-blown cathedral. At the time of its construction, there were only two houses on the block with the church, one being the bishop's, and no others for a block in any direction. Today, the girls from the nearby Loretto day school, on Brunswick, play and stroll through St. Alban's square, watched over by old men in hats sitting on the park benches.

St. George Street

The truly fashionable part of St. George Street was south of Bloor Street adjoining the University grounds. While most of these grand houses have been demolished, a few remain, such as the one at number 89, the residence of Wilmot Matthews illustrated in the postcard on page 94. Influential residents from the early years of the century included Frederic Nicholls (page 81), R. A. Falconer (page 96), the noted physician Julian Derwent Loudon at 83 St. George Street, and the Bank of Commerce president and art collector Sir Byron Edmund Walker at the house called "Long Garth" at 99 St. George Street.

Spilling over into the Annex, north of Bloor Street, were a few more fine houses—most notably, the house of George Gooderham at the northeast corner of Bloor and St. George, a grand home, the equal of any which used to exist south of Bloor Street. Two of the younger sons of George Gooderham also lived north of Bloor—George Horace at 204 and Melville Ross at 190; the unlucky banker James Cooper Mason (page 64) lived at 268 St. George; the railwayman Sir Donald Mann (page 116) lived at 161 St. George.

The George Gooderham house was built between 1889 and 1892, and remains one of the most lavish residences in the city. It has been the premises of the York Club since 1909. Gooderham was able to enjoy it for only fifteen years, until April, 1905, when he was 84 years old. On Monday, the first of May of that year, the newspapers published "extras," describing how "Toronto's Wealthiest Citizen [lay] at Death's Door." He had spent the winter in the south, and returned early in April. The fine weather on the last Saturday of that month lured him outside; he caught cold, which developed into pneumonia. The control of his companies, including the Gooderham & Worts distillery started by his father, the Bank of Toronto, the Manufacturers Life Insurance Company, the Canada Permanent Corporation, and the Toronto Hotel Company (which had built the King Edward Hotel), passed to his son William George. His will, details of which were published in the newspapers on May 16, was valued at $9 million: his widow received $100,000 cash, interest on $500,000, and the family residence and all its contents; the two elder sons, William George and Albert Edward, received half the income from the distillery with power to purchase extra stock; the other sons and daughters received an annuity of $10,000 per year each. The province stood to receive $450,000 inheritance tax, and a family spokesman stated that "in view of the levying of this tax, the late Mr. Gooderham has made no bequests in the will for charitable or religious work."

St. George Street, Toronto

Looking south on St. George Street—the turreted house and its neighbours to the south still stand on the west side of St. George Street south of Prince Arthur. Built early in the 1890s, the house on the corner belonged to Joseph Widdifield, the sheriff of York Township.

Graeme Gibson Adam, who lived at 160 St. George Street, was the son of the literary author and sometime historian G. Mercer Adam, who had been long associated with Professor Goldwin Smith in publishing The Bystander. G. G. Adam had no such interests and joined the Ontario Bank at age 20; when it was absorbed by the Bank of Montreal, he began a rise through the ranks of the latter, culminating in his appointment as manager of the main Toronto branch. His wife maintained at their home one of the best rose gardens in the city, and was president of the Rose Society of Ontario. Their only child, Madeline, was killed in one of the few fatal auto accidents of 1917. Adam had a summer residence called "The Elms" in Weston, where he was a gentleman farmer.

George Gooderham

Looking east along Bloor to the corner of St. George Street. George Gooderham's mansion, now the York Club, still dominates the corner. Shortly after Gooderham's death in 1905, the house was suggested as a candidate to replace the old Government House (page 22); instead, the York Club bought it, and Government House was built in Rosedale (page 245).

Yorkville

In the century and a half since it was first settled, the little Village of Yorkville has been a distinct and separate town, a suburb, a depressed urban area awaiting renewal, the hippie capital of eastern Canada, and a synonym for chic urban restoration. Architectural critic Patricia McHugh's description of modern Yorkville—"the spanking new, the new trying to look old, the old trying to look new, and a little of the old just looking like itself"—captures the curious mixture, the "calculated quaintness," of the former village. The southern area between Bloor and Ramsden Park has altogether too much pavement devoted to too many cars. North of the park, between Roxborough and the Canadian Pacific Railway tracks, there is more of a neighbourhood, which survived the threat posed by the Summerhill Square project in the late 1960s.

Although remote from the Town of York, the area that became Yorkville was easy to reach, even though the Yonge Street artery was so poorly maintained. On the east side of Yonge, just north of the Concession Line which became Bloor Street, stood the area's first landmark, the Red Lion Inn. A place of cheer when all around was prim and bleak, the Inn had the township's best dances in its second-floor ballroom, worth even a two-mile horseback ride from the Town of York on a winter night. Political meetings were also held there, including rallies addressed by the rebel William Lyon Mackenzie. The Red Lion was demolished in 1888, eight decades after its construction.

By that time, Yorkville was a populous suburb of Toronto. The town grew up first as a brewing centre: Joseph Bloor's brewery was built in 1830 in the ravine between Huntley and Sherbourne streets; five years later, John Severn's brewery opened on Yonge Street, just north of the Red Lion Inn. West of Yonge, on the north side of Bloor, was the Potter's

Field, a nonsectarian cemetery. A tollgate was established at the northeast corner of Bloor and Yonge, to tax the farmers hauling their produce in to the St. Lawrence Market. In 1836, Sheriff Jarvis of nearby "Rosedale Villa" worked with Joseph Bloor to subdivide the land between the ravine and Bedford Road. But land sales were slow as the taxes were low. The muddy, corrugated roads made it too difficult to get anywhere, except in winter, when sleighs slid easily over the frozen surface. In 1849, after repeated improvements to Yonge Street and sincere attempts at maintenance, an omnibus line started service between the new suburb and Toronto. The community began to grow. The Potter's Field closed its gates in 1854, and the bodies were exhumed to allow for expansion of the little town.

A campaign for incorporation began. A thousand petitioners were needed, and the story is still fondly told of how everyone voted for it, even the subterranean residents of the Potter's Field. Accordingly, Yorkville became an incorporated village in 1853; its official crest illustrated the industries of the area, which were the businesses of five of the town's biggest boosters: beneath a beaver *couchant*, there was a steer's head for the local butcher, an anvil for the blacksmith, a plane for the carpenter, a brickmaker's mould, and a beer keg.

The clock-towered Yorkville Town Hall, an impressive structure, in size at least, incorporating stylistic elements from wedding cakes to rose windows, was erected on the west side of Yonge Street directly opposite the Park Road (now Collier Street) which wound its way down the hillside into the ravine and thence into Rosedale. Built in 1859, Town Hall served in later years as a public library, then as an armoury, before its demolition in the 1940s. Another landmark with a tower is the Fire Hall, built in

(Next page) The Avenue Road level crossing at Macpherson Avenue, where the Canadian Pacific Railway tracks effectively form the northern boundary of Yorkville. On the west side of Avenue Road, a C.P.R. employee manned a small, square tower, from which he inspected the line and controlled the crossing gates. A similar situation existed a few blocks east at Yonge Street. The C.P.R.'s old North Toronto station was about 150 yards west of Yonge Street, on the south side of the tracks; it was replaced in 1916 by the clock-towered station on Yonge Street—now the liquor store (page 13). The C.P.R. raised its grade and built overpasses at Avenue Road and Yonge Street in 1911. Visible in the distance on the hillside was the splendid Victorian house called "Oaklands," the residence of Senator Macdonald (1824-1890), who had a prosperous drygoods and importing business and a career as member of the legislative assembly for West Toronto. Since 1931, the house has been occupied by the De La Salle Institute, a Roman Catholic boys' school.

Edward Aemilius Jarvis, a banker, military man, yachtsman and horseman, was a prominent figure in Toronto social circles, and lived at 34 Prince Arthur Avenue.

Architect Henry Sproatt (1866-1934) lived at 8 Prince Arthur, a house which has been smartly renovated into offices. Born in Toronto and apprenticed to an architect at the age of sixteen, he was able to travel widely, study in Europe, and work in New York City. He worked for six years with architect Frank Darling, then formed a partnership with Ernest Rolph. They designed a number of significant local buildings, including Bishop Strachan School, Hart House, the library and chapel at Victoria College, St. Andrew's College, and the University of Toronto War Memorial. He and his wife had two daughters and a son, Charles, who won the D.S.C. in the First World War and, as an architect in his own right, continued his father's firm until his own retirement in the 1960s.

1876 and still standing at 34 Yorkville Avenue.

Amongst names and places which evoke the village's past are the Jesse Ketchum park and school, the former Central Public School on Davenport Road. Both were named for the tannery owner and temperance advocate who was one of the big landowners of the city's early years. Ketchum arrived in York at the age of seventeen and a few years later, in 1812, took over a small tannery operation at the southwest corner of Yonge and Adelaide. It is appropriate that a school bears his name, for he was an advocate and supporter of secular education.

Ramsden Park occupies the site of Tannery Hollow, also known as the old Yorkville brick yards, a clay field which was mined in the 1880s. The city, which came into the property partly because of unpaid back taxes and partly by an outright purchase in 1904, named it for Alderman George Ramsden, who lived on Yorkville Avenue.

Bloor Street, named for the brewer who lived on it near Church Street, had become a fashionable address by the 1890s. The most telling transformation from the wild and woolly colonial era took place at the northwest corner of Bloor and Avenue Road. The first building there was a tavern built in 1820 called the Tecumseh Wigwam, a log building, primitive compared with the Red Lion, with a farmhouse-style front porch and a double pitch on the back half of the roof which sheltered a shedlike kitchen addition. It was replaced in 1870 by the fine house of Albert Nordheimer, the brother of the piano-manufacturing owner of "Glen Edyth" on the Poplar Plains Road. In the 1920s, Nordheimer's house was

John Severn

The map shows the district north of Bloor Street at Yonge in 1890—an area which has been radically redeveloped since subway construction in the 1950s and road changes to link Davenport and Yonge with Church Street south of Bloor. Bismarck Avenue, named for the German chancellor, was originally called Jarvis Street, after the Jarvis family of "Rosedale" and elsewhere—its name was changed to Asquith Avenue, after the British prime minister at the outbreak of the First World War, for the same reasons that Berlin, Ontario, became Kitchener. Much of the property to the north, along the unfinished Rosedale Valley Road, had been the estate of Sir D. L. Macpherson, of the house called "Chestnut Park." Yorkville was always noted for its breweries. Joseph Bloor built a brewery in the 1830s along the creek in Rosedale Ravine near what later became the north end of Huntley Street. A bigger and more important brewery, at Severn and Yonge, was that of John Severn (1807-1880), a native of Derbyshire who came to Canada in his early twenties and started brewing in Yorkville in 1835. Brewery Lane, east of Yonge between Severn and Collier, was the site of a row of brewers' cottages (below)—little more sophisticated than the workers' bothies of English rural estates, but nevertheless necessary for the workers, Yorkville being so remote. Severn attempted to establish himself in California in 1850, to take advantage of the gold rush, and built a brewery there which his son was to manage. The latter died, and the project folded. The elder Severn also operated breweries in Davenport, Iowa, and in Belleville. He was the first president of the Canada Brewers and Malters Association.

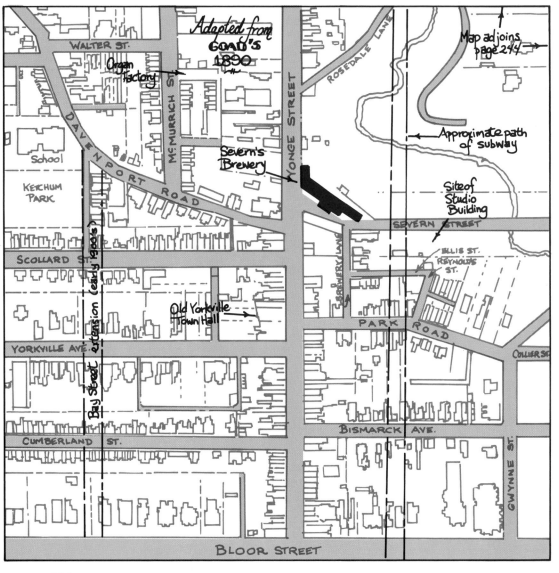

demolished for the construction of the highrise Park Plaza Hotel. The old Yorkville of creeks and hollows had been covered over, but still existed—the land was boggy, a *terra infirma* due to the underground passage of Taddle Creek, and only heroic efforts by the Park Plaza's owners shored up its sagging foundations.

A number of buildings still survive from the days of Yorkville's civic independence. The oldest is probably the cottage at 77 Yorkville Avenue, built in the 1860s for the village constable, John Daniels. The houses on Hazelton Avenue, between numbers 49 and 81, were built in the 1870s, and have in varying degrees survived their updating and renovations. One of the oldest-looking buildings, the Yorkville Public Library at 22 Yorkville Avenue, is in fact one of the newest, having been built in 1906 during the continent-wide spate of library construction which followed American steel magnate Andrew Carnegie's decision to give most of his fortune to that end.

The Studio Building, "a home for Canadian art" erected by Lawren Harris and Dr. J. E. MacCallum in 1913 at 25 Severn Street, can now only be approached from Rosedale Valley Road—the subway line has blocked access to Yonge Street. Designed by architect Eden Smith, it has a virtual wall of windows for north light, and advantageously has almost none on the west side—which is now within several yards of the subway track. It has been home and studio, over the years, to many renowned artists, including several of the Group of Seven; in the early 1920s, Lawren Harris, A. Y. Jackson, Arthur Lismer, J. E. H. MacDonald, and J. W. Beatty lived there. The latter, who has yet to receive the status accorded some of his contemporaries, was born in Toronto in 1869, and had an adventurous life, including service in the Riel Rebellion, and a decade with the Toronto Fire Department. During the First World War, he worked as an official artist in England and on the Western Front. He was one of the first to endure the rigours of painting in Algonquin Park. For two years, he was the president of the Arts & Letters Club, whose founder, choirmaster and music critic Augustus Bridle, described him as "a glorious truculent bigot, ready for action with either fists or vocabulary."

By the early 1880s, about 5,000 people lived in Yorkville, enjoying its friendly, country-town atmosphere. Modest houses lined the streets, shopkeeper lived next to gentleman, cows occasionally escaped from their pastures and wandered the streets, chickens pecked amongst the weeds along the sides of dusty ditches, and nearby, in the ravines and on the rolling land to the north, was forest. Transportation to and from the city had become a simple matter, for the horse-drawn omnibus of the 1850s had been superseded by a horse-drawn street railway.

The influx of commuters, however, brought demands for improvements in muncipal services; as the community became crowded, back-yard wells were suddenly too close to back-yard privies. The village council built a waterworks system near Poplar Plains Road, but it was none too successful in either construction or operation. Taxes rose, and when the City of Toronto suggested annexation in 1883, local ratepayers agreed. The independent village of Yorkville became history.

Bloor Street began to redevelop in the 1920s. Many of the fine old houses became professional offices, their former owners having moved on to areas like Rosedale or Forest Hill. The city widened Bloor Street in 1929, by which time the aforementioned Park Plaza Hotel, the Manufacturers Life Building at 200 Bloor Street East, the Ashley & Crippin Building at 83 Bloor Street West, and the Physicians & Surgeons Building at 86 Bloor Street West had been built, harbingers of a new commercial role for what had been a prestigious residential street. Though stalled by the depression of the 1930s and the Second World War, the redevelopment had regained its momentum by the early 1950s. In the lee of this expensive and fashionable development, Yorkville slumbered and waited.

The bohemian beatnik movement of the fifties flowered on Yonge and Gerrard streets. Jarvis Street, by comparison, was described as "sleazy" and "the sin strip." Yorkville, which had been zoned for commercial use in 1956, was "sophisticated." The *Telegram* ran a series of articles in 1958 called "Toronto's Bohemian World," describing the straight-haired girls with scratchy-wool black sweaters, tight black skirts, and black leotards, wearing heavy black mascara which made their eyes look like two holes burnt in a blanket; the young men imitators of Mort Sahl; the group of hippies living in a former coach house on Huntley Street; the beatnik painter who turned down a $3,000 commission to paint a mural on the history of merchandising; and the threat to the "Gerrard Village," on Gerrard from Yonge to Elizabeth, occasioned by the northward march of the high-rise city.

Commercial development came to Yorkville as an offshoot of the sophisticated shops on Bloor. One of the first was a hat shop opened by Louise Brocklebank on the south side of Cumberland Street, which provoked the rhetorical question of why anyone with a clientele like hers would open shop on a street like Cumberland. A newspaper article in 1957 noted that architects, interior designers and photographers were establishing themselves in Yorkville, as houses were cheap and could easily be converted to commercial uses. Pot Pourri, a clothing boutique, opened on Yorkville Avenue; elsewhere, a few antique shops and art galleries had appeared.

By the early sixties, the incursions of commercial development were becoming more pronounced; during the day, "every Rolls Royce in Toronto is stopping somewhere on [Cumberland] street." At night, however, the streets were thronged with coffee house patrons. Newspapers tumbled over each other to find suitably scornful descriptions of the "air of calculated quaintness" on the streets and the affectations of "the self-conscious set" at the folk music and jazz clubs. There were said to be 200 constant and 800 occasional bohemians frequenting coffee houses such as John and Marilyn McHugh's Halfbeat & Pennyfarthing, Werner ("the epitome of the Beat Innkeeper") Graeber's Inn on the Parking Lot, and Burnie and Pat Fiedler's Mousehole and the Riverboat. Other tastes were satisfied by more flamboyant nightspots such as La Discotheque Kiki Rouge. In April, 1963, according to one story, 90 shops were "competing furiously to flog 75-cent coffees, $80 bathing suits, and gold-plated faucets." The Village of Yorkville Association planned a festival for May 14, to coincide with the presentation of a petition to the Ontario Municipal Board seeking a ban on high-rise development. This "Save the Village" (from high-rises) campaign attracted support from the likes of anthropologist Jane Jacobs. Subsequent festivals and art shows attracted carriage-trade art buyers, espresso-drinking artists, and their respective menageries.

By the mid-sixties, beatniks had become hippies, and Yorkville had become a mecca for aspirants to the counterculture, while maintaining its attraction for the trendy members of the over-the-counter culture. The relaxed morality of the new arrivals prompted much head-shaking and soul-searching, hepatitis and gonorrhea. An incident which caused some hilarity was the visit to the area of conservative alderman David Rotenberg, in August, 1966. A newspaper story, headlined "Peeping David can't find sinning youth in Yorkville," was accompanied by a photograph showing the alderman, in a dark suit and polished shoes, craning to see over a board fence. His tour was prompted by a pending election, as Rotenberg was Ward Three alderman, and by a visit to Yorkville by Metro chairman William Allen, who had declared it to be a "grand place." According to the anonymous reporter, "Alderman David Rotenberg lurked in Yorkville's back yards for three hours last night, looking for evi-dence of teenage sin but couldn't find any. He peered over back fences, stumbled through darkened laneways, tut-tutted at barefoot girls in mini-skirts, lectured a shaggy youth who tried unsuccessfully to sell him a copy of *Satyrday*, the Yorkville newspaper, and knocked on prospective constituents' doors at midnight." One "Yorkville youngster" told Rotenberg that he looked "like a tourist."

The newspaper *Satyrday* and its 34-year-old publisher Andrew Mikolasch became targets of a police crackdown. After allegedly obscene sexual language and imagery were used in a story about "white exploitation of Negroes," police seized 3,000 copies of the paper. In the trial, in a scene repeated in so many cities in North America, established literary and professional figures defended the newspaper and its publisher. Robert Fulford, then a *Star* columnist, called it "quite a contribution to English literature." A social pathologist and a professor of English usage presented their reasoned opinions. The magistrate dismissed all charges.

The climactic event of the "summer of love" was the sit-in on a hot Sunday night in August, 1967. A couple of hundred people blocked Yorkville Avenue to press a demand—supported by a petition from Yorkville businessmen—that the street be closed to cars on weekends and summer evenings. To clear the street, police, "many in plainclothes, struck girls in the face, kneed bearded and sweat-shirted Village types and kicked fallen and limp youths," said the *Star*. In the subsequent retelling, sympathy was heavily on the side of the demonstrators. The "greening" of Toronto was underway. By the time that David DePoe, a "hippie spokesman" active in the sit-in, was acquitted of charges of causing a disturbance, two years had passed, and he had taken a job with the government.

The commercial development of Yorkville scarcely missed a beat. In 1968, the York Square complex opened at Yorkville Avenue and Avenue Road; it combined the old—seven Victorian houses—with a well-thought-out and modern commercial plan. Two other developments, Cumberland Court on Yorkville Avenue, and Hazelton Lanes between Hazelton Avenue and Avenue Road, were built in the early 1970s, and moved Yorkville further away from the serendipity of its beatnik days. The acid generation moved out, replaced by the acid-wash generation.

A somewhat romanticized view of "Rosedale," the home of William Botsford Jarvis which stood until 1905 at Cluny Drive and Rosedale Road. Built amidst rambling, bird-filled hedgerows and rolling fields on a 120-acre farm, the house took its name from the wild roses which dotted the hillsides, drinking up the hot sun— probably the pink-flowered Rosa blanda, *the thornless wild rose of southern Ontario.*

Rosedale

Rosedale would just be another posh suburb were it not for its topography. Sheltered from much of what roars and stinks in the modern city, it is truly an enclave, violated only by the wound of Mount Pleasant Road. Many of its finest residences have fallen to the wreckers and subdividers, austere apartment buildings hug its flanks and threaten its ravines, and almost no places with very grand gardens or much in the way of grounds at all remain, yet it is still a parklike and sylvan retreat, practically in the centre of the city.

Fortunately, no matter what happens to individual houses and properties, the web of roads follows the lay of the land. So leafy and built up are parts of it, and so few views to the outside, that it is quite easy to become disoriented, especially in its rolling southern part. Strollers often find themselves pressed into service as guides, for many residents of the endless straight brown blocks elsewhere in the city get lost while trying to be punctual for an afternoon drink or dinner.

Toronto's rigid grid-plan layout had its advocates, including historians like the Reverend Scadding who was pleased that his city, like Philadelphia and Washington, had been laid out "in accordance with the theories of the idealists" (page 15). A slightly more sympathetic view of the picturesque, in town planning, was expressed by Jessie Edgar Middleton, writing in 1933 for the city's official centennial book: "Rosedale, still a fashionable residential district, is in the 'romantic' style of the later nineteenth century, both in its planning (a labyrinth to the visitor) and its architecture."

As the decades have passed, the street scenes have changed. Most of the old houses have subdivided their grounds, and newer houses have filled in the gaps. An example is "Rose Cottage," the house today of Anthony Adamson, who can trace his ancestors through the Cawthra line of which his mother was a member to the earliest days of the Town of York. From the "widow's walk" on his roof, he can look between the trees and over the rooftops of the several houses which now occupy what was once the garden of "Rose Cottage." Lawns are brick-paved or dug up for swimming pools, cabanas occupy former flower beds, the houses themselves strain to the corners of the lot lines, garages are converted into guestrooms, and front lawns are paved over for parking. Adamson's garden, however, has roses and floral borders, and a sentimental ruin—the Corinthian-capitaled columns from his ancestor's house which stood at

Rosedale Ravine, Toronto, Canada

Rosedale Drive, Toronto

(Above) Looking west from the Glen Road footbridge to the Sherbourne Street bridge. A "toast-rack" open-sided tram is on the bridge. The "Sherbourne" streetcar line connected Rosedale with the Simcoe loop at Front and Simcoe, via Sherbourne Street and King Street; at the northern end of its run, it did a loop at Rachael Street, and connected with the Wellesley-Rosedale bus. In January, 1947, the T.T.C. was obliged to abandon streetcar service across the bridge, as all of its fleet was too wide for the bridge's "devil-strip." (Below) An idyllic scene in Rosedale Ravine. The photograph from which this postcard was printed first appeared in 1898, in a Toronto Board of Trade book delineating local glories, printed for the railway builder and industrialist J. L. Englehardt.

Cor. Cluny Avenue and Crescent Road,
Rosedale, Toronto, Canada

the northeast corner of King and Bay. By contrast, in the house next door lives the drummer of a noted rock-and-roll group, with retinue.

Before the turn of the century, Rosedale was quite cut off from the settled residential Toronto south of Bloor Street. Rosedale Valley Road had not been constructed, and a creek meandered along the bottom of the ravine, eventually draining into the Don River. The first access into the area, to reach "Rosedale Villa" and its farm, which occupied the 120 acres bounded by Lamport, Yonge, Park and Roxborough, was via a road off Yonge Street near Severn Street, which descended to the floor of the ravine and then wound up the other side through bird-filled hedgerows and thickets of shrub roses. The earliest picture of the area—a wash drawing executed in 1835, indicates the rolling fields along the ravine's banks, and a heavy forest behind "Rosedale Villa." The first houses in the area—including "Rosedale Villa," "Caverhill" at Park Road and South Drive, "Lorne Hall" on Meredith Crescent, and "Glenhurst"—could all be reached by carts and carriages using that route. The energetic owner of "Glenhurst," Edgar John Jarvis (a nephew of the William Botsford Jarvis who owned "Rosedale Villa"), built two bridges into the area—one at Huntley Street to allow him more easily to reach his house, the other on Glen road—across the ravine north of Bloor Street. The latter bridge cost him $30,000, and was evidently intended as an inducement to potential buyers of property in the area, much of which he owned. As the historian

(Left) "Hillcrest," later called "Deancroft," on the western side of the southern approach to what was called the North Iron Bridge, on Glen Road. Built by the local property owner Edgar John Jarvis, who lived nearby at "Glenhurst" on Park Road, it was originally given the unimaginative name of "Norcastle." After its 1905 purchase by Mr. and Mrs. A. E. Gooderham, the house was renamed "Deancroft" (in honour of Gooderham's mother, née Harriet Dean). Mary Reford Gooderham (right), though born in Michigan, had a Scots father and a Canadian mother, and was brought to Windsor when still a toddler. She became one of the most active Imperialist women in Canada through her long involvement, including a term as national president from 1912-18, in the Imperial Order Daughters of the Empire, which had its headquarters at "Deancroft." In addition, she was during that period a member of the Red Cross Executive, the Royal Canadian Institute, the Women's Auxiliary of the Conservative Party, and the Canadian Women's Hospital Ship Committee (which raised the funds to equip and send a hospital ship to Europe during the Great War). She inaugurated Queen Alexandra Rose Day in Canada, and arranged for the translation of the Church of England prayer book into Ukrainian. For her war service, she received a medal from the French government—one of only four women in Canada so honoured.

SCENE IN ROSEDALE   TORONTO, CANADA

Warwick Bro's & Rutter, Ltd. Publishers, Toronto   S1280   Compliments of Mrs McFarlane

Lucy Booth Martyn recorded, Jarvis set up a tollgate, which was smashed by M. B. Jackson, the owner of "Drumsnab," when he charged through with his coach and four.

After the city annexed Rosedale in 1887, it paid Jarvis ten thousand dollars of the thirty he had invested in the bridge. Though now too frail and narrow for cars, the bridge still spans the valley today—a remarkable walkway high up among the treetops, with Rosedale Valley Road quite far below, the peaceful greenery of Rosedale on one side, and the hurly-burly of Bloor Street on the other.

The attraction of Rosedale to many nonresidents was its recreational opportunities. An 1890 map of the area shows the Toronto Athletic Grounds west of Sherbourne Street between Elm Avenue and South Drive. Later maps show the Toronto Lacrosse Grounds occupying what is now Rosedale Park, and the Rosedale Golf Club spread over the rolling land north of Binscarth Road. Large crowds of fans walked from the city across the little Glen Road footbridge and through Rosedale to the lacrosse grounds.

The Rosedale Golf Club, which established links on the Scottish and Manitoba Land Company's holdings in North Rosedale, is one of the oldest clubs in Canada. Established in 1893 as the Deer Park Golf Club, the membership hacked its way around a nine-hole layout in Moore Park for two years, then moved to Rosedale, where it shared quarters with the Toronto Lacrosse Club and played over the land immediately to the north and west of the Glen Road bridge. In 1897, the club, having incorporated itself and raised some funds, built the house at the northeast corner of Glen and Beaumont roads (page 257). In 1901, they sold that house to George Watts and built another clubhouse on the south side of Binscarth Road just west of Glen Road. Their links had to be shifted about, too, as the area was rapidly being settled. First to go were the holes to the south and east of the Lacrosse Club; new lands were leased on the hill north of the railway tracks. Finally, in 1909, the club purchased 134 acres of rolling land just outside the city limits at Glen Echo and Mount Pleasant roads; the following year, the Rosedale Golf Club relocated, and remains there to this day.

"Caverhill," the long-time residence of Lt. Col. George Reginald Geary and descendants, at 124 Park Road at South Drive. One of the older Rosedale houses, built about 1865, it is usually called after the maiden name of Geary's wife (he married the daughter of a Colonel Caverhill of Montreal in 1927 when he was 53 years old), though the Gearys were by no means the house's first residents. A man of strong Orange principles, Geary was born in Strathroy in 1874, educated at Upper Canada College, and studied law at the University of Toronto; he was first elected to public office as a school trustee in 1904. He became an alderman, then a controller, and finally mayor of Toronto from 1910 to 1912. Later, he had a distinguished military career, winning a military O.B.E., a Military Cross, and the French Legion of Honour. At the time of his marriage to Beatrice Caverhill, he was Member of Parliament for South Toronto. "Caverhill" still has much of its old grounds, extending into woods above the Rosedale Ravine, and has recently been undergoing a lengthy restoration.

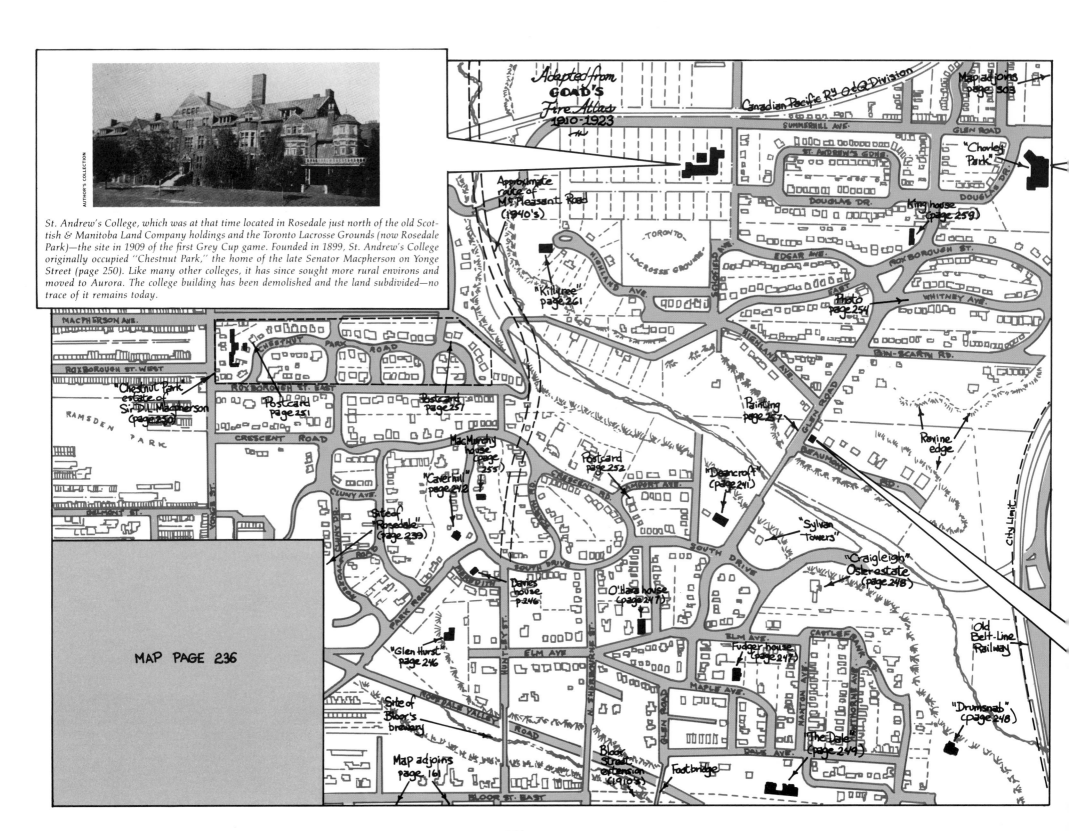

St. Andrew's College, which was at that time located in Rosedale just north of the old Scottish & Manitoba Land Company holdings and the Toronto Lacrosse Grounds (now Rosedale Park)—the site in 1909 of the first Grey Cup game. Founded in 1899, St. Andrew's College originally occupied "Chestnut Park," the home of the late Senator Macpherson on Yonge Street (page 250). Like many other colleges, it has since sought more rural environs and moved to Aurora. The college building has been demolished and the land subdivided—no trace of it remains today.

Adapted from GOAD'S Fire Atlas 1910-1923

Canadian Pacific RY OdQ Division

Map adjoins page 303

"Chorley Park"

SUMMERHILL AVE.

ST. ANDREW'S GDNS.

GLEN ROAD

DOUGLAS DR.

DOUGLAS DR.

King house (page 259)

Approximate route of Mt. Pleasant Road (1940's)

TORONTO LACROSSE GROUNDS

EDGAR AVE.

ROXBOROUGH ST.

"Killyree" page 261

HIGHLAND AVE.

WHITNEY AVE.

Photo page 254

BIN-SCARTH RD.

HIGHLAND AVE.

MACPHERSON AVE.

CHESTNUT   PARK   ROAD

GLEN ROAD

Painting page 257

ROXBOROUGH ST. WEST

ROXBOROUGH ST. EAST

Postcard page 251

Ravine edge

"Chestnut Park" estate of Sir D.L. Macpherson (page 250)

RAMSDEN PARK

Postcard page 251

CRESCENT ROAD

MacMurchy house (page 255)

Postcard page 252

BEAUMONT RD.

"Deancroft" (page 241)

CLUNY AVE.

"Caverhill" page 242

CRESCENT RD.

GLEN RD.

City Limit

Site of "Rosedale" (page 239)

"Sylvan Towers"

MAP PAGE 236

SOUTH DRIVE

"Craigleigh" Oster estate (page 248)

Davies house p. 246

O'Hara house (page 247)

Old Belt-Line Railway

ELM AVE.

Fudger house (page 247)

CASTLE FRANK RD.

"Glen Hurst" page 246

ELM AVE.

MAPLE AVE.

"Drumsnab" (page 248)

Site of Bloor's brewery

ROSEDALE VALLEY ROAD

N. SHERBOURNE ST.

GLEN ROAD

NANTON AVE.

DALE AVE.

"The Dale" (page 244)

Map adjoins page 161

Bloor Street extension (1910's)

Footbridge

BLOOR ST. EAST

244

"Chorley Park," the lieutenant governor's residence, built on property which had originally been owned by Toronto alderman John Hallam, and named by him for his birthplace—Chorley, Lancashire. The land was purchased in 1911 by the provincial government to replace the old Government House at the southwest corner of King and Simcoe (page 22). "Chorley Park" was built in 1915, in the French chateau style popular for

such edifices, and had spacious grounds through which ran a curving driveway, entered from Roxborough Drive. No sooner had it been completed than a clamour began, led by the Toronto *Star*, to abolish it as an extravagance. Towards the end of the First World War, there was a pronounced mood of austerity, and severe fuel shortages; while families were forced to double up in little houses that required only five to seven tons of coal to heat all winter, "Chorley Park" required a staggering 965 tons of it. Fuel was added to the controversy by Lt. Gov. L. H. Clarke, who at a Rotary dinner in 1920 referred to the current political unrest and remarked: "There is nothing which would please the Soviet agitators and Red Bolsheviks more than to abolish Government House, the office of the lieutenant governor, and all those things which are dear to loyal Canadians." Almost apoplectic, the *Star* declared the speech unconstitutional, and obtained legal opinions that the lieutenant governor had exceeded his powers. After a while, the issue ceased to sell newspapers, so it was dropped; the government stated that the sale of the property was impractical, as the land was tied up with covenants preventing its use for other than residential purposes, and there was at the time a lot of vacant residential land, especially in the practically uninhabited Moore Park area north of the C.P.R. tracks. Following Clarke's sudden death in August, 1921, an editorial in *The Farmers' Sun*—effectively the government's house organ—urged the abolition of Government House as "out of keeping with the simplicity of a democratic age." But the United Farmers of Ontario soon found themselves to be out of step with the prosperity and pomp-consciousness of the 1920s, and were defeated. "Chorley Park" finally became a victim of the Great Depression—it was closed in 1937 as an impractical white elephant. In 1940, the dominion government bought it for use as a military hospital; later, the R.C.M.P. and militia used it. The City of Toronto purchased the property for a park in 1960, and demolished the building the following year.

The Rosedale Golf Club clubhouse, at the northeast corner of Glen Road and Beaumont Road, was built in 1897, and was one of the first half-dozen buildings north of the Glen Road bridge. This drawing is from an article in a golf magazine published in 1898.

Huntley Street north of Bloor has effectively disappeared; it used to be a quiet Rosedale residential street, reached by an iron bridge across the Rosedale valley. The name is better known in recent times for the "100 Huntley Street" religious television program, which originates from the studio at that address, south of Bloor Street. In 1949, after years of bitter fighting, the city widened the Rosedale part of Huntley Street, carving strips from the grounds of some of the old houses, and actually biting off a few houses from South Drive, Scarth Road, and Crescent Road; this multilane commuterway connects the widened Jarvis Street south of Bloor Street with North Toronto and beyond.

"Glen Hurst" is the house at the western end of Elm Avenue. Built by Edgar John Jarvis, who moved to Rosedale from Oakville in the 1850s, it had its entrance on Park Road, reached by a winding cart track from Yonge Street. The collapse of a bridge on that route led Jarvis to build another one, at Huntley Street, which gave direct access to what had been the rear of his house.

In 1948, the Branksome Hall Girls School purchased "Glen Hurst." Earlier purchases by the school included the house called "Hollydene," at Ten Elm Avenue, and the house at Three Elm Avenue, which were built respectively by business partners John Blaikie and William Alexander. The latter house was once occupied by D'Alton Lally McCarthy (1871-1963), a barrister of some renown whose silver tongue pleaded many cases before the Privy Council in London. McCarthy married a daughter of Sir John Beverley Robinson. For recreation he was master of foxhounds for the Toronto Hunt Club, and a member of the mysterious Shah-wandahgooze Fishing Club. He was the son of the legendary D'Alton McCarthy, the English-Canadian nationalist who had entered politics as part of "The Noble Thirteen," attacking the Jesuit Estates Bill which he felt to be indicative of the decline of the supremacy of the English in Canada and the rise of a separate French-Canadian culture. The elder McCarthy rocketed to national prominence as an antagonist of bilingualism and separate schools in Manitoba; in the 1896 election, his "McCarthyites" third party helped to split the vote and, ironically, ensured the victory of Sir Wilfrid Laurier's pro-bilingual, pro-separate school, Liberal party.

The pork packer William Davies built the house at Three Meredith Crescent. Called "Lorne Hall," it stood in the midst of his three-acre estate; Meredith Crescent, then called Kensington Crescent, was the old driveway from Park Road to the house. In style, the house is very old-fashioned for Rosedale—its Second Empire mansard-roofed construction was more common on the lower reaches of Jarvis and Church streets. One of the later additions to the block-long street, after the old forest could no longer be seen, is the house of James Dixon Trees, the son of the founder of the tack manufacturing Samuel Trees & Company, at Nine Meredith Crescent. Samuel Trees was an associate of Henry Pellatt in the Toronto Electric Light Company; his house, "Mayfield," was a Sherbourne Street landmark until its demolition in 1966 for a parking lot. The Trees family were among the fortunate who maintained a summer cottage on Centre Island.

The fine house at 50 Elm Avenue was built for Henry O'Hara (1833-1918), partner with his son in the stockbroking firm of H. O'Hara & Company. Born in Newry, County Armagh, Ireland, he immigrated with his parents to Bowmanville. His first business venture was the Dominion Organ & Piano Company there; in 1880, he moved to Toronto, and obtained work managing a territory for the Sun Life Assurance Company. Later, he organized the Temperance & General Life Assurance Company. For more than half a century, he was an active member of the Sons of Temperance, and served for years as Grand Worthy Patriarch of Ontario for that organization. As well, he was chairman of the House of Industry from 1906 until just before his death. The house was later occupied by Joseph Mauns Aitken, an investor and securities salesman who was vice-president of the famed Foley Mine.

The rambling stone and brick house at 40 Maple belonged to Harris Henry Fudger, the long-time president of the Robert Simpson Company (page 48). Born in a house on King Street between Yonge and Bay in 1851, he started his career as an office boy in the wholesale fancy-goods and jewellery business. Besides his business activities, Fudger was a pillar of the Methodist community: on behalf of his church, he visited China and Japan in 1905 to report on Methodist missions; he was a regent of the Methodist Victoria University affiliated with the University of Toronto. His name survives at "Fudger House," a new senior citizens' residence on Sherbourne Street. Originally on that site was the home of Senator Cox, which Fudger purchased as a residence for unmarried female Robert Simpson Company employees from out of town and called the Sherbourne House Club.

The eastern side of Rosedale, on the bank above the Don River, was the location of the first "official" residence in York—the oddly named "Castle Frank," which sounds to modern ears to be of the same ilk as "Prince Chuck." Named for Francis Simcoe, it was a summer house built by his father—Colonel Simcoe, the first governor of Upper Canada—on a 200-acre estate running along the ridge above the west bank of the Don. "Castle Frank" was built in 1795, with log columns in a colonnade around what was effectively a clapboard log house. Today, Castle Frank Crescent, Avenue, and school commemorate the building and its unfortunate namesake, who died on a military campaign against Napoleon's forces in Spain. "Castle Frank" had an even less glorious end, burned down in 1829 by a transient.

The earliest houses built in the southeastern corner of Rosedale were grand estates with extensive grounds: "Craighleigh," "Drumsnab," "The Dale," and a later "Castle Frank." "Craighleigh" was the home of financier Sir Edmund Boyd Osler, the son of a clergyman, born in rural County Simcoe in 1845. After the failure of the Bank of Upper Canada, Osler joined with Henry Pellatt's father in a firm of money brokers and financial agents, then left Pellatt to join H. C. Hammond as Osler & Hammond, Stock Brokers; later, he became the president of the Dominion Bank, and a Member of Parliament for West Toronto—one of the Conservatives who survived the Laurier sweep in the 1896 election. "Craighleigh" was built in 1877 on what was then called Beau Street, now South Drive. As a stipulation of Osler's will, the house was demolished following his death in 1924; his children presented the property to the City of Toronto, as a park. The old gate is still there, as is a plaque commemorating Osler and his wife, Ann Farquharson.

"Drumsnab," at 5 Drumsnab Road, was built in the 1830s by Francis Cayley. According to historian Lucy Booth Martyn, it is the oldest house in Toronto to have been continually occupied as a private dwelling. Nearby, north of the original aforementioned "Castle Frank," Walter McKenzie built a new "Castle Frank," which has since been demolished for the construction of Castle Frank High School. A later occupant of the house was The Hon. Sir Albert Edward Kemp, a sheet metal manufacturer and Conservative who, after several attempts, was elected to Parliament in 1911, and later became minister of militia and defence in Sir Robert Borden's wartime government.

George Herbert Wood, one of the founding partners of Wood, Gundy & Company, lived at 36 Castle Frank Road—a house since demolished in favour of apartments. Born in Cheshire, England, in 1867, he was brought as a child to Toronto and attended Dufferin and Jesse Ketchum schools. Following several years as manager of Dominion Securities Corporation, he resigned, and with Dominion's secretary, J. H. Gundy, founded Wood, Gundy & Company

Frank O'Connor, the founder and owner of Laura Secord Candy shops, lived at 60 Castle Frank Road at the corner of Drumsnab. Born in Deseronto in 1885, he started in the candy business in Peterborough during the First World War.

The Hon. Sir Albert Edward Kemp, the owner of "Castle Frank" above the Don.

(Next page) "The Dale," at 21 Dale Avenue, was the home of the lawyer Dr. John Hoskin, Q.C. Born in Devonshire in 1836, he early attracted attention for his ability, being made a Queen's Counsel while still in his mid-thirties, and subsequently being named the Official Guardian of Infants by the Court of Chancery. He also had business interests, and was president of the Belt Line Railway. In 1866, Hoskin had married the daughter of one of the big landowners in the area—Walter McKenzie of the nearby "Castle Frank." He was subsequently able to build "The Dale," with a sweep of lawn in front that would have done justice to Capability Brown, on the edge of the ravine. Historian G. Mercer Adam, writing in 1891, said that "for beauty of situation, no less than for its fine sylvan setting and the rare attractions of its conservatories, 'The Dale' is well-nigh unsurpassed among Toronto homes." Wealthy men indulged in the fad for conservatories—local enthusiasts included Hart Massey, Sir Casimir Gzowski, and Henry Pellatt. In England, Joseph Paxton, the editor of the Magazine of Botany and head gardener for the Duke of Devonshire, designed a "Great Stove" for exotic plants, using the new technologies of wrought iron, glass, and heat radiated from water circulating in pipes. Paxton's later "Crystal Palace" revolutionized industrial-age architecture; his "stove" created a mania for palm houses.

Chestnut Park

Chestnut Park Road winds through the central part of Sir David Macpherson's old estate, which was called "Chestnut Park," evidently because of a row of horse chestnut trees which lined the property's frontage on Yonge Street. In addition, Macpherson owned a substantial amount of land to the south along the ravine—the land east of Yonge Street which is now traversed by the subway line.

Macpherson rose to prominence as the partner of Casimir Gzowski, the engineer who built several sections of the Grand Trunk Railway. Together, they created the Toronto Rolling Mills, which produced the rails for their contracts. A Conservative and a loyal friend to Sir John A. Macdonald, he organized and was the president of the Interocean Railway Company, one of two syndicates which early in the 1870s sought to build

a railway to the Pacific Ocean. (The other was the first Canadian Pacific Railway, an ostensibly Canadian group led by Sir Hugh Allan of Montreal. Allan's ambition and his connections with American capitalists and railroaders led him to chicanery and boodling which seriously compromised the Conservative government; revelations by the Liberal opposition of Allan's duplicity caused the "Pacific Scandal" and the downfall of Sir John A.'s government.)

Following Macpherson's death, the estate was subdivided; the newly founded St. Andrew's College occupied the old mansion on Yonge Street for six years, until 1905, when it moved to its new building elsewhere in Rosedale. The new subdivision around the winding Chestnut Park Road was very "state of the art," and built to the 1905 plan of S. H. Townsend,

"Chestnut Park," the estate of Sir David Macpherson, facing Yonge Street north of Roxborough.

250

Chestnut Park, Rosedale, Toronto, Canada

CRESCENT PARK ROAD, TORONTO

who conceived the brick sidewalks, paved streets, underground wiring, and distinctive lamp standards—elsewhere in Rosedale, board and plank sidewalks, muddy roads, and a tangle of power lines persisted for years after the first settlement.

Not surprisingly, a number of prominent Torontonians lived on Chestnut Park Road. James Ryrie, the cofounder of Ryrie Brothers Jewellers, built the very large house at One Chestnut Park Road in 1915. Angus MacMurchy, the son of the principal of Jarvis Collegiate Institute and brother of the MacMurchy sisters (page 255), lived at number 67; he was a solicitor for the Canadian Pacific Railway and one of the editors of several volumes on Canadian railway law. Agnes Lind Smythe, the tireless crusader for better care for the "feeble-minded," lived at number 57 with her husband—the prominent King's Counsel Robert Gordon Smythe. The Hon. T. W. McGarry, the president of the Woodstock Rubber Company, a long-time M.P.P., and from 1914-19 the provincial treasurer, lived at number 54. Donald Gordon Ross, the son of Lt. Gov. W.D. Ross, lived at 60 Chestnut Park Road. John Delatre Falconbridge, the Dean of Osgoode Hall Law School, lived at 22 Chestnut Park Road: an authority on commercial law, he wrote extensively on topics such as mortgages, banking, and bills of exchange.

As a very modern subdivision with underground wiring, unique lamp standards, and a universal standard of grooming and grandeur, Chestnut Park not surprisingly attracted the attention of postcard publishers. (Above) The first completely visible house on the right is number 78; to its right is number 74, and so on. (Below) The house on the left with the double-columned porch and the sizeable tree in front is 18 Chestnut Park Road; to its left is number 20. The houses at 20, 22, and 24 Chestnut Park Road were among the earliest in the subdivision, having been built between 1904 and 1906. The card, though published locally by the Richmonde Sales Company, has the street incorrectly named. Neither postcard shows the distinctive lamp standards which are unique to the subdivision.

Henry George Stanton's company published the Canadian Home Journal. *Born in Maryland in 1874, he came to Toronto and started work with R. S. Williams & Company music publishers, becoming the company's general manager when he was 29 years old. Stanton was one of the founders of the Canadian Bureau for the Advancement of Music, and wrote a number of books on diverse musical subjects, including* Sunshine For The Soul *and* Music During The Great War. *He lived at 74 Chestnut Park Road.*

As originally laid out, Crescent Road was a two-block, curving section at the eastern end of a road called North Drive. At that time, North Drive did not connect through to Yonge Street—a one-block extension of Rosedale Road, now called Cluny Avenue, allowed access to Roxborough Street and thus to Yonge. By 1905, the name North Drive had disappeared, the road was connected to Yonge Street, and its entire length was renamed Crescent Road.

Over the years, a number of interesting people have lived on Crescent Road. The rather modest house at number 78, which has recently been renovated into condominiums, was the residence of Sir Henry Pellatt, who moved there when collapsing real estate prices and the debacle of the Home Bank made it impossible to maintain "Casa Loma," his famous white elephant on the Spadina hill.

At number 158 lived Major General Harry Cawthra-Elliott, a career soldier who had been born plain Harry Elliott in Bangalore, India, and later served in the Boer War and in China during the Boxer Rebellion. During the early years of the Great War, he was based in Toronto as head of administrative staff for the Canadian militia; later, he was commissioner of the Ontario Provincial Police. After his first wife died, he married Grace Cawthra, the youngest daughter of Henry Cawthra, and changed his name accordingly. Two doors away, at 162 Crescent Road, another Cawthra—Edith Mary, a daughter of Joseph Cawthra—lived with her husband, the politician Sir Henry Drayton.

The photographer stood in front of 178 Crescent Road, and pointed his camera to the west. Lamport Avenue crosses in the middle distance; the large house fully visible in the centre of the postcard is number 170.

(Left) Walter Page, the occupant of 89 Crescent Road, was a masonry contractor whose firm, Page & Company, constructed buildings such as Hart House, Bishop Strachan School, and Victoria College's Burwash Hall and library. (Middle) Hon. Newton Rowell, K.C., resident at 134 Crescent Road, was leader of the Liberal party in the Ontario legislature from 1911-17—a period when Liberals were in the political wilderness. Because of his pro-conscription beliefs, he was wooed by Conservative Prime Minister Sir Robert Borden into helping form a Unionist dominion government, and then served as vice-chairman of the War Committee of the Cabinet. He was appointed in 1937 as the chairman of the historically significant Rowell-Sirois Commission on Dominion-Provincial Relations, although ill health soon forced his resignation. (Right) Charles Edward Edmonds, who lived at 34 Crescent Road, was president of Christie, Brown & Company biscuit manufacturers. On the death of R. J. Christie in 1926, Edmonds succeeded to the presidency, fifty years after he had joined the company at the age of thirteen in the "handbaking" department.

Sir Henry Lumley Drayton, the owner of the house at 162 Crescent Road, had a varied career, including roles as counsel for the City of Toronto, member of the Toronto Power Commission, chief railway commissioner for Canada, and federal minister of justice. Born in Kingston in 1869, he was educated in England and Canada, and became Toronto's assistant city solicitor at the age of 24. In 1914, he took charge of the removal of Canadian women and children from European countries at war; later, he was the organizer of the movement of foodstuffs and munitions in Canada, for which he was knighted. He was the only Canadian of three commissioners in the 1916 Railway Inquiry, which unravelled the mess of the Grand Trunk and Canadian Northern Railways into the system which became the Canadian National Railway. So great was his reputation that he was appointed as the federal minister of finance in July, 1919; a few months later, a by-election in Kingston sent him to the House of Commons. He remained in the House, often in opposition, until his 69th birthday, when he accepted the chairmanship of the Ontario Liquor Control Board.

Cabbages supposedly grew in the gardens in Cabbagetown and, during the First World War, Victory Gardens flourished, even in some yards in Rosedale. This photograph of a victorious vegetable gardener was taken by William James; the caption with it states simply "Crescent Road Victory Garden," but exactly where this fine garden of corn and potatoes was located remains a mystery. A wartime promoter of the Victory Garden was W. S. Dinnick (page 286), the president of the Dovercourt Company which had such a large stake in the development of North Toronto. In 1913, the Dovercourt Company had offered prizes totalling $1,000 for the best-kept back yard in the city, worked by the owner without any hired help. Flowers gave way to vegetables with the advent of the war, and Dinnick, with arguments later taken up and promoted by the Rotary Clubs of Canada, urged the cultivation of all vacant lots, and said that kitchen gardens could mean a saving of $10 million a year, freeing money and food for the war effort. The Arts & Letters Club was one group which caught the patriotic bug and set out to grow their own food. In the spring of 1917, some members leased farmland in York Mills; their leader, H. B. Lefroy, fought groundhogs and potato bugs with such success that preserving the excess produce became more of a problem than growing it.

James Murdoch (1890-1962) founded Noranda Mines in 1923, and maintained an iron grip on its management until his death. Born in Toronto, he attended Osgoode Hall law school, and was called to the Ontario bar at age 23. As the years went by, his eccentricities became more pronounced; according to Peter C. Newman, he effectively ran Noranda from his living room, and when not giving the orders he was hitting the bottle. Command Centre for Noranda was the house at 30 South Drive.

CTA JAMES 1372

The yet-to-be-groomed suburb—Whitney Avenue, photographed from Glen Road in the autumn of 1907.

The MacMurchys

Helen MacMurchy

Marjory MacMurchy

The comparatively modest house at 122 South Drive was home to the MacMurchy sisters, daughters of Archibald MacMurchy, the long-time rector of Jarvis Collegiate Institute and editor of the *Canadian Educational Monthly*. Archibald MacMurchy had come to Toronto from Argyleshire, and while still in school, began to teach younger pupils. In 1854, he attended the Normal School, then completed a master's degree at the University of Toronto, where he won first-class honours in mathematics, English, French, and sciences. In 1858, he was appointed mathematics master at Toronto Grammar School (later Jarvis Collegiate Institute), and retained the position for over thirty years. He died in April, 1912. His son Angus was a solicitor expert in railway law and lived nearby at 67 Chestnut Park Road. Two of his daughters, Marjory and Helen, had quite exceptional careers.

Marjory was a writer and journalist, and had been special correspondent for a syndicate of Canadian newspapers at King George V's coronation in 1911. She was a crusader for women's rights, her views being expressed in a series of books, including *The Woman—Bless Her*, published in 1916; the "Women and the Nation" chapter in *The New Era in Canada*, 1917; and *The Canadian Girl at Work*, 1920. For many years the president of the Canadian Women's Press Club, she was placed in charge of the women's department of the Canadian Reconstruction Association. In 1926, she married the former director of the Reconstruction Association, newspaperman Sir John Willison (page 49). She continued to write political columns and review books under her maiden name, though she was referred to as Lady Willison elsewhere.

"Dr. Helen" became a household word across the country. As a hospital inspector and educator of expectant mothers, Dr. Helen MacMurchy crusaded against Toronto's notorious infant mortality rate. A graduate *Honoris Causa* from the University of Toronto, she was the first woman to take postgraduate study with Dr. William Osler at Johns Hopkins University, afterwards returning to Toronto to become "a determined young bicycle-riding physician"—later, she owned an electric brougham in which she did her rounds. She first came to public attention in 1906 when asked to prepare reports on the care of the mentally ill. Later, she researched infant mortality, inspected prisons and charitable homes, and worked as assistant in gynaecology and obstetrics at Toronto General Hospital. MacMurchy's reports on the care of children had always been reported in a sensational fashion by the Toronto press. In April, 1910, in response to a city-wide infant mortality rate of nearly 20 percent, her statement, "if the mother works, the child dies," received wide coverage. (Her 1910 book, *Infant Mortality*, is still listed in catalogues as "in print" in Canada, as is her sister's *The Woman—Bless Her*, and some of her brother's legal works.)

In 1913, Dr. MacMurchy was appointed provincial "Inspector of the Feeble-Minded." Part of her duties included visits to country houses of refuge, industrial houses of refuge, and orphanages. That summer, there were a number of sensational stories in the press about baby farming in the city, alleging that nine out of ten of the infants kept in unlicensed baby farms died before they were a year old. Dr. Hastings, the medical health officer, reported that 3,000 houses in the city were occupied by from two to six families.

Dr. MacMurchy left the employ of the provincial government in 1919 and spent the next dozen years working for the Federal Department of Health. During that period, she wrote the *Canadian Mothers Book*, and the nationally distributed series of fourteen "little blue books" filled with tips for mothers and housekeepers, with titles like *How to Cook in Canada*, *How to Care for Father*, and *Rickets*. She retired in 1932, at the age of 70, and promptly accepted an offer to do research for the Canadian National Council of Mental Hygiene. Throughout her career, she found time to write articles on women's and health issues for magazines such as *Saturday Night*, and was a founding member of the Rose Society of Ontario.

She received a number of honours for her lifetime's work. The first was a Commander of the British Empire in 1934; six years later, the Toronto Academy of Medicine held a banquet in her honour, at which a large portrait of her was unveiled. The greatest recognition occurred in 1949, when she was 87 years old: at a convocation at Hobart & William Smith College to mark the hundredth anniversary of the graduation of the first woman to practise medicine in the United States, "Dr. Helen" was named as one of the ten leading physicians in the world. She died in October, 1953.

Glen Road

CTA JAMES 1575

An accident on the Glen Road bridge (according to the original photograph's caption), leaving this little electric brougham inches from the precipice. The iron bridge here was replaced by the current one in 1928.

Glen Road begins at Howard Street, south of Bloor, and winds its way across two bridges—the first of which is now a footbridge—all the way to the top of North Rosedale. At the turn of the century, two of the grand houses of early Rosedale—"Hillcrest" (page 241) and "Sylvan Tower"—occupied opposite sides of Glen Road at the approach to the northern bridge. Both of these houses were built by the ubiquitous and industrious Edgar John Jarvis, the resident of "Glen Hurst" off Huntley Street. Jarvis

built "Sylvan Tower" (so named for its Victorian turret which offered a splendid vantage point over the treetops) for himself in 1881; it was demolished in 1933, and the property subdivided.

(Next page) The handsome house at the northeast corner of Beaumont Road and Glen Road was built in 1897 as the Rosedale Golf Club clubhouse; golfers played over a course laid out on the land to the north and west of the bridge. In 1901, when a new clubhouse was built on the south side of BinScarth Road just west of Glen Road, this house was bought by Col. George Watts (1863-1933). "A great quarter-miler in his day," Watts fought with the Queen's Own Rifles in the Northwest Rebellion, then joined the Canadian General Electric Company at its inception in 1892, and stayed there until his retirement. The "Rosedale" bus service commenced operations about 1922, soon after the Toronto Transportation Commission took over from the Toronto Railway Company, as a feeder service to the Sherbourne streetcars. The buses ran up Glen Road as far as Summerhill, where they turned and made their way back via Highland to Glen Road.

Arthur King

The house at 154 Glen Road at Roxborough Street is distinctive by virtue of being set low to the ground, with a broad, red-tiled roof, rough stonework, and deep, sheltering eaves forming a sort of verandah at the front. It was the home of Arthur King, a manufacturers' agent with a warehouse at 24 Wellington Street West. He served as a sales agent for a few English hosiery companies, but his major client was the K. Ishikawa & Company silk manufacturing company of Yokahama.

King was born in Ottawa, one of a family of ten children. The only one to be a great success in business, he lived in grand style. Following the death of his first wife, he chose a beautiful new bride, much younger than he, named Theola Swanson. He filled their house with expensive Oriental decorations, including exquisite Oriental silk tapestries; his Rolls Royce, when not being polished by the chauffeur, was kept in the garage under a lush, pure silk cover weighted at the corners with silk tassels the size of tennis balls. Their Chinese cook looked forward to the visits of his employer's niece, on which occasions he could concoct the sort of fanciful and fabulous decorated cakes which would delight a child.

King's relatives were treated generously: Frances Findlay—the niece who was the favorite of the Chinese cook—recalls the invitations her mother received from King to visit his warehouse; there, she would be told to pick out her favourite silk or brocade, from which huge, dress-length pieces would be cut. King's reputation as a silk merchant was such that, during the 1920s, tour bus drivers in Rosedale announced: ". . . and on your right is the home of Arthur S. King, the silk magnate. . . ."

Following King's death, his comparatively youthful widow moved to a suite in the Park Plaza Hotel. She was a regular on "best dressed" lists for many years and died only recently.

The King family, photographed around the turn of the century. Silk importer Arthur King is standing, third from the right. His brother Jack, standing on the far right, named his daughter Queenie Victoria King. (Next page) The Arthur King house at 154 Glen Road, built for D. Fitzgerald in 1913.

M.KLUCKNER
© '87

Robert Young Eaton (1875-1956) was Timothy Eaton's nephew; he became president of the T. Eaton Company in April, 1922, following the early death of his cousin, Sir John Craig Eaton. The latter's will had stipulated that one of his four sons, to be chosen by his executors, should eventually assume control of the retailing empire—John David Eaton (1909-73) did so in 1942. R. Y. Eaton had entered the Eaton's buying office in London, England, in 1897, and moved to Canada five years later. He lived at "Killyree" (next page), a rambling estate on the crest of the hill above the route of today's Mount Pleasant Road. R. Y. Eaton and his sons were all well-known horsemen, and at least one of his horses was also called "Killyree"—after the town in County Antrim, Ireland which was his birthplace.

Harry Ryrie was one of the three Ryrie Brothers who owned Toronto's fanciest jewellery store, "Diamond Hall" at the corner of Yonge and Adelaide. He built the large house at One Highland Avenue (next page), and furnished it with rugs and tapestries and furniture which he and his wife had made it their hobby of several years to collect. In July, 1917, their eldest son Evan was killed at Vimy Ridge; two months later, though seemingly in excellent health after a summer of golf, Harry Ryrie collapsed and died. He was only 55 years old. He had been not only a well-known businessman, but a benefactor of the Y.M.C.A. and the Jarvis Street Baptist Church. During his well-attended funeral, amongst uniformly effusive eulogies, W.A. Kemp was moved to adjure "any young men . . . to note that Mr. Ryrie was always punctual in keeping appointments." Harry Ryrie left an estate of $700,000, including a bequest of $10,000 for 100 park benches, 50 of which were to go to Island Park, where the family had kept a summer cottage for many years.

The rambling house at the end of Highland Avenue was built by Harry Ryrie, one of the Ryrie Brothers jewellers. The grounds extended over several rolling, wooded acres down the hillside into the ravine, with fine prospects over the Rosedale area. To this day, its concrete wall indicates something of the property's extent. One of the old garages is now a separate house, with the address 7 Highland Avenue; the grounds have been further cut back by the recent insertion of a new house between the Ryrie house and its former garage. Following Harry Ryrie's death in 1917, his widow found she could not sustain the expense and effort the property required, and sold it to R. Y. Eaton, who named the house "Killyree."

Rebecca Mary Church, the sister of the bachelor mayor Tommy Church, lived with the latter at 98 Binscarth Road. "On the election of her brother to the Mayoralty of Toronto (in 1915), she undertook and graciously carried out the official functions connected with the arduous duties of that position." She had previously had her own career, working as "Critic Teacher" for trainees at the Model School and the Faculty of Education at the University of Toronto. During the First World War, she was active in service groups, such as the British Red Cross, the Amputations Association, the Thrift Committee, and the Imperial Order Daughters of the Empire. She was president of the Women's Canadian Club in 1920-1.

George Anderson was the agent for Borsalino Hats during an era when the hat business could make a man wealthy. Born in Scotland in circumstances "which obliged him to earn his own schooling from his youth," he studied law, then abruptly entered the hat and fur business. His wholesale company was located at 284-286 King Street West. He gained control of the Borsalino Hat agency at the turn of the century, and over the next three decades travelled extensively in connection with his business, making some 60 crossings of the Atlantic. He lived at 85 Highland Avenue.

"Millionaires' Row"

On the steep rise of land north of Davenport Road stood the finest mansions of turn-of-the-century Toronto. Two of them, initially belonging to James Austin and Sir Henry Pellatt respectively, survive today, but without the expansive, parklike grounds which made them true estates. Pellatt's estate was, in fact, always broken up—he had hoped to use his political clout to get Austin Terrace and Walmer Road closed.

The land at the top of the rise—part of a 200-acre lot running from Bloor to St. Clair—was first owned by William Willcocks. He left it to his son-in-law, Dr. W. W. Baldwin, one of the "heaven-sent barristers"—the first local members of the legal profession, so called as their livelihood was created in 1803 by royal proclamation. In 1818, Baldwin built his "very commodious house in the Country," which he called "Spadina," after the Indian word for hill. It stood practically on the site of modern "Spadina," east of the top of the Baldwin steps. A broad avenue, today's Spadina, was cleared from Queen Street northwards to reach it. Following Baldwin's death in 1844, the estate came into the possession of his grandson, William Willcocks Baldwin, who sold 80 acres of it at auction to James Austin; the latter built the current "Spadina" in the 1860s.

Before the turn of the century, James Austin's "Spadina" estate occupied the land bounded by Spadina Road, Huron Street (had it been cleared up the hill), Davenport Road, and St. Clair Avenue. To its east, on the rolling, wooded land near Poplar Plains Road, was "Ravenswood," the house of Austin's relations, Anne and George Arthurs; and Samuel Nordheimer's "Glen Edyth." The extraordinary thing is that Nordheimer could not have built "Glen Edyth" any closer to "Ravenswood" had he tried—the two houses were only about a hundred feet apart. Further east still is the Avenue Road hill, which at the time was the location of the houses of S. H. Janes (page 225) and Senator John Macdonald (page 235). Old Dr. Baldwin's name was preserved in the tract of unsettled land stretching northward from St. Clair Avenue between Forest Hill Road and Huron Street, which was still labelled the Baldwin Estate on maps.

"Spadina" is the second oldest of the grand residences left standing on the escarpment—only "Oaklands," the aforementioned house of Senator Macdonald, is older, and only by a half dozen years. "Spadina" was erected in 1866, added to several times, and occupied until 1982 by the builder's granddaughter. It is now owned by the City of Toronto and the Ontario Heritage Foundation, and operated as a museum by the Toronto Historical Board.

In the early years, the Austins' only neighbours were the Wells family at "Davenport" on Bathurst Street. To the north stretched open, lightly wooded fields separated from each other by hedgerows and the occasional ravine. So empty and lonely was their escarpment eyrie that on many winter nights the only visible civilization was, far in the distance to the southeast, a few lights at Yorkville.

AUTHOR'S COLLECTION

"Casa Loma" in the 1930s, after the estate's grounds to the north of the castle were filled in by housing, isolating the stables a residential block away. Pellatt's declining fortunes and eventual bankruptcy forced him to sell off everything and beg for tax breaks. In December, 1922, for instance, Pellatt appealed the tax assessment of "Casa Loma," arguing that it added nothing to the value of the land, as it had no selling value. By establishing a value for the castle itself, the assessment department had doubled the property's value to $200,000; Judge Coatsworth, however, agreed with Pellatt, and ordered the assessment reduced to $100,000.

James Austin (1813-97) came to Canada from County Armagh, Ireland. Before starting a wholesale grocery business, he apprenticed as a printer to William Lyon Mackenzie. Later, he became the first president of the Dominion Bank. One of his children, Albert William Austin, began his career at the age of seventeen as a junior clerk in the Dominion Bank, but three years later decided to enter the wholesale grocery business of Frank Smith & Company. With a view to establishing a wholesale grocery business, he moved in 1880 to Winnipeg, which was only beginning its spectacular growth above the rutted prairie mud. Instead, he decided that Winnipeg needed a street railway and secured the franchise. Although starting with horsecars in the city itself, he was aware of the new developments in electric traction, and advocated an electric system. Winnipeg City Council opposed him, as it felt that electric cars would be dangerous, so Austin established an electric system in the suburbs, connecting the

Albert William Austin

One of the residents of the new houses built on the "Casa Loma" grounds was Major Samuel John Robins, who lived in the modest house at 4 Castleview Avenue. Robins came to Ontario from Wales in 1907, and became private secretary to the superintendent-general of Indian Affairs, then performed the same function for the future Conservative prime minister Arthur Meighen. During the war, he was special recruiting officer for Canada, then returned to England, where he was a prominent campaigner, yet an unsuccessful candidate for the Conservative cause against the Socialists in the years before the English general strike. Upon his return to Canada, he organized a company which unsuccessfully attempted to capitalize on the Illingworth Process for the low-temperature carbonization of coal—a technology which was unable to survive the popularity of petroleum. More successfully, he was managing director of the Hotel Association of Ontario.

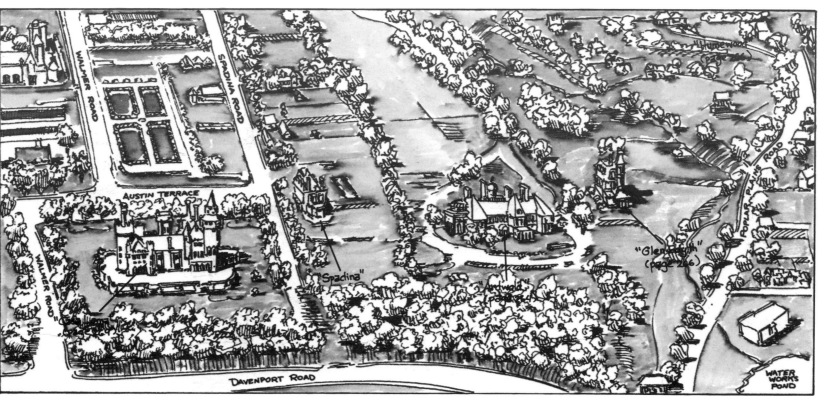

"Millionaires' Row" on the escarpment, as it would have appeared at its height, during the First World War years.

city with parkland and homes along the Red River. In 1892, when he again proposed the electrification of the entire system, he was outflanked by interests led by the Montreal and Toronto financiers James Ross and William Mackenzie—the latter had recently acquired the Toronto street railway franchise. The Ross-Mackenzie interests were allowed to set up a competing system using electric traction, and for a year, as the rivals cut prices and jockeyed for position in the courts, Austin's horsecars and the new electric trams ran along side by side on the Winnipeg streets. Free enterprise has rarely run so rampant. After a protracted legal battle, during which Austin appealed all the way to Privy Council and lost, he sold out and returned to Toronto, where he became vice-president of the Consumers' Gas Company and a director of the Dominion Bank. Following his father's death in February, 1897, he became president of the latter institution. His brother James Henry Austin had shown little interest in business or adventure, choosing instead to remain at home and manage the "Spadina" farm. He always found time to wander the fields, like a country squire, with his dog, pipe, and gun. Unfortunately, such arcadian simplicity did not result in a long life, for he died at the age of 38, in 1891.

In addition to his Toronto business interests, Albert Austin was a fruit

farmer, and maintained a large acreage at Port Dalhousie, "which is one of the largest and finest in that part of the country." He died in 1934. "Spadina" was then occupied by his daughter Anna Kathleen, who had married a nephew of the noted nature writer and artist Ernest Thompson Seton. Her son, the great-grandson of James Austin, wrote about his family's past and their milieu in the book Spadina: A Story of Old Toronto.

The two biggest houses on the escarpment were effectively completed on the eve of the First World War. Sir John Craig Eaton's "Ardwold" had a nominal address of 480 Davenport Road—where there was a simple wooden gate at the bottom of the steep hill—and a carriage entrance several hundred yards to the north at Ardwold Gate. Eaton had purchased the "Ravenswood" property from the Arthurs in 1908, demolished the existing modest house, and erected his own enormous Italianate palace—again, practically on top of Nordheimer's turreted Victorian confection. More ostentatious still was Sir Henry Pellatt's "Casa Loma," which had extensive grounds and greenhouses to the north, but which today seems hemmed in amidst the small houses built on its subdivided estate following the collapse of its owner's empire.

Spadina Hill's salad days were no more than a decade, from 1910 to 1920; after that, two of its squires had misfortunes—Pellatt was financially embarrassed, and Eaton died.

"Ardwold"

Sir John and Lady Eaton's "Ardwold" stood on rolling parkland east of "Spadina." The former's grounds extended northward, wrapping around the "Spadina" property, all the way to the ravine of Castle Frank Creek. At the base of the hill, at 480 Davenport Road, was a modest wooden gate, from which one could ascend a flight of stairs to the gardens and house above. The roadway winding through the property from the main gate and gatehouse on Spadina Road is still called Ardwold Gate.

"Ardwold," meaning "high on a green hill," was enormous and lavish even by Toronto standards. It had 50 rooms, including fourteen bathrooms; the swimming pool and conservatories were covered with an estimated half-acre of glass. No other mansion boasted a private hospital; the one at "Ardwold" contained two bedrooms, a bathroom for patients, a surgery, and a washing-up room. Completed in 1911, the house was occupied for only 25 years before its demolition, and the subsequent subdivision of its grounds. By that time, Lady Eaton was a widow and was most often seen entertaining and riding to the hounds at Eaton Hall, the family estate at King City north of Toronto.

"Ardwold" was built at the climax of a period of exceptionally formalized social behaviour. Like the other grand houses of Toronto, it provided a backdrop for garden parties, amateur theatricals, private concerts by touring string trios, indoor party games such as bezique and cribbage, outdoor games such as croquet and lawn tennis, bicycle parties, striped blazers and boaters, hats bedecked with dried flowers, parasols, *papier poudré* (paper impregnated with scented talcum powder) used by effete young men, monocles, *recherché* suppers of pheasant and champagne, and the ritual of the calling card. Of all the fads of the Victorian and Edwardian period, that of the calling card was the most enduring. Women of the "classes, not the masses" spent much of their time paying calls. A woman would drive in her carriage to the houses of acquaintances, where the door would be opened by a servant; she would enter and generally leave two cards, one of hers and one of her husband's, on a silver plate in the entrance hallway. A woman paying a call had no expectation of a reception or the offer of tea; she was merely performing a social courtesy,

and earning the right to a reciprocal call. Most women had their days when they were "at home" and visitors could expect tea and a chat, while others sent out printed invitations for their parties; this was, however, entirely separate from the calling card ritual. The cards themselves usually only contained the person's name—although there was in the mid-Victorian period a worldwide craze for picture (portrait) cards—and were commonly enamelled or glazed. In addition to leaving her card, the woman paying the visit usually bent over one corner of the card, which had a particular significance: *viz.*, if the upper left hand corner was bent, it signified that the card was left in person, not by a messenger; if the upper right, it signified congratulations; if the lower right, condolences; and, if the lower left, the caller was leaving town. Sometimes, in the last instance, the caller would also write "P.P.C." on the card, meaning *"pour prendre congé,"* or "to take one's leave." Some women had cards printed with the words Visite, Félicitation, Affaires, and Adieu in the four corners of the reverse side, leaving no question, when one corner was bent, of the purpose of the visit.

The calling-card ritual, "Ardwold," the viability of a residence like "Casa Loma," and the affordability and availabiity of servants, all became victims of the world upheaval which led to the First World War. The Eaton family was unusual in that Sir John Eaton's will kept intact the family fortune, and allowed the family to retain control of its business. The old European habit of primogeniture—of the first son's inheritance of the great mass of the family fortune—did not usually transplant to the democratic soil of North America. Sir John's widow, Lady Eaton, lived on into her nineties, and became a dowager-like institution, but her sons died comparatively young. The eldest son, John David (1909-1973) ran and expanded the family enterprises from 1942 until his retirement in 1970; his second son, Fredrik, has continued the direct family control into the fourth generation, and the family has entered into the folklore of the nation through the writings of Peter C. Newman and others. Even Lady Eaton wrote about her own life, in memoirs published in 1956.

Lady Eaton, the daughter-in-law of department store founder Timothy Eaton, was born Flora McCrea in Omemee, Ontario, in 1881. She married when she was 20 years old; after her husband's early death, she lived on for almost half a century, dying in 1970. She was supposedly the first woman in Canada both to drive a car, and to have an accident. She was one of the most active sponsors of and participants in the ritual of riding to the hounds, both at her estate at King, and in club activities at the Toronto Hunt and the Eglinton Hunt. As well, she was a patron of music, and interested herself in charities for the blind and for neglected children. Her autobiography, called Memory's Wall, *was published by Clarke, Irwin & Company in 1956. (See also the photograph on page 47.)*

"Ardwold," the home of Sir John and Lady Eaton, on the escarpment above Davenport Road and east of "Spadina" and "Casa Loma." A splendid house, built at the end of a leisured, gilded age, it lasted for the pitifully short period of 25 years, before being pulled down in 1936. Its red tile roof and Italianate, formal gardens must have contrasted sharply with the rambling, picturesque Victorian gingerbread of "Glen Edyth," visible a mere niblick's pitch away in the right distance. The roadway called Ardwold Gate now winds through the property.

Poplar Plains Road

Poplar Plains Road winds up the hill to what used to be called the Poplar Plains—the flat land at the top of the escarpment. Its "twin," Russell Hill Road, is a comparatively recent addition to the landscape, as it runs along the boundary between two of the old estates from the last century. Walking northwards on Poplar Plains Road, one passes on the left, first the Nordheimer property, then Russell Hill Road, and finally the Gunther property, before reaching St. Clair Avenue.

"Russell Hill" was the name of the Baldwin family farm near Cork, Ireland. William Willcocks Baldwin owned the property called "Spadina," abutting Spadina Road; his brother Augustus owned the adjoining property to the east. Upon the latter's death in 1866, a 22-acre portion of his property was purchased by a German jewellery importer named Edmund Gunther, who built the house originally called "Bellevue" but later known as "Humewood" which is the subject of the painting on these pages. Further south, with a frontage of nearly one-quarter of a mile on Poplar Plains Road, was the 25-acre property of Samuel Nordheimer, one of two brothers who emigrated from Bavaria to New York in 1839.

Samuel's brother Abraham Nordheimer was a pianist, and went to Canada West as music teacher to the governor general's daughter. In 1844, he moved to Toronto and began to manufacture and sell pianos, and was soon joined by his brother. For years, the brothers were prominent members of the congregation at Holy Blossom Synagogue; Samuel, however, courted Edith Boulton (the niece of the builder of "The Grange"), converted to Anglicanism, and married her in 1874. Abraham returned eventually to England; the Nordheimer piano factory was bought out by its chief rival, Heintzman and Company.

On his Poplar Plains Road property, Samuel Nordheimer built a fanciful Victorian house called "Glen Edyth" and developed the grounds surrounding it into a park of great rusticity and tranquillity. The house, built in 1872, stood at the end of Glen Edith Place, a stone's throw from Nordheimer's western property line. Through the middle of the property, along the glen of the shallow ravine, flowed Castle Frank Creek. A four-acre piece of the "Glen Edyth" estate was annexed in 1905 by the city as part of the so-called Avenue Road district; concurrently, Nordheimer received a new city assessment of $1,800 an acre, which he appealed, arguing that it cost him thousands of dollars a year to keep the creek from washing it all away. He had a supporter in a Mr. Defoe, a member of the appeal court, whose conversation with Nordheimer at the hearing on May 9, 1905, was reported in the *Telegram*: "Mr. Nordheimer has been to great expense in benefiting that section, and whatever is reasonable in fixing this assessment should be done. He has made it practically a park." Defoe then turned to Nordheimer, and said: "I sold you that property 24

The enormous building at 49 Clarendon Avenue was originally a quite modest house, built on a splendid 22-acre estate by a jewellery importer named Edward Gunther. The additions which brought it to its current condition were made after its purchase in the late 1920s by Timothy Eaton's daughter, Josephine Burnside (see main text). Before that it was owned by Hume Blake (below), the son of the Hon. Edward Blake. Hume Blake, born in Toronto in 1860, was a lawyer and director of the Union Bank and Canada Trust Company. His father was a stridently Liberal premier of Ontario, a brilliant speaker and logician but a political cold fish—the epitome, at least for ebullient characters like Sir John A. Macdonald, of the "little Ontarian." As leader of the federal opposition, he fought against the French language, national railways, and the trade reciprocity of his successor as Liberal leader, Sir Wilfrid Laurier. He finally left Canada for England in 1892.

Hume Blake

266

years ago, and, don't you remember, you took me to lunch at the Toronto Club and opened a bottle of champagne?" Nordheimer replied: "Why didn't you remind me—I would have taken you to lunch again. It might have had some effect." Much hilarity ensued. After an hour's discussion, the appeal court agreed to reduce Nordheimer's assessment to $1,500 an acre.

At the time of this assessment appeal, Nordheimer was 81 years old. He and his wife lived on at "Glen Edyth" until 1912, when they both died. A son continued to live there until 1924. The Goad's Property Atlas of the previous year shows the house still standing, but indicates the surveyed lots and roadways of a planned subdivision. By 1929, when "Glen Edyth" was torn down, some new houses had already been built on the old estate. A half-dozen years later, the huge neighbour of "Glen Edyth" to the west, "Ardwold," was also demolished, and its grounds subdivided. Today, the two estates are recalled only in the names of roadways through the subdivisions, while Mrs. Nordheimer's family is acknowledged in the name of Boulton Drive.

Looking from the inside out, through the Tudor-style gateway of Samuel Nordheimer's "Glen Edyth" on Poplar Plains Road. The gateway was about all the average citizen could see of the beautiful rambling estate. A coachman lived on one side, and the gardener on the other.

"Casa Loma"

Two photographs of the flamboyant Henry Pellatt—the one on the right taken when he was in his early forties, the one above about a decade later, perhaps 1912, after his knighthood (1910) and the construction of the "Casa Loma" stables, but before the onset of corpulence which so marked his features later in life. The photograph above shows the almost Oriental cast to his features, exaggerated by the moustache in a manner reminiscent of John Wayne's legendary performance as Genghis Khan. The "2" appearing on the Queen's Own Rifles badge dates from its founding, as the Second Battalion, Volunteer Militia Rifles of Canada, in 1861, following several years of controversy about the deployment of local militia forces. In 1863, it became the Queen's Own Rifles of Toronto, and in 1882 the Queen's Own Rifles of Canada.

Henry Mill Pellatt took literally the adage that "a man's home is his castle," and built a preposterous pile on the Spadina hill which has appalled architects and delighted tourists ever since (one recalls the words of Oscar Wilde: "vulgarity is the rich man's modest contribution to democracy"). Pellatt was one of the characters who strode like a colossus across the local stage; ironically, his worthwhile achievements as a pioneering financier, especially in the electrical business, have been all but forgotten by the public; remembered instead is the castle, which even he did not have the wealth to maintain.

Pellatt's father, Henry Senior, was a Bank of British North America employee who went into business as a money broker and financial agent with Edmund Osler, after the failure of the latter's employer, the Bank of Upper Canada. Young Henry, born in 1860, entered the firm when he was fifteen years old. Stories of his youth recount his prowess as a distance runner, and his prescience—especially the oft-repeated tale that he looked from his father's office window at the horse-drawn streetcars and predicted that one day they would be powered by electricity.

Osler and the Pellatts were deep in the mud and the land promotions which were so much a part of the settlement of the west. During one of these, in 1882, they found themselves associated with William Mackenzie (page 39), who became a partner in future ventures. The following year, in Toronto, the younger Pellatt sallied forth on a remarkable business career which lasted for 30 years. Though only 22 years old, he founded the Toronto Electric Light Company, a daring gamble with the virtually untried technology of steam-generated electricity and arc lights. Then, Thomas Edison's invention of the incandescent light bulb revolutionized the industry. In 1889, Frederic Nicholls (page 81) established the Incandescent Electric Light Company; electric traction became feasible, and a syndicate led by William Mackenzie obtained the Toronto street railway franchise and promised to electrify the system. In 1896, Pellatt and Nicholls merged their electricity interests and Nicholls founded the Canadian General Electric Company. Each capitalist bought shares in each other's companies. At the turn of the century, Mackenzie, Pellatt, Nicholls, and Senator Cox (president of the Bank of Commerce) began acquiring monopolistic franchises in Mexican and South American cities for transit and power companies. In 1901, it was Sao Paolo, in 1903 Rio de Janeiro—and eventually a vast web of interlocking companies merged in 1911 to form the company now called Brascan. Prompted by American coalminers' strikes which had disrupted their generators' fuel supply, Pellatt and associates raised a huge pool of capital and proceeded to tap the hydroelectric potential of Niagara Falls.

Meanwhile, Edmund Osler had opted out of his partnership with Henry Pellatt's father, formed another one with H. C. Hammond, and become a Conservative Member of Parliament. The Pellatts, father and son, regrouped as Pellatt & Pellatt, and plunged ever deeper into land speculations. Whereas the electrical ventures usually drew capital from the pool which eventually financed the Canadian Northern Railway, Pellatt & Pellatt generally relied on the funds of the Home Savings & Loan Company—"The Bishop's Bank"—for its land deals. By 1903, the firm was nearly a million dollars in debt to that little bank alone, but as long as the western land boom kept going, cash flow was never a problem.

During this period, three generations of Pellatts lived on Sherbourne Street. Henry Mill lived at number 559, his son Reginald was next door, and his father Henry Senior lived down the street. But Henry Mill Pellatt had grander dreams and sought out a suitable piece of land, at Walmer Road and Austin Terrace, on the bluff above Spadina Avenue. On a trip to England, he visited Nina de Pencier, granddaughter of the pioneer land-owner Col. Joseph Wells and owner of the 25 acres he wanted, and persuaded her to sell. The architect E. J. Lennox, whose previous commissions had included City Hall, began in 1909 to draw the plans for a composite castle. Over the next several years, the sketches evolved into the grand folly "Casa Loma"—an enormous residence of 98 rooms, including 30 bathrooms, a baronial entrance hall, an elevator, a swimming pool, a conservatory and formal gardens, passageways and tunnels; throughout the building, details of extraordinary plaster carving, stonework and wood fitting were rendered with craftsmanship which would rarely be seen again. All Toronto stood agape as the structure rose on the hillside. The deftness of the work—the intricacy with which the detailing and decoration were put together—was matched by the deft interweaving of Pellatt's viper's nest of companies.

Because of his ownership of the electric light system, Pellatt—like his associate William Mackenzie—maintained a sort of adversarial relationship with Toronto. A portion of the population defended him as they defended the capitalist system—questioning whether he operated in the public interest was tantamount to suggesting that public ownership might have its advantages. However, unlike Mackenzie, whose kingly monopoly was evident to all who stood in line in a blizzard to board a streetcar, Pellatt was able to portray himself as a great philanthropist and patriot.

The most public of Pellatt's enthusiasms involved the Queen's Own Rifles, the beloved Toronto volunteer rifle battalion which had seen action in the Fenian Raids and the Northwest Rebellion. Pellatt himself had joined the Q.O.R. when hardly more than a boy and rose through the ranks until in 1901 he assumed its command. He served in highly publicized military roles: major of the Queen's Jubilee Contingent in 1897; commander of the Canadian Contingent at the coronation of Edward VII in 1901; and aide-de-camp to Earl Grey, the governor general. He was

Sir H. M. Pellatt's Stables at "Casa Loma," Toronto, Canada

The postcard says "stables"—the elaborate buildings in the background—but the house in the foreground was occupied by Pellatt's only child, Reginald. The latter was a captain in the Queen's Own Rifles, and accompanied his father, seven other officers, and 600 regular members of the battalion, on the memorable 1910 excursion to Aldershot. On the voyage across the ocean on the White Star liner Megantic, *Reginald Pellatt and his fellow officers caught typhoid fever; all recovered but one—Lt. Gzowski, the grandson of Sir Casimir Gzowski of Bathurst Street.*

created a knight in 1905, and a Companion of the Royal Victorian Order (CVO) in 1910. In the latter year, he had his greatest triumph, when he took 600 members of the Queen's Own Rifles for parade drill in England.

Word of this impending circus had become public on January 21 of that year, when the newspapers announced that the British Army Council had accepted Pellatt's "patriotic and generous offer" to take his regiment to Aldershot. Although there was little hint at that stage of the coming "test of strength," Pellatt felt that the regiment should be prepared for all eventualities, and wanted to "afford evidence of the practical unity and cooperation of British military and Canadian militia" (in the event of war, under the laws then in effect, Canadian contingents were to fight under British command). On August 10, 600 members of the Q.O.R. marshalled and paraded at the Armouries on University Avenue; three days

Lady Mary Pellatt was born in Toronto, was educated at Bishop Strachan School, and married the young Henry Pellatt in 1882. Throughout her life, she was active in the Canadian Girl Guides, the Canadian Women's Club, the Women's Art Association, and the Toronto Women's Musical Club. She collapsed and died in April, 1924, in the midst of the charges and countercharges resulting from the Home Bank's failure.

The stables, formal garden, and greenhouse of "Casa Loma," photographed from the main house about 1913-14. There is still a pile of construction material in the foreground. Pellatt hoped, unsuccessfully as it turned out, to remedy the rather undignified situation wherein public roads—Austin Terrace and Walmer Road—chopped up his estate. Twenty years after this photograph was taken, the view looking north from "Casa Loma" had become distinctly suburban, as in the photograph on page 262.

later, they paraded there again in front of thousands of onlookers. Pellatt received an illuminated address, while Lady Pellatt accepted a gold medal surrounded by diamonds, for the regiment's pending 50th anniversary. The regiment departed by train for Lévis, Quebec, where they trained for a week, then boarded the steamer *Megantic* for Liverpool. On their arrival at the military encampment at Aldershot, they were greeted by 30,000 people and eight bands jamming the decorated streets. Over the next several days, they marched, manoeuvred, toiled, and drilled with the Sixth Infantry Brigade. On September 12, Pellatt and a group of officers were bidden to Balmoral Castle to meet the king. The next day, the entire Canadian contingent visited London "for sightseeing and popular entertainment" and were billeted at a school; finally, on the third of October, they returned in triumph, and marched from the North Toronto station through streets lined with cheering crowds to their dispersal point at the Armouries. Estimates put the cost of the excursion to Pellatt personally at $200,000.

Meanwhile, Pellatt had purchased a 600-acre model farm at King, and he began to speculate heavily in Toronto-area land. By "flipping" the land among his own companies, he was able to inflate the price, and for a time create the illusion that there was a demand for it. Much of his heretofore valuable stock in industrial operations like the Electrical Development Company and the Toronto Railway Company had been watered in order to finance ever bigger houses of cards, such as the Canadian Northern Railway. As the First World War dragged on, his land holdings became effectively worthless paper. After years of warnings, his empire collapsed with the Home Bank in 1923 (see also pages 63-65). Pellatt, at 64 years old, was ruined, as were many of the individual Home Bank depositors who had been gulled.

The corpulent, shambling Pellatt became a pathetic figure. "Casa Loma" was a valueless white elephant—a fact he had publicly admitted since a tax case in 1922. Lady Pellatt died in April, 1924; three months later, his art collection, which had been valued at $1.5 million, was sold off for a quarter of a million dollars. Mary Pickford considered, then rejected, using the castle as a movie set. Pellatt moved to the comparatively modest house at 78 Crescent Road, in Rosedale. "Casa Loma" stood vacant.

Pellatt still had a number of loyal business associates and supporters, and obviously a considerable amount of business experience. His 1930 *Who's Who* biography* lists him as president of three companies: Dominion Telegraph, Dominion Sewer Pipe, and West Dome Mining, vice-

*Curiously, Pellatt was one of the few men of his time who did not bother to list a religious denomination in his biography.

"Casa Loma" guides of the 1940s. This photograph is reproduced from a small folder handed out to "Casa Loma" visitors, published by the Kiwanis. The folder, in addition, had a picture of the castle and the following script: "This little Souvenir of your visit to Casa Loma is presented to you by . . . [the handwritten signature of the guide, in this case one Muriel Martin] . . . who had the pleasure of personally conducting you on your Tour. All of our guides at Casa Loma are University students. These girls thus help to finance their education and render both our guests and Kiwanis a very charming service. Any special acknowledgement of their courtesy you wish to show may be placed in the 'APPRECIATION PLATE' at the end of this Tour."

president of the O'Keefe Brewing & Malting Company (which had connections with the Home Bank dating well back into the nineteenth century), and director of a few others. The depression finally finished him, and he was forced to sell 78 Crescent Road as well as his country estate. In 1936, the Kiwanis Club began to renovate the shambles of the abandoned "Casa Loma" as a tourist attraction; on opening day, one of the first visitors, signing the guest book amidst the popping of reporters' flashbulbs, was the stooped old dreamer himself. He died on March 8, 1939, and his funeral, like so much of his life, was a great spectacle. Thousands lined the streets to watch his casket roll slowly by on a gun carriage, escorted by members of the Queen's Own Rifles, to the beat of their muffled drums and the tolling of the bells of St. James Cathedral.

The Palm Room, with guests enjoying afternoon tea. The rich man's habit of importing exotica such as ferns and palms had begun in the 1840s, a lifetime before this photograph was taken, with the advent of glass roofs and hot-water heating systems (see also the painting caption on page 248).

Wychwood Park

In 1873, a young artist named Marmaduke Matthews bought ten wooded, sloping acres of forest glade through which Taddle Creek ran above Davenport Road. He paid $4,000 for it, and built a yellow brick farmhouse near the edge of the escarpment, at the top of the steep slope overlooking Davenport Road, which offered a fine view southwards to the city and the lake. He named his little estate "Wychwood," after the Wychwood Forest of his Warwickshire childhood.

Scant information remains of Matthews's life. He travelled to New York at the age of 21, in 1860. He was known as a great admirer of the landscape "sketcher" Corot and "a follower of the French school of art"—translated into Canadian English of the time, he believed in the artistic ideals of the Barbizon School, and subsequently the *plein airisme* of Monet and the Impressionists. The historian Lucy Booth Martyn recorded that he had eloped with a colonel's daughter. He became secretary of the Ontario Society of Artists when it was formed in 1875. He had difficulty making a living, and was forced to hand-colour photographs—perhaps postcards for local publishers such as Warwick Bros. & Rutter; and, like many local artists, he solicited the largesse of the Canadian Pacific Railway in order to spend summers painting in the Rocky Mountains.

The Canadian Pacific Railway became one of the great patrons of landscape painting during the first decade after its completion. The railway's general manager, later its president, was Sir William Van Horne, a talented painter in his own right who saw the promotional possibilities in

encouraging photographers and artists to extol the glories of the newly accessible Rockies. Marmaduke Matthews was one of a group of artists, including local resident Frederick Bell-Smith, Thomas Martin, and Lucius O'Brien, who requested free travel passes—Bell-Smith went so far as to ask for a private car—in return for some mountain paintings. Matthews spent the summer of 1889 in the mountains and exhibited the completed works in Toronto that November—one of the paintings became a gift to Van Horne, although evidently it was not used for any promotional publications or railway-sponsored exhibitions, as was the case with works of other artists.

Meanwhile, Matthews was developing plans to turn his Wychwood estate into an artists' colony. He dammed Taddle Creek to form a pond, built a stable and some outbuildings to the northwest of his house, and set up a trust company which was to sell land to artists—the trust deed was registered with the city in 1891. By 1900 only one other house had been built there—that of Alexander Jardine, at number 22, built in 1877. The estate soon gained both a reputation as something of an artists' retreat, and some new residents. By 1909, when the city annexed the district, Wychwood was still private property, and retained its autonomy through its governance by a group of owners. By the outbreak of the First World War, there were about a dozen houses in the little community; since then, about another 35 have been built.

Shortly before Matthews's death in 1913, architect Eden Smith designed a house on seven lots for the solicitor and businessman E. E. A. Duvernet; it sprawls and rambles over 8,000-square-feet at 16 Wychwood, encircled by the community's road, and although it is certainly not

Number Six Wychwood, the "English farmhouse" built in 1874 by the artist Marmaduke Matthews. As the decades have passed, it has become covered with Virginia creeper and settled into the picturesque landscape, much like the cottages of his Warwickshire boyhood. Regrettably, the view of the house and surroundings from the perspective of this painting is blocked by a 1940s-style boxlike bungalow.

Wychwood Park's sylvan setting and reputation as a Ruskinian retreat attracted writers and artists like George Agnew Reid, a long-time member of the Toronto artistic community who was president of the Royal Canadian Academy from 1907-1910, and principal of the Ontario College of Art from 1912-1929. Born in Wingham in 1860, he was educated at the Ontario College of Art, and in Philadelphia and Paris. He painted large-scale, representational works, often on subjects which lent themselves to pathos and arcadian romanticism, and had titles such as Dreaming, Mortgaging the Homestead, The Foreclosure of the Mortgage, Family Prayer, and Berry Pickers. Inside the lobby of Old City Hall are his Pioneers mural panels, executed in 1898; in addition, he painted mural panels in such locations as the Arts and Letters Club and the Earlscourt Library. He was also the architect of record for the Ontario College of Art on McCaul Street, and of his own Wychwood house, "Upland Cottage," at number 81, built in 1906.

Eden Smith, the architect of several Wychwood houses, including the centrepiece, Morrow house, was born in 1860 in Warwickshire—the birthplace also of Wychwood's founder and guiding spirit, Marmaduke Matthews. He came to Canada when he was 25 and farmed in Minnedosa, Manitoba, for three years before moving to Toronto. Though working as a draughtsman in the office of Strickland & Symons, he quickly demonstrated design talent, and won a competition to design St. John's (Garrison) Church on Portland Street. He promptly formed his own architectural firm specializing in the design of churches and houses, the latter showing the influence of the work of English architects such as Edward Lutyens who went to great pains to fit their designs organically into the landscape. This in itself was a great departure for local residential design; Wychwood Park, though built up since with many houses and equally many styles, is still dominated by the loose, landscape-conscious style of his houses. The house he designed for himself is number five, built in 1906. Smith was not shy about his accomplishments, and wrote in his Who's Who listing that he "introduced English Domestic Architecture in Canada," and that he was "recognized as the leading residential Architect in Canada." A building of his which contrasts dramatically with the rambling and picturesque quality of his residential commissions is the Studio Building on Severn Street (page 237).

the sort of house one would expect in an artists' colony, it is a picturesque addition to the landscape. In the decades since, though dozens of unimpressive houses have filled up the empty spaces (there are four houses, numbered 51, 53, 55, and 57, on subdivided sections of the Duvernet lot), and even Matthews' fine farmhouse seems lost in the suburbia created by its neighbours, Eden Smith's masterpiece has remained Wychwood's centrepiece.

The long-time owners of 16 Wychwood were the Morrow family. Frederick Keenan Morrow was a self-made financier, who started as a bank clerk; he became chairman of the board of Loblaw's, and was director of numerous companies including Gooderham & Worts, the Bank of Toronto, the Consumers' Gas Company, and Maple Leaf Gardens. He donated $2 million for a new wing to St. Joseph's Hospital. At his death in May, 1953, when he was only 65 years old, he left an estate valued at more than $3 million.

His widow Edna lived on in the house for more than 30 years; its timelessness, and hers, became symbols of the style of Wychwood which some felt should be preserved. In 1983, when Mrs. Morrow was 93 years old, the presumed fate of the "Morrow mansion"—demolition, after her death—prompted city council to ask the Ministry of Citizenship to declare Wychwood a Heritage Conservation District. A few local residents complained that such a declaration violated the original spirit of Wychwood as an expression of the individualism of its artistic founders; others stressed that, because of the clutter of little houses, all Wychwood had left of its original sense of open space and landscape was reflected in the rambling Morrow mansion. The preservationists carried the day, and in 1985, the year Edna Morrow died, Wychwood was declared a Heritage Conservation District.

The original entrance to Wychwood by means of the steep roadway from Davenport Road is now blocked off, and there is access only from the other direction, via St. Clair and Wychwood avenues. Once past the Wychwood gate, the road itself is private property. Though susceptible to the sound of traffic on Davenport Road, and the clanging and occasional loudspeaker from the T.T.C. shops below, Wychwood remains a world apart from the city's hustle and bustle. Through the birdy trees one can see, far in the distance through the white, hazy light, the skyscrapers of downtown.

Just south of St. Clair, near the ravine along which the "Spadina" subway line now travels, stands "Lyndhurst Lodge," at 153 Lyndhurst Avenue. It was built for Ralph Connable, the namesake of little Connable Drive off Lyndhurst Avenue and Canadian manager of the Woolworth five-and-dime chain. Connable was "a Michiganer who has made all Canada his province, and the Cedarvale golf course his negation." Supposedly Ernest Hemingway lived in the house from January to May, 1920. A later, more settled resident was Nathan Louis Nathanson (right), whose Horatio Alger-type life saw him rise from newsboy to theatrical magnate. Born in Minneapolis in 1887, he came to Toronto at the age of twenty and first operated a concession at Scarboro Beach Park. In 1916, he purchased the old Majestic Theatre from Ambrose Small, renovated it, and reopened it as the Regent Theatre. He founded the Famous Players Canadian Corporation, and soon had a chain of theatres from coast to coast. His other business interests included, in association with J. P. Bickell and Charlie Querrie, the 1922 purchase of the old St. Patrick's Hockey Club; four years later, they sold it to Conn Smythe's Maple Leaf Gardens Corporation. He was a prominent benefactor of various Jewish charities, a staunch member of the Holy Blossom Synagogue congregation, and a supporter of the Toronto Symphony Orchestra; he was a member of the C.B.C.'s first board of governors, and continued as a governor until his death in 1943, when he was just 57 years old. Fifteen hundred mourners attended his funeral; the presiding rabbi came all the way from New York.

Deer Park & Moore Park

The connotations of the name "Deer Park" seem lost when one stands today at the daunting corner of St. Clair and Yonge. Since the last century, when that corner was the centre of Deer Park, the grass has become concrete and the trees high-rises. But the name survives in several shops, the United Church, and the public library branch.

The original Crown land grant, 200 acres on the west side of Yonge Street from St. Clair to Eglinton, belonged to Baron de Hoen. In the 1830s, a widow by the name of Agnes Heath purchased 40 acres of it, centred on Heath Street, which she named Deer Park Farm. She built her farmhouse near the corner of Deer Park Crescent and Heath Street West. Over twenty years later, the twelve-room O'Halloran Hotel opened at the southwest corner of Yonge and St. Clair. It was a modest but prosperous operation; guests could enjoy the football games played on the athletic field to the south, and in the evenings feed the deer which tamely wandered over from the nearby woods. From the 1880s until about 1910, it was called the Deer Park Hotel. A photograph of the corner of Yonge and St. Clair in 1912, taken from immediately in front of the hotel, shows a wild and woolly place: a few power and telephone poles, plank sidewalks and no curbs; on Yonge Street, a single streetcar track amidst an incredible slurry of mud; on the northwest corner, a fine, gingerbread-decorated "Ontario cottage," set well back from the street behind a board fence on a lot which appears also to have an orchard and several large fir trees; occupying pride of place in front of the Deer Park Hotel, almost on the boardwalk, is a cistern pump, probably for watering horses (see also overleaf).

Unlike much of what was to become Forest Hill Village, the Deer Park area around Yonge and St. Clair did not become exclusively an enclave of large, expensive homes. On streets like Oriole Gardens, DeLisle, and Heath, small houses were built, usually three or four to a surveyed lot, but with deep back yards to harbour, if desired, a cow and some chickens. Very few of the small Deer Park houses remain today—due to the proximity of the subway line, the area has been redeveloped with high-rises. The tiniest remaining house is probably the one at 59 Heath Street West.

The abandoned Moore Park Belt Line Station, about 1910, complete with a dog and wandering chickens. The station stood south of Moore Avenue, on the west side of the ravine called Spring Valley; the photograph looks south. The Belt Line was a speculative venture of a group of businessmen who grossly overestimated people's desire and ability to commute from the suburbs. When the real-estate boom of the early 1890s collapsed—even before the Belt Line was completed—it took with it the Belt Line Land Corporation. The railway opened anyway, in 1892, and was operated for a number of years by the Grand Trunk Railway. The writer C. S. Clark, in 1898, described the recently collapsed real-estate boom as "an insane speculative mania which sewered and blockpaved and sidewalked the grassy swards of the county of York's farm lands." He described the ruination of many lenders, "mainly widows and orphans, whose money was advanced through the agency of some rascally lawyer upon worthless second mortgages."

In sharp contrast, there are the two blocks of Forest Hill Road and Avenue Road south of Upper Canada College. They are within the old city limits, having been annexed before the First World War, along with the rest of Deer Park (and might now be considered in Forest Hill). A few of the residents of these large houses were: in the house at the southwest corner of Avenue Road and Heath, the piano manufacturer George Charles Heintzman; in the house at 36 Forest Hill Road, the solicitor James Bain (page 196); and, in the house at 61 Forest Hill Road, the Irishman Harry McGee, vice-president of Eaton's and the Royal Agricultural Winter Fair, and organizer of the Irish Regiment in Toronto during the First World War.

Immediately south of the Deer Park Hotel, on a piece of land adjoining St. Michael's Cemetery, were the maintenance barns of the Toronto & York Radial Railway's Metropolitan division. Before 1921, passengers wishing to travel north on Yonge Street beyond what were then the city limits boarded radial (interurban) cars, initially at the C.P.R. crossing, later at Farnham Avenue; after 1921, the section north to the city limits at Glen Echo loop became part of the Toronto Transportation Commission's one-fare system. Service by rail into the northern suburbs started very early: to Eglinton Avenue in 1885, York Mills in 1890, Richmond Hill in 1896, Newmarket in 1899, and Jackson's Point on Lake Simcoe in 1907.

East of Deer Park, and south of the Mount Pleasant Cemetery, is the Vale of Avoca. Around 1890, the land between there and the next ravine to the east—cheerily named Spring Valley—was subdivided and called Moore Park. The incentive for the subdivision was the availability of transportation, in the form of the Belt Line Railway, of which the Moore of Moore Park was managing director.

Born in Markham in 1844 of Irish parents, John Thomas Moore studied law, and subsequently became the deputy registrar of Waterloo County. But, as his obituary noted, "his genius was creative, and the East hampered him, so at the age of 37 he went West." In that period—the early 1880s—the Canadian Pacific Railway was under construction, and opening up the "Canadian Northwest" to immigration and business. Moore explored the countryside and eventually made some investments in the Red Deer area. He then returned to Toronto, where he "projected Moore Park as a real estate venture." He did not, however, give up his interests in Alberta; on the contrary, he returned to Red Deer at some point around the turn of the century and involved himself in business and political ventures, including membership on the city council and board of trade, the presidency of the Alberta Central Railway, the organization of the Western Electric Company—the town's utility—and, later, presidency of the Alberta Good Roads Association. Following Alberta's achievement of provincehood, in 1905, Moore became Red Deer's first member of the legislative assembly. A 1912 biography indicates that he

Looking north to the corner of St. Clair and Yonge, about 1914. The two-storey clapboard building past the garage was the old Deer Park Hotel (the guests were able to feed the deer which gathered there each evening), later known as Seller's Hotel. Originally built in 1862 as the O'Halloran Hotel, it had twelve modest rooms. The "automobile ambulance" was operated by a Deer Park resident, James Sercombe, who lived a couple of blocks to the north at 109 Lawton Boulevard. His advertisements said: "I have two 5-ton [solid-tired] Peerless Trucks always ready, day or night. Our Automatic Hoisting Bodies enable us to pick up any kind of wreck." Motorists in distress could telephone him at North 1804.

was a Liberal who would "banish the bar," a chartered accountant, *and* a resident of Red Deer. Throughout this period, he retained his interests in Moore Park. His residence there was called "Avoca Villa," a stone house with a wooden turret at the southeast corner of Inglewood and Rose Park avenues. He had started to build another house on a larger property on Inglewood, but it caught fire before completion and was not rebuilt. "Avoca Villa" was demolished in the 1960s.

Irrespective of his wanderings, Moore maintained the nickname "McLintock Moore of Avoca Vale" (according to his obituary) and was known far and wide for his splendid rose gardens. He set out to make Toronto into a "City of Roses," and imported a gardener, Mr. James Bryson, from Scotland, and roses from England and Ireland for his Moore Park estate. In 1913, he was the guiding spirit of the Rose Society of Ontario, and contributed $100 of the $115 which got it underway. The founding meeting was held "on a snowy winter day," February 19, 1913, in the drawing room of the home of Dr. and Mrs. Allan Baines at 228 Bloor Street West. A "who's who" of Toronto were members and patrons; the society even received a letter of congratulations from the world-famous English gardener, Gertrude Jekyll. John Thomas Moore was named lifetime honorary president. An indication of the scale of his Moore Park rose garden was the fact that at the Society's first summer show, held in July, 1913, at St. George's Hall, most of the roses to decorate that large space were his; several months later, at the fall show in the middle of October, his garden still produced enough blooms to decorate the Church House of St. Thomas on Huron Street. Moore died in June, 1917, at the age of 73.

As for the Belt Line Railway, it aspired to be a vehicle to "lift toiling men and women for at least a little while each day out of the grime and scent and smoke of the city" to the Highlands, where the air was clearer—the same sort of appeal held by the hill stations of the Raj. In short, it was a real-estate promotion. In the case of Moore Park, the station stood in Spring Valley, in the sylvan setting shown in the photograph on page 277. The little railway's *raison d'être*—the Belt Line Land Corporation—went bankrupt, but the line continued to be operated by the Grand Trunk Railway. Six trains a day in each direction chuffed in a great loop around the city, generally keeping within two miles of Queen's Park, but in the north and northwest part, above Eglinton Avenue, getting over four miles away. The salutory effect of the clickety-click and the rural scenery did not compensate commuters for the steep fares: a nickel per station, of which there were many.

Three of the northernmost subdivisions and stations on the Belt Line, advertised to the public in 1910 as the "Highlands of Toronto," were called Forest Hill, Fairbank, and Fairbank Junction, strung out like beads northwest of Eglinton Avenue and Bathurst, in what was truly countryside. The streets were unimaginatively laid into a grid: First, Second, and Third avenues ran east to west between Eglinton Avenue and the Belt Line. The north-south roads were also numbered: First Street, Second Street, and so on. The legacy of these streets is the rigid grid northeast of Dufferin and Eglinton, although the street names have been changed.

The popularity of the automobile would eventually have killed the Belt Line, as it killed the much more efficient and direct radial railways. As it happened, the rails in Moore Park were torn up during the First World War, their steel recycled for the war effort. In the 1960s, the Belt Line ended on the west side of Mount Pleasant Cemetery and was still used by the odd freight train servicing the factories along the edge of Forest Hill. Since then, the tracks have been removed and the right of way, still very much in evidence, is used by joggers and dogs and their walkers.

The wealthy inventor Frederick Mercer, who had discovered "many improvements in machinery which are revolving throughout the world," built the house called "Glendoveer" at 120 Inglewood in Moore Park (next page). Born in Tilsonburg in 1866, he had travelled extensively in search of additions to his art collection, and had lived for several years in London, England. Said to be fond of the country life, he owned other rural properties at Islington, Erindale, and Streetsville. When he built "Glendoveer" in 1908, it had five acres of grounds, and was the first house on the west side of what was then called Grace Terrace. Mercer had put in his own electric and water system, and consequently he frowned on the annexation of Moore Park by the city a few years later, as he stood to gain nothing by it. Decades later, the Italian actress Gina Lollobrigida lived for a time at "Glendoveer."

John Thomas Moore (1844-1917), "Toronto's Rose Lover" and the namesake of Moore Park.

M.KLUCKNER
©,1988

North Toronto

Old Ward Nine—the suburb called North Toronto—was the northernmost encroachment into the countryside of the Toronto city limits. In 1912, following a fifteen-year real-estate boom, the city annexed Moore Park and North Toronto, the latter comprising a number of real-estate subdivisions and a few little "towns" which straggled along Yonge Street south of York Mills. It was an area of scattered farms and fields on the one hand, a few board and brick storefronts, picket fences, vacant lots and strips of subdivisions on the other, a pastiche held together by the spine of Yonge Street. Today, the suburbs extend solidly in every direction, but before the Second World War years the march of the little blocks stopped not far outside the city limits.

As laid out in 1793, the land northwards from the lake, to what became Steeles Avenue, was called York Township; however, as the Town of York (Toronto) grew, York Township shrank, and was gradually fractured by the sort of secession that created Forest Hill Village. The 1912 annexation of North Toronto swallowed the area north to Glen Echo Road. Between there and York Mills lay the Hogg's Hollow ravine, with an eight percent grade which was the bane of the radial railway cars. To the west of Yonge Street was the so-called Spadina Heights, which the city had considered annexing, but decided against due to the high costs of servicing it. To the east was Leaside, and more York Township farmland.

One early landmark in the area was the house known as "Castlefield," with a driveway which is now Castlefield Avenue several blocks north of Eglinton Avenue. This strange-looking, turreted medievalism sat on a 200-acre property which James Price, Toronto's first city clerk, had purchased in 1835. It was only a few hundred yards north of the famed Montgomery's Tavern—the rallying point for William Lyon Mackenzie's abortive 1837 rebellion against the powers-that-were. The tavern, which the victorious patriots had burned to the ground to indicate their displeasure with its clientele, was in the "little town" that became Eglinton. Further south, there was another point of civilization at Davisville.

More settlers arrived to fill in the gap, so that in 1889 the two villages were able to incorporate as the Village of North Toronto. The Belt Line Railway and Mount Pleasant Cemetery separated it from Deer Park; Hogg's Hollow separated it from York Mills.

The centre of the village became the intersection of Montgomery and Yonge, where the Town Hall occupied the northwest corner; across the street, Oulcott's Hotel, a three-storey brick building with a mansard roof and a finely turned, wooden front porch and balcony, was built on the foundations of the razed Montgomery's Tavern. A notable early business was that of the potter John Davis, on the east side of Yonge Street between Millwood and Davisville. Two nearby deposits of clay provided him

(Next page) Semirural, unpaved Yonge Street north of Eglinton Avenue in the late 1920s—the electric railway cars of the Toronto & York Radial Railway's Metropolitan division connected the Glen Echo terminal with Lake Simcoe and Sutton. Stiff competition in the form of a car-crazy public forced the abandonment of the interurban line in 1930, although subsequently a segment of it between Glen Echo and Richmond Hill returned to service until its ultimate closure in 1948. Billboards proliferated in the many vacant fields on Yonge Street—the one shown, advertising the 1927 Ford Roadster, features a female passenger wearing a scarf like that of the Bugatti-fancier Isadora Duncan, who was throttled that year when her scarf became entangled in the spoked wheels of a roadster.

Mrs. Archibald Huestis, the owner of the house known as "Birchknoll" at 1184 Mount Pleasant Road on the south side of the Blythwood Ravine, was a lifelong fighter for social welfare and consumer causes. She was active with the Big Brothers and Big Sisters, the Local and National Councils of Women, the National Committee for Combating Venereal Diseases, the Provincial Committee for the Care of the Feeble-Minded, the Canadian Public Health Association, and the Toronto Playground Association.

Mrs. Huestis was most in the public eye immediately following the First World War, when, as the president of the Producers & Consumers League of Ontario, she led the fight against the prices of groceries and consumer goods. Life in Ontario at the beginning of 1920 had been "bathed in the sunshine of popular optimism," but a staggering inflation, blamed by some on the protective tariff, cut into the postwar prosperity. Typical food prices, exposed in a report by the Police Commission that September, yielded profits of from 200 to 1400 percent; rents soared; coal, which in 1918 had cost only $12 a ton, was going for $22 in October, 1920. Mrs. Huestis initially formed a group to boycott potatoes; it was so successful that, at the end of the summer, she formed the Producer's and Consumer's League, to tabulate prices and boycott other selected products. Almost immediately, the price of wool, sugar, and groceries began to decline; by the end of September, price slashing in the U.S. prompted similar actions in Canada, but not before the attorney general, under pressure from Mrs. Huestis and others, had charged the Wholesale Grocers' Association with having a secret price-fixing agreement. On October 6, 1920, A. W. Roebuck of the attorney general's department filed a court action to break the alleged grocers' combine. Controversy and an enquiry also followed the attempts of the Milk & Cream Producers' Association to increase local prices. The enquiries ended inconclusively, with more smoke than fire; prices, however, ceased to be controversial as they continued to fall. In May, 1921, the Globe did a price survey "from the window of a large downtown store," and reported that whereas the year before it had cost $22 to buy a hundred-pound bag of granulated sugar, the same sum would now buy the sugar, plus a twenty-four-pound bag of flour, fourteen pounds of cornmeal and fourteen of rolled oats, a bag of potatoes, five pounds of onions, eight of carrots, six of rice, two of butter, two of tea, two of coffee, two of cheese and two of prunes, two dozen eggs, four tins of tomatoes, two of peas and two of corn, one pail each of plum jam and marmalade, a one-pound tin of shortening, and ten cakes of soap. Prices had fallen all the way back to their 1913 levels! Regardless, it took more than three-quarters of a typical worker's wage just to pay for shelter, food, and fuel for a family of five.

with his raw material—one on Eglinton near the Don River, the other on his own property, near Millwood Road. Early accounts note that a horse, turning a paddle by walking in a circle around a vat, mixed the clay. Because of its location on Yonge Street, which had a radial railway service to the city, North Toronto's isolation soon ceased. A piped water system was operating before the turn of the century; its cordwood-fired steam pump filled a water tower on the high point of land near the well, at Roselawn west of Avenue Road.

Other centres of settlement were Davisville Avenue and Bedford Park Avenue, but they were separated by blocks of vacant land, and muddy, unpaved streets, open ditches, and boardwalks. Excess power from the steam pump and, later, from the radial railway's power system, ran a few arc lights, but there was a lot of darkness in the spaces between them.

These modest beginnings were overshadowed by the development plans of the Dovercourt Land, Building & Savings Company, which flaunted its credentials as "the largest owners and developers of real estate in Canada." Beginning in 1908, Dovercourt spent over $100,000 on 500 acres of what had been the Lawrence, Anderson, and Garland farms, occupying the land from Yonge to Bayview south of Lawrence Avenue. The company's advertisements for its new "Lawrence Park Estates" advised that it had spent $150,000 on developments and improvements and, following the plans of English landscape architect Walter Brooke, had created crescents, boulevards, "winding roads, cement walks, and bowling greens," on an attractive site 400 feet above Lake Ontario which had "pure air" and was "cool in summer, yet free from the lake winds in winter." "High class building restrictions," promised the advertisement, would ensure that only Toronto's prominent citizens built there.

Dovercourt's president, Wilfrid Dinnick, was only 34 years old when he started to develop the Lawrence Park property. He quite rightly considered his efforts to be a cut above those of many other land developers, and he was mortified by the fly-by-night practices of some companies, and the "horror stories" circulating about the frenetic western Canadian real-estate boom. Late in 1913, he travelled to the West and for five weeks examined the speculative mania there at first hand. On his return, he was interviewed by *Saturday Night* magazine, and reported "his disapproval of a certain form of subdivision business, its injury to Western real estate, in particular, and its permanent effect on prices there." The interview, published in the October 18th issue, gained him wide publicity, and local fears were soothed by his optimism about Toronto conditions. (He was right about the West; in some places, prices did not climb back to their 1912 levels until the 1950s.)

On the bank above Blythwood Road, just east of Mount Pleasant Road, stands an old farmhouse, one of two built about 1888 on Alexander Doig's twelve-acre lot. Research by the North Toronto Historical Society indicates that this house and its since-demolished twin, which stood some distance to the east, started life as flat-roofed, roughcast houses, and were later altered, with the addition of a bay and gables and decorative woodwork. Since 1892, the house has been owned by Robert Baillie and his descendants. Blythwood Road was originally called Victoria Avenue, and was to be known as Coronation Avenue in honour of the 1911 ascension to the throne of George V; Mrs. Jane Baillie lobbied the city to rename it Blythwood Road instead. The area along the Blythwood Ravine has until recently retained some rural character; an old house across the street from this one, at the northeast corner of Blythwood and Mount Pleasant, fell victim to the march of progress, and was demolished in the summer of 1987 to be replaced by "Six Custom Homes."

For a time, the Dovercourt Company continued to expand; in early 1914, it acquired an old Royal Bank building on King Street for $700,000; the following year, it acquired another 110 acres of North Toronto farmland. To maintain the enthusiasm, Dinnick published a book called *Tremendous Toronto*. Then the war intervened.

A fair number of the 50-foot lots in Lawrence Park Estates had been bought, for prices beginning at $20 per frontage foot, but few owners had built houses; the lots were easy to hold on to, though, as the tax system drew its heaviest levy from buildings, rather than from land. But at the end of the war, with most of Canada sinking into a depression, the tax law was changed so that unimproved land carried a greater share of the burden. The market was suddenly flooded, as people sought to unload the lots which they could no longer afford to keep. Prices plunged. The Dovercourt Company itself, which had been hanging on by its toenails, was forced in May, 1919, to auction all of its unsold properties for a pittance.

Some of the other landmarks of the old Village of North Toronto fared rather poorly, too. Oulcott's Hotel had lost its liquor license in 1908, when the residents of the village used their Local Option vote to "ban the bar." The hotel struggled on until 1923; subsequently, the building became the North Toronto post office, and was demolished several years later for the new post office which now occupies the site. The old Town Hall was demolished in 1931, around the time the John Davis & Son pottery shop closed its doors. The crossroads of Eglinton and Yonge are, today, a forest of tall office buildings and apartments; there has been heated debate over whether Eglinton Avenue is far enough north to be the second crosstown subway line, as opposed to Lawrence Avenue or even Sheppard.

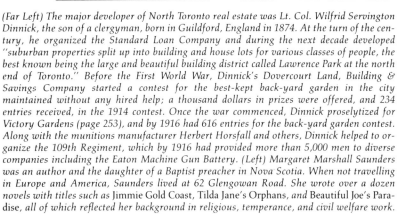

(Far Left) The major developer of North Toronto real estate was Lt. Col. Wilfrid Servington Dinnick, the son of a clergyman, born in Guildford, England in 1874. At the turn of the century, he organized the Standard Loan Company and during the next decade developed "suburban properties split up into building and house lots for various classes of people, the best known being the large and beautiful building district called Lawrence Park at the north end of Toronto." Before the First World War, Dinnick's Dovercourt Land, Building & Savings Company started a contest for the best-kept back-yard garden in the city maintained without any hired help; a thousand dollars in prizes were offered, and 234 entries received, in the 1914 contest. Once the war commenced, Dinnick proselytized for Victory Gardens (page 253), and by 1916 had 616 entries for the back-yard garden contest. Along with the munitions manufacturer Herbert Horsfall and others, Dinnick helped to organize the 109th Regiment, which by 1916 had provided more than 5,000 men to diverse companies including the Eaton Machine Gun Battery. (Left) Margaret Marshall Saunders was an author and the daughter of a Baptist preacher in Nova Scotia. When not travelling in Europe and America, Saunders lived at 62 Glengowan Road. She wrote over a dozen novels with titles such as Jimmie Gold Coast, Tilda Jane's Orphans, *and* Beautiful Joe's Paradise, *all of which reflected her background in religious, temperance, and civil welfare work.*

(Right) James Edmund Jones was also the issue of a clergyman. When not working as a police magistrate at City Hall in Toronto, he wrote a bewildering variety of books melding his favourite themes of singing men and the outdoor life of canoeing, camping, and snowshoeing. He compiled trail manuals and was an authority on songs and "upon work among young men and boys." Some of his publications were In Fane and Forest, Songs for Worship, *and* Mushrooms, Ferns and Grasses; *he also called on his police experiences to write* Pioneer Crimes and Punishments, *which can still be found without much difficulty in old-book stores and on library shelves. He edited the annotated edition of the Book of Common Praise for the Church of England in Canada and compiled the University of Toronto's songbook. He lived at 181 Dawlish Avenue. (Far Right) James Gordon Weir, who lived at the northwest corner of Blythwood and Mount Pleasant Road, was a member of the family which had owned the land extending from Yonge Street to Bayview, east of the old town of Eglinton. After a Harvard education, he joined the* Financial Post *in 1909, won a D.S.O. for his command of the Second Canadian Machine Gun Company during the First World War, and in 1921 helped to establish the firm of McLeod, Young, Weir & Company, investment bankers.*

Forest Hill Village

"St. Timothy & All the Eatons" church—officially, the Timothy Eaton Memorial Methodist Church—on St. Clair Avenue between Dunvegan and Warren. The postcard does not do justice to the size and fine sense of proportion of the building, which was erected beginning in 1910 at the insistence of Timothy Eaton's widow. Before the church was built, the congregation was known as the New Methodist Church on Avenue Road hill.

Forest Hill has a mystique and reputation extending far beyond its boundaries. Most of it *looks* considerably more exclusive than jumbled Rosedale, although the two neighbourhoods share the same substantial houses, walls and gates, weathered curbs and sidewalks, and well-maintained lawns and gardens. In Forest Hill, the houses are usually set further back from the street—they seem to dominate the landscape on the long, straight streets, whereas in Rosedale the houses hunker down amongst the shrubberies, and crowd more closely together.

The area that is now Forest Hill Village just missed the city's big annexation frenzy. In roughly three decades, starting early in the 1880s, Toronto expanded dramatically from its original city limits of Dufferin, Bloor, and the Don River (and the strip between the lake and Queen Street, east of the Don). Deer Park was annexed in 1908, and North Toronto in 1912, but as the future Forest Hill Village's topography was challenging and its population sparse, the city decided to leave it be. It remained as a part of York Township, and was generally referred to either as Spadina Heights, or sometimes as the Baldwin Estate.

About 500 people lived in Spadina Heights in 1910, mainly in the southern part. On its undulating checkerboard were woodlots, dairy farms, the occasional grain field and vegetable garden, little houses and barns, and a few large edifices such as Upper Canada College. Ravines laced its borders, and frog ponds dotted its hollows; deer and cows-at-large completed the scene.

The local equivalent of "squire" was the farmer Lawrence Baldwin, born in a farmhouse at Avenue Road and Heath Street. His family were the big landowners in the area for nearly a century: his house stood at the junction of Old Forest Hill Road, Dunvegan, and Kilbarry, his haybarn was on Russell Hill Road, and he farmed the land in between.

The Township built a two-room schoolhouse, which opened in 1910, because local children whose parents did not wish them sent away to board had either to cross a ravine to the west to get to a school, or else journey two miles to another at Bathurst and Glencairn.

Over the next several years, settlers continued to trickle into the area. More and more of the little surveyed lots were taken up; the new residents wanted the sort of modern urban facilities, such as water, electricity, and gas, which would have been available to them if they had bought a lot in, for instance, Lawrence Park Estates in North Toronto. Their appeals to the officials who ran sprawling York Township fell on inefficient ears; however, York Township and the City of Toronto did manage to sign an agreement in 1916 whereby the latter would supply water to the former; three years later, another agreement provided electricity to the area. These amenities were by no means universally desired—many who lived in other parts of York Township were willing to forego them in return for an independent life with low taxes. However, the new residents of Spadina Heights, who were building substantial houses, even wanted the roads to be paved.

Talk of secession began first in the area to the north. York Township was simply too big—it stretched from the Humber River to Scarborough and northwards almost to Thornhill—to be governed by its five part-time commissioners. In the summer of 1922, the residents to the north voted to secede and establish North York.

Although Spadina Heights had grown somewhat by the time of the northerners' secession, it was still a small country town. The commercial centre was the corner of Spadina and Lonsdale roads, a block north of the city limits; there, a drugstore, a hardware, and two groceries, one with a post office, occupied the four corners. Further north on Spadina, at its junction with Eglinton Avenue and the Belt Line Railway, were a few more stores, some woodyards and a cement plant. Those residents with businesses to operate or land to sell recognized that Spadina Heights was at a standstill; they formed a Ratepayers' Association, and tried to convince Toronto to annex the district. The city wasn't interested—its expansion fever had run its course a decade before—so the Spadina Heights ratepayers organized with like-minded individuals to the west and set out ambitiously to incorporate the large area stretching all the way from Upper Canada College to Mount Dennis, including the areas known as Silverthorn, Fairbank, and Oakwood, as York City. The Belt Line, which ran through the area on a line parallel with and a few blocks north of Eglinton Avenue, would provide access to an industrial tax base, and some local employment. Although the proposition looked positive, and had the backing of many of the local activists, on referendum day it was rejected by both the Spadina Heights and the Mount Dennis residents. In the former, the vote against was eight to one.

The Spadina Heights ratepayers, led by their "squire" Baldwin, then decided their best move was to incorporate themselves as a separate municipality. Throughout the summer of 1923, the group had no trouble gathering signatures on a petition in favour of this procedure. When two-thirds of the ratepayers had signed, York County Council was required by the Municipal Act to incorporate the new municipality. Accordingly, on December 15, 1923, Forest Hill Village, named for the estate of one John Wickson, gained its independence.

Six days later, nominations closed for the first Forest Hill Village council. The residents were so much in agreement on the direction their new corporation should take that only five nominees stood for the five available council positions. Lawrence Baldwin was acclaimed as reeve.*

The council maintained its unanimity when it addressed the first order of business—zoning to protect the village's emerging refined character. At their second meeting, members scrutinized the language on a zoning bylaw to make sure that not only would all new construction be limited to residential, but that residences would be limited to detached and semi-detached houses only. Later amendments detailed lot setbacks and design

*The uncontested first election in Forest Hill Village is certainly not unique in Canada. Elsewhere in the Toronto area, the ratepayers of Swansea found themselves sufficiently like-minded that many of its electoral offices were filled by acclamation. In 1906 in Oak Bay, a prestigious suburb of Victoria, British Columbia, ratepayers first attempted to be annexed by the nearby city, then arranged for incorporation, and then, "to avoid the expense and annoyance of an election," arranged that only enough names be nominated to fill the available council seats.

Upper Canada College, Toronto, Canada

styles, as well as stipulations on square-footage and cost. This policy of exclusivity served to attract home builders, and the population tripled to 6,300 in the first eight years after incorporation. In the 1930s, when many districts within Toronto and its suburbs were wallowing in debt and foreclosing on owners for unpaid taxes, Forest Hill Village was so untouched, insulated, and forward-looking that it passed two remarkable bylaws: the first in 1933, that all new houses must have their front elevations designed by an architect; the second, in 1936, that a board of architects be established to approve all new designs. What dissension there was occurred over whether the existing industry along the Belt Line should be removed; later, when developers attempted to build apartments along the fringes of the area, the village's "one-family" restrictions were challenged in the courts, and eventually rescinded.

Upper Canada College opened at its new location on a 30-acre tract in the rural northern suburbs in October, 1891. The college purchased another two dozen acres in 1901. The edifice shown here which was its old main building had to be demolished because of structural problems, and was replaced, in 1960, by a new building in the same style.

Dr. Augusta Stowe-Gullen, who lived at 461 Spadina Road, was the first woman in Canada to complete the full course in medicine at a Canadian university and to graduate from a Canadian university—the Toronto School of Medicine, Victoria University, in 1883. Her mother, Dr. Emily Stowe, was the first Canadian woman to study medicine and practice in Canada, but she had taken her training in New York City. In addition to her work on children's diseases, Dr. Stowe-Gullen was a tireless supporter of women's rights, and served terms as president of the National Council of Women, the Canadian Suffrage Association, and the International Suffrage Alliance. For a dozen years, she represented the medical profession on the University of Toronto Senate.

In the house at 181 Warren Road lived the contractor Harry Rotenberg. Born in Poland in 1884, he came to Toronto when he was eleven years old; after finishing school he entered the steamship agency and financial business of his father. In 1910, he became a partner with Louis Yolles; Yolles & Rotenberg became one of the largest contractors in the country. Their Toronto-area construction contracts included the Butterick Publishing Company Building, the Hobberlin Building, the Woolworth Building and several motion picture theatres. He was president of a variety of real-estate development and construction companies, including the Federal Building Corporation, the Albert Bay Company, the Richmond Bay Company, and the 347 Bay Street Corporation (347 Bay Street is at the southwest corner of Bay and Temperance, not far south of the corner of Bay and Richmond). Rotenberg was a well-known figure in Toronto's Jewish community, and served as the chairman of the Federation of Jewish Philanthropies and as a trustee of Holy Blossom synagogue.

Those who were attracted by Forest Hill's quiet streets in the years before the Second World War included: at 403 Russell Hill Road, the piano manufacturer Charles Theodore Heintzman; at 404 Russell Hill Road, the radio manufacturer James Hahn, who was president of the local De Forest Crosley Limited and chairman of the board of its parent, the Magnavox Company of Chicago; at 146 Warren Road, Massey-Harris president Thomas Findley; at 237 Warren Road, the *Star*'s owner Joseph Atkinson; at 248 Warren Road, the miner and oilman Joseph Errington, whose activities in Sudbury contributed to the creation of International Nickel Company; at 120 Forest Hill Road, the architect John Pearson, of the nationally renowned firm Darling & Pearson; at 126 Forest Hill Road, the president of Canada Wire & Cable, Herbert Horsfall (page 104); at 101 Old Forest Hill Road, the barrister J. D. M. Spence, partner with Angus MacMurchy (page 255); at 3 Hillholme Road, Main Johnson, who was variously a reporter for the *Star*, principal secretary to Newton Rowell, radio broadcaster, freelance writer, and publicity manager for the Robert Simpson Company; at 10 Ava Crescent, the automobile dealer A. A. Walker (page 70); and, on Spadina Road, Frederick "Big Daddy" Gardiner, the development-oriented first Metro chairman, namesake of the Gardiner Expressway along the lakefront, and reeve of Forest Hill Village for the twelve years before 1949, Even John Labatt, heir to the beer fortune, who was kidnapped from his automobile somewhere between Sarnia and London in the summer of 1934, was released, blindfolded, in Forest Hill Village!

William French's history of Forest Hill, *A Most Unlikely Village*, paints a picture of a peaceful, uncomplicated little suburb: the village's assessor, Harry Tattle, also served as quarantine officer, dog license inspector, weed inspector, and truant officer; a volunteer fire department was sufficient until 1937; in the 1920s, Forest Hill had but a single police constable—a rejected (because he was too short, being only five feet ten inches) Toronto police recruit named Gordon Fraser—whose Coulson Avenue house doubled as the police station, and who, when not patrolling in his cruiser, was on call for the balance of the 24-hour day. Fraser retired as police chief in 1956.

The two schools that, for over a century, have epitomized "proper" education, established themselves in Forest Hill before the 1923 incorporation of the village. Upper Canada College arrived first; it was founded in 1829, under a Royal Charter granted by King George IV, and originally occupied the block bounded by King, Simcoe, John, and Adelaide streets, directly north of the old Government House in downtown Toronto. As the hurly-burly of the expanding city militated against the desired studious and collegial atmosphere, the college's governors purchased 30 acres in the rural northern suburbs, just beyond the boundary of Deer Park. To attend the opening ceremony in October, 1891, a trainload of celebrants journeyed from the smoky city on the yet-to-be-officially-opened Belt Line Railway. The other major edifice in old Forest Hill, a few blocks to the west, is Bishop Strachan School, on Lonsdale Road between Russell Hill and Dunvegan, which sees itself as being to the education of girls what Upper Canada College is to the education of boys. Bishop Strachan is the oldest independent girls school in the country, having been founded in 1867. It is an Anglican institution, as was its stern namesake; initially, it occupied the "Bishop's Palace," Strachan's former home on Front Street between York and Simcoe. Debrett's *Guide to the Canadian Establishment* (Methuen, 1983) unkindly described its graduates as "wily maidens who can turn a curtsy into an effortless bob at debutante balls, then marry promptly and well."

In recent years, Forest Hill Village has acquired a reputation on two counts. The first concerns the number of Jewish residents, who were attracted to the area in the 1930s reportedly because of the good school system. Indeed, statistics show a steady growth in their share of the populace—from eleven percent in 1941, to forty-five percent in 1965. The other is of a kind of mass eccentricity, demonstrated particularly in 1955, when Forest Hill Village successfully took Metro Toronto Council to court to stop the fluoridation of its water supply, and thereby achieved national notoriety. The Supreme Court finally ruled that Metro did not have the legal or moral right to force fluoride into every member of the community.

Just inside the old boundary of Forest Hill Village stands the grand home, built in 1927, of Sigmund Samuel (1868-1962), who at age sixteen joined his father's scrap metal business, Samuel & Son, Importers and Dealers in Iron, Steel and Metals. Samuel spent much of his time in England and maintained another house near Hyde Park in London. He was a benefactor of diverse institutions including the Royal Ontario Museum, the University of Toronto (witness the Sigmund Samuel Library on Hart House Circle), and the Hebrew Benevolent Society. As well, he was active in Conservative politics—both in Canada and in England—and unsuccessfully ran for a seat in Staffordshire. His interests in art were reflected in a book he wrote, entitled The Seven Years' War in Canada *(Ryerson Press, 1934), "a historical scanodrama including 106 rare pictures as illustrations which could only have been chosen by an art connoisseur." His autobiography, called* In Return, *was published by University of Toronto Press in 1963, the year after his death.*

Members of the Eglinton Hunt Club—representing what Oscar Wilde described as "the unspeakable in pursuit of the inedible"—on Bathurst Street north of St. Clair at the Klondyke Ravine, probably about 1910. (Next page) A long-nosed wolfhound, woman and Cord automobile in the parking lot of the Eglinton Hunt Club, during what was elsewhere called the Dirty Thirties. The clubhouse and a judging ring were located at the southeast corner of Avenue Road and Roselawn, just north of Eglinton Avenue. The photograph was taken around the end of the 36-year period during which G. W. Beardmore (1851-1934) was master of foxhounds. In his business life, Beardmore owned a leather tanning company and had been president of the National Life Assurance Company, but horses were his passion—along with his role at the Eglinton Hunt Club, he was president for eighteen years of the Canadian Horse Show Association. A bachelor with a bluff and genial bearing, he was described as "a pleasant combination of the Canadian pioneer and the English squire type"; his home— "Chudleigh" on Beverley Street—now serves as the Italian consulate. The Hunt Club had acquired the Eglinton-Avenue Road property after World War One, and built an indoor arena, stables, a show ring, and a clubhouse. Members also drag-hunted in the vicinity. As the city grew out to meet it, the club decided to move further afield, and sold the property after the Second World War.

293

The Islands

Each time a map is made of the Toronto Islands, it shows a different landform, for they are truly *terra infirma*, a series of sandbars which have been blown apart by winds, dredged, filled, sculpted, and held together by grass, trees, shrubs, and seawalls. The weight of cottages, cottagers, and picnickers perhaps helped to hold them down, for there was no place in the Toronto area which was so popular with so many for so long.

The Islands originated as part of the Scarborough Bluffs which were eroded and moved westward by lake currents. At the time of the founding of the city of Toronto, the Islands formed a single long, narrow hook, the "eye" surrounding a marshy, mosquito-infested pool at Ashbridge's Bay, the "point" almost touching the shoreline at the Western Gap. In the early 1790s, colonial officials, including the lieutenant governor, Colonel Simcoe, saw in the sheltered bay an ideal harbour; they established the town of York at the eastern end of the bay and built a blockhouse on the mainland side of the Western Gap. With wry humour, Simcoe named the island side of the channel—a low, scrub-covered sandy spit—Gibraltar Point. About a decade later, in 1806, his successor erected a lighthouse to mark the entrance to the harbour.

Rising lake levels and bad weather dominated the history of the Islands for the next several decades. The peninsula first became separated from the mainland during an 1828 storm, which opened the eastern ship channel; the storm's effects were enhanced by the same cyclical high water which has recently plagued the Great Lakes. Declining water levels, plus different currents and winds, subsequently refilled the eastern channel with sand, making the Islands once again a peninsula; twenty-five years later, however, severe weather reopened the breach and shifted the sand around to such an extent that it almost closed the Western Gap, with potentially disastrous consequences to the city's shipping business, as well as its water intake and sewage outfall, which shared the bay (see page 168). Civic authorities hastily erected a wooden breakwater, which was washed away for good, and replaced by a 500-yard-wide channel, in a spring storm in April, 1858. The Islands received better stabilization in 1880, in the form of a concrete breakwater; two years later, the dominion government dredged the eastern channel and rebuilt the breakwater, permanently separating the Islands from the mainland. A further modification occurred after a 1906 shipwreck in the western channel—on the recommendation of J. G. Sing, the district engineer for the department of public works, the channel was redredged 1,300 feet to the south.

Four of the dozens of postcards which cast the Toronto Islands in a golden light. The photograph of the lagoon at the bottom left is perhaps the earliest of the four, having been taken about 1898. A favourite spot for spooning under the June moon, it seems to contemporary eyes idyllic and innocent; however, the goings-on attracted disapproval from the city's Sabbath-sayers and allegedly ruined many a maiden's reputation. Three of these four cards were published by John Valentine & Sons of Dundee, Scotland, who clearly had difficulty with the rower Ned Hanlan's name.

Boat Landing at Hanlan's Point, Toronto, Canada

12513—At Island Park, Toronto, Canada.

The Park, Hanlan's Point, Toronto, Canada.

Hanlan's Point at night, Toronto, Canada.

In the mid-nineteenth century, the Islands were home to a successful commercial fishing community, supplying the Toronto market with its piscatorial protein. City residents escaping the sultry summer heat began to visit them by rowboat and small ferry; soon, entrepreneurs built hotels and cottages and created a small resort community. The city gained ownership of the Islands in 1867, and embarked on a plan of improvements: over the next several years, workers planted thousands of trees, dredged lagoons, surveyed the land into five-acre lots, and issued recreational leases to potential cottagers (the intent of the last did not at first sink in, as the few lessees were content to live in tents and shacks, so the city introduced a stipulation that all lessees must, within two years, build "an ornamental summer residence" worth at least $500). Soon, a picturesque, ramshackle cottage community had sprung up on Centre Island. Near the northerly point of the old "hook," at what became known as Hanlan's Point, a group of entrepreneurs built rental accommodation and an amusement ground. One of the earliest of the big hotels was that of the fisherman John Hanlan, who had settled there in the 1840s, and whose son Ned became a world-champion rower. In 1880, the Royal Canadian Yacht Club moved its clubhouse to the Islands from the mainland. That year, city council announced plans to develop a public park on Centre Island, while continuing to issue cottage leases elsewhere. Other additions soon followed: Erastus Wiman, a former alderman, gave the city two floating bathhouses in 1881; on the west side of Gibraltar, or Hanlan's, Point, a commercial bathhouse known as Turner's operated for years (the baths' major function was to provide privacy for individuals, mainly women, who because of contemporary standards of decency and propriety could not bathe in public). At the southwesterly corner of Centre Island, John Ross Robertson built the Lakeside Home for Little Children. A schoolhouse, waterworks, a lighthouse, and a few stores were established next to the Centre Island cottage community. The St. Andrews-By-The-Lake Church was built in 1884—today the only remnant of the old cottage community.

To move the human horde back and forth, a group of businessmen formed the Toronto Ferry Company in 1890, and operated a fleet of a dozen ferries (most of which were named for flowers) from wharves at Dufferin, Brock, Yonge, and George streets; one of the ferryboats, the *Trillium*, was recently rescued from decrepitude, restored, and put back into service following a campaign led by historian and writer Mike Filey. To expand the number of attractions on the Island, the ferry company in

1897 took over the Hanlan's Point amusement park and built a stadium there.

While the Islands' relative isolation, caused by the difficulty of access to them, was an attraction for some, others saw it as a lost business opportunity. The idea of a swing-span bridge across the Western Gap was first mooted in 1891; in 1893, the proposal, now expanded to high-level bridge, became part of the Sunday streetcar debate. Mayor Fleming, later the general manager of the Toronto Railway Company, made streetcar service to the Island a condition of the third (and successful) Sunday streetcar plebiscite, but the Toronto Railway Company never acted on the plan.

* * *

One of the most interesting and amusing (though possibly least accurate) descriptions of the goings-on at Island Park appears in C. S. Clark's lurid 1898 expose *Of Toronto The Good*. Clark described Sundays in the park—the Sally Ann holding forth "with sacred words adapted to the tunes of different waltzes and bar-room songs"—and recounted the sad tale of Joseph Bayley, bandmaster of the Queen's Own Rifles, who was arrested while playing hymns at Hanlan's Point on a Sunday afternoon and subsequently fined for "unlawfully pursuing his worldly calling" in violation of the Lord's Day Act.

Clark also dwelt at length on the alleged seductions of young women who spent their summer afternoons at Island Park. According to Clark, "The Island is simply an open-air place of prostitution or charnel house, a *rendez-vous* not only for prostitutes but for presumably respectable girls." Young men in rowboats hung around the jetties on the Island, and sweet-talked girls into returning with them unchaperoned to the city. Kind souls claimed that in their innocence, the women were beguiled; as far as Clark was concerned, "90 percent" of the single women who went to Island Park or out on boats, unaccompanied by their parents, knew exactly what they were doing, and were "extremely willing victims." Regardless, their reputations were ruined.

The boathouses around the foot of York Street were rented out as summer cottages and "mostly used for immoral purposes." Young men liked the idea of living on the lake, enjoying the cool evenings, eating at restaurants or *al fresco*, and using their airy residences, which were furnished "in an imitation of camp life," for seductions. The seducers were well-paid young clerks and office workers, their victims "shop girls" who landed in rowboats at the boathouses, and were lured inside. Gossip told of one young woman named Sadie Lavelle who was ruined by two brothers—"notorious seducers" who rented one of the boathouses—and died in shameful circumstances on Terauley [Bay] Street in The Ward. In another tale, "the wife of a well-known citizen made a visit to the lakefront . . . and while in a boathouse with her paramour had a $55 diamond ring stolen." A young woman enticed inside, said the scandalized Clark, "rarely leaves without taking a drink of liquor," and even if she managed to repel all boarders, she still had to run the gauntlet of curious onlookers when she left.

Any man who rented a boathouse on the lakefront and furnished it, especially with a camp bed, had his motives questioned. The *Empire* was quoted by Clark as commenting that the rampant immorality along the waterfront brought into question the whole system of boathouse rentals; respectable Esplanade property owners, according to the newspaper, had trouble stopping the practice, for the more barriers they raised the more ingenious the tenants became, in accordance with the adage that "stolen fruit is the sweetest."

* * *

To administer the Islands, city council maintained a six-alderman standing committee which became a fount for long-range development plans. A number of their proposed additions and changes were accomplished, including more lagoons, a fish pond near the Water Works, a bandstand on Centre Island, an athletic field on Olympic Island and, in 1909, the designation of "Hanlan's Memorial Park" in honour of the recently deceased rower. That August, Hanlan's Hotel and most of the amusement area there burned to the ground; subsequently, the amusements and stadium were rebuilt.

Early in the 1920s, an entrepreneur named Lawrence Solman, who owned the Royal Alexandra Theatre, bought the Toronto Ferry Company and the Hanlan's Point amusement park. The Maple Leafs baseball team played at the stadium at the latter. Solman cannily sold the ferry system and amusement park to the city three years later and promptly built Maple Leaf stadium on the mainland side of the Western Gap, near the foot of Bathurst Street, which became the new home of the baseball team and robbed Hanlan's Point of one of its attractions. The amusement park

The location of the ship channels to the east and west of the Toronto Islands is the result of the work of J. G. Sing, district engineer for the department of public works. After the 1911 founding of the Harbour Commission, Sing became its consulting engineer and was one of the members of an advisory board that reported to city council on the city's future pure water needs and chose the locations of new water intakes and sewage outfalls.

Cottages along the shore; girls in World War One-era bathing costumes of heavy cotton and silk, caked with sand and itchy in the heat.

Cottages occupied much of Centre Island, clustered together on narrow roadways with names such as Hooper, Oriole, Cibola, Chippewa, Pawnee, Cherokee, Mohawk, Ongiara, and Shiawassie, all now vanished. The only remnant of that old community is the Island Church, built in 1884. Below are a few of the people who, in the twenties and thirties, had summer cottages on Centre Island. Top row, left: Arthur Eastmure lived at 34 Cheritan Avenue but passed his summers at his "Oriole Lodge"; born in Toronto in 1894, he served overseas with the Canadian Expeditionary Forces and upon his return entered the Casualty Company of Canada—the insurance and financial business established in 1884 by his father. Centre: Percival Mitchell lived at 8 BinScarth Road in Rosedale, and had a summer home on Lakeshore Road. An electrical engineer specializing in hydroelectric developments, he was also an authority on housing and town planning matters and served as managing director of the pioneering Toronto Housing Company (page 184). He married Heasell Dill Holgate, and together they grew roses; Mitchell wrote pamphlets on roses, was president of the Toronto Horticultural Society from 1916-1918, and had an elaborate garden even at his Island cottage, as shown in the drawing on the next page. Right: Douglas Stewart Murray, who lived at 75 Heath Street East, was president and general manager of the Murray Printing Company on Spadina Avenue; beginning in 1961, the Southam company began to purchase shares in Murray Printing and eventually took it over; its fate became national news in 1976, when its largest client, Eaton's, abruptly cancelled future editions of its mail-order catalogues. Bottom row, left: Arthur Moysey, a mining financier, had a cottage on Lake Shore Road; he married the daughter of Orange Jull, who was the inventor of the rotary snow plow. Centre: James Dixon Trees, of 9 Meredith Crescent in Rosedale and Lake Shore Road on Centre Island, was president of the family's tack business, Samuel Trees & Company. Right: Kellogg Sinclair MacLachlan lived in Montreal, managed pulp and paper interests in the Maritimes, but in the summer returned to his boyhood home, Toronto, and stayed in a cottage on Centre Island. During the Great War, he was supervisor of the production and distribution of explosives for the Imperial Munitions Board; his associations with the Gooderham family, who allowed some of their distilling facilities to be converted to the production of the components for high explosives, led him to marry one of George H. Gooderham's daughters.

An Avenue in Centre Island, Toronto

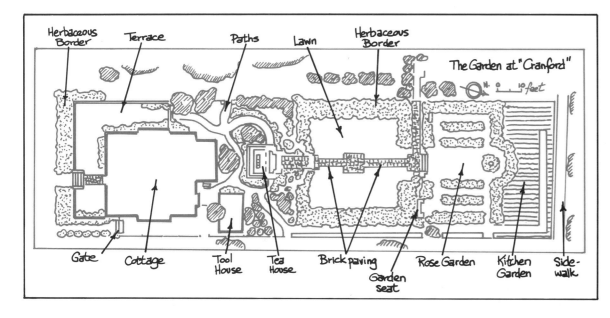

The Garden at "Cranford"

Herbaceous Border — Terrace — Paths — Lawn — Herbaceous Border

N 0 10 feet

Gate — Cottage — Tool House — Tea House — Brick paving — Garden seat — Rose Garden — Kitchen Garden — Side-walk

"Cranford," Percival Mitchell's Island cottage, as depicted in a drawing adapted from a 1918 article in the Rose Society of Ontario annual. The article describes the vagaries of rose gardening on the Island, including the need to bring over all the soil, either in scows or across the ice in carts in the wintertime.

was more or less defunct anyway, as the city had opened the more popular Sunnyside amusement area in Parkdale in 1922. In April, 1927, the city turned over the ferry company and the amusement park to the Toronto Transportation Commission, which lost money on the amusement park and, bedevilled by the noise of seaplanes in the harbour (and later airplanes at the adjoining airport), closed it for good in 1948. The Toronto Parks Department took over the island ferry service in 1962.

Other changes in the Islands' physical form resulted from the formation, in 1911, of the Toronto Harbour Commission. One of its first tasks was to do something with the Ashbridge's Bay marsh; it came up with an ambitious plan involving the marsh's reclamation as industrial land (see the photo on page 189) and, with funding from the federal government, built a new eastern seawall and dredged a ship channel and turning basin. The dredging spoil was dumped near Ward's Island, creating the 45-acre Sunfish (now Algonquin) Island. The Harbour Commission also proposed a boulevard drive, running along the lakefront, across the Western Gap, through the Island, and across the Eastern channel—but that part of the plan was never implemented.

Ward's Island, named for the hotelier William Ward, became a tent city each summer; the city, in 1915, laid out the grid of streets there to put some order into the tenters' existence, and in the 1920s permitted cottages there. Most of the ones built date from the 1930s and later. Algonquin Island became a cottage community in the winter of 1937-8, when 54 cottages were relocated there from Hanlan's Point. Due to wartime housing shortages, authorities encouraged the owners to winterize their cottages, and by the end of the war they were permanent dwellings. Today, the picturesque Algonquin Island community is overgrown with shrubbery and large trees and looks for all the world to have been there for a hundred years.

The idea of an airport at Hanlan's Point dates from 1928, when World War I flying ace and future mayor Bert Wemp suggested an airfield for the West Island sandbar. During the 1920s, seaplanes had become a familiar sight in Toronto harbour, some operating from a wharf near the foot of Yonge Street. For a major North American city which had seen two decades of aeronautical activity, Toronto was very slow in getting a proper airport—at the time of Wemp's proposal, flying club fields dotted the farmlands of North York Township, and some commercial planes used the primitive World War One-era Leaside aerodrome. Council approved $100,000 for development of the West Island site, but lost interest when the federal government changed in 1930 and the Depression slowed the economy to a crawl. Finally, in 1937, city council approved both the Malton and the Island sites; at the latter, crews again modified the geography by dredging 2,360,000 tons of sand for fill. When the airport opened, it was the *coup de grace* for the old Hanlan's Point amusement park; some also thought it spelled the end of the Islands as an attractive park and cottage community.

Since the Second World War, the Islands have changed drastically. They survived a number of planning proposals, including one in 1948 and another in 1951, which recommended apartments, a reduced amount of residential land, and a bridge or a tunnel to allow vehicle access. The summer cottages on Centre Island were removed beginning in the mid-1950s, but in 1968, when the leases on land at Ward's and Algonquin islands expired, the residents refused to move and stood together against omnipotent Metro until the reformist politicians granted them a reprieve. The Ward's and Algonquin communities still exist, but the Centre Island community has completely vanished, replaced with grassy parkland.

"Canada's strongman Fred Beasley amusing himself at Hanlan's Point," taken by William James.

300

Leaside

James Alexander Brand was the secretary-treasurer of Durant Motors, which had its factory just north of the railway line in Leaside, at Laird Drive and Commercial Road. Born in Scotland in 1888, he came to Canada in 1911 with the Canadian National Steamship Company; after several years, he obtained work with Chevrolet at Oshawa, and later moved to the Oldsmobile division as its chief accountant. He accepted the appointment at Durant Motors in 1922, the year after William Durant formed a Canadian subsidiary which built the "Star" and the "Durant" in Leaside. Brand lived at 217 Lytton Boulevard in North Toronto.

Leaside owes its distinctive, curving street layout to the unusual conditions of its birth. Planned before the First World War as a real-estate speculation, it almost failed to get off the ground. However, as it was practically a tabletop, it became an excellent location for a military training aerodrome.

The first settler there was John Lea, a farmer who had arrived in York in 1819 and bought a 200-acre property north of the Don River. A descendant, William Lea, was still farming the land in the 1870s. At that time, the Ontario & Quebec Railway, which was in the process of locating a line to link Toronto with Peterborough and beyond, bought the southeast corner of his property. Lacking the wherewithal to survive on its own, the O&Q was forced in 1884 to lease its line to the Canadian Pacific Railway. Because the land in Leaside was so suitably flat and cheap, the latter decided to locate its maintenance shops there. Thus, over the next few decades, acres of track, shops, and a roundhouse sprawled over the land south of Commercial Road and east of Laird Drive. The C.P.R. built its Leaside passenger station just east of the spot where Millwood Road crossed the railway tracks.

All of this land development was to satisfy solely the operational needs of the railway. The C.P.R. was and is aware, to say the least, of the potential value of serviced land with access to a transportation system, but in the years around 1910 it had other fish to fry, and saw no immediate future in the adjoining farmland at Leaside. Meanwhile, its two rivals in the transcontinental railway sweepstakes—the Canadian Northern Railway and the Grand Trunk Pacific Railway—were astutely amassing fortunes by providing a transportation system to connect with serviced land, mainly in western Canada. The railways had been able to attract seemingly limitless numbers of private and public dollars and pounds sterling, a significant portion of which was kited into the wildest speculations. The Grand Trunk Pacific Railway had sunk millions into creating an instant town called Prince Rupert, on the west coast of British Columbia, for its Pacific Ocean terminus, as it was on a more or less level line between London and Yokohama—a shorter and quicker route to the Orient than the C.P.R.'s through Vancouver. Similarly, the Canadian Northern Railway, headed by the Toronto-based financiers William Mackenzie and Donald Mann, was deeply involved in the rankest land speculation—the metropolis of Factoria in Saskatchewan, populated by a few gophers; and Port Mann, the Canadian Northern terminus near Vancouver, destined to be a fabulous city; and so on. In Toronto and else-

where, Henry Pellatt and his associates had for years played the land speculation tune, and prospered when the gullible and greedy danced to it.

In the case of Leaside, the Canadian Northern Railway had little operational interest in the area. Its line snaked along the Don Valley, crossing and recrossing the river as it went. Similarly, its major shareholders, Mackenzie and Mann, who owned the Toronto street-railway system and a number of affiliated radial lines, showed little interest in servicing the area with an electric transit system. However, the price of land was right and Toronto was booming, so they decided to speculate with a model subdivision on the old Lea farmland, and engaged the Montreal landscape architect Frederick Todd to create a layout. Todd, who sometimes worked with the Danish engineer L. E. Davick, had been employed by the Canadian Northern's principals on several projects; furthermore, he was a favourite of Lord Shaughnessy, president of the Canadian Pacific Railway, and had designed some of the latter's most prestigious subdivisions.

Mackenzie and Mann moved quickly—they purchased over 1,000 acres between Bayview and Leslie, from the C.P.R. yards northwards to well beyond Eglinton Avenue; Todd came up with an attractive plan of curving streets, interspersed with garden cul-de-sacs, which looked remarkably like his earlier plans for elsewhere in Canada. Streets received names of suitable friends and luminaries: Donald for Donald Mann; Hanna for David Blythe Hanna, the third vice-president (page 116); McRae for the prairie-land tycoon Alexander Duncan McRae; Aird for the vice-president of the Bank of Commerce, which was the C.N.R.'s major Canadian financial backer (page 229). All of this was cobbled together and prepared for sale in the early months of 1912. Then came four events: firstly, the withdrawal of foreign—mainly British and German—investment in Canada, due to the "battleship crisis" and rumours of war; secondly, the disunity and uncertainty over whether Canada should have its own navy or should raise money to give to Britain for *her* battleships; subsequently, the collapse of the western Canadian real-estate bubble, which further dried up credit and operational revenue for the C.N.R. and the G.T.R. Finally, there was that most symbolic event—the sinking, in April, of the *Titanic*.

The Leaside townsite, which had been touted by the *World* as "the biggest real estate operation ever carried out in Toronto," came on the market too late. In the harsh light of 1913, with real-estate prices falling and repeated war scares, Leaside seemed to be just a remote location—the site of some unattractive railyards and the Canada Wire & Cable Company factory.

Although the depression and the war which followed ended for a time Leaside's chance to be a prime residential area, it created the conditions to put Leaside firmly on the map as "Toronto's New Business & Railway Centre." Its remoteness and flatness—two factors militating against its desirability as a residential area—suddenly became advantages. In the first instance, the Canada Wire & Cable Company obtained munitions contracts from the Shell Committee; in the second instance, aviators found Leaside to be an ideal location for an aerodrome.

The Leaside Munitions Company, formed as a division of Canada Wire & Cable Company, built extensive facilities at the corner of Laird and Commercial Road. Some accommodation was built for the workers; others commuted daily on a C.P.R. "special" from the North Toronto station. As men enlisted and went overseas, women were drawn into the labour force to fill their positions in the munitions factories. At remote plants like Leaside, the special needs of women in the work force needed special attention. A committee of the Y.W.C.A., at the behest of the Imperial Munitions Board, appointed a Miss Wiseman to supervise the introduction of canteens and "comforts" in the factories. (Miss Wiseman's public statement that educated women were not needed for munitions work was regretted by a Miss Boulton, who called it a "slur upon the leisured women who had accepted the patriotic call of the Munitions Board.")

North of the Leaside Munitions Plant, on fields which had been popular for flying demonstrations, a Royal Flying Corps aerodrome was established in the summer of 1917. Prior to that, any Canadians who wished to volunteer for the Royal Flying Corps had to obtain a flying license at their own expense from a civilian school (there was no Canadian air force until after the First World War); however, the number of volunteers with these credentials could not keep pace with either the mortality rate or the increased availability of aircraft, so the Royal Flying Corps established training stations at Camp Borden, Deseronto, and North Toronto. The latter consisted of aerodromes at Long Branch, Armour Heights (roughly the intersection of Avenue Road and Highway 401), and Leaside. Cadets received basic training at Long Branch, then attended the School of Military Aeronautics at the University of Toronto. After a brief period of training at the Canadian Aeroplanes plant on Dufferin Street—which produced the JN-4 trainers—the cadets took to the air. There ensued an extraordinary carnage, with 125 cadets and instructors killed between the summer of 1917 and the end of the war. Planes stalled and spun, augering themselves into the soft earth; at Mohawk, part of the R.F.C. Station Deseronto, a cadet brought his "Jenny" down into a hangar, burning it to the ground; pranged airplanes were fixed, then pranged again. Fortunately, the Rosedale Military Hospital was nearby, at St. Andrew's College at MacLennan and Summerhill in Rosedale.

The Leaside aerodrome survived its wartime pilots and continued in regular use for commercial aviation until eventually superseded by airports at Hanlan's Point and Malton. The last of the old aerodrome hangars were removed in 1971.

After the war, one of the old munitions plant buildings was taken over by Durant Motors. William Durant had been the star of Buick and, for a time, controlled General Motors, but in 1920 he had a falling out with his employer and established a new company to build a car to be named after him. In September, 1921, he incorporated Durant Motors of Canada, which was to build under license the low-priced "Star" and mid-priced "Durant" models. Production started early in 1922 under the direction of Roy "Golden Rule" Kerby, a super-salesman who was one of the investors with shares in the fifty percent of the company not owned by Durant. The Canadian firm was well-managed and prosperous; eventually, the factories expanded to occupy over eighteen acres and twelve buildings. When its American parent collapsed in 1930, the Canadian directors gained control and changed the name to Dominion Motors. The new company built a variety of new vehicles and old Durants, including the Frontenac, the Reo Flying Cloud, and the Reo Speed Wagon, and manufactured Rugby trucks under license. It was no match for the severity of the depression, and only in Ontario did the sales figures hold up. When it ceased production in December, 1933, Dominion Motors was the last independent piece of the Canadian automobile industry.

The other landmark in Leaside was Thorncliffe Race Track, laid out in 1920 east of Leaside Station. A venture of a syndicate from Baltimore, it had a stadium seating 4,000, and stables for over 600 horses. The last race at the track was in 1952; today, a large apartment development covers the site. The old C.P.R. shops, yards, and the Leaside aerodrome have vanished; the land along the tracks is a windswept wasteland of broken concrete, shattered glass, weeds, and litter.

The map on the next page is an adaptation of one in a promotional article published in the Toronto World *on September 18, 1918. It did not indicate the extent of housing development— which at the time was minimal— but showed clearly the few features for which Leaside was known, namely its Aerodrome, the Leaside Munitions Plant, and the Thorncliffe Race Track.*

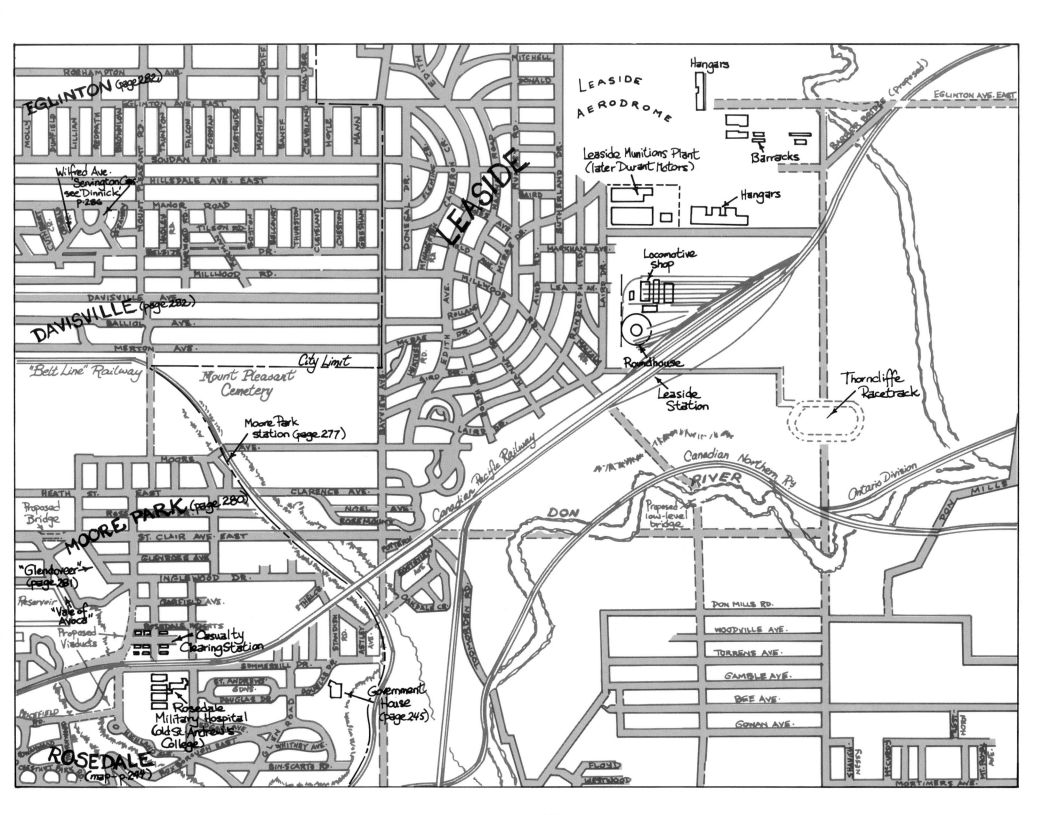

EGLINTON (page 282)

Wilfred Ave.
Servington Cres.
see 'Dinnick'
p. 286

DAVISVILLE (page 282)

LEASIDE

"Belt Line" Railway

Mount Pleasant
Cemetery

City Limit

Moore Park
station (page 277)

MOORE PARK (page 280)

"Glendoveer"
(page 281)

Reservoir in
"Vale of Avoca"

Proposed
Bridge

Proposed
Viaducts

St. Clair Ave. East

Casualty
Clearing Station

Rosedale
Military Hospital
(old St. Andrew's
College)

Government
House
(page 245)

ROSEDALE
(map - p. 244)

LEASIDE
AERODROME

Hangars

Barracks

Leaside Munitions Plant
(later Durant Motors)

Hangars

Locomotive
shop

Roundhouse

Leaside
Station

Bayview Bridge (proposed)

Eglinton Ave. East

Thorncliffe
Racetrack

Ontario Division

Canadian Pacific Railway

Canadian Northern Ry.

DON RIVER

Proposed
low-level
bridge

Don Mills Rd.

Woodville Ave.

Torrens Ave.

Gamble Ave.

Bee Ave.

Gowan Ave.

Mortimers Ave.

303

Aviation

Early aviators and airplane manufacturers used farmers' fields in North York Township for many of their feats and experiments. The most famous was de Lesseps Airport, "1,500 feet of mowed cow pasture" on the Trethewey Farm, northeast of the corner of Trethewey Drive and Jane Street on land now suburbanized and traversed by Black Creek Drive. In addition, there were flying club and testing fields occupying the current Downsview Airport site between Wilson and Sheppard on either side of Dufferin, for the Toronto Flying Club and Canadian Airways. The old Armour Heights Aerodrome, renamed Barker Airport, occupied a tract of farmland between Dufferin Street and the Canadian National Railway tracks, midway between Lawrence and Wilson. Elsewhere in the metropolitan area in the 1920s and early 1930s, airplanes could land at the Leaside Aerodrome (see also page 303), and seaplanes regularly used Toronto Bay and moorings near the Harbour Commission Building at the foot of Bay Street. The two current airports, on the Island and at Malton (Toronto International, now known as Lester B. Pearson Airport), were opened in 1937.

Toronto saw its first flying machine in the summer of 1909, about six months after J. A. D. McCurdy made the first flight in a heavier-than-air machine in Canada. A pilot named Foster Charles Willard brought his Curtiss *Golden Flyer* to Toronto to perform a flying demonstration at Scarborough Beach; the promoters prepared a short runway, which ended at the lakefront, "so when Willard starts the engine going, the aeroplane has either to fly, or he and the machine will get a dunking." Willard had an abrupt swim. A few days later he tried again and successfully made a five-minute flight, but a third demonstration ended in ignominy and the water when the engine failed. According to aviation historian Larry Milberry, Willard later had the questionable distinction of being the first aviator to be shot down, by a farmer annoyed at his noisy low flying.

Toronto saw its next big demonstration in July, 1910, at the Trethewey Farm in the Mount Dennis-Weston area. (Frank Trethewey was an aviation enthusiast who became one of the founders of the Toronto Flying Club.) The star attraction was the French aviator Count Jacques de Lesseps with his *Bleriot*, in which he had crossed the English Channel; in addition, there were several pilots and planes from the Wright organization in the United States. The Royal Canadian Dragoons provided security, and private detectives watched for pickpockets among the huge crowd. One of the aviators came down in a tree; on July 13, de Lesseps made the first flight over the city of Toronto.

The flying demonstrations of 1911 brought the aviation pioneer J. A .D. McCurdy to the city. As a prelude on August 2, McCurdy raced Charles Willard to the city from Hamilton; the former landed on Fisherman's Island and the latter at the Exhibition Grounds, evidently because it was too smoggy to fly up the Don River to the Donlands Farm, where the air meet was scheduled to take place the next day. Like its predecessors,

(Left) John Alexander Douglas McCurdy was born in Baddeck, Nova Scotia; when he was 21 years old, in 1907, he became acquainted with Alexander Graham Bell, who had established the Aerial Experimental Association at his home in Baddeck. Bell, McCurdy and some others built an airplane, which McCurdy flew in 1909—the first-ever flight by a British subject (the first airplane designed and built completely in Canada was W. W. Gibson's, in Victoria, British Columbia, which flew in 1910). McCurdy formed a commercial organization to build airplanes, but found it difficult to attract interest, so entered into an association with the American Glenn Curtiss, whose airplanes were popular in the United States. McCurdy became the president of the Curtiss subsidiary in Toronto, which became Canadian Aeroplanes Limited during the First World War. He lived at 83 Crescent Road in Rosedale. (Middle) Lt. Col. William Avery "Billy" Bishop was born in Owen Sound in 1894. At the age of 21 he joined the Royal Flying Corps and ended the war as the most-decorated Canadian airman, with a Victoria Cross, Distinguished Service Order, Military Cross, Distinguished Flying Cross, Croix de Guerre, and Légion d'Honneur. He was lionized by the public, and married Margaret Burden, the granddaughter of Timothy Eaton, at a glittering, celebrity-packed wedding in 1917. After the war, he wrote a book called Winged Warfare, gave lectures, and had a checkered career as president of Bishop-Barker Aeroplanes. He lived at 50 Poplar Plains Road. (Right) Bishop's partner was another Victoria Cross winner, the Manitoba-born Lt. Col. William George Barker; the two were the same age—both turning 24 in 1918. Barker was unassuming compared with his brash partner; he shot down 52 enemy planes, 20 fewer than the amazing Bishop, whose exploits have been the subject of several recent plays and films.

the function drew large crowds, but after two days the aviators refused to continue flying as the field was so bumpy.

Although aviation had progressed considerably between the 1909 Scarborough demonstrations and the air meets of the following few years— especially after it was proven that the planes could defy gravity for a controlled period of time—military authorities remained uninterested in its potential. McCurdy and his associates were repeatedly unsuccessful in attempts to get the government, through Minister of Militia and Defense Sam Hughes, to sponsor the development of aviation and pilot training.

American-built Curtiss-Hawks at the Leaside Aerodrome in 1929.

Hughes was quoted as telling McCurdy that "aviation is of no value in war, and I do not propose to tie the government up financially to such a ridiculous scheme."

He changed his mind in September, 1914, and approved the formation of the Canadian Aviation Corps, with the goal of helping to train pilots who would then join the Royal Flying Corps. Within a year, aviation proved its value in the war zone—at least for reconnaissance—and the demand for pilots increased rapidly. Pilots were required to be between nineteen and twenty-five years of age, "well-educated, athletic and thoroughly fit with excellent eye-sight," and to pay for their own flying lessons, for which they would be partially repaid if they survived and were accepted by the Royal Flying Corps. The first school opened in Toronto in 1915, run by the American-based Curtiss Aviation Company (with which McCurdy had long been associated), offering flying-boat training at Hanlan's Point and wheel-equipped-airplane instruction at an airfield at Long Branch. With McCurdy as president, the Curtiss company established a factory in Toronto to build the JN-3 and JN-4 trainers it required. The trainees paid $1,000 each, an enormous sum at the time; Toronto City Council granted eight dollars a week to each local student attending the course, and the British government announced that it would guarantee $375 of each accepted aviator's expenses. The trainees were inspected by the governor general, H.R.H. the Duke of Connaught, at Long Branch on September 7, 1916.

Later that year, Canadian Aeroplanes Limited was organized under a board composed of representatives from the Admiralty, War Office and the Imperial Munitions Board, to take over the Toronto factories of the Curtiss Aeroplane Company at 70-76 Pearl Street and on Strachan Avenue near the Massey-Harris works. Controlled by Joseph Flavelle, E. R. Wood and managing director F. W. Baillie—a munitions manufacturer based in Hamilton—the company soon expanded into a larger plant at 1244 Dufferin Street which turned out the JN-4 Canuck, a modified Curtiss design with a four-cylinder, in-line engine whose valves and heads stuck out through the fuselage on the right-hand side of the airplane. The company bought its engines from the Curtiss factory in Buffalo, its structural wood from the Queen Charlotte Islands off the British Columbia coast (the same wood used in World War II for the famous Mosquito fighter-bombers), and its fabric from a cotton plant in Trois Rivières (initial plans to use Irish linen had been disrupted by marauding U-boats). At its wartime peak, the Toronto plant employed 2,400 workers, but it closed down soon after the armistice.

Aviation received a boost early in 1917 when the Royal Flying Corps took over the Curtiss operation at Long Branch and established airports and fields at Camp Borden and locally at Armour Heights and Leaside. During the winter, the R.F.C. flew to Texas to continue training, having rejected Vancouver on account of its fog and rain. Training was a risky business—in the last eighteen months of the war, 125 flight cadets and instructors were killed in flying accidents.

Two of the war's most famous aviators, the Victoria Cross winners Billy Bishop and William George Barker, moved to Toronto in 1919 and formed the Bishop-Barker Company, with headquarters at 93 Spadina Avenue and a variety of flying operations, including an air-taxi service between Toronto Bay and Muskoka using Curtiss HS-2L flying boats. Recollections of their seat-of-the-pants flights include overcrowding (five passengers in the front cockpit which was supposed to hold two or three), a forced landing in Lake Ontario, and a descent into trees near Brooklin, Ontario. The firm never had any casualties, although some passengers must have wondered whether they were witnessing a re-creation of the danger on the Western Front. In addition to their charters, Bishop-Barker sold used JN-4s at the Armour Heights aerodrome, and at one low point painted streetcars for the Toronto Transportation Commission.

Canada's own air force (designated the Royal Canadian Air Force in 1923) formed in 1920, and outfitted itself with De Havilland aircraft from England. The director of the Ontario Provincial Air Service, Captain Roy Maxwell, was impressed with the De Havilland Moth, the firm's first civilian design, and ordered four of them on floats for patrol duty in the Ontario north; De Havilland's Canadian sales director saw the potential market, and in 1928 opened an aircraft sales and service centre on Frank Trethewey's cow pasture, now renamed de Lesseps Field. Although they had barely enough space there to assemble the Moths shipped from England, the enterprise prospered. In the years that followed, De Havilland Canada adapted Moths to the Canadian terrain, built Mosquitos during the Second World War, created the famous line of bushplanes including the Otter and the Beaver, and, recently, introduced the Dash 7 and Dash 8 commuter airplanes.

Other aircraft manufacturers gravitated to Malton late in the 1930s and set up manufacturing plants around the periphery of the airport. Among them was National Steel Car, which changed its name to Victory Aircraft and built 430 Avro Lancaster bombers during the war. The most famous of all was probably Avro Aircraft, established at the end of 1945 as part of the English Hawker Siddeley Group. Its Jetliner flew at 500 miles per hour and made the first international jet transport flight in North America, from Toronto to New York, in April, 1950; the Jetliner was ahead of its time, and not even the government-owned Trans Canada Airlines could be induced to purchase it. During the Korean War, the Canadian government ordered Avro to concentrate its efforts on producing the CF-100 interceptor, so the Jetliner was abandoned. The CF-100's successor, the Avro Arrow, was a watershed in Canadian design and manufacturing. A state-of-the-art warplane, it was ready to begin production in the late 1950s, which unfortunately was the time when ballistic missiles and satellites, according to some military experts, were about to render obsolete the manned supersonic fighter and bomber; in February, 1959, the federal government cancelled the Arrow program.

Metro

In the late 1940s, after nearly forty years of slow and steady growth, the City of Toronto exploded from its old boundaries into the surrounding countryside. Until that time, Toronto had been a comparatively compact city—suburban settlement extended westwards down the lake through Mimico and Long Branch, north along Yonge Street to about Steeles, northwest in scattered communities to Weston and beyond, and east along the lakeshore to Scarboro Junction. North York and East York townships had the least development—in fact, development was very uneven throughout the metropolitan region, as taxes and the quality of municipal services available to potential residents varied greatly.

The city planning board had been busy during the Second World War years, studying new permutations of industry, business, and housing in the city and its suburbs. The board's landmark 1943 report proposed a metropolis of suburban towns, each of which would have its own industrial zone; a ring system of superhighways would link these suburbs with each other, the city, and distant points. Most of the arteries delineated in the plan were eventually built, although some were built as subways, rather than highways. On only one matter, population growth, was the planning board off the mark; it greatly underestimated the number of returned servicemen and families who would want to settle in the Toronto area, and had no conception of the waves of immigration which would so completely transform the city in the 1950s.

One of the great peacetime lessons of the Second World War and—in the United States, at least—the war against the Great Depression was the value of centralized planning. The 1940s and 1950s became the era of the "expert," with fingers in every planning pie and, according to the logic of

the time, the good of the public at heart. However, development of Toronto was stalled, not by lack of a good plan, but by an inefficient and inequitable political system which was allowing the city to grow in an amorphous, organic fashion.

A former reeve of Forest Hill Village, Frederick Gardiner, became the self-appointed advocate of centralized planning and full-speed development. Gardiner became the head of the Toronto and Suburban Planning

Port Credit was too distant from the city for people who had to be at work at an early hour, but for those who had some flexibility and could afford the lengthy drive, it was an attractive place to live. The first four of these five people gave Port Credit addresses in their Who's Who listings in the early 1930s. Leo Charles (far left) was an Australian who became the president and managing director of several specialty paper and twine companies and the Canadian Vegetable Parchment Company, manufacturers of "Purity Brand Genuine Vegetable Parchment." He lived at a property called "Arrowfield" on the Mississauga Road. Samuel John Moore (left), of "Breezy Brae," rose from an apprenticeship as a printer with the Barrie Gazette to become president of the Bank of Nova Scotia; like many Baptists, he supported missionary efforts on the world's "frontiers," including the Chinese Famine Fund of 1911. J. P. Bickell (centre) was the president of McIntyre-Porcupine Mines, vice-president of Famous Players Canadian Corporation, and a financial associate of Conn Smythe at Maple Leaf Gardens; the son of a clergyman, he was born in Toronto and established his own brokerage business at the age of 23. He is the namesake of the Bickell Memorial Cup, given at the discretion of team management to a member of the Maple Leafs for excellent play. Charles Burgess (right) was a bond dealer specializing in the financing of municipalities. (Far right) James Franceschini was one of a few Italian-born Toronto residents who prospered in the period before the Second World War. Born in Pescara in 1890, he came to Canada as a youth and organized the Dufferin Construction Company when he was 28 years old. The firm grew into a large paving, concrete, crushed stone and building supply concern on Fleet Street. Franceschini joined the Eglinton Hunt Club and the Ontario Jockey Club, and enjoyed exhibiting hackney show horses. He lived at "Myrtle Villa," named after his daughter, at 415 Lakeshore Road at Mimico Beach.

Board and issued a report in 1949 urging the amalgamation of Toronto with its suburbs. This amalgamation movement gathered strength, and four years later was approved by the Ontario Municipal Board. Metro, the new supercity, assumed power in 1954 over the pit of hissing snakes which had been Toronto and its suburbs.

The political machinations which created Metro were to ensure that the postwar economic boom, fueled by immigration and later by Korean War contracts, would be well channelled and continuous. *Toronto Boom Town*, a National Film Board short feature which had its first showing at the Imperial Theatre on Yonge Street on February 15, 1951, spread the word of this phenomenon to the rest of the country. Everywhere were the sounds and smells of money being made.

Amidst all the prosperity, Torontonians began to indulge in their favourite civic pastime—self-analysis. In a sort of inverted Calvinism, commentators questioned whether the Tory mass psyche was stopping everyone from having enough fun, whether Toronto was embarrassingly dull, inhabited by too many people who only wanted to make money. Were Torontonians a strange throwback to a Presbyterian age? Were they at odds with the hedonism of the postwar world? Toronto was rapidly approaching Montreal in size, prosperity, and importance; was it still true that people had to go to Montreal to have a good time? How much *was* that doggie in the window? The Curly-Larry-and-Modigliani world of the C.B.C. trotted out new analyses, especially Lister Sinclair's classic radio play *We All Hate Toronto*, first broadcast in January, 1946, on the "Panorama" series—its premise being that Canada was united only in its hatred of Toronto.

There was some justification for these suspicions about the city's character. It was impossible to get a drink other than in the "beverage rooms" of standard hotels, nor could one see a sporting event on Sunday (plebiscites in 1947 and 1950, respectively, overturned those regulations). A spate of articles appeared in the newspapers describing what opportunities existed for entertainment and dining in the city. The list was quite a short one. Aside from the offerings from Hollywood in local cinemas, one could see live theatre at the Royal Alexandra, attend prom concerts Tuesday evenings at the Varsity Arena, or see the midnight floor show in the Roof Garden at the "King Eddie." Diners who did not cherish the thought of creamed salmon, chicken à la king, and cup custard sought out the roof restaurant at the Park Plaza, the Stoodleigh under the *Star* building on King Street, or the Winston Grill ("which attracts all the performers after their shows at the Royal"); more daring gourmands ate at the atmospheric Chicken Palace on Yonge near Carlton, or took in the smorgasbord at the Little Denmark, on the west side of Bay at Gerrard, in a house

Grounds and Office Building, Mimico Asylum, Toronto, Canada.

decorated with murals of Norse legends and enlivened with the ambience of operatic music and candlelight. "Whipper Billy" Watson and colleagues wrestled at the Gardens. On Sundays, one could visit Sunnyside for rides and games, hot dogs and candy floss, or attend the performances at Chinese theatres on Elizabeth Street.

Along with the cultural change in the city, provoked in part by massive immigration, there was a physical change as suburban housing development expanded swiftly into the countryside. Probably the first and most famous subdivision was Don Mills, assembled by E. P. Taylor on 2,000 acres of former farmland, and developed with a mix of housing and industry. It was followed in the mid-1950s by land assembly projects which resulted in sprawling communities such as Erin Mills and Bramalea. Concurrently, there were shopping developments, the most notable being Yorkdale, at what was to be the intersection of the 401 and the Spadina Expressway. Developments, such as those in Mississauga, combined shopping malls and offices with some light industry and residential complexes. Although each of these developments had some distinctive and laudable components, they all extended Toronto's suburban sprawl, and thereby contributed to the disappearance of the farmland which had so recently ringed the city. *Sic transit agricolae mundi.*

This was the precursor of the new Toronto.

Picnickers along the Humber River in the twenties drove their cars into the river and washed them.

Painting Sources

All of the paintings were sketched and done in rough at their locations between the spring and the end of 1987, with the exceptions of the painting of "The Dale" on page 249 which is a straight adaptation of a single photograph, and the paintings on pages 230-1 and 281 which were done in February, 1988. The paintings on pages 2-3, 162-3, 165, 177, 181, 185, 217, 230-1, 235, 242-3, 259, 261, 266-7, 275, 281, 284-5, and 290-1 have no photographic references, although in some cases I have added appropriate cars and people. Sources of material and research for the other paintings are delineated below. All James Collection and "Department of Public Works" (DPW) photographs are in the City of Toronto Archives. The Goad's Fire Insurance Atlases are in the Metropolitan Toronto Reference Library. Names of authors within this list refer to the bibliography overleaf.

Page 13: the Rosedale Hotel appears in a 1914 photo, DPW Yonge 238. Details of the signs on the Yonge Street crossing and the William McGill & Company coal shack appear in DPW Yonge 28 and Yonge 193. None of these photographs shows both the hotel and the railway station.

Page 17: the lettering and signs on St. Lawrence Hall appear in a photograph in Careless page 88.

Page 21: the "street patrol cart" is illustrated in DPW "Street Cleaning" photographs, circa 1930.

Pages 28-9: the Fairweather's store at 88-90 Yonge stood until the autumn of 1987 (its façade has been preserved, as has that of Dunfield & Company at 102-4 Yonge); the Georgian shop to its north at 92 Yonge, and the Dunfield & Company block, were demolished at the same time. The building at 94-100 Yonge, between Rathbone and Dunfield, was torn down in 1930, and replaced with the Tip Top Tailors shop which was torn down in 1987; the pre-1930 building appears in the distance in a number of photographs (all of which were taken before the construction in 1918 of the "new" Fairweather's store), including one in Careless page 185. The shop occupants are all those in the 1923 directory. The *Star*'s radio van appears in a number of photographs, including one in Stewart page 41.

Page 43: the bus station still exists; its signs and the 1940-vintage bus appear in Toronto Transportation Commission page 84. I angled the painting to show the Ford Hotel (see page 33) and City Hall in the distance. The "Waste Paper Cabinet" is a 1930s model, DPW "Streetcleaning."

Page 53: the old *Star* building appears in dozens of newspaper photographs from the late 1960s, shortly before its demolition. In order to "get close" to it without too much foreground clutter, I put the point-of-view about three storeys in the air, and made up the office and secretary to fill out the picture's horizontal dimension.

Page 69: the buildings—at least at the corner and the tavern tower in the distance, are unchanged. The lettering detail of the New Method Laundry truck appears in James 1161.

Page 75: the Goad's Atlases show three townhouses, and architectural historians such as Eric Arthur and Patricia McHugh state that the three were identical. The only photograph I could find of Bond Street looks south from Dundas, DPW Bond Street 12, and shows the boulevard trees and fences, but little else. The truck appears in DPW Streetcleaning 93.

Pages 102-3: the billboard, photographed from much closer and looking northward (without any view of Osgoode Hall), appears in James 725. The 1915-model Toronto Hydro trouble wagon is DPW Hydro 7.

Pages 130-1: Details of the Toronto Railway Company's Shaw Street "wye" onto King Street appear in Bromley, map number one. A T.T.C. photograph of Massey-Harris shift workers boarding a T.T.C. tram in 1927 at the bottom of Crawford (a new routing) appears in Bromley, page 44. Portions of the works still exist; a bird's-eye view in Careless, page 113, can be located with reference to the corner of King and Shaw streets using the 1923 Goad's Atlas.

Page 133: a straight-on photograph of the driveway into Euclid Hall, showing the conservatory details, appears in Lucy Booth Martyn's "Aristocratic Toronto."

Page 136-7: the exceptionally dilapidated building on the left appears in two photographs looking east, DPW Elizabeth Street 27—showing it when the city condemned it in March, 1937—and 28—after renovation and replastering by the landlord. Of the old buildings to the south of the lane, only the three-storey one, at 105 Elizabeth, remains, although the "imprint" of a gabled cottage is still clearly visible on its northern sidewall.

Page 139: the corner of Kensington and Baldwin is still relatively intact, although at the "T" of Baldwin (on the right side of the painting), part of a rowhouse has been removed and replaced with a modern building—the sawn-off end of the easternmost gable is still visible above the new building's rooftop. The addresses on Kensington Avenue in 1927 were all listed as shops. There are very few old photographs of Kensington Market—it seemed to hold little interest for photographers; one of the few, which shows poultry cages and awnings and a scattering of customers but no building detail, is Public Archives of Canada PA 84811, reproduced in Speisman.

Page 143: the full "Bargain Benny's" building, photographed from a different angle and with an empty foreground, appears in Greenhill, photo 23.

Page 149: I added the buildings which still exist on the east side of Church Street, plus a foreground, to a different angle of the photograph in Adam, page 10.

Page 156-7: photographs in DPW "Sherbourne Street," taken in the early 1950s straight on at 609 Sherbourne, show a picket fence, four identical houses there (now only two remain), and the boulevard trees. I have changed the angle so that the picture looks southward along the line of the picket fence.

Page 159: a pamphlet published by Rosar-Morrison Funeral Home, in commemoration of its 125th anniversary, shows one of its 1930s hearses. The house between Rosar-Morrison and the Ernescliffe Apartments, demolished in 1954, evidently was not photographed by anyone, but appears in the 1923 Goad's to have had a very prominent turret. The rest of the scene has remained more or less intact, although the boulevard trees are gone.

Page 183: the cupola, which has since vanished, appears in Adam page 180.

Pages 198-199: the level crossing appears in DPW "Dunn Street," but with no view of Springhurst or the corner.

Page 207: the 1890 Goad's clearly shows the profile of the original hotel (which can still be discerned from within the dross of later additions) and the emptiness of the surrounding streets. The turret, which has since been removed, appears in a photograph in Filey.

Pages 210-1: The bizarre loading procedure is delineated in a T.T.C. photo and accompanying explanation in Bromley, page 64—the photograph there looks directly north, showing little of the distinctive building at the northwest corner of Keele and Dundas.

Page 213: the double-decker bus appears in Toronto Transportation Commission page 36 and elsewhere.

Page 221: The double line of power poles, one for high voltage and the other for household current, appear in DPW "Ossington Avenue."

Page 223: The cobbled street appears in DPW "Bloor Street." The William Davies Company logo of white cut-out letters fastened to a scaffolding appears in a number of photographs showing company stores throughout the city. The other building tenants are listed in the 1921 Directory. Nasmith's Bakery is James 32.

Page 227: Bedford Road, looking directly north from the sidewalk in front of Varsity Stadium, appears in DPW "Bedford Road" 4, although it shows just the edge of the British American gas station, and is looking at it from a more easterly point than the painting. The building on the northeast corner of Bloor and Bedford still exists, though it has been greatly modified.

Page 239: "apologies to Monet" refers to the oft-reproduced painting "Les Coquelicots à Vertheuil." I have replaced the poppies with wild roses—the pink *Rosa Blanda* common to southern Ontario and the most likely candidate as the rose of Rosedale. The background is adapted from a nineteenth-century wash drawing of "Rosedale," now in the collection of the Metropolitan Toronto Reference Library, which was probably sketched looking northeast from Yonge Street. My point of view is near the bottom of the ravine, along the old Park Road.

Page 249: "The Dale" no longer exists, but contemporary accounts describe its fine, spacious grounds. A number of photographs survive of the house, but none really shows the extent of the property.

Page 257: the 1920s-vintage "Rosedale" bus appears in various T.T.C. photographs, and in Bromley page 38.

Page 278-9: two photographs of the corner of St. Clair and Yonge appear in Kinsella, pictures 52 and 53. The former looks southwest from the corner, and takes in the hotel and the garage; the latter looks north from directly in front of the hotel. Using these photographs, I have painted from a point of view further south on Yonge, looking north past the garage and hotel, and added the Sercombe truck, which appears in an advertisement in a 1914 issue of *Canadian Motorist*.

Page 283: a typical radial car appears in Bromley page 11. I have switched the point of view around so that I could include a 1927 Ford Roadster billboard, an example of which appears in Collins, page 45.

Page 297: the cottages, photographed full-frame from a spot on the edge of the boardwalk, appear in James 228.

The Postcards

The heyday of the picture postcard was in the two decades before the First World War. Although "The Kodak" and other so-called detective cameras were available throughout that period, and were easy to operate, they had to be loaded and unloaded in a darkroom, and usually gave only mediocre results; by comparison, professional cameras took superb photographs, especially of static objects such as buildings, but were bulky, expensive, and complex to operate. However, postcards could be bought almost anywhere *of* anywhere, and were in many cases in colour. Rather than drag photographic equipment with them, travellers collected cards voraciously—even armchair travellers kept postcard books. The seven dozen postcards in this book are a small fraction of the hundreds of cards published on Toronto alone.

During this period, there was no colour photography as we now know it; these cards are reproductions of black and white photographs, coloured with printed ink overlays in a similar manner to the hand-tinting of original photographs. The "structure" of the printed postcard is a standard black and white half-tone photograph, to which colours were added in layers. Before the card was printed, the manufacturer had the option to retouch and remove anything which he thought detracted from the original photograph, such as power lines and garbage, as well as to add objects such as horses and wagons—the result, in many cases, is an edited, idealized version of the original scene.

The colouring process is slightly different from that used in "Sunday colour comics," in that the overlay colours on these old postcards are not half-tone mixtures of the printers' primary inks (cyan, magenta and yellow), but custom-mixed inks, their tone ranges indicated usually by stippling, rather than through the medium of a photomechanical half-tone screen. To keep costs down, the colour range is simplified, giving the cards their charming pastel "posterized" quality. In some instances, the colouring was crude—colour patches did not fit "within the lines"—and/or the colours were printed "off-register," producing an effect of weird floating patches such as the blue dresses of the children in the Balmy Beach postcard on page 166.

The most skilfully executed cards, using the most natural colours, are in my opinion those of the John Valentine & Sons Company, which had its headquarters in Scotland and offices all over the world. Many of their early cards were coloured and printed in Germany, but by the First World War the company was printing everything in the United Kingdom and making a point of the fact that its cards were "British made." The "nighttime" cards of Scarborough Beach and Hanlan's Point amusement parks, on pages 168 and 295 respectively, are cleverly retouched daytime photographs, as is the amusing one on page 25 of King Street West under an enormous harvest moon. Successors to Valentine & Sons were the Valentine & Sons United Company and the Valentine-Black Company, both of whose cards, such as the Sunnyside card at the bottom left of page 205, or the Yonge Street card in the centre of page 32, have a stark, crude look.

As the years went by and the old artisans quit or retired, the quality of postcard colouring became rougher and less natural. Some of this could perhaps be blamed on changes in colour fashion, as in the Coliseum postcard on page 124, or on a desire to achieve a more "contemporary," sleek look, as represented by the Maple Leaf Gardens postcard on page 155. By the 1940s, colour photography had become common, and most postcards were the four-colour reproductions typical of today. Probably the most recent card reproduced in this book that was printed by the overlay method described above is the Sunnyside bathing beauty card (probably from the late 1940s) on page 205, which uses a fine mezzotint screen for the black and white halftone. By contrast, the Warwick Bros. & Rutter postcard of "Deancroft" at the bottom of page 241, is a "rescreen," and probably a rip-off, of a turn-of-the-century colour card of the type described above and is clouded by a coarse version of the nubbly moire pattern common to all four-colour reproduction (it looks like a colour screen-printed billboard or newspaper photograph seen from too close). Two other oddities are the Royal York hotel card on page 119, and the card of Sir Henry Pellatt on page 269, which have backgrounds of metallic ink.

I have no idea who took the original photographs. To further confuse the issue, some of these photographs have appeared many times in black and white collections and old books, and were reproduced in different colour schemes by different companies. The probable source for several of the Valentine & Sons postcards is the book (printed of course in black and white) called *Toronto—Its Board of Trade*, printed by R. G. McLean in 1897-8. The photographs within it are not credited to any photographer, but some appeared later as postcards—in this book, they are the ones on pages 70, 94 top right, 150, 158, 178, 219, 240 bottom, and 294 bottom.

Bibliography

Adam, G. Mercer, *Toronto Old & New*, (The Mail Printing Company, 1891).

Arthur, Eric, *Toronto—No Mean City*, (University of Toronto Press, 1964).

Berton, Pierre, *The New City*, (Macmillan, 1961).

Betcherman, Lita-Rose, *The Swastika and the Maple Leaf*, (Fitzhenry & Whiteside, 1975).

Boyer, Barbaranne, *The Boardwalk Album—Memories of The Beach*, (Boston Mills Press, 1985).

Bromley, John F. and May, Jack, *Fifty Years of Progressive Transit*, (Electric Railroaders' Association, New York, 1973).

Bullen, Frank T., *The Royal Road to Fortune*, (Canadian Northern Railway, 1910).

Careless, J.M.S., *Toronto To 1918* (Lorimer and National Museum of Man, 1984).

Clark, C.S., *Of Toronto The Good—The Queen City As It Is*, (Toronto Publishing Company, 1898).

Collins, Robert, *A Great Way To Go—The Automobile in Canada*, (Ryerson, 1969).

Creighton, Donald, *Canada's First Century*, (Macmillan, 1970).

Dumford, Hugh and Baechler, Glenn, *Cars of Canada* (McClelland & Stewart, 1973).

Filey, Mike, *I Remember Sunnyside*, (McClelland & Stewart, 1982).

French, William, *A Most Unlikely Village*, (The Corporation of the Village of Forest Hill, 1964).

Granatstein, J.L., *Marlborough Marathon*, (A.M. Habbert Ltd. and James Lewis & Samuel, 1971).

Greene, B.M. (editor), *Who's Who & Why*, (International Press Limited, various editions from 1910 through 1930).

Greenhill, Ralph, *The Face of Toronto*, (Oxford University Press, 1960).

Harkness, Ross, *Atkinson*, (1964).

Hopkins, John Castell, *Canadian Annual Review of Public Affairs*, (Review Publishing Company, issued annually by him from 1900 until his death at the end of 1923; sporadically thereafter until the mid-1930s by his son and others).

Hotson, Fred W., *The De Havilland Canada Story*, (Canav Books, 1983).

Kelly, Colleen, *Cabbagetown in Pictures*, (Toronto Public Library Board, 1984).

Kinsella, Joan, *A Walking Tour of the Old Deer Park Farm Area*, (Deer Park Branch, Toronto Public Library, 1984).

Lemon, James, *Toronto Since 1918*, (Lorimer and National Museum of Man, 1984).

Lorimer, James, *A Citizen's Guide to City Politics*, (James Lewis & Samuel, 1972).

Lorimer, James & Phillips, Myfanwy, *Working People*, (James Lewis & Samuel, 1971).

Martyn, Lucy Booth, *Toronto—100 Years of Grandeur*, (Pagurian Press, 1978).

Martyn, Lucy Booth, *Aristocratic Toronto*, (Gage, 1980).

McHugh, Patricia, *Toronto Architecture—A City Guide*, (Mercury Books, 1985).

Macpherson, Mary-Etta, *Shopkeepers To A Nation*, (McClelland & Stewart, 1963).

Middleton, Jesse Edgar, *Toronto's 100 Years*, (Centennial Committee, 1934).

Milberry, Larry, *Aviation In Canada*, (McGraw-Hill Ryerson, 1979).

Myrvold, Barbara, *The Danforth*, (Toronto Public Library Board Local History Handbooks, 1984).

Newman, Peter C., *The Canadian Establishment, Volume I*, (McClelland & Stewart, 1975).

Newman, Peter C. (general editor), *Debrett's Illustrated Guide to the Canadian Establishment*, (Methuen, 1983).

North Toronto Historical Society, *Blythwood-Sherwood Park Walk*, (1985).

Piva, Michael J., *The Condition of the Working Class in Toronto, 1900-1921*, (University of Ottawa Press, 1979).

Rempel, J.I., *The Town of Leaside*, (East York Historical Society, 1982).

Robertson, John Ross, *Landmarks of Toronto*, (1894).

Rose Society of Ontario, *Annual Reports, 1914-1918*, (Bryant Press).

Rust-D'Eye, George H., *Cabbagetown Remembered*, (Boston Mills Press, 1984).

Scott, John G., *The Parkdale Register*, (Bengough, Moore & Bengough, 1881).

Speisman, Stephen A., *The Jews of Toronto*, (McClelland & Stewart, 1979).

Stephen, A.M. (editor), *The Voice of Canada*, (J.M. Dent & Sons, 1927).

Stevens, G.R., *History of the Canadian National Railways*, (Macmillan Co., New York, 1973).

Stewart, Sandy, *A Pictorial History of Radio in Canada*, (Gage, 1975).

Tigert, D., *Corporate Background Report, Royal Commission on Corporate Concentration*, (1976).

Toronto Board of Trade, (Geo. W. Englehardt, 1898).

Toronto Transportation Commission, *Wheels of Progress*, (1941).

Index

(Where relevant, the major page reference is in *italics*)

Acetylene gas, 111, 190
Adam, Graeme Gibson, 232
Adam, G. Mercer, 24, 35, 128, 151, 182, 186, 208, 225, 232, 248
Adamson, Anthony, 240
Adaskin, Harry, 92, 161
Ahrens, Carl, 58
Aird, John, 229, 301
Aitken, Max, 98, 120, 121, 144
Alexandra Palace Apartments, 87
Allan, William, 20, 156
Allan Gardens, 156
Allward, W.S., 88, 145
Ames, A.E. 48
Anderson, A.J., 212
Anderson, George, 260
Annex, The, 225-233
Applegath, Albert Walter, 34
"Ardwold," 263, 264-265
Argus Corporation, 30, 132, 169
Armouries, 100
Art Museum of Toronto, 147
Arthur, Eric, 30, 54, 87, 88, 91, 128, 136, 176
Arts & Letters Club, 57, *84-85*, 101, 237, 253
Ashbridge's Bay, 18, 172, 176, 189, 294, 299
Ashworth, E.M., 83
Asylum *see* 999 Queen Street West
Atkinson, Joseph, 39, 49, *51, 52,* 79, 98, 170, 195, 289
Austin, James and Albert, 262
Automobiles (including their effects on personal behaviour and development of the city), 15, 40, 42, 46, 83, 86, 90, 119, 191, 216, 280, 282
Avenue Road, 234
Aviation, 100, 120, 299, 302, *304-306*
Avro Aircraft, 306
Aylesworth, Allan, 152, 229

Baby, Frank, 210
Baillie, Robert, 284
Bain, James William, 196, 197, 278
Baldwin, Lawrence, 287, 288
Baldwin, William Warren, 20, 23, 262
Ballard, Harold, 155
Balmy Beach, 164, 166, 167
Banfield, William Henry, 104
Bank of Hamilton, 64
Bank of Montreal, 20, 22, 32, 60
Bank of Toronto, 188
Bank of Upper Canada, 20
Banking industry, 60-65
Banting, F.G., 91, 226

Bargain Benny's, 142
Barker, W.G., 304, 306
Baseball, 113, 296
Bassett, John, 49, 52, 155
Baxter, Arthur Beverley, 121
Bay Street, 23, 30, 55, 61, 68, 117, 120
Beaches, 16, 164-168
Beardmore, G.W., 81, 141, 292
Beattie Nesbitt, William, *60, 62, 76*
Beatty, J.W., 85, 237
Beaverbrook, Lord *see* Aitken, Max
Beck, Adam, 39, 40, *80-83*, 90
Bedford Road, 226
Beer, George Frank, 180, 184
Beer and brewing, 72, 73, 180, 219, 220, 234
Bell, Marilyn, 125
Bell-Smith, Frederick, 274
Belt Line Railway, 248, 277, 278, 280, 288, 290
Bennett, R.B., 27, 28, 98, 102
"Benvenuto," 225
Berkeley, 172
Berton, Pierre, 16
Best, C.H., 91
Bickell, John Paris, 155, 276, 307
Birks, Earl, 66
Birks Jewellers, 66
Bishop, Billy, 46, 108, *304*, 306
Bishop Strachan School, 290
Blackstone, Milton, 92
Blake, Edward, 160, 266
Blake, Hume, 266
Blewett, Jean, 206
Bloor, Joseph, 234, 236
Bloor Street (and subway), 215, 222, 229, 230, 233, 234, 236, 237
Bloor Street Viaduct, 174, 178
Bongard, Robert Ross, 161
Borden, Robert, 49, 98, 108, 153
Boulton, D'Arcy, 145
Boulton, H.J., 23
Boydell, H.C., 229
Brand, J.A., 301
Branksome Hall Girls School, 156, 246
Brazilian Traction, Light and Power Company (Brascan), 44, 228
Bredin, Mark, 144
Bridle, Augustus, 57, 85, 237
British American Oil Company, 187
Brock, General Isaac, 20
Brockton, 198
Brown, Caroline, 220
Brown, George, 49
Brown, Jane, 108
Bruce, Helen, 101, 182

Burden, Charles Elbridge, 46
Burden, Margaret, 108
Burgess, Charles, 307
Burnside, Josephine (Eaton), 46, 266
Burton, Charles L., 28, 48
Bus (services and depot, *see also* Toronto Transportation Commission), 33, 41, 42, 119, 212, 257

CN Tower, 110
Cabbagetown, 11, 16, 179-197
Cadillac-Fairview Corp., 212
Calvert, A.E., 63
Cambrai Avenue, 86
Campbell, Judge William, 20,
Canada Life Assurance Company, 87
Canada Packers, 197
Canada Permanent Trust, 188
Canada Steamship Lines, 120, 121
Canada Wire & Cable Company, 302
Canadian Aeroplanes Limited, 306
Canadian Bank of Commerce, 40, 64, 98, 118, 119, 141, 228
Canadian Bank of Commerce building, 32
Canadian Bankers' Association, 63, 64
Canadian Broadcasting Corporation, 85, 135, 154, 162, 229, 308
Canadian Cycle & Motor Company, 132, 209
Canadian Fishing & Sporting Association, 209, 210
Canadian General Electric Company, 37, 81, 209, 269
Canadian Home Journal, 251
Canadian Horological Institute, 222
Canadian National Exhibition, *122-125,* 128,
Canadian National Railway, 65, 116, 119, 179, 186
Canadian Northern Railway, 39, 40, 83, *116-119,* 228, 252, 301
Canadian Pacific Railway: *118-119,* 208; builds overpasses and North Toronto station, 12, 119, 234; builds office tower, 22, 32; opposes Beck, 90; operations in the Junction, 212; sponsors artists, 274; Leaside operations, 301
Canadian Reconstruction Association, 49, 108, 255
Capreol, Frederick, 23, 115, 116
Careless, J.M.S., 74, 116
Carswell, Robert, 200
"Casa Loma," 54, 262, 263, 269-273
Casino Burlesque, 58, 59
"Castle Frank," 248
Catholic Army Huts Association, 154
Caulfield, W.G., 206
"Caverhill," 242
Cawthra, Joseph (and Cawthra family), 20, 240, 252
Central Prison, 126, 128
Central Supply Association, 60
Charles, Leo, 307
Charlesworth, H.W., 85
Chestnut Park Road, 250, 251

Chinatown, 134, 142
Chown, Rev. S.D., 76
Christie, R.J., 228
Christie-Brown Company, 100
Christie Pits, 224
Christie Street Military Hospital, 84
Church, Rebecca M. 260
Church, Thomas L., 24, 40, 41, 82, 83, 90, 97, 141, 191, 260
Church Street, 148-149, 150, 155
Churches (see Religion for issues of public morality and behaviour):
    148-151
  Holy Trinity Church, 134
  Jarvis Street Baptist Church, 160
  Little Trinity Church, 180
  Metropolitan Methodist Church, 149, 151
  St. Alban-The-Martyr, 230
  St. Anne's Anglican Church, 203
  St. James Cathedral, 16, 18, 150
  St. James Square Presbyerian Church, 70
  St. Michael's Cathedral, 73, 151
  St. Paul's, 151
  Zion Congregational, 61
City Dairy, 94
City Hall: Front Street, 18; Old, 23, 54, 93, 101, 102; New, 59,
"Chorley Park" see Government House
Clark, C.S., 60, 135, 150, 277, 296
Clark, Gregory, 52
Clark, John Murray, 226
Clarke, Charles Kirk, 128
Clarke, Lt.Gov. L.H., 245
Clarke Institute of Psychiatry, 128
Clarkson, G.T., 64, 65, 197
Clarkson, Gordon & Dilworth, 65, 196
Clothing industry, 22, 27-28, 46, 100, 135, 136, 141, 179, 180
Clysdale, W.G., 162
Coal, 18, 108, 190-191, 192
Coatsworth, Emerson, 64, 81, 262
Cody, Canon Henry John, 153
College of Pharmacy, 70
College Park, 46
Colonial Theatre, 30, 57
Confederation Life Association (and building), 23, 26, 32, 93
Connable, Ralph, 276
Consumers' Gas Company, 112, 127, 179, 188, 192-193, 263
Cooke, Jack Kent, 113
Copp, William, 156
Cosgrave, Patrick, 72, 220
Cost of living, 27-28, 101, 108, 180, 184, 190, 191, 194-197, 282
Couzens, Herbert, 41, 44, 82
Cox, Alfred Herbert, 161
Cox, Senator George, 50, 158, 161, 228, 269
Crescent Road, 252
Crystal Palace, 123, 128
Culver, Frank, 200

"Dale, The," 169, 248
Daly, Herbert, 63-65
Danforth, The (and Danforth Avenue), 16, 172-178
Darling, Frank, 229, 234
Davies, William, 246
Davies, The William, Company, 98, 108, 179, 194-197
De Havilland Canada, 306
"Deancroft," 241
Deer Park, 277, 278
Degrassi Street, 176
Denison, George Taylor III, 60, 108, 202, 203
Denison, Merrill, 58
Depressions: 1860s, 192; 1913, 209; 1919, 286; 1930s, 42, 182, 209,
    212, 245
Dinnick, W.S., 253, 284, 286
Distillers Corporation, 170
Dolittle, Dr. Perry, 100
Dominion Bank, 64
Dominion Motors, 302
Dominion Public Building, 20
Don Jail, 176, 178
Don Mills, 308
Don River, 18, 116, 172, 176, 178, 180, 188
Dovercourt Company, 253, 284, 286
Drayton, Henry, 82, 212, 252
Drury, E.C., 77, 78, 79, 90, 170
Dufferin Race Track, 204
"Dundonald," 70, 95
Dunfield & Company, 28
Durant Motors, 302
DuVernet, E.E.A., 27, 60, 274
Dyment, A.E., 169

Easson, C.H., 226
East Toronto, 176
East York Township, 178
Eastmure, Arthur, 298
Easton, Alexander, 36
Eaton, Edward Young, 46
Eaton, John Craig, 46, 51, 100, 102, 108, 228, 263, 264
Eaton, John David, 46, 47, 264
Eaton, Lady (Flora McCrae), 47, 264
Eaton, Margaret W., 229
Eaton, R.Y., 28, 46, 260
Eaton, Timothy, 45, 46, 50
Eaton, T., Company, 22, 27, 28, 45-47, 48, 135, 141,
Education, 15, 71, 96
Eglinton, 282
Eglinton Hunt Club, 292, 293
Electric Diner, 114
Electrical Development Company, 81-83
Elizabeth Street, 136, 142, 308

Ellis, P.W., 41, 82
Ellis Brothers, 28
England (see also Imperialism): competition for colonies, 14;
    retention of English ways, 15; titles for Canadians, 49, 50, 98;
    drinking habits, 77; Canadian attitudes during World War One,
    100-109; as land of opportunity, 120-121; Goldwin Smith's
    ideas, 147
Ernescliffe Apartments, 158
Esplanade, 116
"Euclid Hall," 132
Exhibition Stadium, 113

Fairweather's, 26, 28
Falconer, R.A., 96-97, 99, 232
Family Compact, 20, 49, 74, 91
Farmers Bank, 50, 60-62
Fashion, 171, 205, 264, 296
Ferguson, G. Howard, 64, 79
Financial Post, 80, 81, 90
Findley, Thomas, 132, 289
Fire: of 1849, 16, 150; of 1904, 35, 118,
Fire department, 35
Fire Hall Number One, 61
Fire Hall Number Three, 68
Fitzpatrick, Alfred, 92, 93
Flavelle, Joseph, 48, 50, 51, 76, 90, 98-99, 104, 108, 184, 194-197,
    306
Fleming, R.J., 60
Ford Hotel, 33, 42
Forest Hill Village, 287-293
Fort York, 112, 113
Foster, George Eulas, 26
Fox, E.C., 196
Franceschini, James, 307
Frankel, Leo, 140
Fraternal organizations, 23, 24,
Fred Victor Mission, 94, 132, 182
French, William, 289
Fricker, H.A., 57, 92, 93, 124
Front Street, 20, 22, 86, 110, 116,
Frontier College, 92, 93
Fudger, H.H. 48, 158, 247
Fulford, Robert, 238
Furniss, Albert, 18, 166, 192

Gage, William, 50, 108, 229
Gardiner, Frederick, 289, 307
Gardiner Expressway, 90, 113, 115, 123, 124, 205
Geary, Reginald, 82, 242
"Glen Edyth," 265, 266, 268
"Glen Hurst," 246
Glen Road, 256-257

"Glendoveer," 280

Globe, The, 11, 15, *49,* 50, 52, 81, 96, 102, 127, 153, 170, 197, 206, 228

Globe & Mail, 52

Gooderham, A.E., 101, 102, *188*

Gooderham, Mrs. A.E., 100, 104, 241

Gooderham, Charles H., 156

Gooderham, George, 232, 233

Gooderham, George H., 2, 123, 160, 170

Gooderham, William George, 188, 232

Gooderham & Worts distillery, 101, 179, 188

Gough, R.P., 65

Government House: Wellington Street, *22, 23,* 88; Rosedale ("Chorley Park"), *22,* 108, 191, 233, *245*

Granatstein, J.L., 12

Grand Trunk Railway, 90, 98, 116, 118, 119, 172, 176, 179, 186, 208, 216, 252, *277,* 280

"Grange, The," 145-147

Grant, W.L., 15,

Gray Coach Lines, 42

Great War Veterans Association, 109

Great Western Railway, 116, 118

Greenwood Race Track, 169-171

Grier, E. Wyly, 85

Gunther, Edmund, 266

Gwynne family, 198, 201

Gzowski, Casimir, 115, 117, 248, 250

Hague, Dorothy, 216

Hambourg, Boris, 85, 92, 161

Hamilton, 116

Haney, Michael, 51, *63,* 64, 65

Hanlan, Ned, 295

Hanlan's Point, 295, 296, 299

Hanna, D.B., *116,,* 301

Hanna, W.J., 77, 206

Harbour Commission, *110*

Harbour Master's house, 112

Harris, Lawren, 237

Harris, R.C. (and water purification plant), 16, 166, 168, 190

Harris, W. & Company, 176

Hart House, 91, 92

Hart House Quartet, 91, 92, 161

Hastings, Dr. Charles, 135, *138,* 180, 255

Hatch, Harry, 188

Havergal Girls College, 162

Heintzman family and piano company, 209, 210, 212, 278, 289

Hellmuth, Isidore, 79

Hemingway, Ernest, 52, 276

Hepburn, Mitchell, 90

Hermant, Percy, 140

Hewitt, Foster, 28, 52, 155

High Park, 218

High Park Sanitarium, 212, 214, 215

Highland Avenue, 260

Hindmarsh, Harry C., 52

Hiram-Walker distillery, 188, 193

Hocken, H.C., 40, 82

Hockey, 50, 155

Holt Renfrew and Company, 34

Holy Blossom Synagogue, 135, 140, 141

Home Bank, 25, *63-65,* 272

Home for Incurables, 198

Home Savings & Loan Company, 63, 270

Honderich, Beland, 52

Hopkins, John Castell, 11, 15, 24, 60, 62, 74, 77, 96

Horne-Payne, R.M., 118, 228

Horsfall, Herbert, 104, 289

Hoskin, John, 248

Hospital for Sick Children, 50

House of Industry, 135, 136, 182, 247

House of Providence, 186

Howard, John, 128, 218

Hudson's Bay Company, 27

Huestis, Mrs. Archibald, 104, 282

Hughes, James Laughlin, 15

Hughes, Sam, 100

Humberston, Clara, 206

Hydro-Electric Power Commission of Ontario, 40, 81, 83, 90, 161

Imperial Order Daughters of the Empire, 46, 100, 101, 182, 195, 229, 241

Imperialism, 15, 49, 52, 77, 96, 97, 100-109, 123, 147

Independent Order of Foresters, 23-27, 30,

Independent Order of Odd Fellows, 24, 68

Influenza epidemic (1918), 109, 191

Inglis, John Company, 126

Inkster, J.G., 230

Insurance industry, 23-27

Island airport, 299

Islands, The Toronto, 294-300

Italian community, 142, 178

Jackson, A.Y., 237

Jackson, M.B., 242

Jacob, Fred, 56

James, William, 10, 171, 253

Janes, Simeon, 225, 262

Jardine, Alexander, 274

Jarvis, Aemilius, 100, 234

Jarvis, Edgar John, 256

Jarvis, William Botsford, 18, 160, 234, 238, 241, 242

Jarvis Street, 2, 114, 132, 160-163

Jarvis Street Collegiate Institute, 160

Jewish community, 51, 134-143, 166, 224, 290

John Valentine & Sons, 123, 294, 312

Johnson, Main, 52, 289

Jones, J.E., 286

Jones, Lyman, 50, 51, 132

Junction, The, 16, 208-215

Keay, Arthur, 114

Keith, Alexander, 111

Kellogg, Rev. Samuel, 70

Kelso, J.J., 152

Kemp, A.E., 248

Kensington, 11, 142, 143

Kensington Market, 11, 138, 142

Ketchum, Jesse, 70, 235

Kew Gardens, 164

"Killyree," 260

King, Arthur, 258

King, William Lyon Mackenzie, 51, 74, 116, 136

King Edward Hotel, *33,* 54, 84

King Street, 16, 18, 23, 25, 46, 63

King's College, 86, 91

King's Plate *see* Queen's Plate

Kingston, Ontario, 14, 18, 20

Knox, Ellen Mary, 162

Knox College, 94, 141

Labour, 39, 46, 50, 51, 77, 90, 108, 184

Lakeside Home for Little Children, 50, 295

Lamb, Daniel, 184

Lanphier, Rev. Charles, 154

Larkin, Peter, 50

Lash, Miller, 228

Lash, Zebulon, 82, 118, 184, *228*

Laurier, Wilfrid, 50, 108, 118, 150, 228, 229

Lawrence Park, 284, 286

Le Sueur, W.D., 74

Leacock, Stephen, 77, 79, 146

Leaside, 301, 302

Leaside airport, 119, 302, 304

Leaside Munitions Plant, 104, 302

Lennox, E.J., 54, 270

Leslieville, 172

Lindsey, G.G.S., 74

Liquor *see also* Prohibition, 60, 76-79, 162, 169, 182, 206, 308

Liquor Control Act, 79

Lismer, Arthur, 237

"Little Belfast" *see also* Orange Order, 15, 24

"Little Trinity," 180, 186-187

Living conditions, 134-140, 180, 182, 190, 191, 195

Loblaw, T.P. and Loblaw's, 90, 113, 144, 164

Lord's Day Alliance (*see also* Religion), 39, 50, 229

Loretto Convent and Abbey, 73, 127

Lorimer, James, 184, 212

Macauley, Dr. James, 20, 135
MacCallum, J.E., 85, 237
McCarthy, D'Alton, 141, 150, 246
McCarthy, D'Alton Lally, 65, 246
McCarthy, J.O., 201
McCullagh, George, 52
McCurdy, J.A.D., 304
Macdonald, John Kay, 26
MacDonald, J.E.H., 85, 237
Macdonald, Senator, 234, 262
Macdonald, Sir John A., 51, 88, 98, 250
Macdonald, Wilson, 158
MacGregor, D.C., 206
McHugh, Patricia, 234
Mackay, Donald, 70
Mackenzie, William, 36, 37, 39, 40, 41, 60, 80, 81, 82, 83, 116, 118,
    119, 191, 225, 263, 269
Mackenzie, William Lyon, 20, 49, 74, 234
McKenzie, Walter, 248
McKishnie, Archie, 206
MacLachlan, K.S., 298
McLean, J.S., 27, 197
MacLean's, 121, 142
McLennan, J.C., 91
MacLeod, J.J.R., 91
McLeod, Young, Weir & Company, 169
McMaster, Arthur, 132, 225
McMaster University, 93
MacMillan, Ernest, 92
MacMurchy, Angus, 251, 255
MacMurchy, Archibald, 255
MacMurchy, Dr. Helen, 94, 152, 255
MacMurchy, Marjory, 49, 255
McNaught, W.K., 40,
Macpherson, D.L., 236, 250

Magann, G. Plunkett, 50, 82, 200
Magrath, C.A., 190, 191
Mail & Empire, The, 25, 50, 52, 56, 63, 86
Makers of Canada, 74
Mann, Donald, 37, 116, 118, 119, 232
Manufacturers Life, 188, 237
Maple Leaf Gardens, 155
Maple Leaf stadium, 113, 296
Maple Leafs, 155
Marathon Realty, 119
Marshall, K.R. and N.G.L., 191
Martyn, Lucy Booth, 202, 242, 248, 274
Mason, James Cooper, 63-65, 232
Massey family, 91, 130-132
Massey, C.D., 132

Massey, Hart, 130, 132, 160, 248
Massey, Vincent, 85, 132
Massey, W.E.H., 50, 209
Massey-Harris, 101, 126, 130-132, 136, 209
Massey Music Hall, 56, 92
Master Plumbers & Steam Fitters Cooperative, 60
Matthews, W.D., 94, 228, 274
Mendellsohn Choir, 56, 92
Mercer, Frederick, 280
Mercer Reformatory, 126, 128, 198
Metcalf, George, 144, 203
"Metro," 16, 307, 308
Middleton, Jesse Edgar, 15, 56, 91, 124, 169, 206, 240
Miles, Madonna, 58
Milk, 94, 138
Miller, Fred, 41
Mirvish, Ed, 57
Mitchell, Percival, 298, 299
Montgomery's Tavern, 74, 282
Montreal, 14, 20, 77, 120, 151, 308
Moore, J.T., 278, 280
Moore, S.J., 307
Moore, Rev. T.A., 78
Moore Park, 278, 280
Morang Company, 74
Morden, Walter Grant, 120-121
Morrow, Frederick, 276
Mossop, F.W., 77
Motion pictures, 57, 84, 101, 121
Mount Pleasant Road, 2, 246
Mowat, Oliver, 90, 91
Moysey, A., 298
Mueller, P.W., 96
Muirhead's Cafeterias, 24
Mulock, William, 50, 51, 65, 160, 161
Munro Park, 164
Murdoch, James, 254
Murray, D.S., 298

Nash, A.E., 65
Nasmith, G.G., 94, 168
Nathanson, Nathan, 276
National Life Assurance Company, 292
National Trust Company, 98
Neilson, Morden, 126, 203
"New Town," 23
New York, 20, 171
Newcombe, Octavius, 219, 220
Newman, Peter C., 254, 264
News, The, 49, 50, 51, 76, 81, 98
Newspapers, 49-52. See also Globe, Mail & Empire, News, Star,
    Telegram, World

Nicholls, Frederic, 37, 39, 50, 60, 80, 81, 100, 104, 118, 228, 232,
    269
Nickenson, John, 56
999 Queen Street West, 36, 126, 128-129, 219
Noranda Mines, 254
Nordheimer, Albert, 236
Nordheimer, Samuel, 262, 266, 268
Nordheimer Piano Company, 209
Noronic, 121
North Toronto, 282-286
Northern Railway, 116, 118
Norway, 172

Oakley, George, 176
O'Connor, Frank, 248
O'Hara, Henry, 247
O'Keefe, Eugene, 63, 72-73, 220
"Old Town," 23
Ontario Jockey Club, 169-171
Ontario Motor League, 40
Ontario Temperance Act see Prohibition
Orange Order, 15, 24, 49, 50, 150-154
Oronhyatekha, Dr. Peter, 26, 27
Osgoode Hall, 101, 102,
Osler, Edmund, 97, 184, 248, 269

Page, Walter, 252
Pantages Theatre, 73
"Park lots," 18, 156, 160
Park Plaza Hotel, 237
Parkdale, 198-207
Parliament Buildings: foot of Berkeley Street, 18, 88; Front Street,
    23, 88; Queen's Park, 88-90
Parliament Street, 179
Parsons, S.R., 187
Patterson Ice Cream, 123, 126
Pearson, Lester, 230
Pellatt, Henry, 39, 60, 64, 80, 81, 82, 228, 246, 248, 252, 262, 263,
    269-273
Pellatt, Henry Senior, 248, 269, 270
Pellatt, Lady Mary, 270, 272
Pember, William Thomas, 34
Phillips, Nathan, 140
Pickford, Mary, 57, 84, 142, 272
Piva, Michael, 136
Playter, John Lea, 173, 176,
Plumptre, Adelaide, 104
Pollution, water, 166, 168
Pope, W.W., 226
Poplar Plains Road, 266-268
Port Credit, 307
Post office buildings, 30

Powell, William, 23, 119
Price, W.H., 206
Price Spreads Commission, 27
Prince of Wales, 84
Prohibition, 76-79, 90, 100, 169
Protestant Orphans Home, 198, 203,
Protestant Radio League, 135, 154

Quebec: political clout thwarts Dominion-wide Prohibition, 77;
    Goldwin Smith's ideas about Quebec culture, 147; conflicts with
    Ontario over Catholicism, 150-154; Imperialism during World
    War One, 154
Quebec City, 14, 108
Quebec-Gothic area, 212, 214, 215
"Queen City" (see also Imperialism), 15,
Queen Street, 22, 58, 59, 109, 142
Queen's Hotel, 23, 110, 116, 118
Queen's Own Rifles, 101, 269, 270, 272
Queen's Park, 88-90, 109
Queen's Plate, 155, 169, 170, 171
Queen's Rangers, 18, 70

Radial railways (see also Toronto Transportation Commission and
    Toronto & York Radial Railways), 90, 210
Radio, 52, 132, 154, 161, 205
Radio League of St. Michael, 154
Railways (see also Canadian Pacific Railway, Canadian National
    Railway, Canadian Northern Railway, Grand Trunk Railway,
    Great Western Railway): 115-119; expansion of Toronto due to,
    14; effect on New Town, 23;
Raney, W.E., 78, 79, 169, 170
Red Lion Hotel, 36, 234
Red Triangle Club, 2
Reed, Le Grand, 226
Regent Park, 184
Reid, G.A., 274
Religion: issues of public morality and behaviour, 14, 39, 45, 46, 50,
    56, 60, 102, 150-154, 169, 170, 202, 229, 296; anti-Catholicism,
    49, 135, 150-154; separate schools, 50, 51, 150; Sundays in the
    city, 58, 296; anti-Semitism see Jewish community; Roman
    Catholics and the Home Bank, 63, 72, 73; Methodism & its
    influence on public morality, 76-79, 132, 151, 170, and
    education, 92; Baptist faith, 160
Renfrew, Allan Edmund, 34
Ridout, Thomas, 156
Riverdale, 172-178
Riverdale Park, 178, 179, 184
Robertson, James & Company, 60
Robertson, John Ross, 49-50, 98, 115, 116, 118, 295
Robins, Samuel John, 263
Robinson, John Beverley, 20, 91, 98
Rochdale College, 96, 230

Rogers, Elias, 179, 190
Rosar-Morrison Funeral Home, 158
Rose Society of Ontario, 280, 299
Rosedale, 15, 238-260
Rosedale Golf Club, 242, 245, 256
Rosedale Hotel, 12
"Rosedale Villa," 238
Rotenberg, David, 238
Rotenberg, Harry
Rowell, Newton, 65, 197, 252
Royal Alexandra theatre, 57
Royal Bank of Canada, 32
Royal Conservatory of Music, 93
Royal Ontario Museum, 98
Royal York Hotel, 20, 115, 119
Russell, Peter, 18
Russell Motor Car Company, 104, 132, 209
Russill, F.J.B., 65
Ryan, Tommy, 132
Ryerson, Egerton, 49, 71, 92
Ryerson Polytechnic Institute, 71
Ryrie, Harry, 66, 260
Ryrie, James, 66, 251
Ryrie Bros. Jewellers, 28, 66

Sabbath laws see Religion
St. Alban's Square, 230
St. Andrew's College, 244, 250
St. Clair, Rev. R.B., 56
St. George Street, 94, 232, 233
St. George's Hall, 85, 280
St. James Square, 70, 71
St. James Town, 184
St. Lawrence Hall, 16, 56, 203
St. Lawrence Market, 18, 36
St. Leger family., 169, 215
Salvation Army, 182
Samuel, Sigmund, 290
Sandy, F.G., 78
Santa Claus parade, 46
Saturday Night, 56, 85, 102, 142, 196
Saunders, M.M., 286
Saunders, Robert, 184
Scadding, Rev. Henry, 15,
Scarboro Beach Park, 25, 39, 168
Scholes, Thomas E., 206
Scott Mission, 135, 182
Seagram, Norman, 170
Selby Hotel, 156
Severn, John, 234, 236
Sewell, John, 184, 212
Sheedy, J.J., 68, 187

Shenstone, J.N., 132, 209
Sheppard, E.E., 50, 85, 150
Sherbourne Street, 156-159
Simcoe, Colonel John Graves, 14, 18, 248, 294
Simpson, James, 39, 71, 104, 176
Simpson, Robert Company, 27, 48, 98
Sinclair, Gordon, 52, 79
Sinclair, Lister, 58, 308
Sing, J.G., 294, 296
Singer, Henry, 134
Singer, Louis Michael, 140
Small, Ambrose, 58
Smith, Eden, 85, 184, 237, 274
Smith, F.D.L., 52
Smith, Goldwin, 15, 49, 90, 145-147, 219
Smythe, A.E.S. 50
Smythe, Agnes, 251
Smythe, Conn, 50, 155
Solman, Lawrence, 296
South African War Memorial, 102
"Spadina," 262, 263
Spadina Expressway, 44
Spence, Rev. Ben, 77, 78
Spence, F.S., 76, 80
Spracklin, Rev. J.O.L., 78, 79
Sproatt, Henry, 85, 234
Standard Bank, 64
Stanford, J.H., 222
Stanton, H.G., 251
Stapells, Richard, 58
Staples, Owen, 172
Star, The (and Evening Star and Star Weekly), 11, 15, 24, 28, 39,
    40, 50-53, 79, 81, 83, 86, 90, 101, 136, 140, 145, 170, 191, 210,
    228, 229, 245
Star building, 24, 53
Stevens, H.H., 27-28, 197
Stewart, J.F.M., 65
Stoodleigh Restaurant, 24,
Stowe-Gullen, Augusta, 289
Strachan, Dr. John, 20, 23, 150, 160, 219
Stuart, George Okill, 160
Studio Building, 237
Subway see Toronto Transportation Commission
Summerhill Square, 12
Sun, The, 52
Sun Life Assurance Company, 247
Sunnyside, 205
Swansea, 216

Tamblyn's, 144, 164
Taylor, Edward P., 132, 169, 308
Taylor, Eleanor, 222

Telegram, The, 11, 40, *49*, *50*, 86, 96, 97, 109, 127, 140, 142, 172, 202, 210
Temple Building, *30-31*, 59, 93
Theatres, *56-59*, 142
Thomson, Roy and Kenneth, 120
Thorncliffe Race Track, 302
Tilley, Norman, 197
Timothy Eaton Memorial Church, 108, 287
Tindale, Arthur Stanley, 24
Titles (British ones for Canadians) *see* England
Todmorden, 172
Toronto & York Radial Railway Company, 39, 41, 42, 81, 83, 208, 278, 282
Toronto Centennial (1934), 84, 124
Toronto Civic Railway, 39, 40,
Toronto Collegiate Institute, 96
"Toronto Eighteen," 15, 51, 119, *228*
Toronto Electric Light Company, 40, 80, 81, 82, 83, 101, 178, 269
Toronto Ferry Company, 117, 295
Toronto General Hospital, 98, 182
Toronto Harbour Commission, 40,
Toronto Housing Company, 180, 184, 298
Toronto Hydro, 40, *80-83*
Toronto Lacrosse Grounds, 242
Toronto Model School, 71
Toronto Municipal Abattoir, 112
Toronto Normal School, 71
"Toronto Purchase," 14
Toronto Railway Company, *36-41*, 51, 81, 82, 101, 164, 168, 178, 179
Toronto Street, 30
Toronto Suburban Railway Company, 39, 41, 42,
Toronto Symphony Orchestra, 92
"Toronto The Good" (issues of public morality and behaviour) *see* Religion
Toronto Trail, 14, 115
Toronto Transportation Commission (and Toronto Transit Commission), *36-44*, 168, 205, 210, 240, 299
Torrington, F.H., 56
Traders Bank, 23, *32*
Travers, W.R., 60, 62
Trees, James Dixon, 246, 298
Trefann Court, 184
"Trinity," 219-221
Trinity College, 219
Trinity Street School, 180
Tudhope Motor Company, 73
Turley, W.E., 109
Turner, Enoch, 180

Union Bank, 64
Union Station, 20, 115, 116, 119
Union Trust Company, 26
Unions *see* Labour
United Farmers of Ontario, 40, 77, 78, 79, 83, *90*, 98, 102, 109, 147, 170, 245
United States of America: consequences of American Revolution, 14; influence on fashions and lifestyles, 15, 57, 98, 171; reciprocity and/or free trade with, 15, 90, 132, 145, 147, *228*; old rivalries, 56; business ethics, 60; banking industry, 63; Prohibition, 76-79; energy interdependence, 80, 82, 83, 161, 190-191; attitudes during First World War, 96, 97, 101; Goldwin Smith's opinions, 145-147
University Avenue, 86-87, 91, 102
University College, 92, 95
University of Toronto, *91-97*, 98, 99, 100, 155, 219, 230
Upper Canada, 18, 20, 74
Upper Canada College, 23, 88, 288, 290

Vankoughnet, Gertrude, 100, 101, 226
Vankoughnet, Philip, 56
Varsity Stadium, 91
Vella family, 210, 212
Victoria College, 92, 132
Victoria Park, 164
Vogt, Dr. A.S., 56, 92

Wages (and working conditions), 27-28, 135, 136, 140, 180, 182
Walker, A.A., 70, 289
Walker, Edmund, 39, 154, 228, 232
Walker House Hotel, 33
Wallace, E.W., 99
Warburton, G.A., 76
Ward, The, 94, *134-142*
Warren, Sarah Trumbull, 161
(Wars:)
War of 1812, 20
Boer War, 64
First World War, 49, 57, 76, 77, 79, 83, 90, 91, 96, 97, 98, *100-109*, 119, 120, 130, 140, 141, 154, 166, 190, 191, 194, 195, 196, 197, 253, 286, 301, 302
Second World War, 42
Warwick Bros. & Rutter, 127
Waterfront, 90, *110-111*, 115-119, 179, 186-197
Waters, H.W., 124
Waterworks, 18, 110, 166, 168
Watts, George, 242, 256
Weir, J.G., 286
Western Gap, 20, 112
Weston, 209
Weston, George and W.G., 113, *144*, 203

Wheaton, C.F., 208
White, Arthur
White, Thomas, 64
Whitney, James, 39, 62, 76, 80, 81, 82, 90, 170, 209
Who's Who, 140
Wilkinson Plough Company, 208
Willan, Healey, 92
William Neilson Company, 100, 123, 144, *203*
Williams, Joseph and Kew, 164
Willinsky, A.I., 229
Willison, John, 49, 50, 98
Willys-Overland, 209
Winchester Hotel, 182
Windmill Line, 186, 188
Winnipeg General Strike, 39, 40, 51,
Withrow, J.J., 123
Women's suffrage, 104, 108
Wood, G.H., 248
Woodbine Race Track, 169-171, 172
Working conditions *see* Wages
World, The, 11, 50, 51, 52, 81, 96, 171, 301, 302
Worts, James, 188
Wright, George, 33, 41
Wychwood, 274-276

Yonge Street, 12, 18, 20, 22, 26, 32, 45, 66, *68-70*, 109, 234, 277, 278, 280, 282
York, 14, *18-20*, 70
York Club, 232, 233
York County Loan & Savings Company, 60
York Township, 216, 282, 287, 288
Yorkville, 36, 192, 234-238
Young, George, 84, 125

Zeidler, F., 206
Zeidman, Morris, 135, 154